Amaravati: The Art of an Early Buddhist Monument in Context

Edited by Akira Shimada and Michael Willis

The British Museum

Published with the generous support of

European Research Council
Established by the European Commission

Publishers
The British Museum
Great Russell Street
London WC1B 3DG

Series editor
Sarah Faulks

Amaravati:
The Art of an Early Buddhist Monument in Context
Edited by Akira Shimada and Michael Willis

ISBN 978 086159 207 4
ISSN 1747 3640

Front cover: Drum slab depicting *stūpa* from the Amaravati *stūpa*, *c.* 3rd century CE, British Museum, 1880,0709.81

Printed and bound in the UK by 4edge Ltd, Hockley

Papers used by The British Museum are recyclable products made from wood grown in well-managed forests and other controlled sources. The manufacturing processes conform to the environmental regulations of the country of origin.

Further information about the Museum and its collection can be found at britishmuseum.org.

Contents

Preface

This volume is the outcome of 'Amaravati: The Art of an Early Buddhist Monument in Context', an international conference held at the British Museum and the Courtauld Institute of Art, London, on 4–5 September 2014.

After the conference, we took the editorial decision to develop the volume from a simple collection of conference papers into a more comprehensive study of Amaravati and the early visual culture of India. We therefore asked participants to revise their paper for publication and called on additional scholars in the field to contribute. After peer review we decided to publish ten papers, together with an introduction based on the keynote address presented by Akira Shimada at the Courtauld Institute during the conference. Seven chapters are based on papers presented at the British Museum by their authors (Skilling, Zin, Becker, Ślączka, Barnard, Willis and Vardhan). The three further contributions (by Johansen, Bhandare and Stone) are additional to the proceedings proper. We are very grateful to all our contributors for sending their papers in good time and for enthusiastically supporting this publication despite other projects and professional obligations.

It is our pleasant duty to thank the Courtauld Institute and the British Museum for handling the planning and implementation of a complex international conference. It is difficult to name everyone who helped, but here we would like to give special thanks to David Park, Professor and Director, Conservation of Wall Painting Department, Courtauld Institute of Art, and Jan Stuart, former Keeper of the Department of Asia at the British Museum. Without their energetic support, the conference would not have gone forward. Also essential was the financial support given by the British Museum and The Robert H.N. Ho Family Foundation Centre for Buddhist Art and Conservation. To both many thanks are due.

This publication came under the rubric of *Beyond Boundaries: Religion, Region, Language and the State*, a project hosted by the British Museum and funded by the European Research Council (ERC Synergy Project no. 609823). We are especially grateful to the ERC whose support allowed the publication to go forward without delay. Dr J.D. Hill, Head of Research at the British Museum, has warmly supported the project throughout and sanctioned the publication of this volume in the British Museum Research Publication Series. Sarah Faulks, the Senior Editorial Manager of the series, assisted us at every stage and kept the publication on target and in good order. Dr Jason Hawkes, Project Curator at the British Museum and a member of the 'Beyond Boundaries' team, created two excellent maps of Buddhist sites which do much to enhance the present book. Last but not least, we would like to express our sincere gratitude to our colleagues, friends and families who encouraged us to finish this book and offered support in an inconceivable number of ways.

Akira Shimada
Michael Willis

Abbreviations

ARIRIAB: *Annual Report of the International Research Institute for Advanced Buddhology at Soka University*
ARASI: *Annual Report of Archaeological Survey of India*
ASI: Archaeological Survey of India
BL: British Library
BM: British Museum
CII: *Corpus Inscriptionum Indicarum*
EI: *Epigraphia Indica*
IAR: *Indian Archaeology: A Review*
IOR: India Office Records, the British Library
LIMC: *Lexicon iconographicum mythologiae classicae*, 1981–2009, Zürich/Munich
MASI: *Memoirs of the Archaeological Survey of India*

Notes on transliteration

The transliteration employed for words in Indic and other languages follows, as far as possible, the standard modern scholarly system. The spelling of modern place names, including the ones of archaeological sites such as Amaravati and Nagarjunakonda, follows the spelling in the Survey of India maps. In terms of ancient names of places, those listed in *Archaeological Remains: Monuments and Museums* (Archaeological Survey of India, New Delhi, 1996) are used. As for proper names and various technical terms mentioned in the historical texts and inscriptions, the spelling of the original documents is employed rather than Sanskritized versions. If inscriptions record multiple spellings for one term, the most common one is taken. Names of Indic scripts and languages, such as Pali, Gandhari, Sanskrit and Brahmi, are spelt as naturalized English terms without diacritical marks. Other Indic terms are transliterated with diacritical marks.

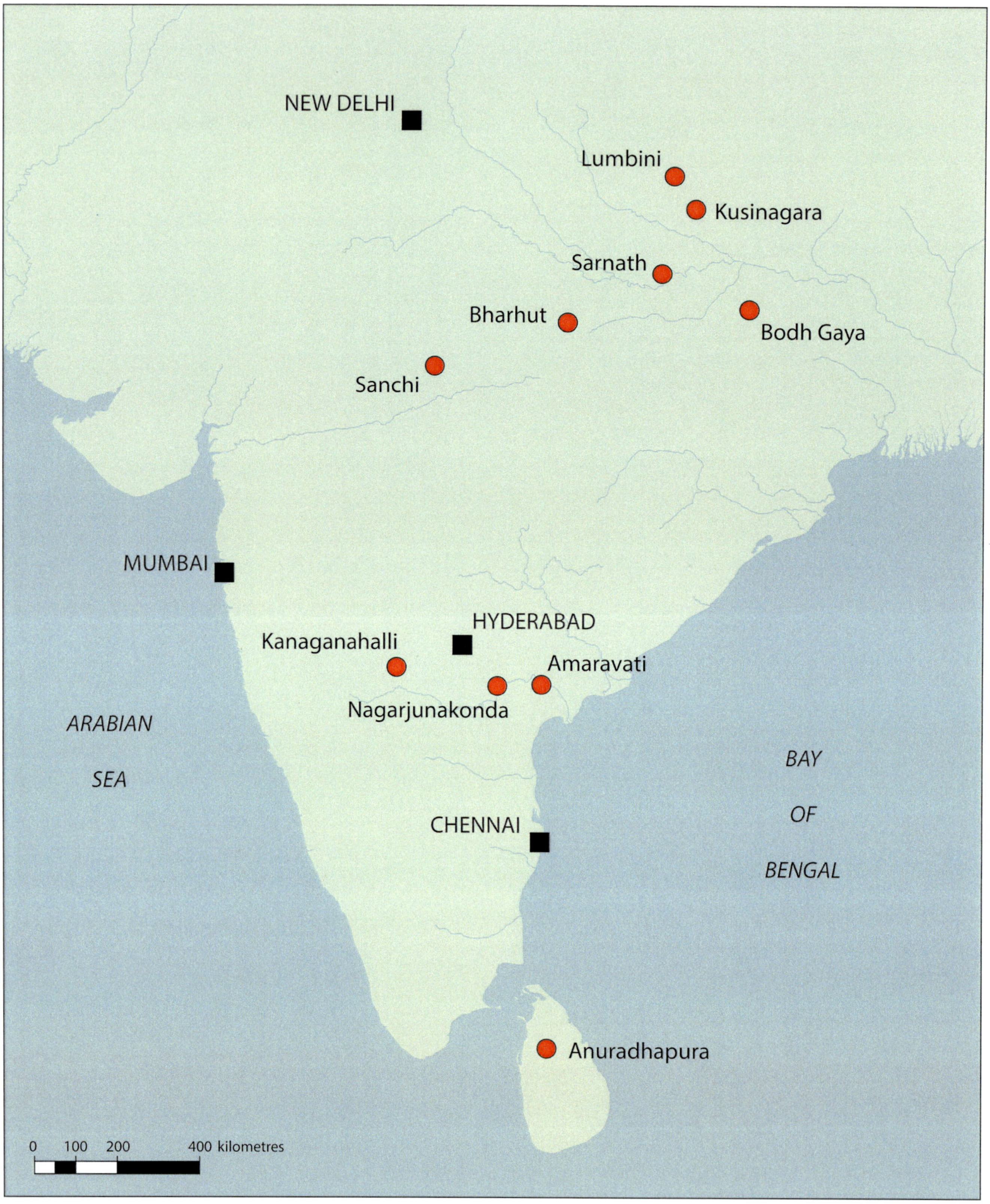

Figure 1 Map of early Buddhist sites in the Indian subcontinent (red circle: Buddhist site; black square: modern city)

Introduction
Discovery of the Amaravati *Stūpa*: Early Excavations and Interpretations[1]

Akira Shimada

Between approximately the 2nd century BCE and the 3rd century CE, Buddhism burgeoned in the coastal area of south-east India, the part of the country that was traditionally known as Andhra (**Figs 1–2**). Among the more than one hundred Buddhist sites and remains in this region, particularly in the lower Krishna River valley, the great *stūpa* (a hemispherical monument enshrining relics) at Amaravati (ancient Dhāñyakaṭaka) is undoubtedly the most outstanding (**Fig. 3**). Since its discovery at the end of the 18th century the *stūpa* site has yielded numerous sculptures and votive inscriptions, which constitute the richest sculptural and epigraphic corpus of Andhran Buddhism. As indicated by Sri Lankan and Thai inscriptions that mention Dhāñyakaṭaka (Paranavitana 1935: 97; Chirapravati 2008: 20–1) as well as a Tibetan account of Dhāñyakaṭaka as an esoteric Buddhist centre (Lama Chimpa and Chattopadhyaya 1990: 107, 192, 209, 345, 440), Amaravati/Dhāñyakaṭaka was known as an important Buddhist centre as late as the 14th century, even though many Andhran Buddhist monasteries had entered a period of decline after the 3rd–4th centuries CE. The excavated sculptures that decorated the *stūpa* are masterpieces of early Indian Buddhist art, and are exhibited in several museums in India, Europe and the USA.

Despite its great reputation as an early Buddhist centre and place of art production, however, Amaravati is an enigmatic site with many unanswered questions about its foundation, development and decline – a situation largely caused by the destruction of the *stūpa* by early excavations. Why and how was the *stūpa* dismembered despite the British effort to understand the monument? What kind of problems did Indian archaeological monuments encounter in the colonial

Figure 2 Map of early Buddhist sites in the Andhra region (red circle: Buddhist site; black square: modern city)

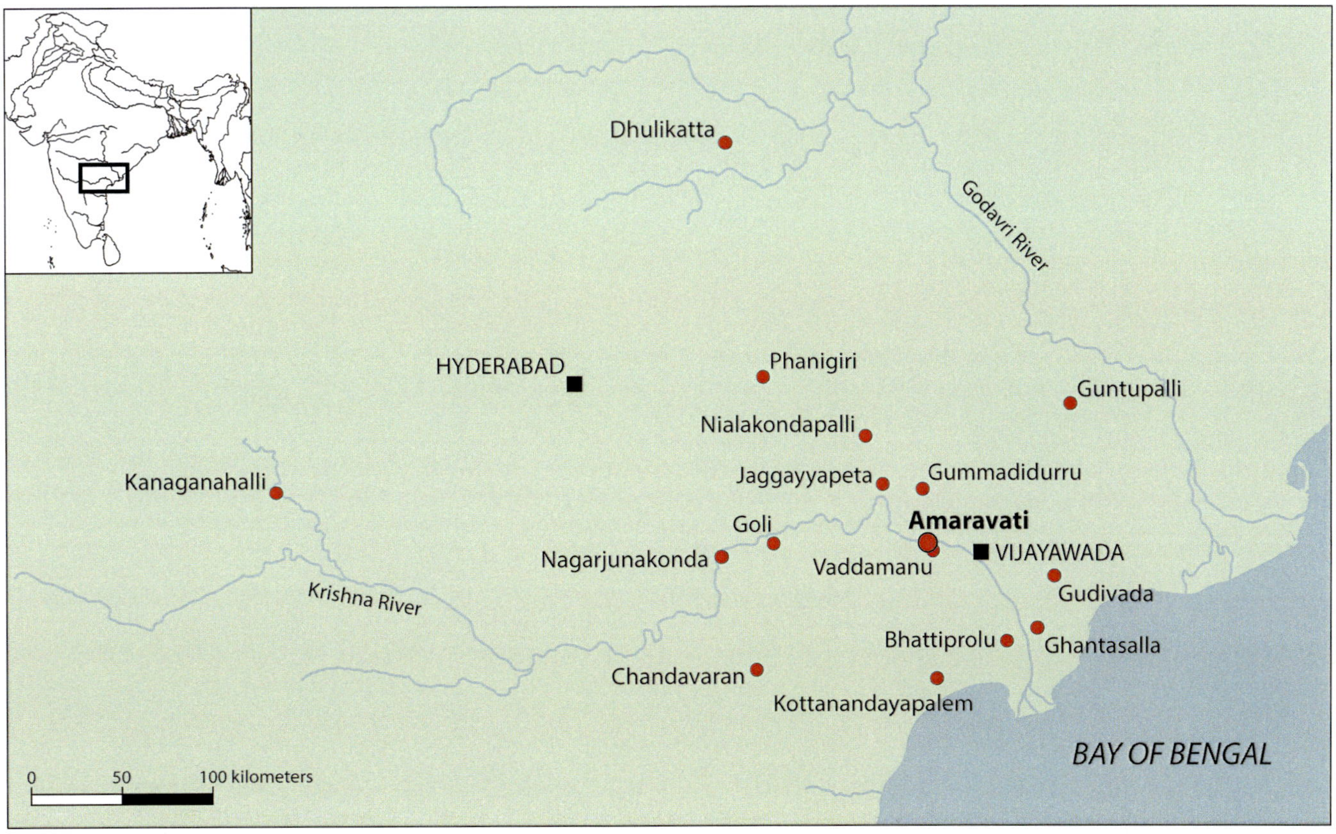

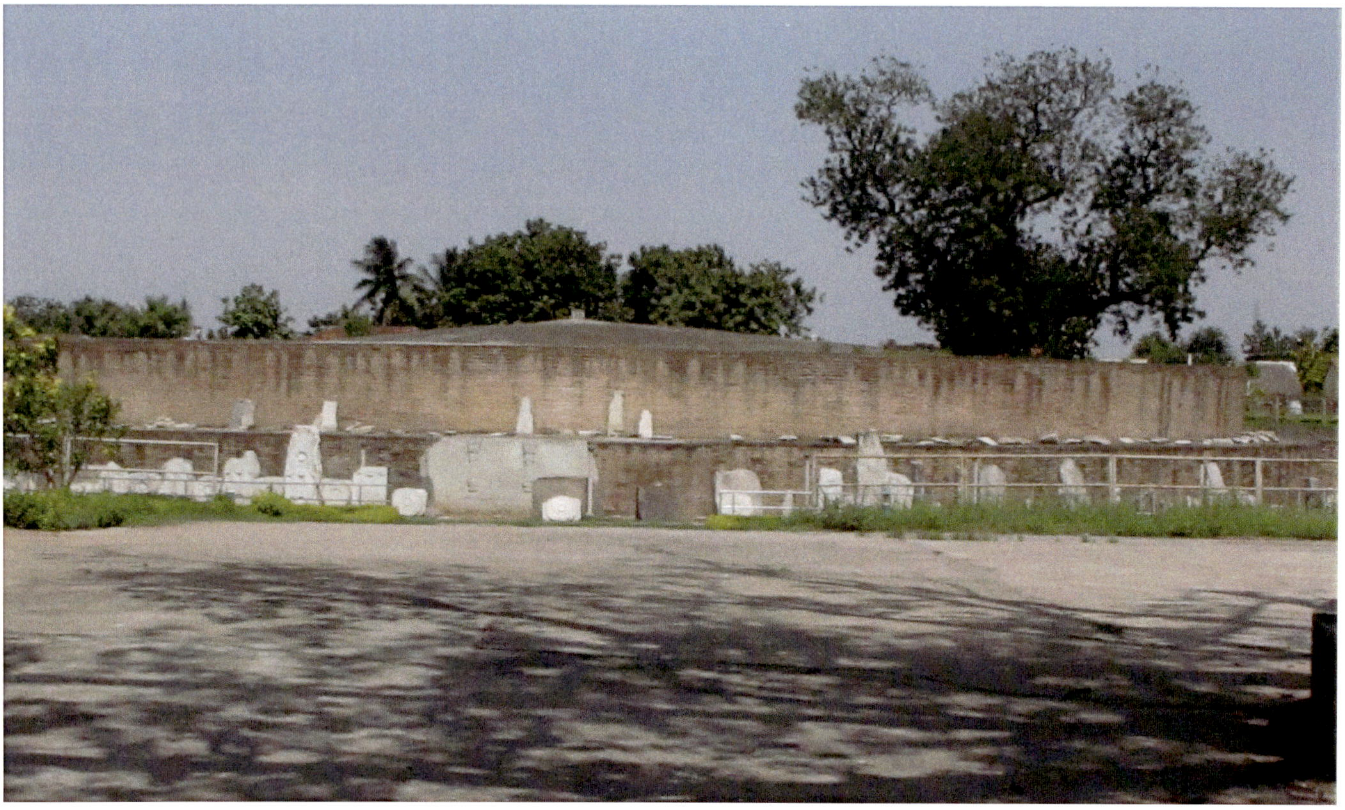

Figure 3 The Amaravati *stūpa* from the east, 2011

era? How has scholarship, both early and recent, addressed these problems? This introductory chapter will examine these questions by investigating the research history of the Amaravati *stūpa* and Andhran Buddhist material culture.

Discovery and dismemberment of the *stūpa*

As discussed in previous publications (Singh 2001; Howes 2002; 2009; Shimada 2013), early surveys of the Amaravati *stūpa* between the end of the 18th century and the end of the 19th century were beset by much confusion and many problems. The discovery of the *stūpa* was made around 1797 by Raja Vesireddy Nayudu, a local landlord who had decided to move his residence to Amaravati because of the East India Company's annexation of Guntur District (Mackenzie 1807: 273). In the process of searching for building materials to renovate Amaravati town as his new capital, Nayudu and his subjects came across the *stūpa* mound, which had been covered with soil. Numerous bricks and stone pillars were found inside the mound, and Nayudu used them for his building projects. The Madras government, having heard about the discovery of a mysterious mound, sent Colonel Colin Mackenzie, a military engineer and surveyor, to Amaravati in 1798.[2] He made a brief observation of the site and the excavated sculptures, but did not (or could not) stop the project of the powerful *zamindar*. When Mackenzie came back to Amaravati in 1816 as the Surveyor General, the dome of the *stūpa* had been destroyed and the centre of the mound turned into a reservoir, as yet unfinished (**Fig. 4**) (Mackenzie 1823: 465). On this second visit, however, Mackenzie and his team conducted an intensive survey of the *stūpa*, working until the end of 1817, and made detailed drawings of the excavated sculptures.[3] They also removed a considerable number of sculptures from the site and sent them to Masulipatan, Calcutta, Madras and London (Taylor 1856: 36; Sewell 1880: 13). Although there are no good records of the final destinations of these pieces, some of those sent to Calcutta formed part of the collection of the Asiatic Society of Bengal and the Indian Museum (Anderson 1883: I, 195–7). Pieces sent to Masulipatan in coastal Andhra were used to embellish a monument built by Francis W. Robertson, the Head Assistant to the Collector at Masulipatan. As one of Mackenzie's drawings records a plan of Robertson's monument, one of the purposes of the 1816–17 survey may have been to find sculptures for the monument (Howes 2002: 59–61). Pieces shipped to London via Calcutta and Madras seem to have gone either to East India House in Leadenhall Street (Wilson 1841: 33) or to private individuals. A drum frieze purchased by the British Museum in 1860, for example, was probably sent to private individuals, as the sculpture was found lying in the backyard for a barber's in Great Marlborough Street near the museum (**Fig. 5**) (Fergusson 1868: 205, n. 1).

This kind of archaeological survey, tinged by the antiquarian interests of various surveyors and officials, continued at Amaravati after Mackenzie. In 1845 Walter Elliot, a civil servant who had a wide interest in South Indian languages, flora and fauna, coins and antiquities, excavated the *stūpa* and collected a large number of sculptures during a mission that lasted for a few months (Elliot 1872: 346). Since the excavation took place in the year when he was appointed Commissioner of Guntur and that he expressed a wish to present the pieces to the Court of Directors of the East India Company (Taylor 1856: 30), we may assume that one reason for his excavation may have been to find a gift for the top executives of the Company Raj.

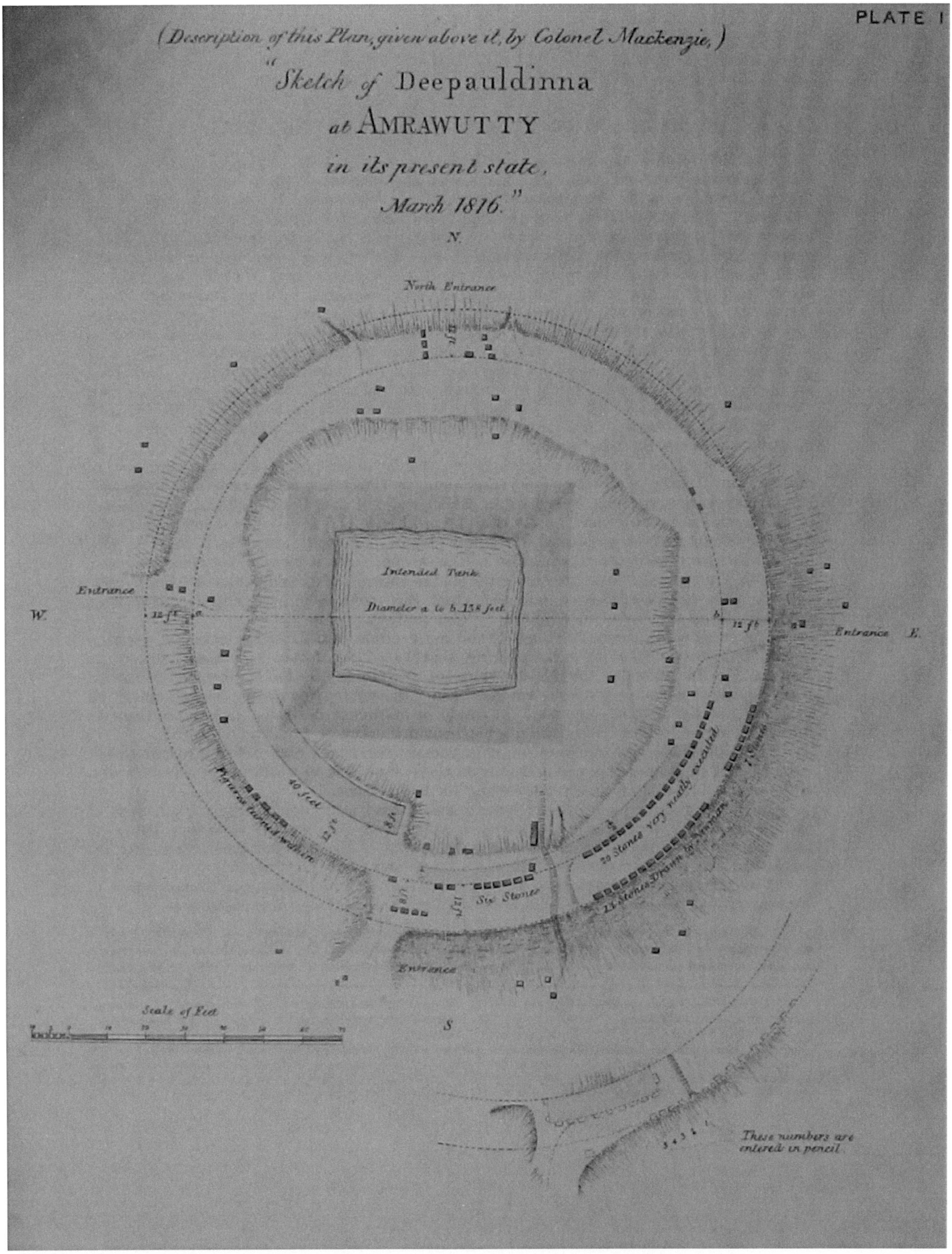

Figure 4 The Amaravati *stūpa* observed by Colin Mackenzie in March 1817 (after Sewell 1880: pl. 1)

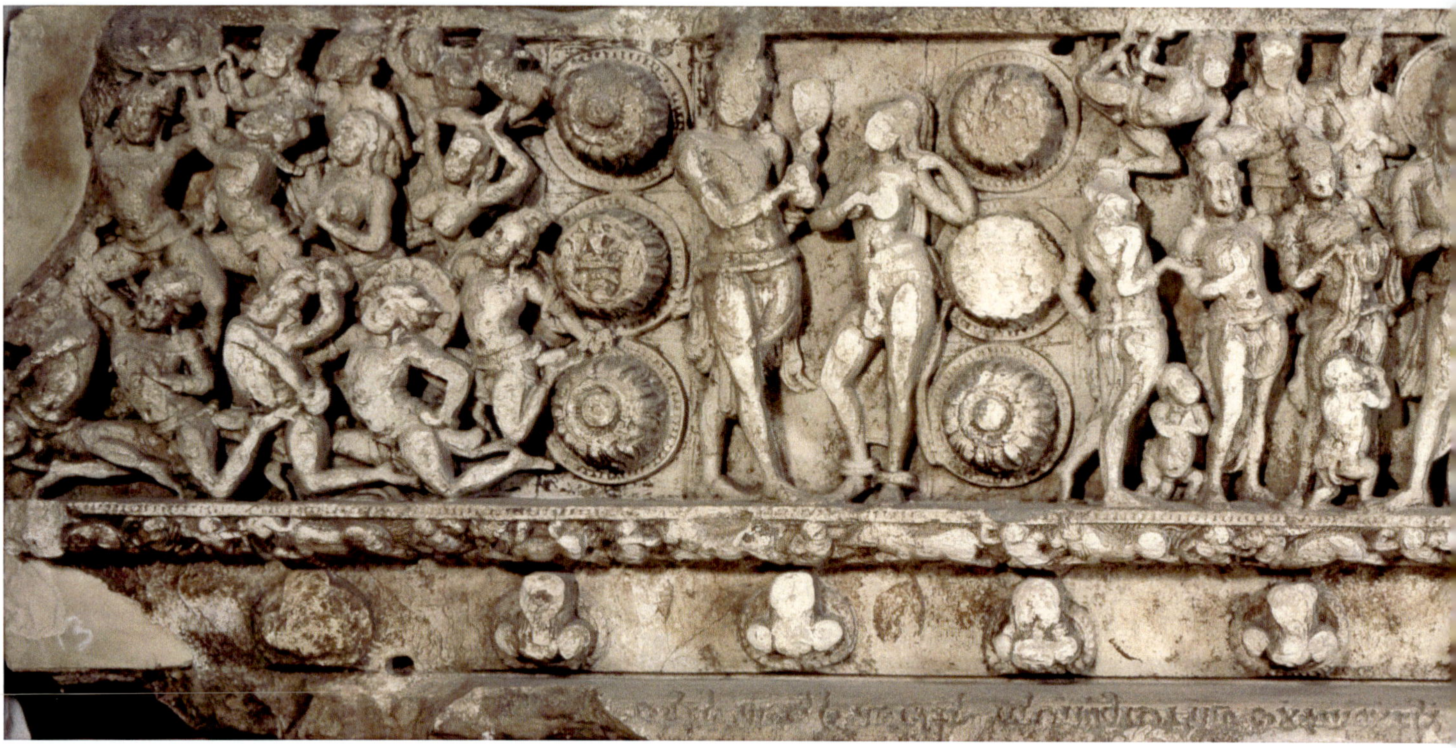

Figure 5 Drum frieze, Amaravati, *c.* 3rd century CE, British Museum, 1880,0709.77

Despite this, the pieces were abandoned for a long time in the Old College at Fort St George in Madras. When drawings of the sculptures were made in 1854 'to enable the Honorable Court to decide whether the marbles are worthy of transmission to England or not', two of the 79 sculptures collected by Elliot (ibid.: nos 63 and 85) had been lost.[4] This incident seems to have alarmed the Madras government, as it was around this time that they decided to assemble the Amaravati sculptures in the newly opened Madras Central Museum. When the Revd William Taylor compiled a list of the Amaravati sculptures in the museum in 1856, the pieces at the Old College had been moved to the museum (ibid.: 6). The government had also successfully acquired 37 sculptures that had embellished Robertson's monument and sent them to the museum (Sewell 1880: 21; Howes 2002: 61). When Linnaeus Tripe, official photographer to the Madras government, took the first photographs of the Amaravati sculptures in Madras in 1858, six more pieces (Tripe 1859: nos 130/135, 131/134, 132/133, 136/137, 138/139, 140/141) had been added to the museum either from Masulipatan or Amaravati (Howes 2009: 25). These sculptures, 120 pieces in total, were shipped to London in 1859.

Unfortunately, the sculptures arrived in London at an inopportune time. After the abolition of the East India Company as a result of the Indian Rebellion in 1857, the India Museum, attached to East India House, which kept Mackenzie's Amaravati collection, was closed.[5] Until it reopened temporarily in 1861 at Fife House, Whitehall, under the administration of the Secretary of State for India, there was no space to accommodate the sculptures. For a year after their arrival in 1860, therefore, the Amaravati sculptures stayed at Beale's Wharf in Southwark before they were transported to Fife House. Even then, as the museum could not exhibit such a large number of sculptures, they were stored in the attached coach house, and a few pieces were exhibited outside. By the time James Fergusson rediscovered the pieces in January 1867 (Fergusson 1867: 135), the dust in the coach house and the polluted air of 19th-century London had seriously damaged them, especially the ones exhibited outside (BM nos 1880,0709.1, 1880,0709.93; Knox 1992: nos 8, 88). When the museum had to move again to smaller premises at the India Office in 1869, the Amaravati sculptures were sent to a storehouse in Lambeth (ibid.: 18) until the museum acquired new galleries at South Kensington in 1875. As this new India Museum lasted for only four years, the sculptures were transferred again in 1880 to the British Museum, where they at last found permanent residence. Again, however, their large numbers, monumental size and damaged condition meant that finding an appropriate space to exhibit the collection became a challenge, one which was not effectively solved until the opening in 1992 of the Asahi Shimbun gallery.

After Elliot's survey the *stūpa* went through another period of neglect until 1870, when J.A.C. Boswell, the Officiating Collector of the Krishna District, undertook an exploration of the ancient remains in the Krishna District and recommended a further survey of the Amaravati *stūpa* to the Madras government (Boswell 1871; Singh 2001: 25). To investigate the possibility of finding more sculptures and architectural remains, Robert Sewell, the Acting Head Assistant Collector of the Krishna District, undertook a test excavation at Amaravati in April 1877. In a one-week mission, his team excavated the north-west quadrant of the processional path and found a good number of sculptures, including a portion of *in situ* railing (Sewell 1880: nos 26–8; Knox 1992: fig. 16). To preserve the original context of the site, his team recorded the find-spot, shape and size of each sculpture without moving it. They also conducted a survey of loose sculptures surrounding the *stūpa* and found 89 pieces through excavation and exploration. Sewell's effort to study

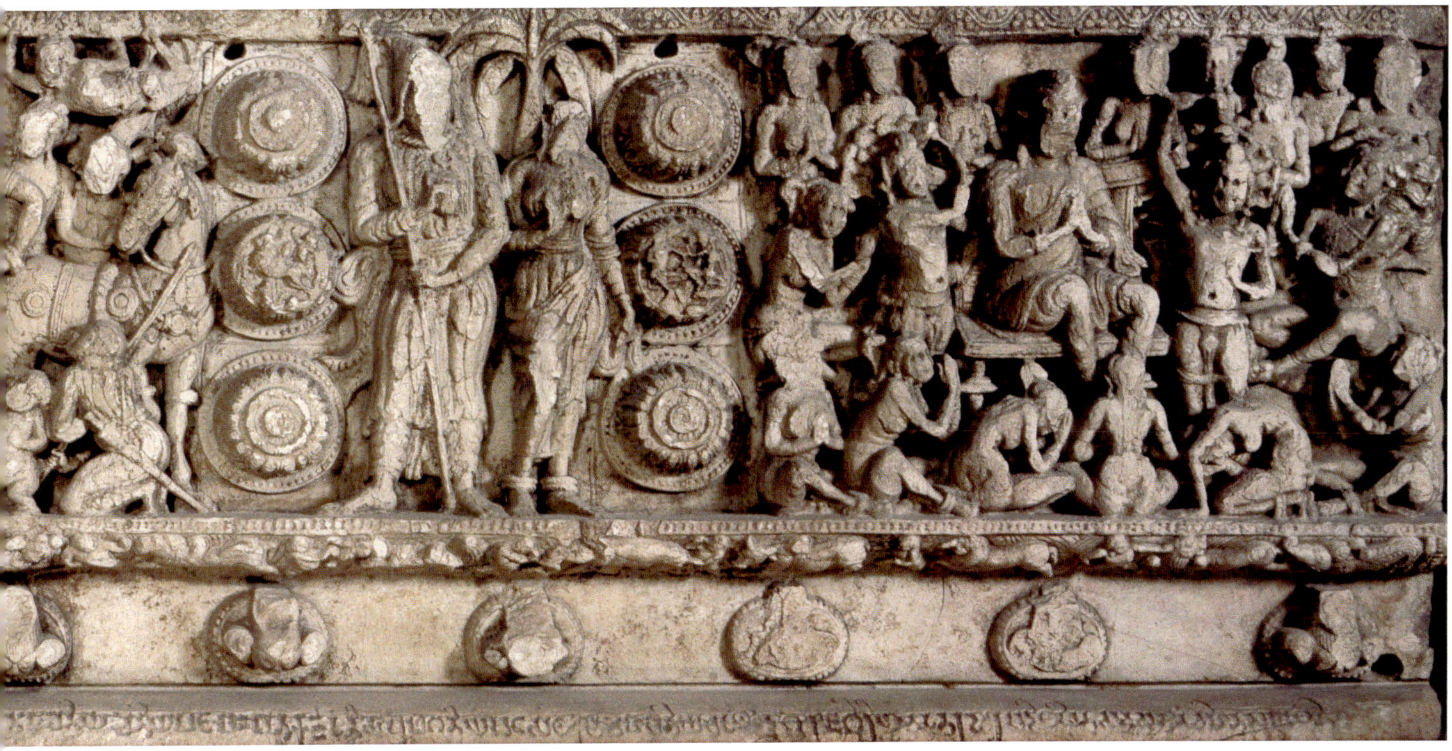

the *stūpa* with no further destruction, however, was in vain. In February 1880, Richard Temple-Grenville, the Governor of Madras, visited Amaravati and ordered the immediate completion of the Amaravati excavation without waiting for the sanction of the Secretary of the State (Burgess 1882b: 3). Following the order, J.G. Horsfall, the Collector of the Krishna District, uncovered the entire passageway around the *stūpa* in about two weeks and numbered, photographed and drew the excavated sculptures (**Fig. 6**). The results of the excavation, according to Horsfall, were 'somewhat disappointing' (Horsfall 1880). Because of the lack of financial and professional support from the central government, the excavation focused exclusively on finding sculptures by hiring local labour. Owing to his lack of archaeological knowledge, Horsfall was not able to take any detailed notes on the excavated sculptures, inscriptions and other excavated objects. When the Archaeological Survey of India (ASI) sent James Burgess to inspect the condition of Amaravati in December 1881, the *stūpa* had been turned into a circular area of ground with a scattering of sculptures. Seeing the highly disturbed condition of the site, Burgess decided to ship 175 fine pieces to Madras. This plan was suspended by H.H. Cole, who was appointed as the first Curator of Ancient Monuments in 1881. In an attempt to restore the monument Cole insisted that the sculptures should stay at the site and criticized Burgess, saying that he had 'ransacked the place' and 'monopolized the ground particularly important to my department' (Cole 1882a; 1882b). Burgess accused Cole of ignorance about the condition of the site, and even suggested that his real aim

Figure 6 The south gate of the Amaravati *stūpa* excavated by J.G. Horsfall, 1880

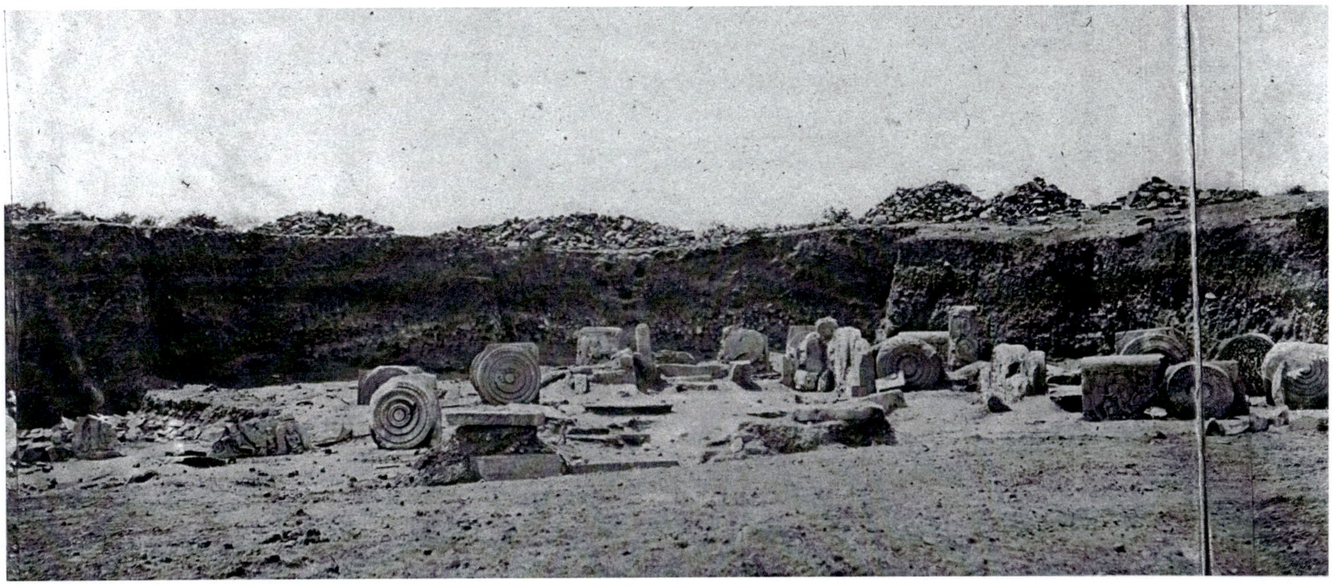

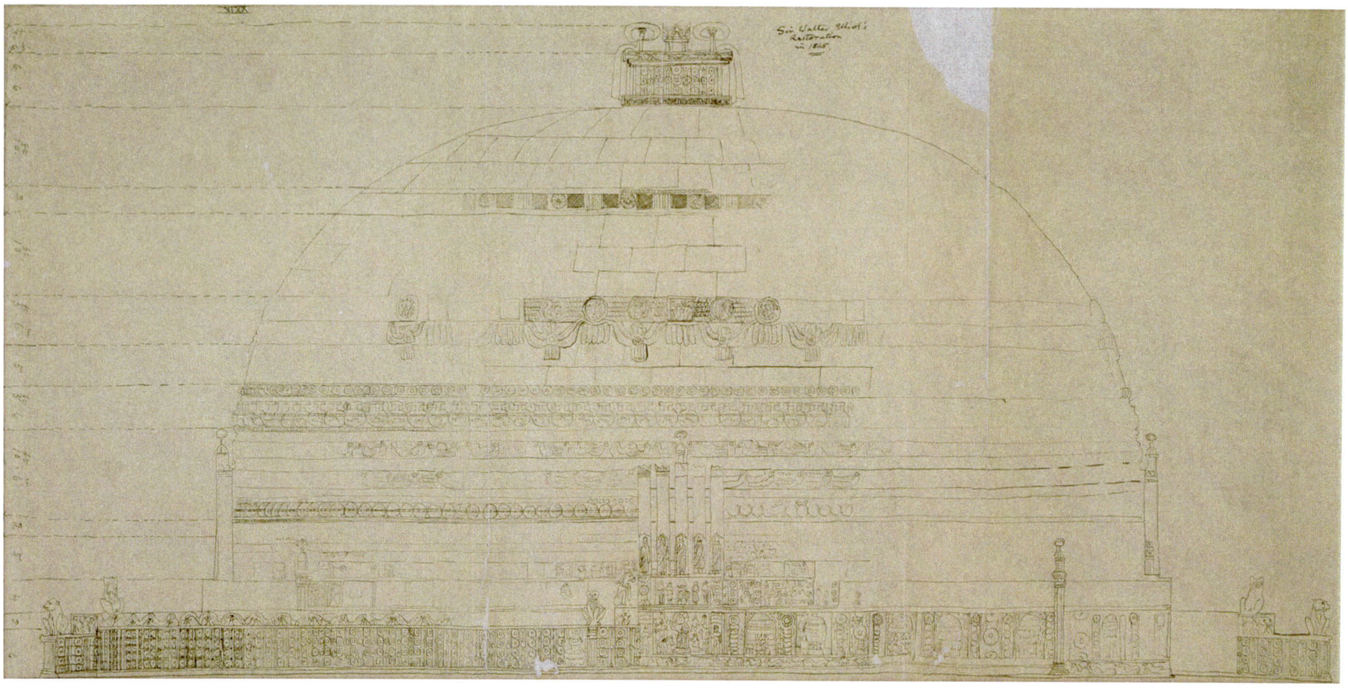

Figure 7 Reconstruction of the Amaravati *stūpa* by Walter Elliot, 1845 or after, British Museum, 1996,1007,0.3

was to deprive the ASI of the right to survey South Indian architecture (Burgess 1882a). Although this conflict was settled by the government's decision to move the sculptures from the site in 1883, it delayed the shipment of the sculpture for two years (Singh 2001: 32–7). After their arrival at Madras, the sculptures were stored at the museum for another two years. When the reliefs were finally installed in the museum gallery in 1886, they suffered again. Surgeon George Bidie, the Superintendent of the Museum, arranged the sculptures according to his own idea and embedded them in the concrete walls of the gallery (ibid.: 37). This infamous installation caused serious damage to the sculptures, although the Government Museum, Chennai has recently removed all the sculptures from the wall and placed them in the new Amaravati gallery.

After the destruction of the mound, the excavations at Amaravati continued in the hope of finding more sculpture and other monastic remains in the surroundings of the *stūpa*. In April 1888 and February 1889, Alexander Rea of the ASI excavated around the west, east and south gateways and found more than 200 pieces of sculpture and brick structures, particularly at the west side of the *stūpa*.[6] Between 1905–6 and 1908–9, Rea extended the scope of excavation to the surrounding area of the *stūpa* between the gates and the area to the north, and found further objects and structures, such as bronze Buddhas, a gold relic casket, granite rail pillars and votive *stūpas* (Rea 1909; 1912). After India's independence, R. Subrahmanyam of the ASI excavated the surroundings of the *stūpa* in 1958–9, and uncovered the damaged portion of the original *stūpa* drum, four projections of the drum, and circumambulatory way of the despoiled *stūpa*. The excavation also found several objects that show extended activity at the *stūpa* between the 3rd–2nd century BCE and the 9th century CE (*IAR* 1958–9). In the latest surveys, in 1973–5, I.K. Sarma excavated underneath the former sculpture shed at the north-east of the *stūpa* and obtained stratigraphical data of the site (*IAR* 1973–4; 1974–5; Sarma 1975; 1980a; 1985). As the largest part of the site had been heavily disturbed by early excavations, these recent excavations could not provide any conclusive answers about the detailed plan of the monastic complex as it would have existed at Amaravati or its chronological development.

The above history of the Amaravati excavations exemplifies the problems typically faced by Indian archaeological monuments in the 19th century. Early surveyors of archaeological monuments, such as Mackenzie, Elliot, Sewell and Horsfall, were military officers or civil servants with varying levels of skill and personal interest in Indian antiquaries. Even early professional archaeologists from the ASI, such as Cunningham and Burgess, developed their research discipline largely through their experience at the sites. Since there was no standard method for surveying and recording the sites, the quality of the surveys varied significantly with each surveyor. As the study of early Indian Buddhism and Buddhist art developed so little in the early 19th century, the early surveyors excavated the site with scant knowledge of the monuments and objects (Almond 1988: 7–32). Preserving the architectural remains was not their main interest, as the primary aim of the excavations was often to find treasures. This certainly seems to have been the basic attitude of the British India government in the early and mid 19th century because, despite the removal of a large number of sculptures by Nayudu, Mackenzie and Elliot, the government did not take any effective action to preserve the monument. In 1871, the Public Works Department of the government even destroyed an early *stūpa* at Gudivada to use the materials for road-making (Rea 1894: 18). The British India government started addressing this issue around the 1870s, as is manifested by the institutional foundation of the ASI (1871), its administrative expansion to the Madras Presidency (1881) and the appointment of the Curator of Ancient Monuments (1881). As described above, these institutions did not function well in their early stages and were not able to save Amaravati from destruction. The

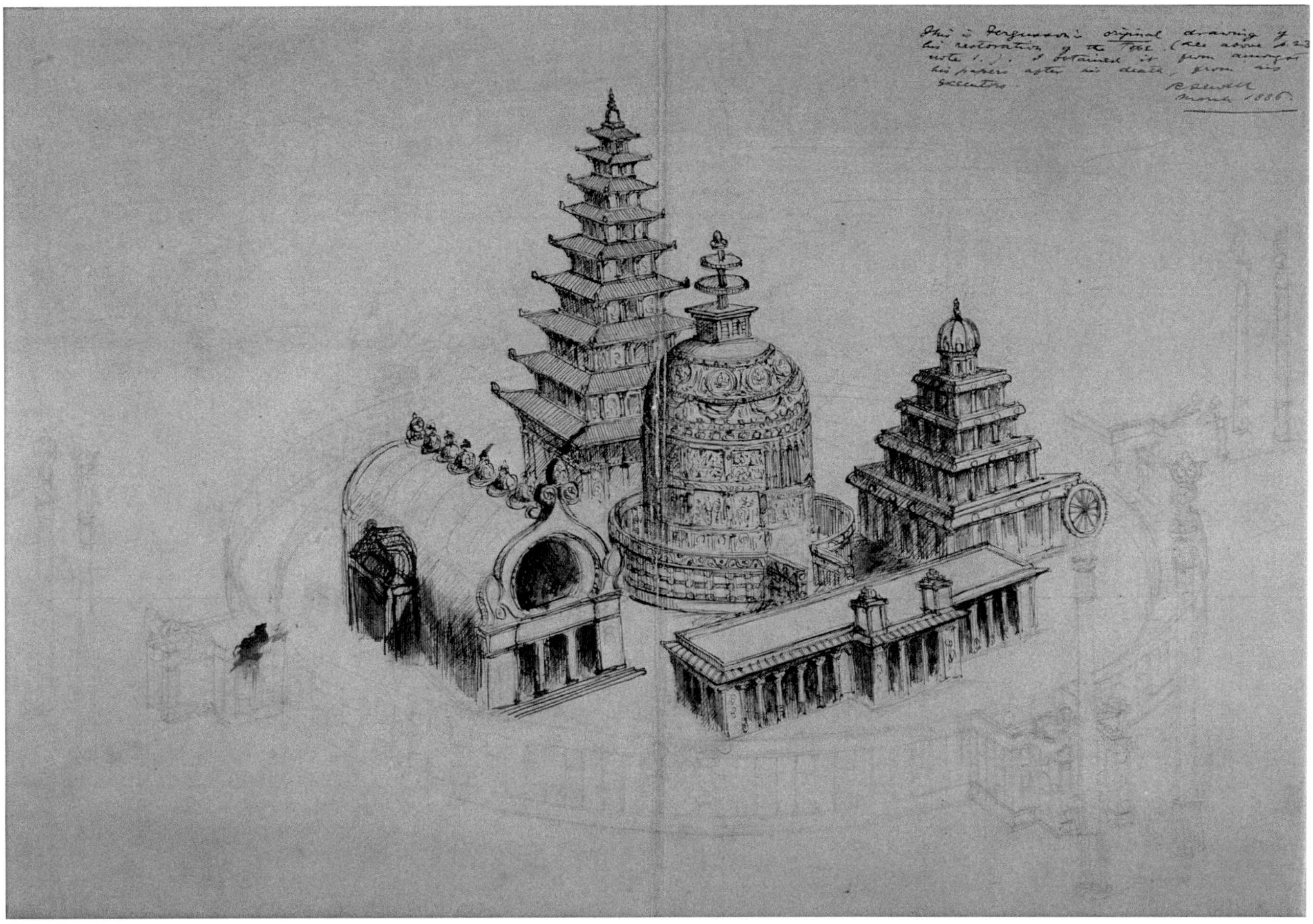

Figure 8 Reconstruction of the Amaravati *stūpa* by James Fergusson, drawn before 1869, British Museum, 1996,1007,0.2

devastation of the Andhran Buddhist sites continued to be a major problem even in the 20th century, when Andhran Buddhist sculpture became the subject of interest among antiquarians and art dealers. While the ASI kept exploring and registering early Buddhist remains in Andhra for protection, their work could not catch up with the spread of treasure-hunting at many unprotected sites. Jouveau-Dubreuil's collecting of sculptures at Nagarjunakonda and other sites in the lower Krishna valley in the 1920s under the direction of an art dealer, C.T. Loo, is a famous example of these kinds of 'excavations' (Delatour 1996: 37; Kaimal 2012: 133–47). Sculptures obtained through such methods were sent to the European and US markets with no excavation data, labelled as Amaravati or 'Amaravati school' sculptures.

Studies of Amaravati

In spite of the disappearance of the monument itself, the Amaravati *stūpa* has been a major subject of academic research since the 19th century. As the late 19th and early 20th centuries were the foundation period of modern academic disciplines concerning the investigation of history and material culture, scholars of each discipline applied their methods to analyse excavated objects, particularly sculptures and inscriptions, in order to address a set of questions about the *stūpa*. Broadly speaking, these questions sought information on three topics: (1) the architectural features of the destroyed monument; (2) the contents of the narrative sculptures and inscriptions; (3) the chronology of the *stūpa* and the excavated artefacts.

Architectural reconstruction

Since the main structure of the *stūpa* had been destroyed before Mackenzie's survey in 1816–17, the original shape of the demolished monument was the immediate concern of early surveyors. The presence of Buddhism in ancient India was hardly recognized in the early 19th century, so they struggled to understand the religious affiliation of the monument. Colin Mackenzie, the first British surveyor of the *stūpa*, did not make any conclusive comments about the nature of the monument, while briefly noting its possible affiliation with a religion other than Hinduism and Jainism (Mackenzie 1807: 278; 1823: 469). Walter Elliot, according to his letters, started the excavation in 1845 with little idea about the character of the mound. During the course of the excavation, however, he noticed that the sculpture carved on drum slabs resembled that of Ceylonese *dagoba* (= *stūpa*) (Elliot 1871; Sewell 1880: 68). Based on this observation and the measurements of the slabs and mound, he made the first elevation plan of the monument (**Fig. 7**). He was, however, discouraged from publishing his elevation plan, since it did not get support from James Fergusson, an authority on the history of Indian architecture at that time (Elliot 1871). Indeed, Fergusson's first catalogue of the Amaravati sculpture in 1868 and his reconstruction plan, which is preserved in the British Museum, proposed a very different shape for the monument from that of Elliot (Fergusson 1868: 164) (**Fig. 8**). He assumed that the *stūpa* was relatively small and occupied the centre of the mound, being then surrounded by a monastic complex with *vihāras*, a nine-storeyed pagoda, a *caitya* hall and so forth. Although Sewell's 1880 report persuasively argued that the monument was a large single *stūpa* (Sewell 1880: 23–5), the debate about the detailed shape of the *stūpa* and the precise location of the excavated sculpture on the *stūpa* continued (Jouveau-Dubreuil 1932: 5–16; Brown 1942: 45–7; Barrett 1954a: 27–39; Knox 1992: 23–30; Kuwayama 1997: 148–9) and still remains one of the unsolved questions concerning Amaravati.

Content analysis of sculptures and inscriptions

Apart from the continuing discussions about the shape of the demolished *stūpa*, many academic researchers have developed minute analysis relating to the contents of the sculptures and the accompanying inscriptions. Initial efforts to read Amaravati inscriptions based on Mackenzie's drawings started immediately after the decipherment of Brahmi script by James Prinsep in 1837 (Prinsep 1837: 218–23; Sewell 1880: 63–6).[7] Fergusson's Amaravati catalogue includes Cunningham's tentative transliterations and translations of 20 inscriptions, although his readings suffered from the poor facsimiles of inscriptions that he used (Fergusson 1868: 238–40). More accurate readings appeared in the late 19th and early 20th centuries, when professional epigraphists began publishing rigorous studies (Hultzsch 1883; 1886; Burgess 1887; Lüders 1912; Chanda 1925; Sivaramamurti 1942). With the continual discovery of new inscriptions after Independence, the total number of published Amaravati inscriptions has now reached more than 300 and is still growing (Ghosh and Sarkar 1967; Sarkar 1971; Sarma 1975; Ghosh 1979; Sarma 1980a). Since these epigraphic studies have been published in several different epigraphic journals and archaeological reports, however, it has become difficult to capture the entire picture. Even the latest comprehensive catalogue of Indian Buddhist inscriptions by Tsukamoto does not include a full list of the published Amaravati inscriptions (Tsukamoto 1996).

In terms of the identification of the narrative sculptures, the first attempt was made by Fergusson, although his interpretation of the sculpture is heavily tinged by his controversial theory of tree and serpent worship, the ancient Turanian cult he postulated as being widely spread among non-Semitic and non-Aryan races (Fergusson 1868). With the significant increase of knowledge of early Buddhist narrative texts, sculptures and paintings in the late 19th and early 20th centuries, his interpretation was fully revised by more objective and comprehensive analyses of the sculptures (Burgess 1887; Vogel 1926; Foucher 1928; Coomaraswamy 1928b; 1929; Linossier 1930; Kempers 1932; Ramachandran 1932). Sivaramamurti's catalogue, which tried to identify all the narrative sculptures in the Madras Museum collection, was the culmination of such scholarly efforts (Sivaramamurti 1942). Since the Amaravati narrative sculptures often include iconography that does not correspond with any surviving texts and artistic examples, their identification has had to be tentative in many cases. As rightly noted by Monika Zin (Chapter 4), the most reliable clues for identifying the reliefs are often the reliefs themselves.

Date and historical background of the stūpa

More warmly debated, compared to the consistent but relatively low-key discussions on the contents of inscriptions and narrative sculptures, and involving different fields of scholarship, has been the issue of the dating and nature of the cultural and political circumstances under which the *stūpa* was constructed with the attendant flowering of artistic production. To address this question, scholars have noted in particular two historical events of the early Deccan: first, the cultural interactions between Andhra and outside regions, particularly the western classical world; and, second, the rule of the Sātavāhana dynasty. As exemplified by Mackenzie's report praising the sculptures' 'correct' representation of the human figure, the use of perspective and their qualitative superiority to any ancient or modern Hindu art (Mackenzie 1823: 469), British officials and scholars were highly impressed with the Amaravati sculptures' naturalistic style and their affinity with western classical art. When subsequent archaeological and historical studies amply proved the flowering of Greco-Bactrian art in north-west India and Indo-Roman trade in the early centuries CE (Sewell 1904; Warmington 1928), such observations developed into a conviction that there was a connection between the Amaravati style and Greco-Roman art. The most explicit example of this line of interpretation is William Taylor's list of the Amaravati sculptures (Taylor 1856). He called the sculptures 'the Elliot Marbles', most likely to compare them with the Elgin Marbles in the British Museum. With the strong conviction that the Amaravati sculptures were made on the basis of a Greek model, he misinterpreted the accompanying Brahmi inscriptions as localized Greek letters and even published his translation! Unsurprisingly, the aesthetic value of Amaravati sculpture in Indian art was elevated by this theory. Fergusson, for instance, regarded the history of Indian architecture and sculpture as the process of artistic and moral decay from the purest prototype brought by Aryans (Mitter 1977: 263–8). However, he evaluated the Amaravati sculptures more highly than the earlier Buddhist sculpture at Bhārhut and Sānchī since they were produced under the influence of Greco-Bactrian art, which, in his opinion, temporarily arrested the process of decay of Indian art (Fergusson 1891: 34–5, 99). While such a eurocentric understanding of Indian sculpture became unpopular during the 20th century, serious scholarly efforts to seek a source for Amaravati style in western classical art, particularly in Roman art and architecture, have continued (Rowland 1953: 128, nn 6, 10; Stone 1985; Kuwayama 1997; Stone 2008). Stone's article in this volume (Chapter 5), for example, is the latest result of this aspect of research. When scholars started discussing the 'Indianization' of south-east Asia in the early 20th century, the far-flung presence of Amaravati-style sculpture in Sri Lanka and south-east Asia was noted as important evidence of the early expansion of Indian religious culture into the Indian Ocean world (Coomaraswamy 1927: 161, 197). The precise stylistic and iconographical relationship between the Amaravati sculpture and Sri Lankan and south-east Asian Buddhist art has thus been a major concern among scholars (see Chapter 6).

In terms of the political circumstances that supported the flowering of the *stūpa*, what has been particularly noted by former studies is the rule of the Sātavāhanas, the imperial dynasty that emerged in the post-Mauryan Deccan. The first scholar who highlighted the link between the *stūpa* and the dynasty was probably Fergusson. Because of the similarity between the design of the Amaravati railing and that of railing motifs carved at Buddhist caves at Kanheri and Nasik, and on account of the palaeographic resemblances among the inscriptions at all three sites, he assigned these sites to the same period. He dated the Nasik caves to the early 4th century CE because of their association with the Sātavāhana king, Gotamīputa, and so the Amaravati railing was also dated to the 4th century CE (Fergusson 1868: 84, 156–7). Subsequently, Burgess's Amaravati excavation in 1882 found a Sātavāhana inscription mentioning King Puḷumāyi, the son of Gotamīputa. While Burgess revised the date of the two Sātavāhana kings to the early–mid 2nd century CE based on Gotamīputa's contemporaneity with Nahanāpa, a famous ruler of the Kṣaharātas, the chronological link between the *stūpa* and the dynasty was confirmed (Burgess 1887: 4–5, 100). After Rea's excavations at the end of the 19th and the beginning of the 20th centuries, R. Chanda (1925) studied newly discovered inscriptions and classified them on the basis of the palaeography into four periods between the 2nd century BCE and the 3rd century CE. Since this dating corresponded well with the traditional chronology of the Sātavāhanas based on a group of the Purāṇas, it was fully accepted by Sivaramamurti, who labelled the *stūpa* 'a glorious monument of the Sātavāhana period' (1942: 8).

In 1954, however, this so-called long chronology of the Amaravati *stūpa* and sculpture was strongly contested by Douglas Barrett. In his catalogue of the Amaravati sculpture of the British Museum, Barrett agreed with Sivaramamurti in admitting the Sātavāhanas' crucial role in providing the Andhra region with the political and economic stability that enabled the erection of Buddhist monuments (Barrett 1954a: 40). However, he dated the beginning of the dynasty's rule in Andhra to the second quarter of the 2nd century CE, since he identified the homeland of the Sātavāhanas with the north-west Deccan, not with Andhra (ibid.: 13). He also supported the much shorter chronology of the dynasty that was proposed by D.C. Sircar, who relied on another group of Purāṇas (Sircar 1951: 195–211). Barrett thus concluded that the construction of the Amaravati *stūpa* and sculptures was achieved in a relatively short period between *c.* 125 and 240 CE (Barrett 1954a: 45).

This co-existence of two significantly different chronologies of the *stūpa*, relying on different chronologies of the Sātavāhanas, generated much controversy among scholars. While Barrett's short chronology was, with minor modifications, well accepted among art historians outside India (Spink 1958: 100; Huntington 1985: 174–9; Miyaji 1992: 101; Koezuka 1994: 18, 22), Indian archaeologists contested it by providing new archaeological and epigraphic data that indicated that the *stūpa* was founded much earlier (Ghosh and Sarkar 1967; Sarma 1975; Ghosh 1979; Sarma 1985). As scholars in different fields discussed the validity of their supporting chronologies of the Amaravati *stūpa* and the Sātavāhanas by analysing their own materials, such as Purāṇic accounts, inscriptions, sculptures, coins and architecture, the chronological argument became complicated and hard to comprehend for non-specialists. On the other hand, all studies accepted the validity of the historical assumption on which the chronological debates were based, i.e. the causal link between the rule of the Sātavāhanas and the development of the *stūpa*, because 'the historical model presented here by the Sātavāhana/Amaravati combination, i.e. the juxtaposition of economic prosperity, royal patronage and religion, remains unaffected by the dating controversy' (Knox 1992: 14).

In short, since the unfortunate destruction of the site in the 19th century, scholars have studied the architectural and historical developments of the Amaravati *stūpa* mainly by analysing excavated objects such as sculpture, inscriptions, coins and pottery, in isolation from their site contexts, and by connecting their material analysis with textual sources, particularly the Purāṇas. Their studies thus approached the Amaravati *stūpa* not as an integrated monument, but as a depository containing much sculptural and epigraphic data awaiting scholarly classification and analysis. This approach was successful in revealing the stylistic and iconographical features of each of the sculptures, deciphering the contents of inscriptions and identifying kings mentioned in the Purāṇas. Their efforts to understand a variety of objects also enhanced the specialization of disciplines, such as epigraphy, archaeology, art history and numismatic studies, and developed different scholarly narratives to understand their objects. Since the site had already been destroyed and early excavations were poorly recorded, serious efforts to examine the original integration of the objects with the *stūpa* and the monastic complex at Amaravati tended to be dismissed among scholars. For instance, even now, there is no full *catalogue raisonné* listing all Amaravati sculptures and inscriptions and providing detailed acquisition records. As a result, in the discussion of Amaravati sculpture many 'Amaravati-school' sculptures whose association with the Amaravati *stūpa* is unconfirmed are often included without distinguishing them from genuine Amaravati pieces. This situation undermines our precise understanding of the Amaravati sculpture and creates considerable confusions in the discussion of 'Amaravati-style' art in Andhra, Sri Lanka and south-east Asia (Brown 2014: 14–18). By assuming the causal relationship between the rule of the Sātavāhana dynasty and the development of the *stūpa*, early studies have tended to avoid in-depth discussions about the immediate social surroundings in which the *stūpa* flourished. Amaravati thus tended to be studied as if it had an autonomous existence, lacking any relationship with the local habitations or with the other Buddhist sites in Andhra (Sarkar 1987: 631–2). In the main it has been compared to famous early Buddhist sites outside Andhra, such as Bharhut, Sanchi, Ajanta and Gandhara. This has been a major methodological problem for the study not only of the Amaravati *stūpa*, but for Indian archaeological monuments in general.

Recent approaches

Fortunately, recent developments in archaeological and historical research on early India have helped somewhat in enabling us to address such methodological problems. Of particular note is the substantial growth of our knowledge about Indian Buddhist sites, particularly those of Andhra. Throughout the 20th century, apart from a few sites like Amaravati and Nagarjunakonda, Andhran Buddhist sites received very little serious scholarly attention in comparison to their counterparts in the western Deccan, owing to the poor documentation and protection of the sites. In the last few decades, the situation has changed significantly. As a result of extensive surveys by AP State Archaeology and the Archaeological Survey of India, more than 100 Buddhist remains are now documented in the lower Krishna and Godavari valleys (Shimada 2013: Appendix B). While many of these sites await further intensive research, some of the newly discovered sites, such as Chandavaran, Dhulikatta, Vaddamanu, Nellakondapalli, Kottanandayapalem, Phanigiri and Kanaganahalli, have become well known, since they yielded a significant number of new sculptures and inscriptions. Perhaps the two most impressive sites are Phanigiri and Kanaganahalli, located on the tributary of the upper Krishna valley. Recent re-excavations at Phanigiri in Nalgonda District, to the south of the new state of Telangana, revealed an extensive monastic complex of the Ikṣvāku and the Viṣṇukuṇḍin periods on a monolithic hillock (Reddy *et al.* 2008; Skilling 2008; Skilling and von Hinüber 2011). As is highlighted by Becker in this volume (Chapter 6), the excavated objects include unique pieces, such as the narrative sculpture on the gateway (*toraṇa*) and a large statue of a princely figure. Excavations at Kanaganahalli, which had been known as Sannati, yielded a well-preserved *stūpa* with numerous relief sculptures in good condition, dated roughly to between the 1st century BCE and the 3rd century CE (Poonacha 2011; Nakanishi and von Hinüber 2014). Since the excavated sculptures include many reliefs of narratives and portraits of Aśoka and several Sātavāhana kings with label inscriptions, they provide a new set of evidence to identify Andhran Buddhist narrative sculptures and also to establish their chronology. Recent archaeological research in the Deccan has provided more data not only on the Buddhist period, but also on the pre-Buddhist or 'megalithic period', as discussed by Johansen in this volume (Chapter 1).

This increase in archaeological and epigraphic data on Andhran Buddhist sites has certainly raised scholarly and public interest in Andhran Buddhism and Buddhist material culture in recent years. In terms of scholarly research, a notable development is the interdisciplinary discussion about the excavated objects. As exemplified by a series of works by Gregory Schopen (1988; 1991), textual Buddhologists have started revising traditional theories on early Indian Buddhism, such as the monastic avoidance of *stūpa* worship, by making active use of archaeological and epigraphic data from Andhra. Peter Skilling's study of *mahācaitya* in this volume (Chapter 2) demonstrates the advantage of such scholarship, which combines the careful analysis of the texts with a comprehensive survey of the epigraphic and archaeological evidence. Moreover, a series of studies by J. Heitzman, H.P. Ray and A. Parasher-Sen show how a historical approach can reveal more refined pictures of the political and economic development of the eastern Deccan in the Early Historic period on the basis of archaeological and epigraphic data (Heitzman 1984; Parasher-Sen 1991; Ray 1988; 1994; 1997; 2008). In the field of research into Andhran Buddhist monuments, Lars Fogelin's study of Thotlakonda and my own work on the Amaravati *stūpa* employed this method in order to reveal the immediate historical landscape in which the monastic complex flourished (Fogelin 2006; Shimada 2013).

The growth of data on Andhran Buddhist sites has also brought a better understanding of the old Andhran collections in museums. Scholars have started to re-examine so-called Amaravati-school sculptures in order to identify their original locations and recover their site context by combining the early acquisition records of the objects in the museums with new data on Andhran Buddhist sites, sculptures and other excavated objects. The studies of Barnard, Ślaczka and Willis in this volume (Chapters 7–9) are examples of this. One of the major discoveries resulting from this type of research is that of the Sadas, an important local dynasty that ruled the coastal Andhra region before the expansion of the Sātavāhanas. As noted by Bhandhare in this volume (Chapter 3), their coins in the British Museum were discovered more than a century ago but were given obscure identifications. Accumulation of epigraphic and numismatic data through recent excavations at Vaddamanu and other sites, however, has enabled scholars to find out about this unknown dynasty and even construct a chronology of the kings. According to my study on the construction process of the great limestone railing at Amaravati, the sculptural production of Amaravati seems to have reached a high point under the Sadas' rule (Shimada 2006: 127–8, 131–2; 2013: 40–2, 111–12). This suggests that the construction of the *stūpa* was not simply the accomplishment of the Sātavāhana dynasty.

It is also important to note that continual discoveries of new Buddhist sites in Andhra have greatly increased people's consciousness of the legacy of Buddhism in Andhra. Since the legacy is used to promote tourism and enhance local pride, Buddhist remains are given new layers of significance as symbols of the glory of Andhran history and culture. As discussed recently by Becker (2009; 2015) and in Vardhan's report of Sriparvata Arama in this volume (Chapter 10), the Amaravati *stūpa* is seen as the most important monument in this movement of promoting the legacy of Buddhism as a cultural identifier for Andhra. The recent selection of Amaravati as the new capital of Andhra Pradesh after the split of the Urdu-speaking Telangana region may not be completely unrelated to this movement.

In short, the Amaravati *stūpa* and its sculptures, which had been treated as outstanding but rather solitary and fragmented examples of early Buddhist monuments and art in Andhra, have attracted significant scholarly and non-scholarly interest in recent years through the acquisition of new kinds of knowledge and fresh perspectives that have led to a clearer understanding of the monument. This volume presents such new scholarship on Amaravati and the related Buddhist material culture of early Andhra, in the hope of enhancing further discussions on this remarkable Buddhist monument of early India.

Notes

1 This topic is taken up in my monograph (Shimada 2013: 1–30) and consequently the contents here overlap in part. For this article, I have incorporated new scholarship and discoveries as far as possible. Owing to the word limit in this volume I have not repeated the detailed references in my monograph to the early surveys of the Amaravati *stūpa*, particularly the India Office Records.

2 Mackenzie's report indicates that his visit to Amaravati took place around February 1797 (Mackenzie 1807: 272). Howes' recent study of Mackenzie's surveys in South India, however, shows that his visit to Amaravati took place in February 1798 (Howes 2002: 54; 2009; 21; 2010: 49).

3 A set of the drawings is preserved in the British Library (BL, WD 1061). They are available online at http://www.bl.uk/onlinegallery/features/amaravati/homepage.html (accessed 17 June 2016).

4 This set of drawings is now in the British Library (WD 2242–2283). About the drawings, see Howes 2009.

5 The British Museum Amaravati collection includes 12 sculptures that have no record of arrival in London (nos 1880,0709.8, 9, 34, 67, 70–72, 77, 79, 82, 92, 129; illustrated in Knox 1992: nos 22, 27, 30, 40, 55, 60/72, 69, 70, 81, 84, 105, 130). As six of them (nos 1880,0709.8, 34, 67, 79, 71, 72; illustrated in Knox 1992: nos 27, 40, 60/72, 70, 81, 130) are recorded in the Mackenzie Amaravati drawings, it is likely that they were sent by Mackenzie and were kept in the India Museum of East India House. Unfortunately, the archive of the India Museum kept in the Victoria & Albert Museum does not include records of Mackenzie's Amaravati pieces. I thank Nick Barnard for sharing this piece of information.

6 The report of these excavations was not published. Brief records are available in Madras Public Proceeding, 11 September 1888, no. 896 (BL, IOR, P/3284) and Madras Public Proceeding, 30 April 1889, no. 383 (BL, IOR, P/3511).

7 One of the two inscriptions discovered by Mackenzie is in the British Museum (no. 1880,0709.67; illustrated in Knox 1992: no. 130).

Chapter 1
The South Deccan Iron Age: Antecedents to Early Historic Andhradeśa

Peter G. Johansen

Before the establishment of cities, states and Buddhist monastic institutions in Early Historic Andhradeśa, agro-pastoral communities across much of peninsular India participated in a common, or at least related, suite of commemorative-memorial practices, craft production and consumption activities. The material record of these practices, which includes a range of megalithic monuments and tombs, slipped and polished ceramic wares, bronze and copper items, iron weapons and tools, has a wide distribution across peninsular India during the South Indian Iron Age (*c.* 1200–300 BCE) or 'megalithic period' as it is also known (Leshnik 1974; Allchin and Allchin 1982; Moorti 1994; Brubaker 2001). During the Iron Age many regional settlement communities across South India began to create and maintain politically transformative social distinctions through a range of material practices that involved settlement, land use, mortuary ritual and monumentality (Bauer 2011; Johansen 2011; 2014a; Bauer and Johansen 2015). The political implications of these material practices, which included differential social access to material and symbolic resources, places, power and decision-making, has led to considerable speculation on the formative relationship between Iron Age social and political organization and the development of cities, states and economies during the subsequent Early Historic period (*c.* 300 BCE–400 CE).

This chapter examines the South Indian Iron Age in an effort to historicize the social, political and economic contexts antecedent to Early Historic period urbanism, states and Buddhist monasticism in Andhradeśa, developments that are exemplified by the monastic settlement at Amaravati and its contemporary, adjacent urban community at Dharanikota (see Shimada 2013) (**Fig. 9**). Historicizing the Iron Age and its relationship to the developments of the Early Historic period are beset by a number of empirical and conceptual constraints. A lack of systematic survey and data recovery has left many regions without adequate information to evaluate the range of activities critical to addressing questions of social, political and economic practice and change (e.g. settlement, land-use practices, craft production, trade), while a paucity of radiometric dates from well-documented archaeological contexts continues to impede the ability of archaeologists to examine change and continuity across time, especially amongst data sets with important variation, such as megalithic monuments and burial contexts (Brubaker 2001). Conceptually, the framing of the Iron Age as an 'archaeological culture' (i.e. the Megalithic Culture) has also obscured matters by collapsing a myriad of temporally dynamic and geographically diverse social, political and economic practices into a normative, homogenous and homeostatic Megalithic Culture, people or 'folk' (Johansen 2003).

Despite these constraints it is possible to address some Iron Age social and political practices, and investigate how and why these developed and changed in historically unique contexts across South India. For many Iron Age communities an emergent concern with constructing, maintaining and contesting a range of social differences and affiliations, distinct from those practised during the preceding Neolithic period (*c.* 3000–1200 BCE), restructured

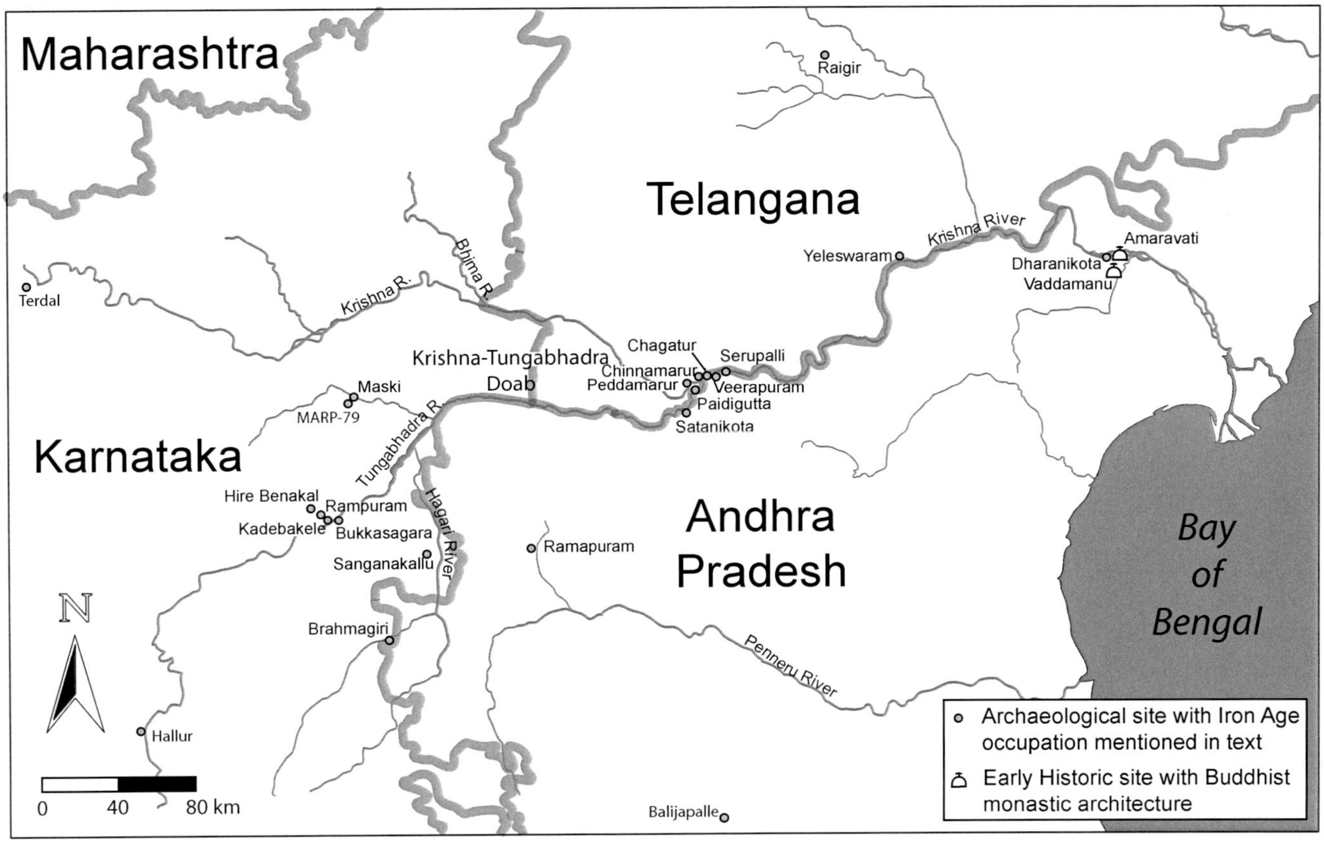

Figure 9 Location of archaeological sites mentioned in Chapter 1

and reordered social and political relations within and between communities across landscapes in many regions. At the end of this chapter, I return to some of the potential consequences and implications of Iron Age socio-political relations for a suite of more localized developments in the regional politics of Early Historic Andhradeśa. As a whole, however, this chapter examines Iron Age social and political practice in the south Deccan region, honing in primarily on the Krishna River and Tungabhadra River drainages to explore data from regional studies where Iron Age socio-politics are the focus of research.

Investigating the South Indian Iron Age: the legacy of a 'Megalithic Culture'

The archaeological remains of the South Indian Iron Age are among the most obtrusive and well distributed of any prehistoric period in South India. From the early 19th century megalithic features were among the first archaeological materials to capture the attention of colonial administrators as well as those of amateur and, later, professional archaeologists (e.g. Babington 1823; Taylor 1853; Branfill 1881). Early investigations typically consisted of the 'opening' of megalithic tombs, and when reported, the itemization of their form and content, but it was not until the pioneering work of R.E.M. Wheeler (1948) at the multiperiod site of Brahmagiri that stratified Iron Age archaeological deposits were placed into a systematic, albeit relative, chronological scheme. Wheeler's ceramic typology and periodization enabled the relative dating of Iron Age archaeological sites, including many megalithic mortuary features, to a time after the Neolithic period and antecedent to the Early Historic and medieval periods. With the onset of radiocarbon dating the Iron Age was further refined to date between *c.* 1200 and 300 BCE.

Wheeler's ceramic typology and periodization remain among the most significant developments in South Indian archaeology, but his framing of the Iron Age as an archaeological culture (i.e. the 'Megalithic Culture') has had lasting, albeit less productive effects. Wheeler's Megalithic Culture became the predominant interpretative framing for the Iron Age, synonymous with a singular people, who were often characterized as a 'race' or ethnolinguistic group (e.g. Fürer-Haimendorf 1953; Banerjee 1965; Sarkar 1972; Leshnik 1974), their normative customs, beliefs and behaviours straightforwardly reflected in the widespread distribution of seemingly uniform material markers (Black-and-Red ware ceramics, iron and megaliths). In spite of the eventual recognition of regional differences in Iron Age material culture, especially megaliths (e.g. Leshnik 1974; Sundara 1975; McIntosh 1985), the notion of a uniform and homeostatic Megalithic Culture persists to this day.

Investigation into the actual workings of Iron Age societies remained only thinly pursued through much of the 20th century, with research dominated by descriptions of the material markers of the archaeological culture. For decades, efforts at explanation focused almost exclusively upon the issue of cultural origins or ethnogenesis and the postulated diffusionary mechanisms that were responsible for an extraneous megalith-building people displacing an indigenous Neolithic culture in South India.[1] Generations of archaeologists and historians have argued that the transition to the Iron Age was the result of an invasion or migration of new people from North India or indeed farther afield (cf. Childe 1947; Gordon 1958; Banerjee 1965; Nilakanta Sastri

1966; Gururaja Rao 1972; Leshnik 1974; Allchin and Allchin 1982; Padma 2008). Archaeologists saw the appearance of archaeological 'traits' (e.g. megaliths, ceramic wares, iron and even skull shapes) as evidence for the influx of a new people into South India. Archaeological data from several sites (e.g. Balijapalle, Hallur, Maski, Ramapuram, Sangankallu, Terdal) document localized transitions in mortuary practices and ceramic production during the latter part of the Neolithic Period (Sundara 1969–70; Nagaraja Rao 1971; *IAR* 1985; Walimbe *et al.* 1991; Fuller *et al.* 2007; Bauer and Johansen 2015), and today it is increasingly recognized that the Neolithic/Iron Age transition was a more gradual and localized period of change (Moorti 1994; Brubaker 2001; Bauer and Johansen 2015). Other developments such as early iron metallurgy may have had their origins in the exchange of goods and knowledge with northern India (Johansen 2014a), a relationship that would have precedence with the introduction of North Indian crops (e.g. wheat, barley and rice) to the south during the early third millennium BCE (Fuller 2005; 2006).

The notion of a homogeneous South India-wide Megalithic Culture has been an equally persistent and detrimental legacy of the culture-history approach. However, by the mid-1970s an increasing number of studies were identifying regional variations in the distribution of megalithic monuments (Gururaja Rao 1972; Leshnik 1974; Sundara 1975; Deo 1985; McIntosh 1985; Rao 1988). At first this variation was seen by some (e.g. McIntosh 1985; Rao 1988) as representing the further diffusion of megalithic peoples and mortuary practices *within* South India from postulated origins in northern Karnataka and western Andhra Pradesh. It was with U.S. Moorti's landmark study (1994) of previously recorded mortuary and settlement data that a cohesive socio-economic explanation for Iron Age social organization was first proposed. Moorti (1994) and, later, Brubaker (2001) argued that Iron Age societies were socially ranked with disparities in power probably configured through differential participation in trade, craft and agricultural production within regional contexts. Moorti (1994) considered regional ecologies to be important conditioning factors in socio-political organization, while Brubaker (2001: 287) suggested that the degree of Iron Age social control varied across regions, falling into a range of political arrangements best characterized as 'chiefdoms', an ethnographically derived political form used to denote ranked, non-state social organization in socio-evolutionary approaches to past political organization. A number of recent field surveys (e.g. Selvakumar 2000; Abraham 2003; Sinopoli and Morrison 2007; Sugandhi 2013; Bauer 2015; Johansen and Bauer 2015) have demonstrated even greater and more fine-grained regional variation in the distribution of all manner of Iron Age sites, which increasingly draws attention to the importance of locality in understanding Iron Age social and political practices.

Despite culture history's blurring of regional variation in the distribution of archaeological materials, there was widespread participation in a common suite of commemorative-memorial practices, ceramic and metals production and consumption activities throughout Iron Age South India. However, rather than a uniform and normative 'culture', regional variation in the distribution of megaliths, slipped and polished ceramics and metals suggests participation in temporally perduring ritual, technological and aesthetic 'communities of practice' (Wenger 1998; Stahl 2013: 54). These multi-scalar social networks were where ideas, values, knowledge, technologies and materials were formulated, transmitted and exchanged, in what Stahl (2013: 54) calls 'shared domains' (e.g. craft production, ritual complexes). Placing Iron Age social and political practices in historical context requires the investigation of how and why this more widely distributed suite of socio-material practices was developed, mobilized, incorporated or reformulated by individuals, groups and communities to produce social relations of difference and affiliation in accordance with the circumstances of localized contexts, rather than the construction of historicist (i.e. culture history) or socio-evolutionary metanarratives of the past. For most regions of South India this goal requires further problem-oriented research and data with greater chronological resolution. I turn now to a discussion of the Iron Age in the south Deccan plateau, specifically the watershed of the upper Krishna–Tungabhadra River (**Fig. 9**).

Iron Age society and politics

Across the semi-arid plains and hill chains west of the confluence of the Krishna and Tungabhadra Rivers, the social and material landscape of the region's agro-pastoral communities was undergoing significant change by at least *c.* 1200 BCE. Potters gradually began producing new slipped and polished ceramic wares, with an increasing emphasis on small serving vessels, while the chipped and ground stone industry of the Neolithic period was increasingly replaced by iron (and later steel) tools smelted and smithed by local producers (Sinopoli 2009; Gullapalli 2009; Johansen 2014a; Morrison *et al.* 2016). Objects of adornment made from non-local semi-precious stones (e.g. carnelian, lapis lazuli) and marine shell, or from rarer metals such as gold, point to increasing trade within South India, between the south and the north, and perhaps farther afield (Kelly 2013). Subsistence practices appear to have been one important area of continuity with Neolithic times but there is increasing evidence for both intensifications and other changes in the social organization of food production. Multi-scalar settlement data demonstrate considerable change in the size, location and configuration of many settlements but also reveal continuity of occupation at some sites. The most remarkable changes were in commemorative-memorial practices and the megalithic monuments and mortuary interments these produced. When viewed together many of these changes and their subsequent development in regions across the south Deccan plateau document the creation and maintenance of social affiliations, distinctions and inequalities within and between Iron Age settlement communities, differences which had profound political consequences, transforming the character and organization of social relations.

Monumentality and mortuary ritual: social distinctions and claims

Megalithic monumentality and mortuary ritual were two important media for the creation and maintenance of Iron

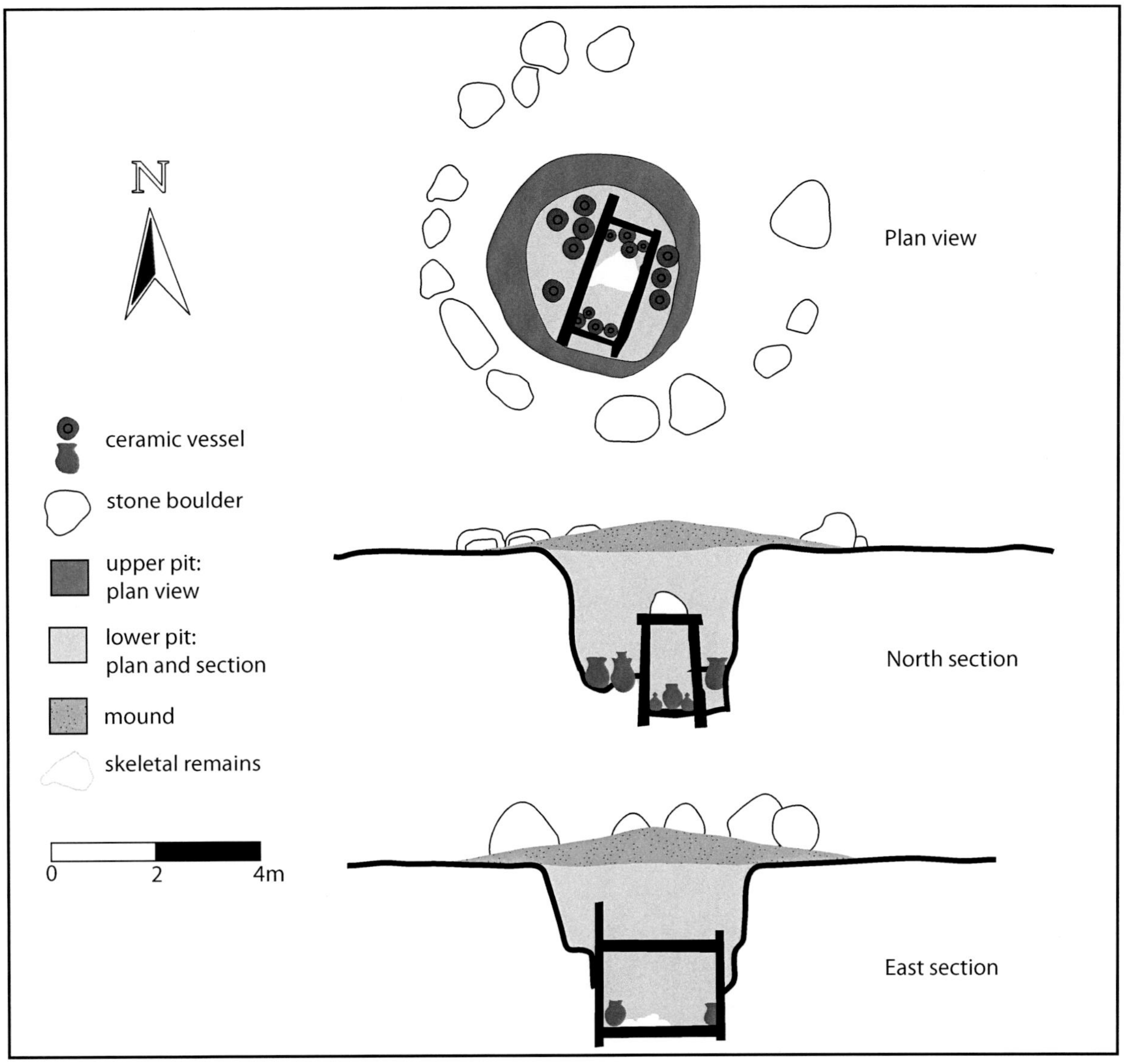

Figure 10 Excavated cist-circle megalith from Raigir, Telangana State, original drawing by G. Yazdani (based on an unnumbered drawing in Hunt 1916 between pages 180 and 181)

Age social distinctions. Efforts by Iron Age communities to produce social differences through mortuary ritual appear to have begun very early, during the period sometimes referred to as the Neolithic–Iron Age transition (*c.* 1400–1200 BCE). At the site of Maski in the Krishna–Tungabhadra *doāb*,[2] B.K. Thapar (1957) excavated and defined three classes of 'megalithic' burial in strata intervening between Neolithic/Chalcolithic and Iron Age settlement deposits. Nearby, the Maski Archaeological Research Project (MARP) recently recorded a large Neolithic–Iron Age cemetery at MARP-79, further examples of variation in mortuary treatments, which were radiometrically dated to *c.* 1800–1200 BCE (Bauer and Johansen 2015). The differences among these interments are considerable (e.g. pit burials, jar burials, terracotta sarcophagi, with and without small capstones or stone slab coverings). Like the burials documented by Thapar (1957), those at MARP-79 anticipate the more labour-intensive developments in mortuary preparation exhibited by the larger, later-dated megalithic interments (Bauer and Johansen 2015).

Iron Age megaliths include a wide range of commemorative-memorial stone and earth features such as dolmens, stone circles, cairns, barrows, menhirs, alignments, avenues, slab wedge and passage chamber features, located in a variety of mortuary and non-mortuary contexts (Leshnik 1974; Moorti 1994; Brubaker 2001; Bauer and Trivedi 2013; Haricharan *et al.* 2013; Morrison *et al.* 2016). In the south Deccan they are found in large and small complexes, as well as in small groups or as individual features, the latter often without clear mortuary associations. Megalithic complexes are typically located close to settlements (Moorti 1994; Brubaker 2001; Bauer 2015), but small groups of megaliths are also found in, and on the immediate margins of, settlements as both pre-abandonment and post-abandonment features (Bauer *et al.* 2007; Johansen 2010; Morrison *et al.* 2016; Wilcox 2015).

Megalithic features are most frequently associated with Iron Age and Early Historic mortuary practices (**Fig. 10**). Mortuary ritual and monumental practice inscribed a range of social meanings on people and places through the commemoration and memorialization of the dead during both periods. Excavated mortuary contexts display considerable variation in the size and type of associated megaliths, the type of interments (e.g. pits, urns, stone cists and slabs, terracotta sarcophagi), the number of interred

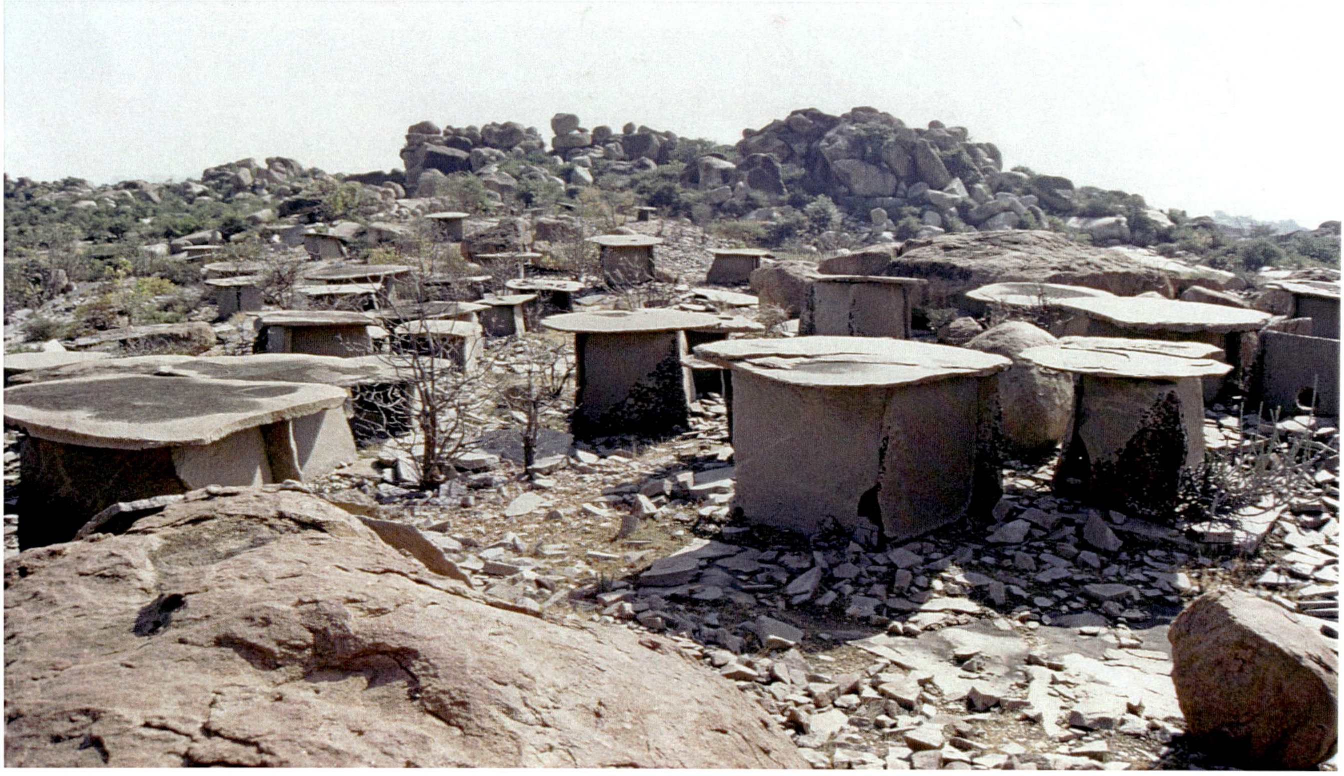

Figure 11 Dolmen megaliths at the apex of the mortuary complex at Hire Benakal, Karnataka

individuals (e.g. single, double, multiple), the treatment of the body (e.g. extended articulated, excarnated, partial, cremated) and the number and kind of grave goods (e.g. ceramic vessels, iron weapons and tools, ornaments and objects of gold, copper, bronze and semi-precious stone) (Leshnik 1974; Moorti 1994; Brubaker 2001). This variation has been widely accepted as evidence for Iron Age social differences and inequalities (Sundara 1975; Leshnik 1974; Moorti 1994; Brubaker 2001; Johansen 2014b; Bauer 2015). Unfortunately, there have been very few detailed and comprehensive studies of variation within individual Iron Age cemeteries, and there remains an extreme paucity of radiometric dates from individual interments. This has severely hampered efforts to assess the specific local contours of Iron Age social ranking and political organization.

The proximity of many megalithic mortuary complexes to settlements suggests that particular cemeteries were populated by members of specific, adjacent settlement communities (Bauer 2015). Brubaker (2001: 279, 297), using Leshnik's (1974: 252–3) demographic analysis of cemetery data, has argued convincingly that the individuals buried in most megalithic mortuary complexes must represent only a portion of much larger Iron Age settlement communities (cf. Hunt 1916). He further suggests that the remainder of the population is buried in less imposing, less well-marked interments, in as-yet-undiscovered cemeteries (Brubaker 2001: 297). Several cemeteries surrounding the Iron Age settlements near Maski that fit this criteria have been recorded (Gordon 1958; Bauer and Johansen 2015).

Bauer's (2015; Bauer and Trivedi 2013) pioneering analysis of monument production at the mortuary site of Hire Benakal (**Fig. 9**) documented distinct spatial patterning in the distribution of megaliths, strongly suggestive of inequalities both in access to place and in the capacity to muster labour for megalith construction among the social groups who incrementally built the site. At Hire Benakal the largest, most labour-intensive and formalized monuments (i.e. massive stone slab dolmens) were located at the apex of the cemetery surrounding a large, constructed, rock-cut reservoir (**Fig. 11**). Ever smaller, less formalized and less labour-intensive features were placed along the lower slopes and margins of the site (**Fig. 12**), a pattern repeated on a smaller scale at other cemeteries nearby and elsewhere (Bauer and Trivedi 2013: 57–8). Spatial clustering of megaliths in Iron Age cemeteries is a frequently observed pattern. However, Bauer's study convincingly links differences in monument form and size with the production of a mortuary landscape with tangible social contours. Clusters of megaliths here and at other mortuary complexes may equally represent social affiliations such as kin, lineage or residential groupings (Bauer 2011; Wheeler 1948; Sundara 1975; Krishna Sastry 1983).

While much further research is clearly required, archaeological patterning suggests several dimensions of social difference and inequalities were produced and expressed through Iron Age mortuary ritual. Mortuary complexes appear to have been the relatively exclusive domain of nearby settlement communities, yet within those communities it would appear that only some possessed the rights or privilege to inter their dead at megalithic cemeteries. Furthermore, within large megalithic mortuary complexes (e.g. Hire Benakal) there appear to have been inequalities both in access to particular places within the cemetery and in the capacity to recruit and deploy the requisite labour to construct many of the larger features (Bauer and Trivedi 2013: 59). This spatial patterning suggests a localized socio-politics of mortuary ritual practised within a ranked political hierarchy of social groups. Inequalities of

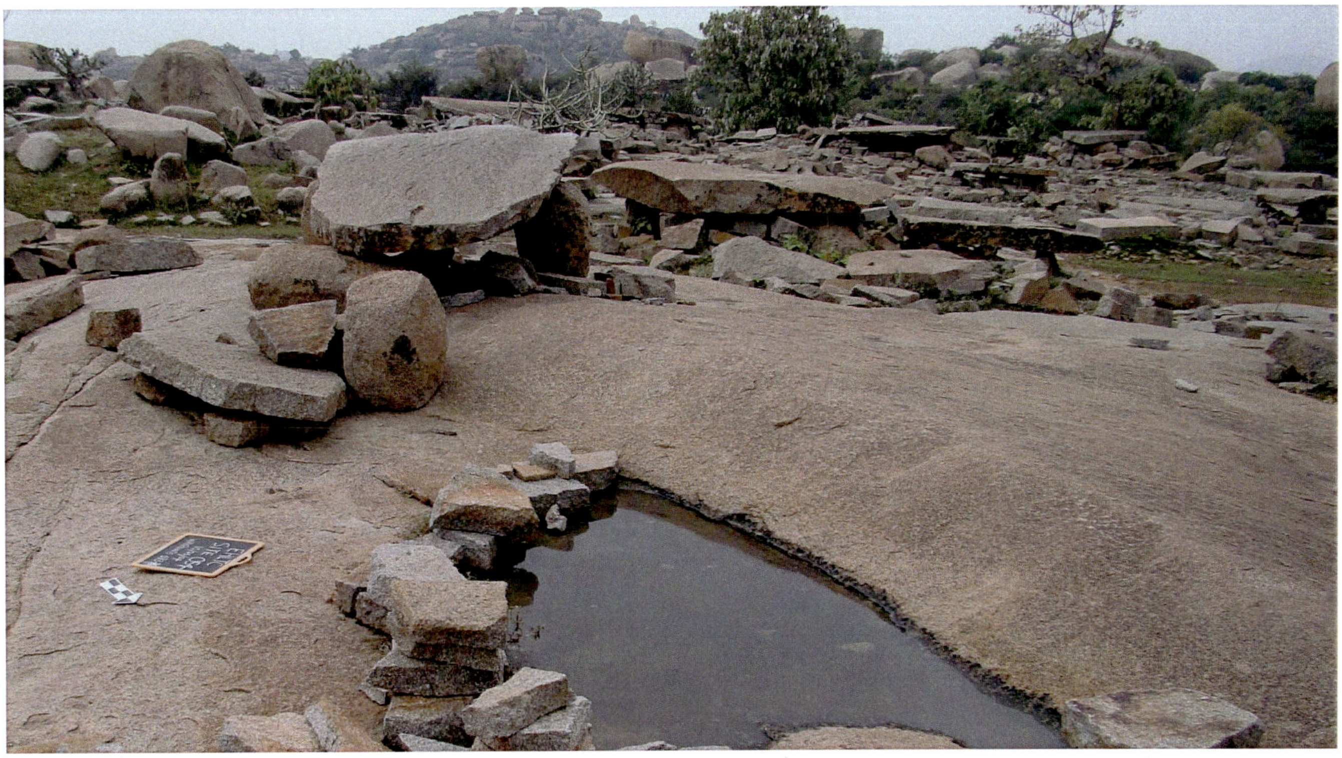

Figure 12 Smaller less formalized megaliths on the margins of Hire Benakal overlooking a small modified rock pool (photograph: courtesy of Andrew Bauer)

access to place and to other socio-symbolic resources (e.g. labour) find compelling parallels in the design and spatial organization of some settlements as well (see below).

The type of interment and the kind and quantity of grave goods further support the idea that some Iron Age communities were creating and expressing ranked social differences and inequalities of access to particular kinds of goods and materials (e.g. iron weapons and tools, non-local semi-precious stone, other metallurgical specialist products) through mortuary ritual (Moorti 1994). Additionally, the frequent presence of weapons, tools and other items suggests that occupational differences, such as martial activities, were further aspects of Iron Age social distinctions produced in part through mortuary practices. Iron Age mortuary practices created a multitude of social relations of difference and affiliation through the commemoration of the dead that at the least included community membership, residential group differences, martial skill and success, occupational distinctions and social ranking. The extent and degree of social ranking we may infer from variation in the mortuary record are far less certain and require considerable further research in localized contexts with evidence that can be more precisely dated.

Megalithic features have also been found away from large mortuary contexts. In north-eastern Karnataka and western Telangana there are large complexes containing multiple alignments of standing stones. Some of these appear to have marked or commemorated the passing of important annual astronomical events such as the solstices and equinoxes, which were perhaps linked to seasonal crop cycles (Allchin 1956; Rao and Thakur 2010). These complexes seem to have been associated with places of communal ritual or purpose, and their design and construction would have required not only considerable specialist skill (e.g. astronomical, engineering) but also the managerial capacity to recruit and mobilize labour to cut, dress and move the massive stone elements erected at these places.

In the Krishna–Tungabhadra *doāb*, megaliths were constructed and maintained near important water, soil and perhaps mineral resources, demonstrating the claims of particular social groups to important material and symbolic resources (Bauer 2011; Bauer and Trivedi 2013; Johansen 2014a; Bauer 2014; 2015). Bauer's systematic survey (2011; 2015) in the Benakal Forest has documented the association of megaliths with small constructed soil- and water-retention features, which he convincingly argues were individual or group claims to important agro-pastoral resources (i.e. water, pasturage) (see **Fig. 12**). The Maski Archaeological Research Project (Johansen and Bauer 2015) has recorded the occurrence of passage chamber megaliths with small rock shelter herding camps as well as the limited access routes to a gold mineral source and ore-processing facility. This latter observation suggests passage chamber megaliths may also have been used to make social claims to mineral resources.

Megalithic features were also built in and around active or abandoned Iron Age settlements. On the margins of the Iron Age settlement of Kadebakele, a stone circle megalith was built on top of a series of prepared surfaces, pits and other deposits that were used in repeated feasting events contemporary with the site's residential occupation; the megalith appears to have commemorated the place of these activities (R. Bauer 2007; Bauer *et al.* 2007; Sinopoli 2009; Morrison *et al.* 2016). Stone circles and smaller, less formally constructed megalithic features are also found on the margins of nearby Iron Age settlements at Bukkasagara, Rampuram and elsewhere (Johansen 2009; 2014a). On the margins of the main residential area at Kadebakele, a group of small intersecting and overlapping megalithic features (circular and linear alignments, small cists) were constructed, renovated, disassembled and maintained for hundreds of years as part of punctuated ritual events involving small- and large-scale burnings, the burial of small offerings and the butchering and sharing of domesticated animals (R. Bauer 2007; Bauer *et al.* 2007; Sinopoli 2009; Morrison *et al.* 2016; Wilcox 2015).

The association of megalithic features with the mortuary rituals of particular individuals and social groups suggests the provisioning of labour and resources to build megaliths established and contested claims to important places and resources. The construction of large complexes of menhirs that appear to have been linked to seasonal astronomical events may be evidence for the practice of seasonal agricultural rituals, and perhaps community claims to agricultural lands. The construction of small groups of single megaliths associated with constructed water pools, sedimented terraces and herding camps points towards the maintenance of claims to important agricultural and pastoral resources (Bauer and Morrison 2008; Bauer 2011; 2015). Finally, the construction and maintenance of megaliths on settlements both during their occupation and following abandonment suggests the active maintenance of further claims of affiliation and difference by resident social groups, claims which may have extended to historical associations to places no longer occupied by claimant groups. Regardless, Iron Age megalithic monumental practices were deeply entangled with claims of social difference and affiliation, and with the making and maintaining of inequalities of access to places and a range of other symbolic and material resources.

Settlement practices: design, organization and sociality

Iron Age settlement research was widely neglected until the mid 1970s, largely because many archaeologists assumed incorrectly that Iron Age peoples were nomadic pastoralists who only rarely inhabited anything but the most seasonally occupied settlements (Moorti 1994: 5–6). While this 'myth' was firmly dispelled by a number of regional surveys, beginning with Sundara's (1975) work in northern Karnataka, systematically recorded studies of Iron Age settlements remain uncommon and excavations of settlements are, with some exceptions, largely under-reported. In spite of this, recent research suggests that many of the social distinctions and inequalities inferred from Iron Age mortuary and monumental practices were also being produced in some regions through settlement practices.

Moorti's (1994) study of Iron Age social organization collated previously collected data on settlement sizes and locations from across South India. Using this admittedly rudimentary data, largely without adequate contextual information, Moorti observed regional settlement size patterning that he took to represent two-tier settlement hierarchies in many regions, a pattern he used to substantiate claims for regionally ranked societies corresponding to ethnographic 'chiefdoms'. Systematic regional surveys conducted in recent years in South India have challenged the notion of a tidy two-tiered settlement hierarchy, instead recording considerable regional variation in both the size and the distribution of Iron Age settlements across a number of study regions (cf. Abraham 2003; Sinopoli and Morrison 2007; Sugandhi 2013; Bauer 2015; Johansen and Bauer 2015; Morrison *et al.* 2016). Regional surveys in the Raichur, Koppal and Bellary Districts of Karnataka record a rise in the number of Iron Age settlements and of other sites such as smaller, more ephemeral, herding camps and agricultural field stations compared to the preceding Neolithic period, suggesting an expansion in population in this region (e.g. Sinopoli and Morrison 2007; Bauer 2014; 2015; Johansen and Bauer 2015). Yet in the western Bellary District there is clear evidence for site abandonment early in the Iron Age (Roberts *et al.* 2015), which underlines the importance of considering the role of locality in regional socio-political and economic practices.

In northern Karnataka, where some of the most extensive research on Iron Age settlement has been conducted, settlements are primarily located on adjoining hilltop and hillslope terraces in the region's granite-gneiss hills (Sinopoli and Morrison 2007; Johansen 2010; Bauer 2011; 2015). At many sites in the region there was a concern with boundary maintenance: access to settlements was through narrow pathways and passages on the rocky slopes and these were then controlled by constructing stone walls and formalized entrance architecture (e.g. constructed passages, alignments, terracing). At Paidigutta, an Iron Age settlement on the open peneplain in western Andhra Pradesh (**Fig. 9**), a large stone enclosure wall was exposed, demonstrating that a concern with defence was also a feature of Iron Age settlements beyond the rocky hill tracts of Karnataka (Sastry 2000).[3] This concern with boundary maintenance supports the notion that settlement communities may have been relatively politically autonomous, and that the settlement community was an important unit of Iron Age social affiliation. It also suggests, together with images of martial activities in rock art and high frequencies of iron weaponry in burials, that violent conflict between communities was a significant if not a persistent concern.

Hilltop and hillside settlements in northern Karnataka appear to have been designed to distinguish, spatially and symbolically, the residential places of socially distinct groups (Johansen 2010; 2011; Bauer 2015; Johansen and Bauer 2015). This was achieved by constructing separate residential zones with elevated and sometimes tiered stone and earth terraces surrounding larger open extramural areas (Johansen 2010; 2011). At several well-documented sites in the Bellary and Koppal Districts of Karnataka, larger residential terraces abut extramural activity areas closer to the architecturally formalized entrances to settlements, while smaller and more secluded terraces were constructed at higher elevations (Johansen 2010; 2011; Bauer 2015). At the site of Bukkasagara, adjacent residential zones were constructed to be distinct from one another with walls and alignments clearly separating each area, while at Kadebakele and Rampuram discrete residential zones were built in two areas physically separated by topographical and architectural features (Johansen 2010; 2011). In each of these cases movement between residential zones and the architecturally formalized entrances to the sites was controlled by a limited number of access points, often with architectural elaboration. At

Paidigutta, the pattern has interesting similarities to and differences from the hill settlements further west. Here four rows of small houses were constructed in two rows on either side of a large extramural area (Sastry 2000).

The practical and symbolic separation of residential spaces within settlements into two or more architecturally distinct areas suggests that there were important social differences practised within settlement communities between residential groups (e.g. extended families, lineage groups). The elevated, visually prominent, yet more secluded location of a smaller group of residential terraces within individual residential zones at some settlements suggests further social differentiation that may have involved ranked hierarchical relationships within residential groups.

As was the case with many forms of larger megalithic monuments at mortuary and non-mortuary complexes, the construction and design of residential terraces, enclosure walls, stone pathways, passages, alignments and revetments would have required considerable consensus and/or authority to organize labour and other resources (cf. Bauer and Trivedi 2013). The overlapping and agglutinative remains of smaller megalithic features on the margins of settlements and residential zones at well-studied sites points towards the possibility of ritualized political practices through which resident social groups negotiated their positions and prerogatives. The remains of repeated feasting events on the margins of Kadebakele (R. Bauer 2007; Sinopoli 2009; Morrison *et al.* 2016) and surface deposits with high proportions of small serving vessels observed in the vicinity of megaliths at other settlements (e.g. Rampuram) (Johansen 2010) suggest that political authority and consensus at Iron Age settlements may have required regular negotiations between resident groups.

The subsistence economy

Data for Iron Age subsistence practices in the south Deccan are limited in comparison with those of the preceding Neolithic period, particularly regarding plant foods (cf. Fuller 2005; 2006). However, available data show a persistent emphasis on cattle-, sheep- and goat-herding, the farming of locally domesticated legumes and millets with a secondary focus on grains such as rice, wheat and barley, and the hunting and gathering of wild plants and animals (Kajale 1984; 1989; Moorti 1994; Fuller 2005; 2006; Bauer *et al.* 2007; R. Bauer 2007; Morrison *et al.* forthcoming). The growing of winter-sown crops such as wheat and barley, and rice intensified agricultural production by extending the growing season past that of monsoon-sown millets and pulses, with rudimentary irrigation (Fuller 2005; Bauer and Morrison 2008; Roberts *et al.* 2015; Morrison *et al.* forthcoming). Other crops such as banana, recently identified from mid-Iron Age (*c.* 800–400 BCE) trash deposits at Kadebakele, would have required some irrigation as well (Bauer and Morrison 2008; Morrison *et al.* forthcoming), suggesting that small constructed reservoirs at Iron Age settlement sites (e.g. Kadebakele and perhaps Maski) were used for small-scale pot irrigation, watering fields with non-local domesticates during the dry season. In spite of the presence of this non-local package of domesticates at several south Deccan sites (e.g. Hallur, Heggadehalli, Kadebakele, Veerapuram), Morrison *et al.* (forthcoming) argue that these crops account for a rather small portion of overall agricultural production. They also point to the likelihood of important regional differences in cropping regimes (e.g. the increased planting of rice in wetter environs at Hallur). Regardless, growing irrigation-dependent crops would have required greater investment in labour to construct and maintain water- and soil-retention features, something unlikely to have been practised by all residents of Iron Age settlements.

Iron Age faunal assemblages demonstrate some regional variation in animal food production and procurement. While early Iron Age faunal assemblages at Sannarchamma (at Sanganakallu) show that goat- /sheep-herding increased in importance in comparison to cattle, elsewhere assemblage variation in later Iron Age deposits suggests cattle was the dominant domestic species (Thomas 1984; 1992; Bauer *et al.* 2007; R. Bauer 2007; Roberts *et al.* 2015). Indeed at Kadebakele, cattle appear in higher proportions to sheep/goat in both domestic and ritual contexts (Bauer *et al.* 2007; R. Bauer 2007). The demography and taphonomy of cattle bone assemblages from both sites suggest that cattle were primarily raised for secondary products (e.g. milk) as well as for traction in farming, yet were consumed less frequently in special ritualized contexts (e.g. feasting) (R. Bauer 2007; Boivin *et al.* 2008; Roberts *et al.* 2015).

Survey data from the Benakal Forest (Bauer 2011; 2015) and the MARP (Johansen and Bauer 2015) study areas note marked increases in small herding camps and constructed soil- and water-retention features in hillslope and peneplain contexts, which indicate that pastoral production was intensifying through the expansion of range, increasing logistical mobility and investments in water retention and slope management (Bauer 2011; 2014; Morrison *et al.* forthcoming). The building of megaliths adjacent to many of these features suggests social claims by those who built, used or expropriated these places, claims that produced practical and symbolic inequalities of access (Bauer 2011).

Currently there is little direct evidence for the production of social differences through dietary practices but the foregoing discussion points to differential access to, and management of, agro-pastoral resources and places, differences that almost certainly involved consumption as well as production. Comparisons of faunal data from feasting deposits with data from generalized midden deposits at Iron Age Kadebakele show significant differences: wild avian and riparian fauna outstrip cattle in middens but in feasting deposits cattle predominate, demonstrating variation in quotidian and non-quotidian dietary profiles (Bauer *et al.* 2007; R. Bauer 2007; Wilcox 2015). Isotopic studies of human skeletal remains from Iron Age mortuary contexts hold much promise for a better understanding of the entanglement of dietary and social differences.

Iron metallurgy and social differentiation

By the middle of the Iron Age, smiths themselves were highly skilled specialists producing a range of iron and steel weapons and tools crafted specifically for a range of needs and tasks (Mudhol 1997; Srinivasan *et al.* 2009). The curation of iron weapons, tools and other items in Iron Age burial

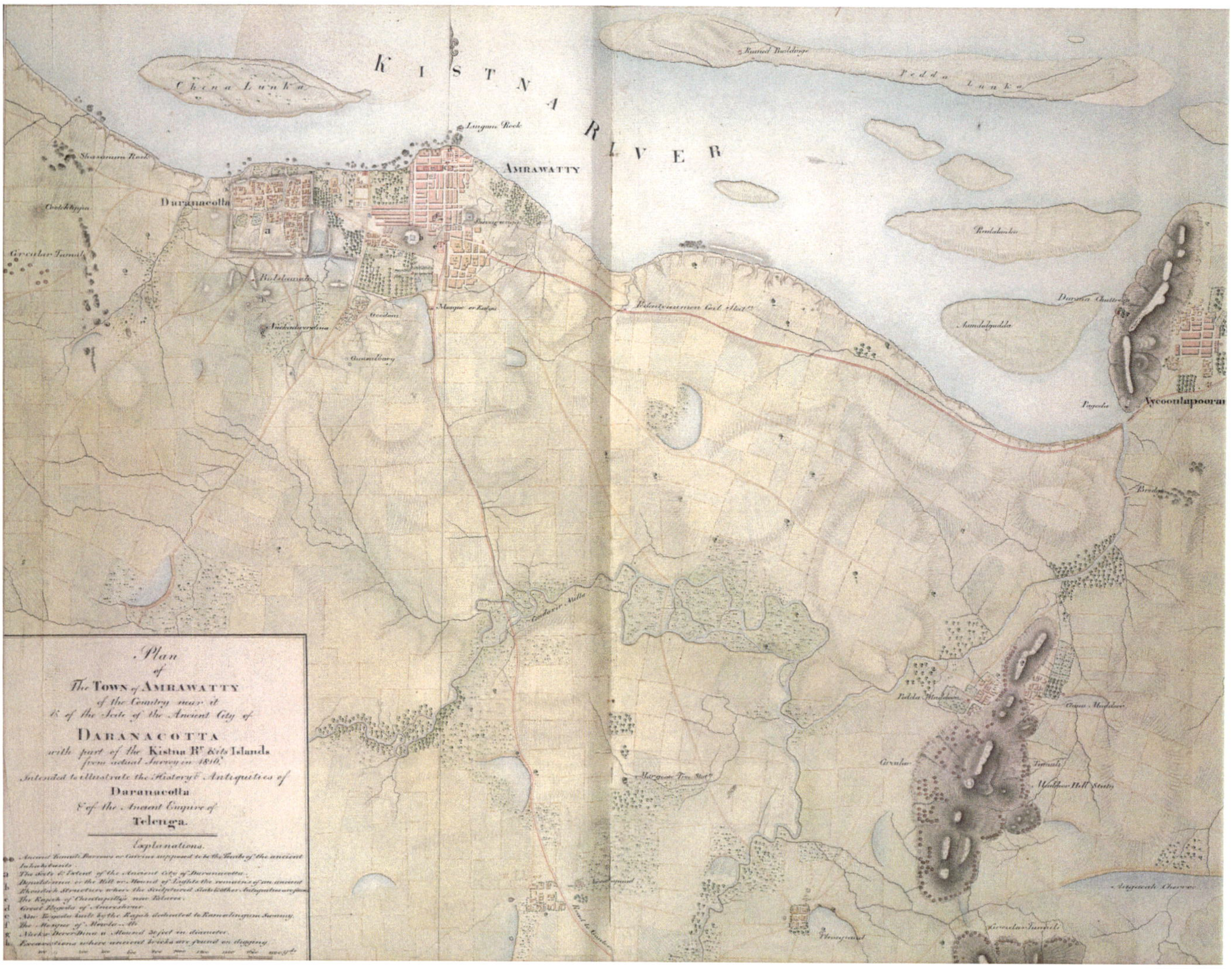

Figure 13 Colonel Colin Mackenzie's 1816 map of the region surrounding Amaravati with extensive distribution of stone circle megaliths, British Library, WD 1061, fols 4–5

contexts demonstrates the value finished iron products had in creating and maintaining social distinctions in mortuary display and ritual. Iron tools and hardware were also integral for agricultural, pastoral, building and other more quotidian practices as well as martial activities. The use of iron in this wide range of Iron Age socio-economic practices suggests that iron production was a venue for the creation and maintenance of social distinctions and a vector for inequalities of access to materials and places of production.

The earliest recorded evidence for ironworking in South India is at Bukkasagara (**Fig. 9**), where a smithing facility is dated to *c.* 1300–1000 BCE (Johansen 2014a). A small number of smelting furnaces have been recorded across South India that have been radiometrically dated to later in the Iron Age (e.g. Banahalli, Guttur, Naikund) (Deo and Jamkhedkar 1982; Mudhol 1997; Sasisekaran and Raghunatha Rao 2001). Iron slag has been reported from many additional Iron Age sites across the south Deccan, but only rarely has that slag been distinguished as smelting- or smithing-related debris. Systematic survey in northern Karnataka has demonstrated that iron smithing was practised at many or most Iron Age settlements as well as in some more ephemeral occupations such as camps, and even in cemeteries (Johansen 2014a; Johansen and Bauer 2015). On the other hand, iron smelting facilities were located in far fewer places, demonstrating that smelting[4] was a less well-distributed occupational speciality than smithing (Johansen 2014a). While this pattern is elucidated from an arguably small sample of regional survey it suggests that smelting specialists, their patrons, or the larger social groups to which they belonged, controlled the distribution of iron bloom to a more widely distributed group of smiths working among individual settlement communities (ibid). At settlement sites where the location of smithing activities has been investigated metalworking facilities were associated with particular residential zones, suggesting that smiths practised their craft in the architectural spaces of specific residential groups in larger settlement communities (Johansen 2010; 2011; 2014a). Access to primary products (i.e. bloom), technical proficiency (e.g. smelting, smithing) and finished products appears to have been socially contoured, at least among some Iron Age communities.

Discussion: Iron Age socio-politics, locality and the transition to the Early Historic in Andhradeśa

Archaeological research on Iron Age social and political practices documents how settlement communities in several regions of the south Deccan produced a variety of social affiliations and distinctions that created and maintained a number of important inequalities of access to places, symbolic and material resources, managerial capabilities and decision-making. This transformed the relatively egalitarian social order of the Neolithic period into a political landscape of social differences that included distinctions in rank, residential affiliations and occupational specialization. There appears to have been social ranking within residential social groups and a palpable degree of conflict and negotiation between settlement communities, yet there is little we can currently say with certainty about regional structures of authority. Social distinctions and inequalities developed in response to localized needs and contexts largely through shared domains of practice that included mortuary ritual, monumentality, residence, commensality and craft production and consumption (e.g. ceramics and metals). These social differences operated within a transforming Iron Age economy in which intensifications in agro-pastoral production grew in many regions and iron metallurgy, trade and exchange increased, expanded and escalated especially during the transition to the Early Historic period (Kelly 2013; Morrison *et al.* forthcoming).

In the mid–lower Krishna River watershed many megalithic mortuary complexes and settlements have been documented as Iron Age or megalithic-period sites. Krishna Sastry (2003: 109) lists 15 Iron Age settlements, 270 mortuary sites and 111 settlement/mortuary sites in the Krishna River drainage within the modern-day states of Andhra Pradesh and Telangana. Yet adequate dating and empirical description at most of these sites are not well developed[5] and most of the small number of radiocarbon dates from 'megalithic' deposits (e.g. Satanikota, Veerapuram, Polakonda) clearly date to the Early Historic period. The paucity of radiocarbon dates has led some scholars to employ relative chronologies (bracketed by absolute date ranges) to organize the internal chronology of the Iron Age (or Megalithic period) (Margabandhu 1985; Ghosh 1986; Parasher-Sen 2007 – also Sundara 1975 and McIntosh 1985), but these are neither accurate nor reliable. What is telling about the available radiocarbon dates is that megalithic mortuary and settlement practices continued in several (if not all) regions well into Early Historic times in spite of significant regional changes in ritual, economy and politics (e.g. Sramana and Brahmana religious practices, intensified regional trade and the formation of regional states) (see Schopen 2004 [1996]; Johansen 2014b). However, very early radiocarbon dates at Iron Age sites from adjacent regions (e.g. at Ramapuram, **Fig. 9**), and the depositional histories at settlement sites without (or with incomplete) radiocarbon assays (e.g. Paidigutta, Peddamarur, Serupalli, Veerapuram), suggest that the mid–lower Krishna River watershed was occupied through much of the Iron Age (Krishna Sastry 1983; Sastri *et al.* 1984; Sastry 2000; Krishna Sastry 2003).

By the dawn of the Early Historic period in Andhradeśa (*c.* 300–400 BCE) there is evidence for a transition to larger, fortified and perhaps urban settlements (e.g. Dharanikota, Kotalingala) in some regions.[6] Settlement patterning further suggests that in some localities the development of larger, more spatially complex, settlements was accompanied by constellations of smaller, perhaps co-dependent, settlements that together constituted small pre-state polities (Parasher-Sen 2007). While this argument is predicated upon data collected by multiple researchers without systematic survey, it does appear plausible, particularly given the localized distribution of early (i.e. pre-Mauryan) coinage (Chattopadhyaya 2003; Parasher-Sen 2007). Yet the constitution of these incipient Early Historic polities and their Iron Age antecedents are not well understood. Any evaluation of the political and social practices that configured these localities and how they developed over the course of the Iron Age must await further problem-oriented archaeological research.

The Iron Age antecedents of the Buddhist monastic complex at Amaravati, the adjacent fortified urban settlement at Dharanikota and the wider social and political geography of the surrounding region remain opaque. The region's only radiocarbon assays at Dharanikota date the earliest known occupation at the settlement to *c.* 475 BCE (*IAR* 1973), very late in the Iron Age, while basal deposits at the nearby settlement at Vaddamanu (8km south of Amaravati) contain ceramic assemblages that consist of a mixture of South Indian slipped and polished ceramic wares (e.g. Black-and-Red Ware) together with North Indian Early Historic wares (e.g. Northern-Black-Polished Ware and Rouletted Ware), suggesting a very late or post-Iron Age origin for the settlement (Sastri 1992: 3, 6).

When Amaravati was initially recorded by Colin Mackenzie in 1816 he mapped several extensive distributions of stone circle megaliths, including an area immediately south-west of Dharanikota as well as throughout the granite hill chains to the south-east, adjacent to the Early Historic Buddhist monastery at Vaddamanu (Fergusson 1873; Shimada 2013) (**Fig. 13**). While these megaliths remain undated, two threads of data suggest that some may pre-date Early Historic-period settlement. First, at Amaravati, Alexander Rea (1912) excavated 17 Iron Age urn burials beneath a small *stūpa c.* 75m north-west of the *mahāstūpa*. At Vaddamanu an early *stūpa* appears to have been constructed to incorporate the remains of a large stone cist-circle megalith (**Fig. 14**) (Sastri 1992: 4–5). Indeed, further upstream on the Krishna River at Yeleswaram excavations exposed an Early Historic *stūpa* built atop megalithic burials (Khan 1963). This pattern suggests the Buddhist *sangha* (monastic communities) were selecting pre-existing mortuary complexes as locations for monastic architecture – acts of spatial appropriation (DeCaroli 2007; Morrison 2009; Johansen 2014b; Schopen 2004 [1996]). While the presence of megalithic mortuary features beneath Early Historic-period monastic architecture does not necessarily imply that the former were Iron Age features it demonstrates regional temporal precedence. If these mortuary features and the other reported megaliths were Iron Age in origin, then we might anticipate systematic survey to discover settlements in the region as well, given patterns recorded elsewhere.

The early dates at Dharanikota demonstrate that the social, economic and political processes that gave rise to the fortified, urban, Early Historic settlement began in the Iron Age, perhaps involving a settlement consolidation process similar to those that are coming to light in nearby regions of

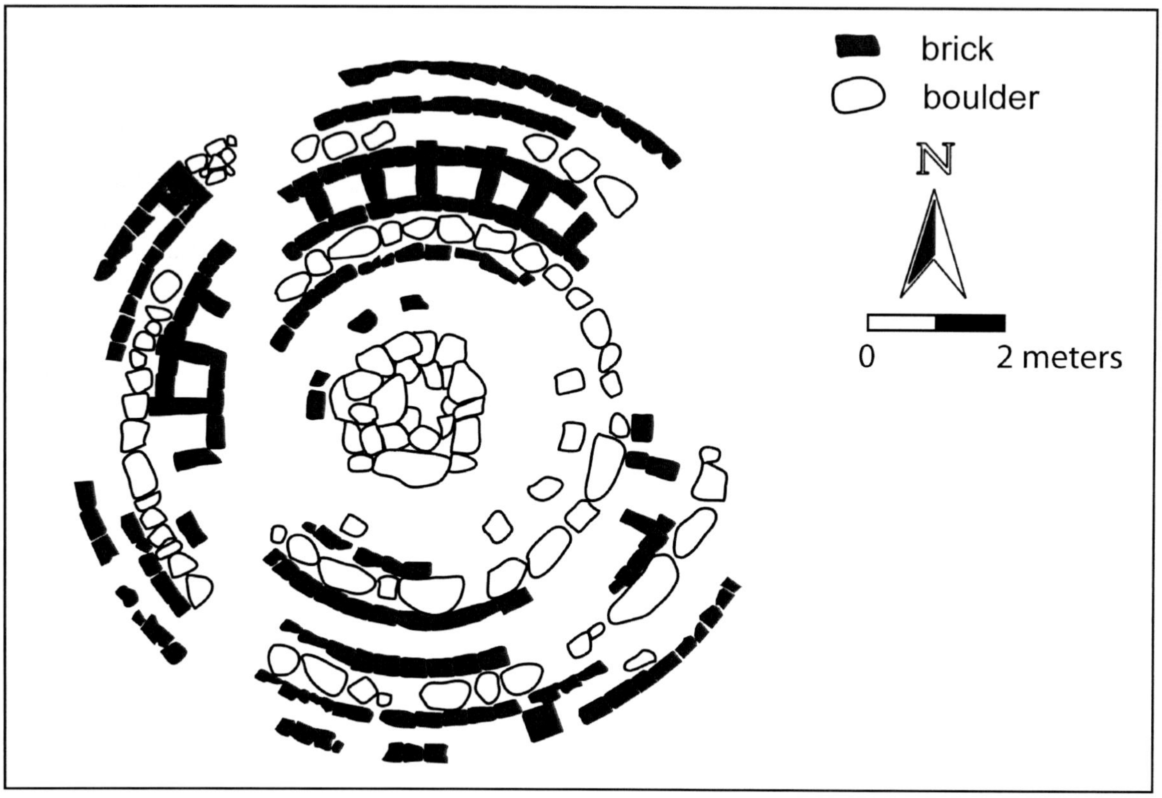

Figure 14 Base of excavations of brick *stūpa* (feature VDM-II) at Vaddamanu built to incorporate stone circle megalith (based on Sastri 1992: fig. 1)

the south Deccan (e.g. the central Tungabhadra River corridor and the Raichur District of Karnataka) (Sinopoli 2009; Johansen and Bauer 2015). Yet here, unlike central Karnataka, there appears to be evidence of a more intensified socio-economic interaction with North India in the centuries that followed the establishment of Dharanikota. This is demonstrated by unquantified proportions of North Indian ceramics and, eventually, coins and monastic architecture. The interaction with North Indian traders, as well as with religious and perhaps political (e.g. Mauryan) emissaries, provided opportunities for local settlement community members to contest, maintain and create novel social relationships, affiliations and differences within a dynamic societal field of practice, one that was steeped in the history and structure of Iron Age social and political relations.

The gradual establishment of monastic architectural complexes, many with well-documented donative inscriptions such as those of Amaravati, demonstrates that Buddhism provided an ideology and field of socio-ritual practice that was accepted and adopted by some members of local settlement communities. Like megalithic monumentalism and mortuary practices, participation in Buddhist rituals and the construction of monastic architecture (as donors, lay practitioners, *bhikkhus*/*bhikkhunis* (Buddhist monks and nuns)) soon became a new idiom of socio-ritual practice through which social relations were created, reproduced and modified in the lower Krishna River drainage. Together with megaliths these new religious monuments colonized the spatial margins of several Early Historic settlements across the region (see Shimada 2013), becoming important vectors for both the strengthening and contesting of traditional social distinctions and affiliations and for the production of novel others (e.g. Buddhist communities of practice), at a time when Andhradeśa was developing regional states, more rigidly defined forms of political authority and increasingly stratified social relations from the ranked social relations, inequalities and affiliations created, fostered and maintained during the Iron Age.

Notes

1 Interest in the ethnic origins of Iron Age megalith-builders pre-dates the entanglement of culture-history with South Indian archaeology by more than a century. Some of the earliest reflections on megaliths by British colonial scholarship argued that their builders were the descendants of migrating Hebrews, Celts, Druids and Scythians (see Kennedy 2000: 328–37), a diffusionary logic with its origins in what Thomas Trautmann (1997) has described as a 'Mosaic ethnology', a biblical ontology for the diversity and distribution of the world's population.

2 The area west of, and between, the confluence of the Krishna River and Tungabhadra River.

3 Siva Naga Reddy (1998: 116) reports similar enclosure walls from Iron Age settlements nearby at Chagatur and Chinnamarur in western Andhra Pradesh. However, published reports are not available for these sites.

4 Pre-industrial iron smelting required considerable technical skill and knowledge. It produced a spongy mass of unrefined iron (i.e. bloom), which smiths refined into workable billet stock (a purer iron) then smithed into finished objects.

5 With some notable exceptions the majority of Iron Age and Early Historic-period archaeological sites remain unreported or restricted to short descriptions in annual review publications.

6 Despite the likelihood that these settlements were indeed urban by 300 BCE, most published accounts of research at these sites do not provide adequate detail with which to make a conclusive evaluation.

Chapter 2
Caitya, *Mahācaitya*, *Tathāgatacaitya*: Questions of Terminology in the Age of Amaravati

Peter Skilling

The *stūpa* or *caitya* takes us back to the beginnings of Indian Buddhism, in both archaeology and language.[1] The Prakrit word *thupa*, counterpart of Pali *thūpa* and Sanskrit *stūpa*, occurs in the earliest written records of India, the Aśokan inscriptions (**Fig. 15**). The oldest surviving Indian manuscripts are birch-bark scrolls from the north-west (present-day Pakistan and Afghanistan). They are inscribed in the Kharoṣṭhī script in the Gandhari Prakrit language. There we find the forms *thuba*, *thupa* and *thuva*. Nearly two thousand years later, we meet this word again in the Anglo-Indian word 'tope', about which *Hobson-Jobson* says the following (Yule and Burnell 1903: 934–5):

> **Tope**. An ancient Buddhist monument in the form of a solid dome. The word *tōp* is in local use in the N.W. Punjab, where ancient monuments of this kind occur, and appears to come from Skt *stūpa* through the Pali or Prakrit *thūpo*. … The word was first introduced to European knowledge by Mr. Elphinstone in his account of Manikyala in the Rawal Pindi district.[2]

The original title of this essay, 'Amaravati in the age of Great Caityas', seemed straightforward enough. But the 'Great Caitya' proved elusive as a documentable historical phenomenon, and this led me to question the idea of an 'Age of Great Caityas' (**Fig. 16**). There are no written records and no chronicles of the *caityas* of South Asia, with the exception of those compiled at Anuradhapura in Sri Lanka, and I was unable to find any authoritative Indian source that defines *mahācaitya* or explains the difference between a *caitya* and a *mahācaitya*. Similarly, there is no traditional source that defines *mahāstūpa* or explains the difference between a *stūpa* and a *mahāstūpa*. There is no inventory of *Mahācaityas* or *Mahāstūpas* beyond the liturgical and narrative lists connected with eight *prātihārya* or sites of marvellous events in Śākyamuni's life. We do not know the ancient names of the scores of large *stūpas* in the Indian subcontinent, much less those of the hundreds of medium-sized *stūpas*. The names that we use today were given by local villagers or by explorers and archaeologists. The original names of only a small number of this profusion of *stūpas* are preserved in epigraphic or literary sources, and of these only a handful are described as *Mahācaitya* or *Mahāstūpa*.

South India, especially the Andhra country and the Krishna River valley and delta, is rich in *caitya* sites. The

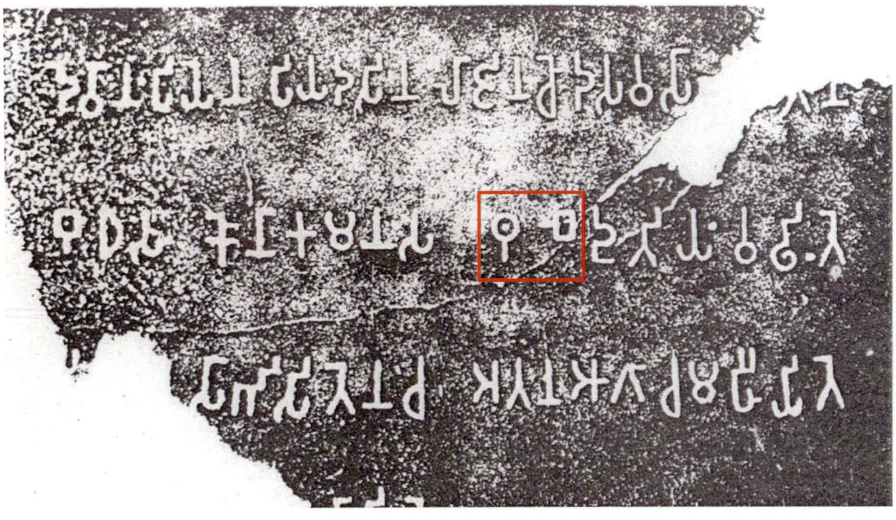

Figure 15 Aśokan pillar inscription, Nigali Sagar (Nigliva), Nepal: earliest record of the word *stūpa* (*thupa*, line 2) (after Hultzsch 1925, 165), c. mid 3rd century BCE

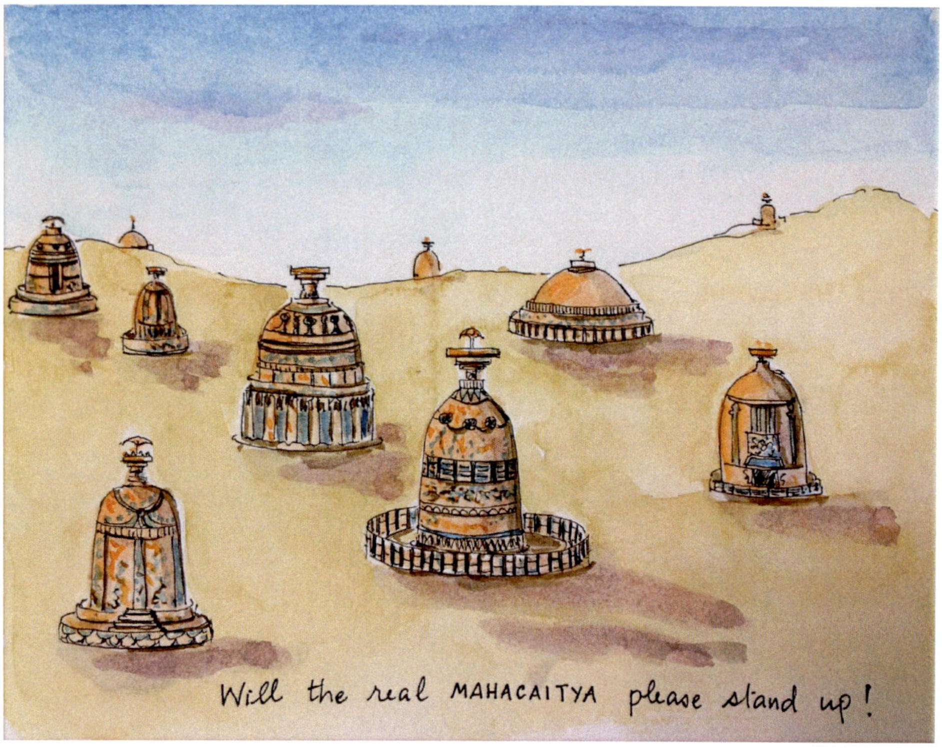

Figure 16 ***Will the Real Mahācaitya Please Stand Up?*** **Watercolour by Paritta Chalermpow Koanantakool, Bangkok, September 2014**

gates, casing slabs and railings of the *stūpas* – above all those of the Great Cetiya at Amaravati – are adorned with narrative and devotional reliefs. The presence of several monastic schools is attested in the area, and these schools, such as the Caitīyas, Bahuśrutīyas and Śailas, are known to have transmitted their own collections of scriptures – of Piṭakas and Śāstras.[3] In the study of local and regional art and architecture, we need to bear in mind that the scriptural collections, the Piṭakas, of the South are all long lost. Not even a single manuscript survives. In general, modern knowledge of Buddhist canons derives from those of the North; this includes the texts translated into Chinese and Tibetan, which, for historical reasons, were those of the North Indian schools. Further, we have no local chronicles or histories from the South. In the absence of the canons of the monastic schools that were active in the South, scholars who seek to identify the narratives depicted on the *stūpas* have had to resort to the collections of the Sri Lankan Theravādins, written in Pali, or the Sanskrit, Buddhist Sanskrit and translated texts of the Lokottaravādins and Sarvāstivādins.[4]

What, then, is a *mahācaitya*? What is a *mahāstūpa*? The two words are used freely in archaeological reports for the 'main' or 'biggest' *stūpa* at a site. But when we look for epigraphic records, many of the *mahācaitya*s and *mahāstūpa*s disappear. Scholars tend to take the terminology of their trade for granted and neglect to define or justify their terms. The report on the Thotlakonda *stūpa* in Andhra Pradesh is an exception insofar as the writers address the question of terminology: 'While describing the Main Stupa at Thotlakonda Buddhist complex, there arose a doubt whether to name it as a Maha Stupa or simply as the Main Stupa' (Krishna Sastry *et al.* 1992: 26). They refer to inscriptions from Nagarjunakonda, Jaggayyapeta and Amaravati that use the word *Mahācetiya*, as well as a Bhattiprolu inscription that records the installation of relics of the Buddha (but does not itself use the terms *mahāstūpa* or *mahācetiya*).[5] The authors then state that 'it is not known whether the Stupa at Thotlakonda contained the relics of Lord Buddha or *Arhat*s, as there is no epigraphical evidence or otherwise'. From this it appears that for them the definition of *Mahāstūpa* is the presence of epigraphs that use terms like *Mahāstūpa* or *Mahācetiya* or that refer to the installation of relics. The first proposition is quite practicable, and in what follows I too define a Great Cetiya as a structure that is described as *Mahācetiya*, *Mahāthūpa*, *Mahāstūpa*, etc. by an inscription or inscriptions. I also assume that a *Mahācetiya* would contain relics of the Buddha, but that is a much more complicated question.[6]

Dates

Even if the age of the Great Caityas dissolves as this essay advances, I have to assign a date to it, or, at least, to the period under discussion. My chronological frame is 300 BCE to 300 CE, following that of Shimada's *Early Buddhist Architecture in Context* (Shimada 2013). Unlike the legendary 84,000 *stūpas* made to order for King Aśoka, the historical monumental *stūpas* were not built overnight. Like the great temples of India in later periods, or like the great cathedrals of Europe, the construction and periodic renovation of the great *stūpas* was a matter of centuries. Von Hinüber writes that the latest donation to the Adhālaka Mahācaitya at Kanaganahalli was made somewhere around 230 CE, and concludes that 'donations to the Adhālaka Mahācaitya must have gone on for about two centuries, if not even two centuries and a half' (Nakanishi and von Hinüber 2014: 24). It would seem that 300 BCE to 300 CE is a reasonable frame for the development of the sites discussed below. Most of the inscriptions cited here fall within this period, as do many of the texts that I draw upon – with the proviso that with the exception of the Gandhari scrolls, the physical copies and translations on which we rely today are centuries younger.

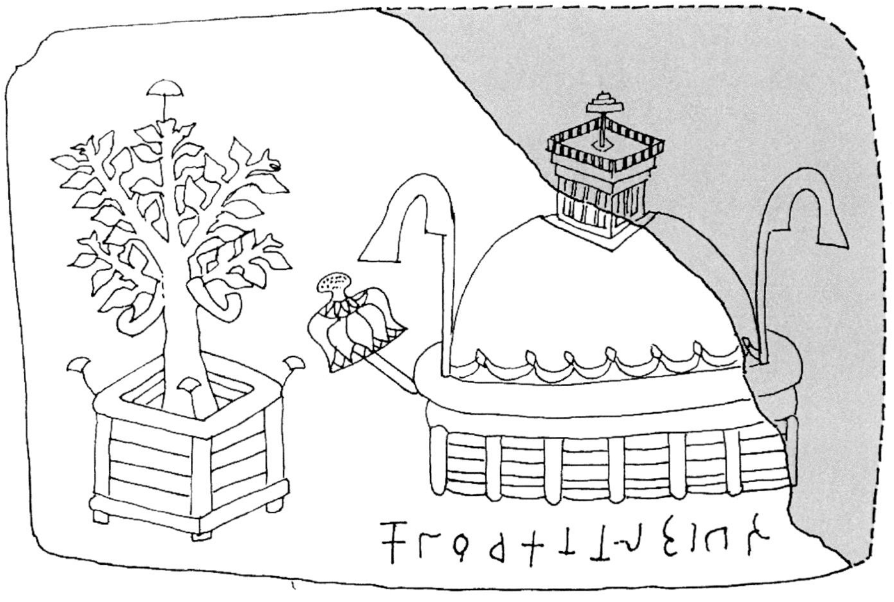

Figure 17 Engraving of a tree-shrine and a *stūpa*, Amaravati, Archaeological Museum, Amaravati, no. 50, *c.* 2nd–1st centuries BCE. Drawing by Paritta Chalermpow Koanantakool. The *stūpa* has been tentatively restored in the drawing (indicated by shading)

What is a *Mahācaitya*?

Caitya has a broader meaning than *stūpa*. *Caitya* shrines existed long before the Buddha's time as features of the natural landscape that had an ethereal presence and were associated with supernatural forces – with vegetal and elemental spirits like *vṛkṣa-devatā*, *nāga*s and *yakṣa*s (**Fig. 17**). Each shrine had its own identity and history, its own local name. The Fortunate One (*bhagavat*) visited contemporary shrines, which were the places where local society would gather. Rather than break with the past, his followers and supporters appropriated the model of the *caitya* as a sacred, open-air and open-access space, and developed their own sites for the new teaching. These sites centred increasingly on *stūpa*s, which within a century or two of the Buddha's death dominated the landscape along the routes of commercial and social circulation.[7]

The 'Great Parinirvāṇa Sūtra' records the Awakened One's final journey in North India. He stopped in the land of the Vṛjis, a confederation whose territory lay north of the Ganga River in today's northern Bihar. The *sūtra* reports that the Vṛjis paid respect, revered, venerated and made offerings to their *caitya*s in the four directions, and that they did not allow this ancient practice to be interrupted. This was one of the strengths of their society.[8] The Teacher stayed at the Pāṭalaka-caitya (§§ 4.2, 3; 6.1), and at the Cāpāla-caitya at Vāiśālī he said to Ānanda:[9]

> Beautiful, Ānanda, is Vaiśālī, as is the land of Vṛji – the Cāpāla Shrine, the Seven Mangoes Shrine, the Many Children Shrine, the Gautama Banyan Tree Shrine, the *śāla* forest, the Putting Aside Burdens Shrine and the Tying a Crest Shrine of the Mallas! Jambudvīpa, the Black Plum Island, is wonderful, and sweet is the life of humans![10]

Mahācaitya (*mahā* + *caitya*) means 'great shrine'. But I do not think that here *mahā* refers simply to size, that a *mahācaitya* is *necessarily* big, large or extra large. The meaning of *mahā* would have changed as *stūpa*s, originally relatively small, were progressively enlarged, a process that can be deduced from excavation, epigraphy and literature. *Mahācaitya* is rather a great shrine, a grand shrine, an outstanding shrine. I suspect that a *mahācaitya* would enshrine physical relics of a Buddha, in most cases those of Śākyamuni, but perhaps also of past Buddhas (such as those of Konāgamana of the Aśokan pillar at Nigliva (Nigali Sagar) in Nepal or those recorded by the Chinese scholar-pilgrims Faxian and Xuanzang). But there is no evidence to support this, and as mentioned I have not seen any definitions of *mahācaitya* or *mahāstūpa* in literature. Relic caskets have been recovered across South Asia but for the most part they do not bear inscriptions. We do not know whose relics they are meant to contain, the name of the *stūpa* in which they were installed or whether it might have been thought of as a *Mahācaitya*.[11]

Mahācaitya and *Mahāstūpa* in epigraphy

I have come across only a few epigraphic records of the term *Mahāstūpa*. A gold sheet from Mata in Swat, Pakistan, states in Gandhari Prakrit that King Ajitasena installed relics in Tira 'in the southern part of the Great Stūpa'.[12] This took place about 9 CE. A reliquary from Devnimori in Gujarat uses the Sanskrit term *Mahāstūpa*: 'this Great Stūpa, a banner on the earth in the grounds of the Great Monastery, erected to benefit many beings, in which the Śākya monks find joy'.[13] The date is not certain; the editors suggest the 4th century CE.

Inscriptions refer to the *stūpa* at Amaravati as a Mahācetiya, and more specifically as 'the *Mahācetiya* at Dhañakaṭaka [the ancient name for Amaravati]'.[14] In several cases it is described as 'the Great Cetiya of the Fortunate One' (*bhagavato mahācetiya*: 140.2). One inscription records that a Wheel of the Dhamma (*dhammacakka*) was set up at the western gate of 'the Mahācetiya of the Fortunate One' for the 'acceptance of the Cetiya monastic order'.[15] Jaggayyapeta is described as a 'Great Cetiya of the Fortunate One, the Buddha'.[16] Inscriptions at Nagarjunakonda refer to the main monument there as a Great Cetiya, as noted by Vogel (*EI* XX, 3), for example on the *āyaka* pillar inscriptions (*EI* XX: 15–21) and apsidal temple inscriptions.[17] Kesanapalli is also a Great Cetiya (here spelt *Mahācetika*).[18]

The *stūpa* complexes of the Krishna delta have been known and studied for a long time; nonetheless, we very

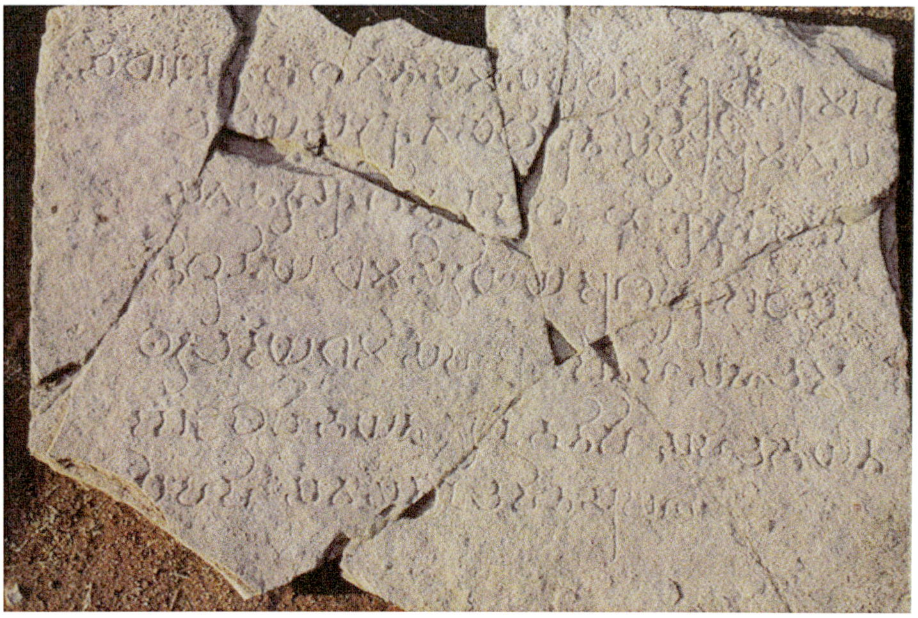

Figure 18 'The Great Cetiya at Adhālaka', a label inscription from Kanaganahalli (after Nakanishi and von Hinüber 2014, § I.8 (pp. 31–3) and pl. 2), *c.* late 1st century BCE to early 1st century CE

much need a new and comprehensive review of the current epigraphic corpus. Recently the Great Cetiya at Kanaganahalli in Karnataka has been added to the map of South Indian *stūpa* sites; it has a rich body of architecture, art and inscriptions that has yet to be adequately presented, let alone integrated into the ever-changing landscapes of Indian Buddhism, Indian history and art history. There are approximately 130 inscriptions, from which we learn that the

Figure 19 'King Sātakaṇi donates silver lotus flowers to the Great Cetiya', Kanaganahalli, *c.* 1st century CE (photograph: Maiko Nakanishi)

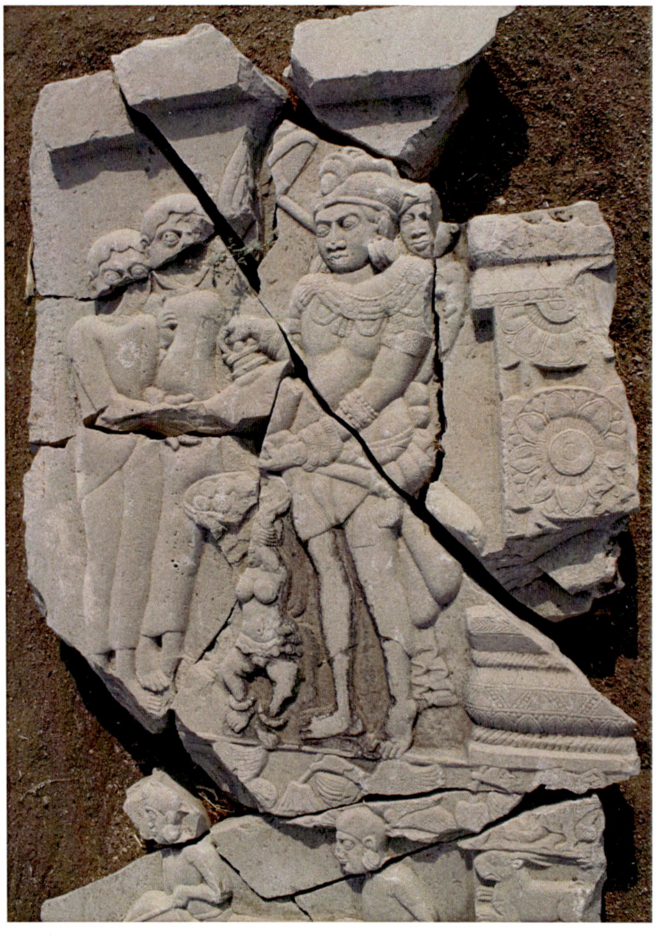

monument at Kanaganahalli was called Adhālaka Mahācetiya (**Fig. 18**).[19] The meaning of 'Adhālaka' is unknown; the little we know about the naming of *stūpas* in the South suggests that it might be a toponym: 'the Great Cetiya at Adhālaka'.

The monument is called Great Cetiya in several inscriptions. A relief of a royal figure making a donation to two monks is labelled 'King Sātakaṇi donates silver lotus flowers to the Great Cetiya' (**Fig. 19**).[20] Two slabs bearing Buddhapādas were donated by 'the respected Sihakasapa, pupil of the respected Senior Monk Buddhatāta' at the Great Cetiya.[21] Another example is on a ledge for flower offerings (*puphagahani*): 'The gift at the Great Cetiya of the pupil [name lost] of the Venerable Elder Mahārakhita'.[22] The Great Cetiya at Kanaganahalli is related to the Great Cetiya of Amaravati insofar as about 10 of the benefactors of the former record the fact that they were from Dhañakaṭaka. They include a female renunciant named Āryā Mitrā (**Fig. 20**).[23]

Both *mahāstūpa* and *mahācaitya* were used in Sri Lanka for the ancient monuments erected from the 3rd century BCE. The inscriptions were indited in Sinhala Brahmi in Old Sinhala Prakrit.[24] Unlike those of India, the Lankan *stūpas* have written histories preserved as the 'Chronicle of the Island', the 'Great Chronicle' and the 'Chronicle of the Stūpa' (*Dīpavaṃsa*, *Mahāvaṃsa* and *Thūpavaṃsa*, respectively). A fragmentary inscription of King Goṭhābhaya (249–62 CE) on the pavement of the Ruvanväli Dagoba refers to the *maha-ceta*, which the editor reads as a reference to the Mahāthūpa or Ruvanväli itself (Paranavitana 2001: no. 110, B1–2, pp. 188–9). This edifice (**Fig. 21**), which goes under several names, became the *Mahāstūpa* par excellence, perhaps the only *Mahāstūpa* with a continuous identity for over two thousand years up to the present,[25] and the only *Mahāstūpa* with dedicated biographies in Pali and Sinhala – both of them translated into English.[26] Amaravati, Kanaganahalli and all the other *Mahāstūpas* have archaeological but no literary records. Although earlier *stūpas* were enlarged and bigger *stūpas* were erected, not only in Anuradhapura – for example at the Abhayagiri and the

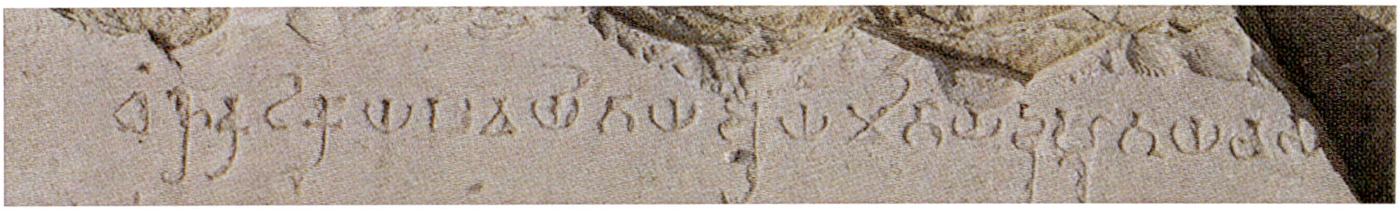

Figure 20 Donation inscription of Āryā Mitrā, a female renunciant, one of the benefactors from Dhañakaṭaka (*dhañakaḍikāya pavayitāya aya mitāya*), Kanaganahalli (after Nakanishi and von Hinüber 2014, IV.8, 106–7), *c.* 1st century CE

Jetavana Vihāras – but also elsewhere on the island – such as the Tissa Mahārāma on the southern coast – the Ruvanväli remained the *Mahāthūpa*.[27]

Outside the capital, the term Great Stūpa is used in the 'Kāsimottai Rock-inscription' from Batticaloa District, which refers to the construction of a Great Stūpa and land grants made to it for a variety of purposes. It uses the term *mahātuba* three times and *tuba* twice (Paranavitana 1983: nos 48, 73–5).[28] The inscription is from the reign of King Vasabha (60–7 CE).[29]

Other Old Sinhala records refer to Great Cetiya. The Ratanapāsāda slab-inscription at Anuradhapura from the reign of Gajabāhu, son of Vasabha (114–36 CE), refers to the '*Abhaya-Gamini-Utara-mahaceta*', that is, the Great Cetiya of Abhayagāminī in the Northern [monastery], Uttaravihāra or Abhayagiri (Paranavitana 1983: no. 59, line 4, p. 88). The Uttara-mahācetiya is the subject of a donation record of Kaniṭṭha Tissa (167–86 CE). A large but fragmentary rock inscription in Anuradhapura District refers to a *Mahāceya* (ibid.: no. 114, line 11, 195–293). A fragmentary rock-inscription near the Kaṇṭaka-cetiya in Mihintale lists donations to the '*Kaṭaka-ceta*' and uses the term *mahaceta* (Paranavitana 2001: no. 135, line 8, p. 228).

In sum, the following monuments were Great Caityas or Great Stūpas in India and Sri Lanka:

India
Amaravati
Jaggayyapeta
Nagarjunakonda
Kesanapalli
Kanaganahalli
Devnimori

Pakistan
Taxila
Mata, Swat

Sri Lanka
Mahāthūpa at Anuradhapura
Mahācetiya at Abhayagirivihāra
Kaṇṭaka-cetiya at Mihintale
Mahāthūpa at Kasimottai, Batticalloa Dist.

Another type of *stūpa* is the Dharmarājika, known mainly from the legend that King Aśoka caused 84,000 Dharmarājika

Figure 21 Ruvanväli Dagoba, Anuradhapura, Sri Lanka. According to the chronicles, the Dagoba was originally built in the 3rd century BCE, but it has been enlarged and restored many times up to the present (photograph: Akira Shimada)

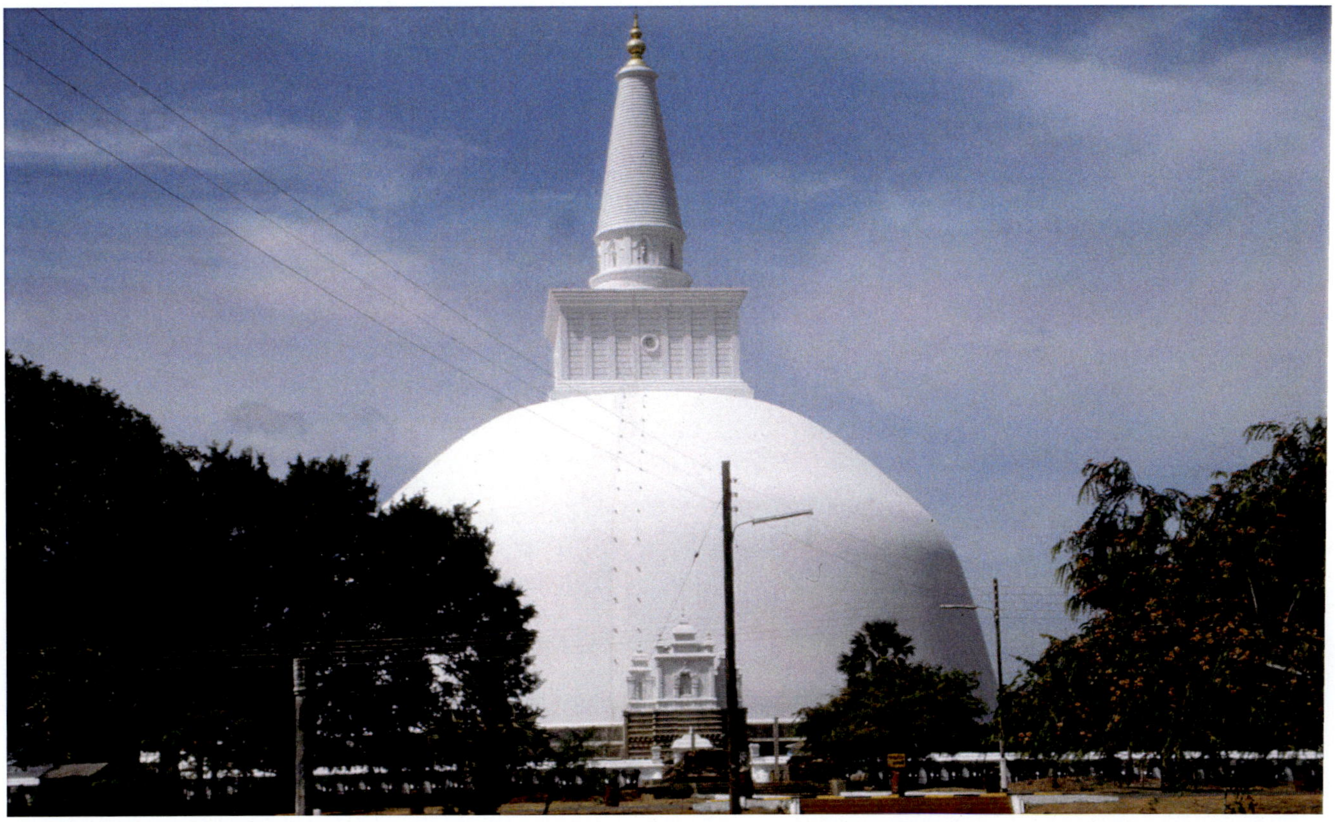

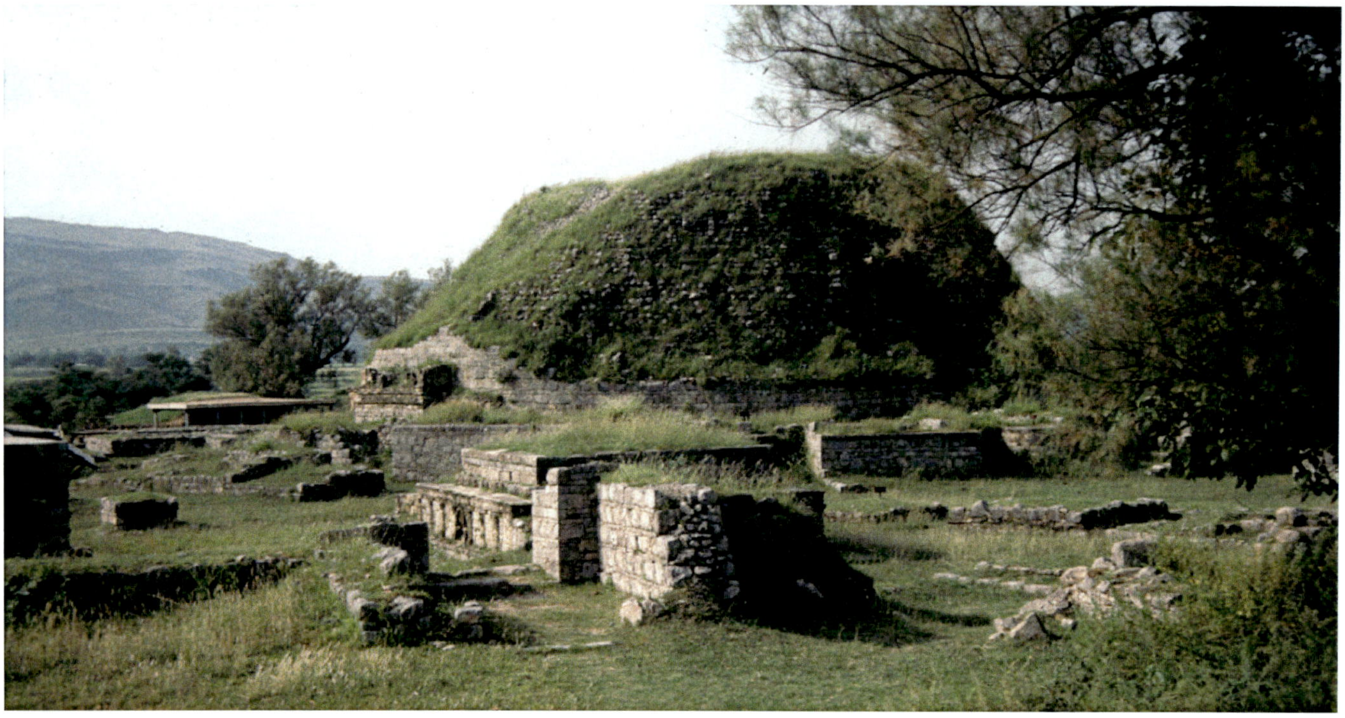

Figure 22 Dharmarājika *stūpa*, Taxila (photograph: Kurt Behrendt)

stūpas to be erected (**Fig. 22**). The term may mean a *stūpa* enshrining a relic of Śākyamuni, King of the Dharma, or a *stūpa* built by Aśoka, the Righteous King. Xuanzang visited Dharmarājika *stūpas* in north-western India during his travels in the 7th century CE. A silver scroll in the Gandhari language refers to relics installed in the Dharmarājika at the ancient metropolis of Taxila (Jongeward *et al.* 2012: § 30, 237). The inscribed pedestal of a stone Bodhisatva image from Mathura states that the Bodhisatva was 'installed at the Dharmarājika, into the acceptance of the teachers of the Mahāsāṃghikas' (Falk 2012: 13–18 and pl. 4).

Mahāstūpa and *Mahācaitya* in literature

The term *mahāstūpa* seems rare in literature. It occurs several times in the 'Stanzas recited on the shores of the Anavatapta Lake'. This is a collection of poems or songs in which Śākyamuni's personal disciples gather by the Anavatapta Lake in the high Himalayas and describe acts of merit that they performed in their previous lives. It survives in several versions: Sanskrit from Turfan in Central Asia, Gandhari from the north-west of the subcontinent, and in translation in Tibetan and Chinese.[30] In the Gandhari version, one of the disciples, Kusuma by name, recounts the following (Salomon 2008: 313–25):[31]

> 'Putting a jasmine flower on my ear, and putting a garland on my head, I went out to the park, accompanied by my friends.
>
> There I saw a **great *stūpa*** [Gandhari *mahathubu*] of the glorious Vipaśyin. A crowd of people had assembled and was paying homage and worshipping it.
>
> Those friends of mine, having assembled, took their own garlands and placed them on the ***stūpa*** [Gandhari *thuva*, also in the verses that follow] with pure hearts and minds.
>
> Seeing them and watching them one after another, I took the jasmine flower from my ear and placed it on the ***stūpa*** myself.
>
> For no gift is small when given by one who is pure in mind to an enlightened Tathāgata and to those who are the personal disciples of the Buddhas.
>
> If I had paid homage to the ***stūpa*** while knowing the Buddha-virtues in the Tathāgata, I would have been all the more without a superior [?].
>
> Therefore, indeed, by one who understands the many virtues of the Teacher – make homage at a ***stūpa***. Thereby you will escape bad birth.
>
> Having donated just one flower, for a thousand crores of years I enjoyed pleasures among the gods, and in the end now comes my calming [i.e. *nirvāṇa*].
>
> This, O venerable ones, I remember: having donated just one flower, I experienced its result, for karma does not disappear.'
>
> Thus did the elder Kusuma, a monk and personal disciple of the Buddha, explain his karma himself on the great lake Anavatapta.

I cite this song at length for more than one reason. It describes the veneration of *stūpas*, and it traces the efficacy of one simple act of worship towards the *stūpa* of a past Buddha to an enormously long reward enjoyed as a deity. It emphasizes the importance of the heart of serene faith, and of conjoining material worship with an understanding of the Buddha's virtues (*buddha-guṇa*), one of the fundamental spiritual exercises of early Dharma practice. Kusuma exhorts us to understand these virtues and to make homage at a *stūpa*.

The Gandhari stanzas of the senior Vāgīśa (Salomon 2008: 276–99) are another testimony to the karmic power of *stūpa* veneration. Like Kusuma's, they show how worship begins with emulation:

> In this ninety-first aeon since then [?], I do not recall having had a bad birth; as a god and a human, I have had only good birth, because of worshipping at a ***stūpa*** [Gandhari *thubu*].

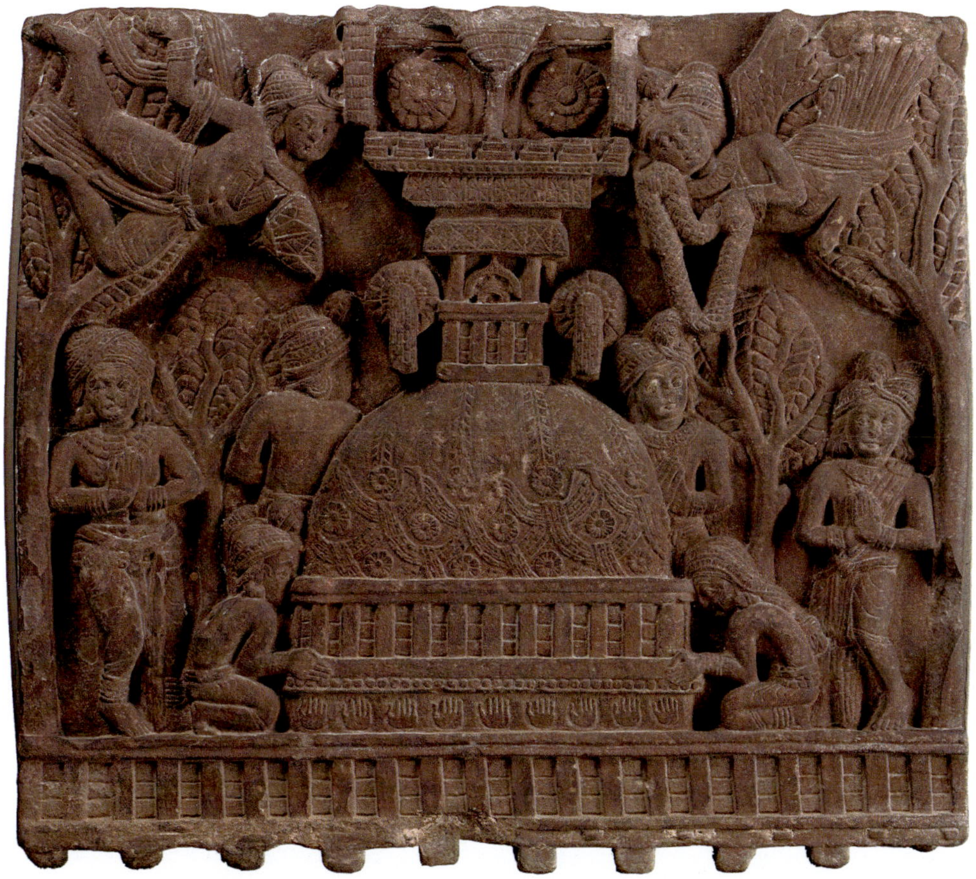

Figure 23 Making offerings to a *stūpa*, Bharhut, c. 2nd century BCE. Freer Gallery of Art, Smithsonian Institution, Washington, D.C.: Purchase, F1932.26

Without knowing the merit of it, having watched others doing it one after another, I went to the ***stūpa*** [*thubu*] of the Buddha Vipaśyin and made homage to it then.

Joyful, I placed a garland, incense, and unguent of three *kākinīs* value on the ***stūpa*** [*thuva*]. As a result, I was not reborn into a bad birth.

It is clear from the Anavatapta stanzas that, at least in poetry, *stūpa* and *mahāstūpa* are interchangeable. Where the Gandhari version of Kusuma's verses has *mahāstūpa*, other versions have *stūpa* (with the exception of the Turfan fragment). In Kusuma's other verses, the Gandhari and all other versions have simply *stūpa*. This interchangeability is confirmed by Nanda's verses from Central Asia. According to the Turfan fragment, Nanda gained serene faith when he saw the *Mahāstūpa* of the Buddha Kāśyapa. In the Gandhari version and the Tibetan translation, however, it is simply Kāśyapa's *Stūpa*. In all versions, Nanda is inspired to offer a parasol to the *Stūpa* (Salomon 2008: 197–8).[32]

The British Library scroll may be as early as the first half of the 1st century CE, but if not, then the first half of the 2nd century CE.[33] The verses of Kusuma, Vāgīśa and others attest to the practices and ideology of *stūpa* worship before the beginning of the Christian era, practices that we already know from the devotional and narrative reliefs at Bharhut, Bodh Gaya and Sanchi that may be dated to the 2nd to 1st centuries BCE (**Fig. 23**).

In certain instances *mahācaitya* refers to specific pilgrimage sites in North India. In the 'Chapter on Robes' (*Cīvara-vastu*) of the *Vinaya* of the Mūlasarvāstivādin school, it refers to four sites in north-eastern India: the places where Śākyamuni was born, was awakened, gave his first teaching and passed away.[34] These four *Mahācaityas* are the same as the four 'inspiring sites' (*saṃvejaniyaṭṭhāna*) of the 'Great Discourse on the Buddha's Final *Nibbāna*' (*Mahāparinibbāna-sutta*) and the four 'great sites' (*mahāṭṭhāna*) of Pali liturgy.[35] In terms of historical and spiritual import these four have first rights to *mahācaitya* status (**Fig. 24a–c**).

The 'Great Evaluation of Deeds' (*Mahākarmavibhaṅga*) lists 12 benefits (*anuśaṃsa*) gained from raising one's hands in homage (*añjali*) to the Tathāgata-*caityas* that are the four great *caityas* in the Middle Country, that is, Lumbini, the Mahābodhi, etc.:[36]

One is reborn in the Middle Country; one obtains excellent clothing, excellent family, excellent reputation, excellent voice, excellent eloquence, excellent faith, excellent morality, excellent learning, excellent relinquishment, excellent mindfulness, and excellent wisdom.

It is the promise of such rewards that drew, and continues to draw, devotees to the holy sites.

There are also groups of eight 'great caityas', which usually subsume the four 'great sites'.[37] One source for these is a eulogy (*stotra*) that pays homage to the eight great events of Śākyamuni's career. The original Sanskrit title is not certain; according to the Tibetan it may be *Aṣṭa-mahāsthāna-caitya-vandana*, 'Veneration to the Caityas at the Eight Great Sites'.[38] These eight sites codify key events in Śākyamuni's life – eight marvels/miracles, each of which is associated with a particular place and each of which is a *caitya* or a *stūpa*. Eight great *chöten* (*mchod rten* = *stūpa*/*caitya*[39]) are listed in the 'Prophecy Regarding the Li Country [Khotan]'. The text uses the term *chöten chenpo* (*mchod rten chen po*) several times, but since it is preserved in Tibetan translation only it is impossible to say whether this represents *mahāstūpa* or *mahācaitya*.[40]

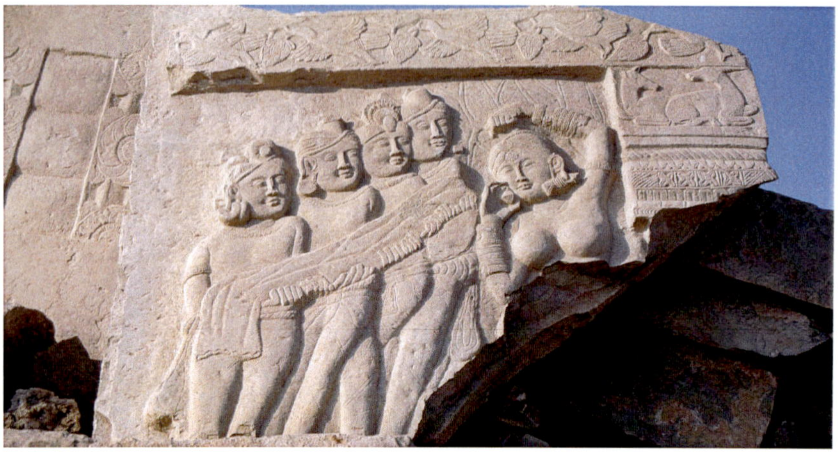

Figure 24a Birth of the Buddha at Lumbini, Kanaganahalli, *c.* 1st century CE (photograph: Christian Luczanits)

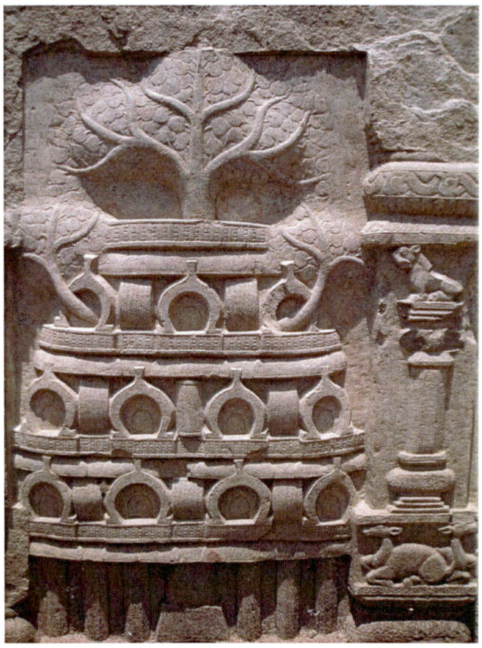

Figure 24b An early depiction of a bodhi-tree shrine, possibly Vajrāsana (Bodh Gaya), Kanaganahalli, *c.* 1st century CE (photograph: Christian Luczanits)

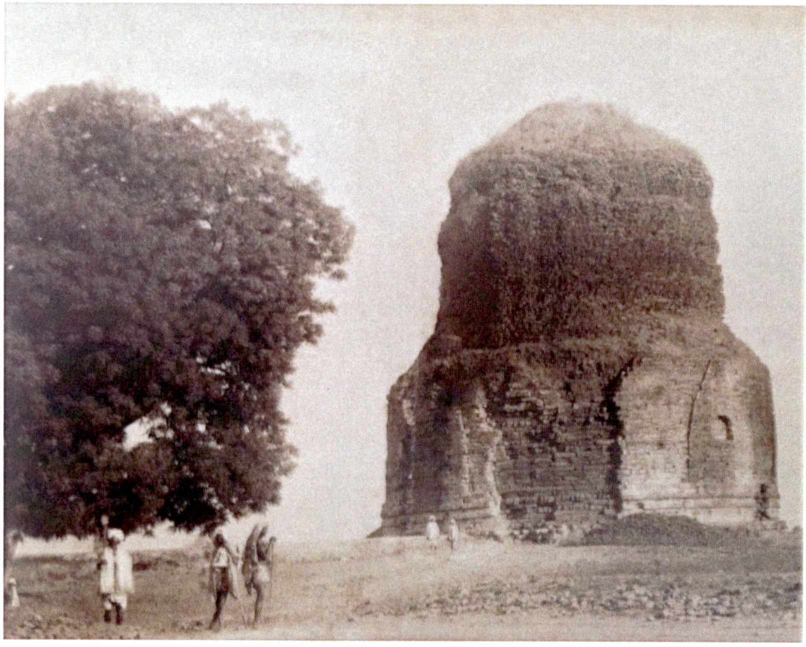

Figure 24c Buddhist tope, Sarnath, 1888 (photograph: Raja Deen Dayal)

In an Avadāna called the 'Past Exploits of King Candraprabha', Candraprabha is a king who is devoted to generosity, to fulfilling the wishes of each and every supplicant who comes to him. He takes care of his subjects to the point that he gives all of them jewellery, regalia, crowns and diadems, and the city resounds with merriment and joy. But one day there comes Raudrākṣa, a heartless brahman, who asks Candraprabha to sacrifice his head: overjoyed at the prospect, the magnanimous king agrees. Before doing this, he makes an 'appropriate vow' (*samyak-praṇidhāna*) in which he uses the three terms *mahāstūpa*, *mahācaitya* and *caitya* in the same breath.[41] When compared with the Sanskrit, the Tibetan translation provides a good example of how both *(mahā)caitya* and *(mahā)stūpa* are translated by a single term, *chöten (chenpo)*.

> By this truth, by these words of truth, may this exertion bear fruit! When I have passed away in *nirvāṇa*, may there be relics the size of mustard seeds! May there be a **great *stūpa*** (*mahān stūpaḥ/mchod rten chen po*), one that surpasses all other ***stūpas*** (*sarva-stūpa-prativiśiṣṭaṃ/mchod rten thams cad las khyad par du 'phags pa*). Should there come beings who are physically worn out and want to pay homage to the **great *caitya*** (*mahācaitya/mchod rten chen po*), when they see that excellent relic, surpassing all other ***stūpas*** [Skt, Tib. as above], may they be restored. When I have passed away in *nirvāṇa*, may the crowds who come and do worship to my ***caityas*** (*mama caityeṣu/nga'i mchod rten la*) all be destined for heaven and liberation.

There are other references to *chöten chenpo* in the Tibetan translation of the *Vinaya* of the Mūlasarvāstivādins. In the 'Chapter on the Rupture of the Saṃgha' of the *Vinayavastu*, a great *stūpa* is erected for the relics of the past Buddha Aranābhī.[42] Here again we have the great *stūpa* of a past Buddha. Otherwise, the Tibetan translations contain isolated references, for example in the *Sumukha-dhāraṇī*, which opens with the Bhagavā staying at the foot of the bodhi tree, 'at the great *mchod rten* of the Bodhi-maṇḍa'.[43]

I have not seen any research on these terms in literature, and what I have given here are only random examples. The *mahācaityas* and *mahāstūpas* of literature are narrative and legendary, and how they relate to the landscapes of history is another story.

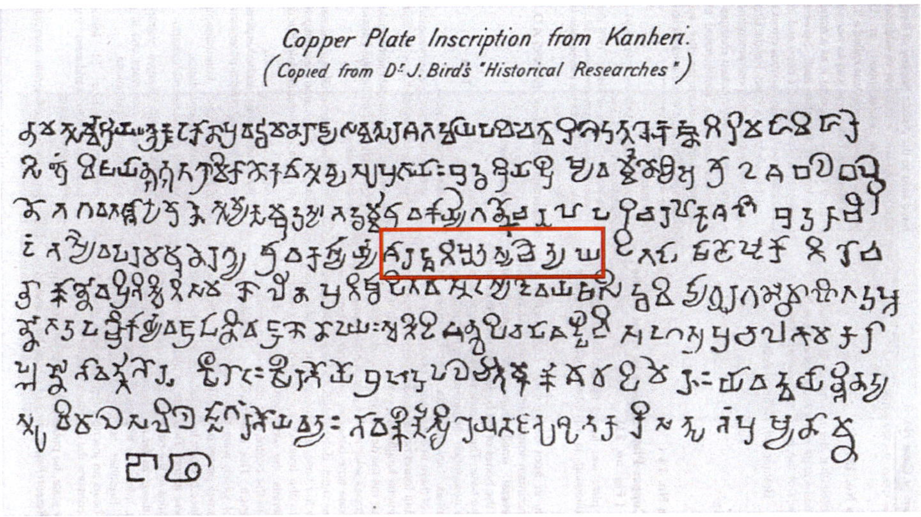

Figure 25 Eye-copy of copperplate inscription, now lost, referring to the *caitya* dedicated to Śāriputra at Kṛṣṇagiri at Kanheri (after Bird 1847), 494/495 CE

Varieties of *caityas*

The nature of the relics enshrined defines the typologies of *caitya*s. Texts mention two main types: that of a Tathāgata and that of a Śrāvaka (that is, *tathāgata-caitya*, of a Buddha, and *śrāvaka-caitya*, of a 'hearer' or direct disciple).[44] Across a broad spectrum of texts, the *caitya* of the Tathāgata is by far the most frequent. It is regularly mentioned in *Vinaya* texts, in independent texts like the 'Great Evaluation of Deeds'[45] or the '*Sūtra* on the Gabled Hall',[46] in the *Lalitavistara* – the grand biography of the Buddha – and in Mahāyāna *sūtras*, including the 'Perfection of Wisdom' (*Prajñāpāramitā*), '*Gaṇḍavyūha*', 'White Lotus of the True Dharma',[47] 'King of Concentrations' (*Samādhirāja*), 'Cloud of Gems',[48] 'Questions of Pūrṇa',[49] 'Scriptural Basket of the Bodhisatvas', 'Heap of Jewels'[50] and others. The 'Chapter on Worship' in the 'Bodhisatva Stages' uses the term repeatedly.[51] Literary preference shows that *caitya*s were seen primarily as containing relics of the Tathāgata, the Buddha, and that they were sites of worship and sources of merit.

Śrāvaka-caityas are attested in literature – the *Āgama*s and the accounts of the Chinese pilgrims – but they have rarely been discovered archaeologically. The few examples include the *caitya*s at Sanchi and Satdhara in central India, which contained the inscribed reliquaries of Śāriputra and Maudgalyāyana (Willis 2000), and a Śāriputra *caitya* at Kanheri near Mumbai, long ago reduced to rubble but known from a copperplate inscription (itself now lost) (**Fig. 25**).[52] The *Mūlasarvāstivādin Vinaya* has a passage on the institution of a festival for Śāriputra's *stūpa*.[53] In the 'Story of Sesavatī' in the Pali 'Stories of the Celestial Mansions', the young woman Sesavatī offers golden flowers and fragrances to Śāriputra's *stūpa* at the town of Nālaka in Magadha (his birthplace) and the site of his *parinirvāṇa* and cremation.[54] This *caitya* is of a different order than that of the 'institutional *caitya*s' of the *Mūlasarvāstivādin Vinaya*, and must be related to the Śāriputra *stūpa* in the vicinity of Nalanda reported by Chinese and Tibetan pilgrims.

Otherwise, *śrāvaka-caitya*s may be subdivided into the *caitya*s of the *arhat*, the non-returner, etc., but these are infrequent even in dogmatic texts. *Stūpa*s of 'Solitary Buddhas' (*Pratyekabuddhas*) feature in pious narratives, but not in archaeology, since dogma has it that *Pratyekabuddhas* appear in the world only when there is no Buddha. Two broad categories are '*caitya* without relics' and '*caitya* with relics' (*adhātuka*, *sadhātuka*);[55] the latter include '*stūpa* for physical relics' and '*stūpa* for relics', which differ only in choice of words.[56] The clippings of Śākyamuni's hair and nails were collected and venerated as memorials of the Master; references to these 'hair and nail' *stūpa*s (*keśanakha-stūpa*) are frequent in Mūlasarvāstivādin literature. A short Avadāna states a general principle:[57]

> It is a natural rule that while the Fortunate Ones, the Buddhas, are still living, are alive, continue to exist, there are *stūpa*s for their hair and nails. When the Fortunate Ones, the Buddhas, are withdrawn for meditation … monks perform ceremonies at these *stūpa*s for hair and nails.

It goes on to give a vivid description of one monk's devotions.

In the chronology of the Buddha's biography, two of the earliest *stūpa*s – belonging to his pre-Awakening and Awakening cycles – are those made to enshrine the Bodhisatva's topknot and the hairs that he presented to the two merchants Trapuṣa and Bhallika. The northern Thai narrative of Śākyamuni's travels across northern Siam, 'The Lord Crosses the World' (*Phra chao liap lok*), mentions many places with hair *stūpa*s, each with its own foundation story.[58] Today numerous hair *stūpa*s are found in northern Thailand. Memorial *stūpa*s commemorating sites where the Bodhisatva performed heroic deeds or the visits of past Buddhas were noted by the Chinese pilgrims in north-western and central India. In south-east Asia there are a variety of memorial *stūpa*s, commemorating, for example, royal victories in war.

In addition to *stūpa*s for the disciples of the Buddha, there are *stūpa*s and '*stūpa* galleries' from centuries later with inscriptions that show they enshrine relics of what Schopen has called the 'local monastic dead'. Prominent examples are at Kanheri and Bhaja in the Western Ghats (Gokhale 1991; Schopen 1991 [1997]).[59] The Lankan chronicles have a lot to say about the cremation and *stūpa*s of *Arhat* Mahinda, who brought the Dharma to the island, and his remains are said to be installed in the Mihindu Seya and the Ambasthala Dagaba at Mihintale to the north of the capital of Anuradhapura.[60] In Thailand, secondary *stūpa*s are more broadly those of the 'local dead': of kings or members of the royal family, abbots or leading monks, donors and their descendants, or dignitaries connected with the temple. Most are anonymous; if they ever had plaques, they are lost. The

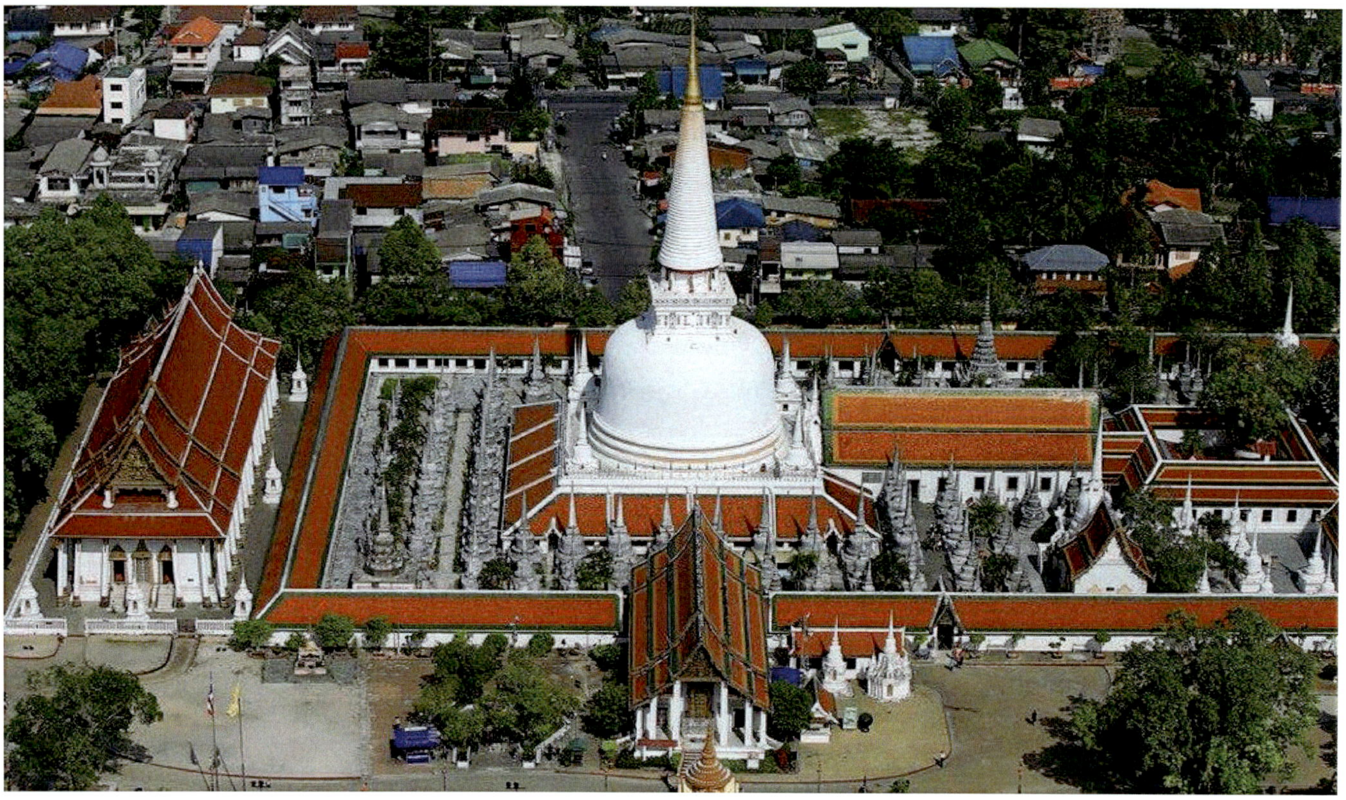

Figure 26 Wat Phra Boromathat at Nakhon Si Thammarat, southern Thailand. A much-venerated *stūpa* with legendary beginnings, restored and expanded many times up to the present (photograph: Chaibancha Prachong 2015)

courtyard of the great relic *stūpa* of Wat Phra Boromathat at Nakhon Si Thammarat, southern Thailand, is filled with lesser *stūpa*s, very few of which have identifying plaques (**Fig. 26**).

One type of *stūpa* that is frequently mentioned in modern writing is the 'votive *stūpa*'. Never clearly defined, it seems to be used for any or all of the smaller monuments in a *stūpa* cluster. The *New Oxford Dictionary of English* defines 'votive' as 'offered or consecrated in fulfilment of a vow' (Pearsall 2001: 2072). It is possible that *stūpa*s have been built for this reason, but this was never a primary reason, and in order to call a monument a 'votive *stūpa*' we should have explicit evidence, from an inscription or a historical document, that this had indeed been the case. For the vast numbers of lesser *stūpa*s that fill the courtyards of the Great Caitya complexes, there is no evidence whatsoever to show why or for whom they were erected. The dedications inscribed on reliquaries state that the relics were installed to make merit for the sponsor and his or her extended family and ancestors, with the provision that this is 'for the benefit of the many, for the good of the world' – easily the most common expression used in reliquary inscriptions across South Asia (Skilling forthcoming b).

In contemporary Thai practice, devotees request something in front of a *stūpa* (the relic being the Buddha), a statue of the Buddha, or a deity, and promise something in return if their wishes are fulfilled. If the wish is granted, the devotees return to make offerings as promised. This, the 'exchange vow', is central to Thai religious behaviour. In it, the 'votive process' – the vow and the fulfilment of the vow – may take place in front of a *caitya* or image, but the vow is not the reason for the erection of the *caitya* or image. Rather than project alien concepts like 'votive' on to ancient Indian or Buddhist religious architecture, it makes better sense to use non-committal terms such as 'lesser', 'minor' or 'subsidiary' *stūpa*s.

Stūpa clusters and *caitya* complexes

Strictly speaking, we should not consider just '*stūpa*s' or '*caitya*s', but '*stūpa* complexes' or '*caitya* complexes'. No *stūpa* stands alone. A Great *Stūpa* is a part, the very heart, of an interactive agglomeration of structures – the heart because the *stūpa* is enlivened by relics and it animates the precincts.[61] The built environment may include apsidal temples, image halls, halls for devotion, meditation and study, residences, refectories, kitchens, baths, steam-baths and toilets, all landscaped with paths and platforms, gardens, wells, reservoirs and water-control systems. The lesser *stūpa*s make up *stūpa* or *caitya* clusters. These conglomerations were located along trade routes, waterways and pilgrim routes, which linked up with mountain passes, river crossings and ports. The *caitya* complexes were storehouses or treasure houses of cultural and spiritual information. Relics were installed and buried; they were not meant, under normal circumstances, to be seen again. The caskets were sealed; relics emanated their posthumous or post-*nirvāṇa* power on their own, through the supernormal will power of the Buddhas. The Great Caityas attracted donations (Sanskrit *deyadharma*; Prakrit *deyadhama*; Pali *deyadhamma*) to the *stūpa* itself and to the monastic order; they drew pilgrims, festival-goers and those in search of blessings such as members of the court, merchants and traders. Townspeople and travellers came as proto-tourists. The primary rituals were donation, homage, recitation and circumambulation, just as they are to this day. It is probable that one of the recitations was the *Āṭānāṭiya sūtra*, one of the most prominent early Buddhist ritual texts, which is still chanted in Paritta and healing ceremonies.[62]

Practices and benefits

The circumambulation of sacred objects is an ancient practice in many societies. The earliest record of the practice in Buddhist textual chronology might be the account of Śākyamuni's funeral in the 'Great Parinirvāṇa Sūtra', which reports that 500 monks circumambulated the Buddha's coffin three times and bowed their heads at his feet, after which it burst into flames of its own accord.[63]

The 'Verses on the Circumambulation of *Caityas*' preserved in Tibetan translation describe the benefits of the exercise.[64] These benefits are both worldly and spiritual: from beautiful complexion to wealth and high status to heavenly rebirth to the realization of the stages of Arhat, Solitary Buddha and, ultimately, full Buddhahood. The concluding verses (p. 231) emphasize two essential points. One is that the veneration of the Buddha is as productive of merit after his death as when he was alive. This had been a point of contention after his passing; it was eventually resolved by the assertion of the ideology of merit in tandem with metaphysics of the several bodies of the Buddha. The other is that the Buddhas are ineffable and the merit of veneration is beyond conceptualization, a move steeped in faith that sidesteps the need for exegesis:[65]

> There is no difference between the merit of those
> Who make offerings while I am here, and those
> Who make offerings after my *nirvāṇa*,
> If their virtuous intentions are the same.
>
> Such is the inconceivable Buddha;
> So also the inconceivable Buddhadharma;
> For those with faith in the inconceivable,
> The rewards are inconceivable.

Other meritorious deeds are washing the *stūpa* and performing ritual ablutions for the reliquary. Whitewashing the *stūpa*, covering it with gold leaf or with plates of precious metal (bronze, silver or gold), offering garlands, streamers and banners, raising ceremonial parasols – the merits of these are extolled in the Avadāna and Ānisaṅsa literature, in the Vaidalya *sūtras* and in another verse text also preserved in Sanskrit and in Tibetan translation, the 'Questions' or 'Verses of King Prasenajit'.[66] Many of these activities are depicted in early *stūpa* reliefs, in which *stūpas* are bedecked with banners, streamers and garlands, and clusters of parasols hover over the *stūpa* like giant blossoms (**Fig. 27**). As mentioned earlier, no contemporary texts from the Krishna delta have survived to guide us in our study of the rich material remains that are the heritage of an extraordinary and flourishing period, from 300 BCE to 300 CE. We have no evidence that the texts cited here ever circulated in the region. But the narrative and devotional reliefs chosen to decorate the monuments that spread along the river valleys show that the ideology of offerings would have been similar to that expressed in the texts (**Fig. 28**).

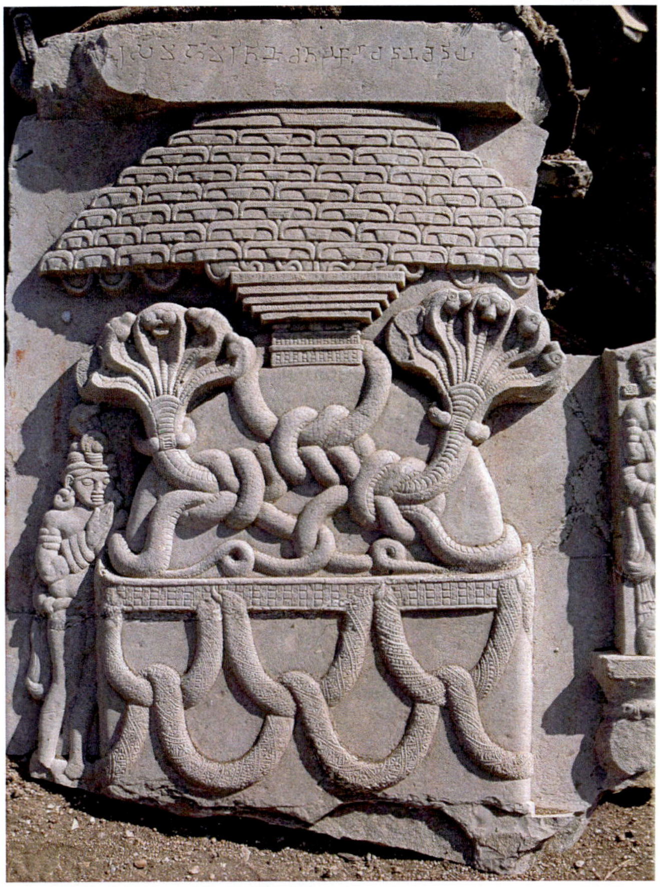

Figure 27 Relief showing a *stūpa*, Kanaganahalli, *c.* 1st century CE (photograph: Christian Luczanits)

The long age of *caityas*

The *stūpa* complexes are records of the organic development of devotional focal points during the early centuries of Buddhism. They are also records of technological and aesthetic achievements: of architecture using stone, brick, plaster and stucco and of landscaping and irrigation/water control. The complexes were nodes in networks of communication and patronage that centred on devotional and ritual relations. As social monuments, the *caitya* complexes were shared by societal groups; they were built and maintained for the benefit of individuals and extended families, of monastic and teacher–student lineages and of all beings. Centres for ritual, for the exchange of knowledge and goods, the monuments were anything but static. What remain today, uncovered by the excavators' spades, are layers of growth – and decline and renovation – characteristic of living monuments.[67] The monuments live on today, driven by the diktats of preservation, heritage and tourism.

Caitya and *mahācaitya*, *stūpa* and *mahāstūpa*, are conventional terms that would have been adopted according to context, circumstances and current fashion. Buddhism never developed a centralized hierarchy in which certain monasteries or *stūpas* would have had a special status as administrative seats like the cathedrals of certain Christian denominations. *Caitya* or *mahācaitya* would not be a status conferred from above, but rather a matter of common acceptation. We have seen this flexibility in the literary examples cited above. *Caityas* and *mahācaityas* were equal, but some were bigger than others, and may have been more

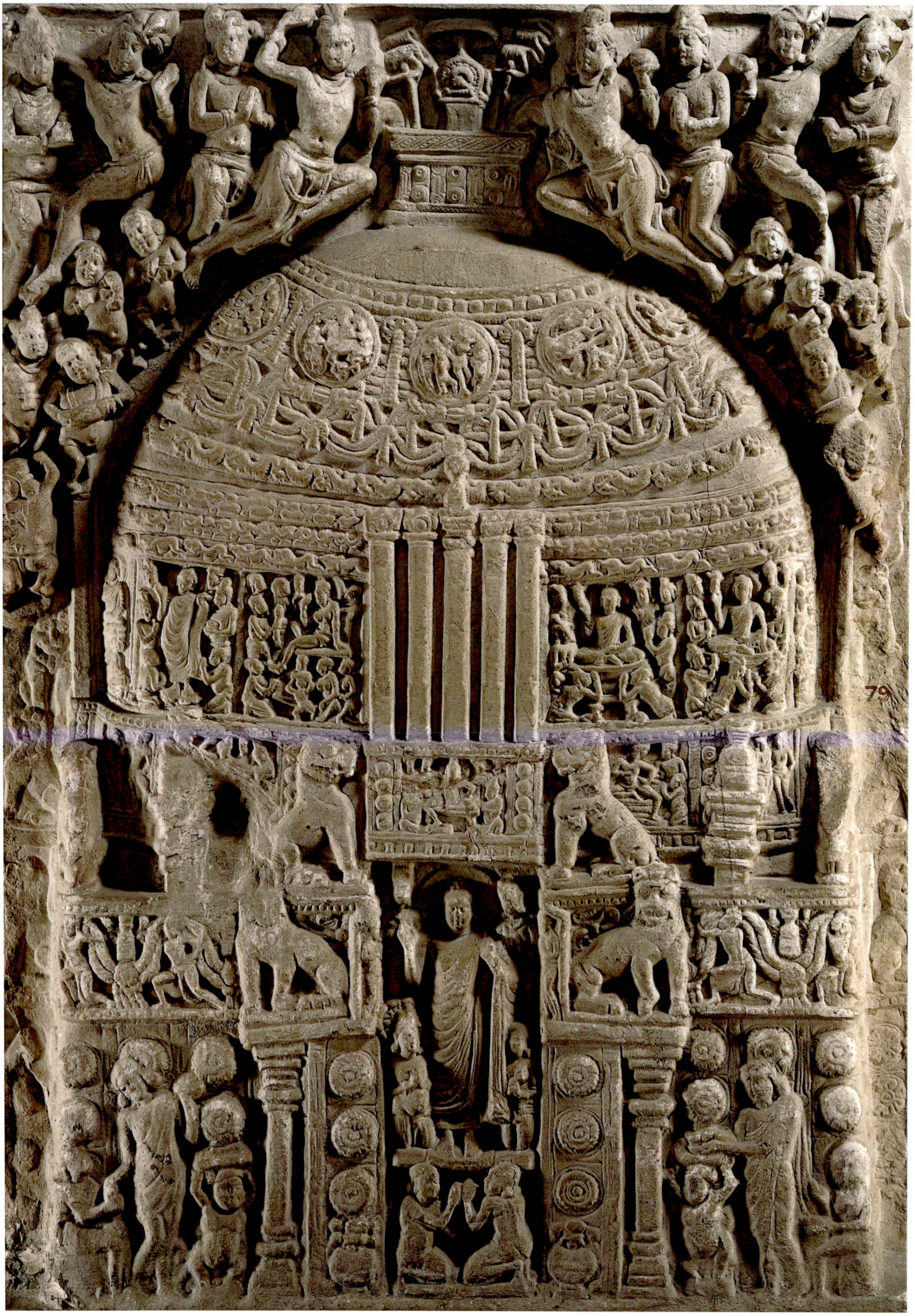

Figure 28 Relief showing a *stūpa*, Amaravati, *c.* 3rd century CE, British Museum, 1880,0709.79

frequently described as *mahācaityas*. In the history of South Asian architecture there was a long 'Age of *Caityas*', when in many areas *caityas* or *stūpas* would have been the most prominent monuments. Some of these would have been *mahācaityas* and *mahāstūpas*, side by side in the same landscape.

Acknowledgements

I express my gratitude to Christian Luczanits, Alexander von Rospatt, Franz-Karl Erhard, Saerji, Seishi Karashima, Mattia Salvini, Bhikṣuṇī Dharmadinnā and others for supplying materials and giving advice. I thank the Courtauld Institute and the British Museum for arranging the seminar, especially David Park and Michael Willis. It is a pleasure to thank Akira Shimada for his patient and conscientious editing of this volume.

Conventions

Unless otherwise indicated, translations are my own. My translations of titles are interpretative rather than literal. The original Sanskrit, etc., titles are given in the notes.

Buddhist texts use a wide range of terms for the figure whose name is routinely reduced to 'the Buddha' in modern English and European writings. To relieve the monotony, I use a sampling of these names: the Fortunate One (Bhagavat), the Teacher, the Master, Śākyamuni, the Awakened One (the Buddha). Epithets of the Buddha open classical lexicons like *Amarakośa*, *Abhidhānappadīpika* and *Mahāvyutpatti*.

I generally use *stūpa* and *caitya* interchangeably. I use the Sanskrit terms for general statements, and specific forms in Pali (*thūpa*, *cetiya*), Prakrit (*thuba*, etc., *cetiya*, *ceta*) or Tibetan (*chöten*) in direct citations or references. I capitalize *Mahācaitya* and *Mahāstūpa* as names of a particular monument.

For my choice of the spelling 'Bodhisatva' see Skilling 2013. This spelling is already adopted in, for example, Mitterwallner 1987 (241, n. 17).

Notes

1 A bibliography on the *stūpa*, even the South Asian *stūpa* alone, would fill at least a hefty volume. One of the most complete is that in Kottkamp 1992. More recent is Ulrich Pagel's '*Stūpa*, Pagoda, Caitya', available online at http://www.oxfordbibliographies.com/view/document/obo-9780195393521/obo-9780195393521-0087.xml (subscription required; accessed 23 June 2016). In the following notes, references to Pali texts are to the editions of the Pali Text Society (PTS), UK; references to Tibetan texts are to the Derge xylograph edition.

2 The reference is to Elphinstone 1815; see Wilson 1841, 28ff. For cognate forms see Turner ([1966] 1999): 790, §§ 13709–12.

3 See Skilling 2009; 2010a.

4 Mahāvihāra Theravādins were also present in the region, but they were only one of many schools – and their early *caityas* in Sri Lanka lacked a narrative relief tradition. One text that *might* have been composed or compiled in the South, and does survive in Sanskrit, is the *Gaṇḍavyūha* of the *Buddhāvataṃsaka*. It describes the spiritual journey of the youth Sudhana to sites many of which are in the South, but it is hardly a travelogue or a useful handbook of geography.

5 *budha-sarirānaṃ nikhetu*: see Tsukamoto 1996. Part I (II): Bhat. 2.

6 The most impressive study of the *stūpa* is that by Kottkamp (1992), who focuses more on archaeology, structure, style and symbolism than on terminology and narrative.

7 For a well-illustrated presentation of early Hindu and Buddhist architecture enhanced by excellent maps, see Singh 2008: 445–60.

8 *Mahāparinirvāṇasūtra*: ed. Waldschmidt 1950–1: § 1.32–4; Pali *Dīghanikāya* (ed. PTS) II 74–5.

9 Translation after Rotman 2008: 337, with a few minor changes, for which I beg the translator's kind indulgence.

10 The Pali (*Dīghanikāya* II, 102) has here 'Delightful, Ānanda, is Vesālī: delightful is the Udena Cetiya, delightful the Gotamaka Cetiya; delightful is the Sattambaka Cetiya, delightful the Bahuputta Cetiya; delightful is the Sārandada Cetiya, and delightful is the Cāpāla Cetiya.'

11 For a good sampling of reliquary and *caitya* dedications see Tsukamoto 2007: 123–33.

12 Jongeward *et al.* 2012: inscr. no. 11: *mahathubami dhakṣiṇami bhagami.*

13 *kṛtam avaniketubhūtam mahāvihārāśraye mahāstūpaṃ, satvānekānugraha-niratābhyāṃ śākyabhikṣubhyāṃ*, Mehta and Chowdhary 1966: 121; Tsukamoto 1996. Part II (III): Devnī Mori 1 line 2; Chowdhary 2010: 134–6. 'Śākya monks' (*śākyabhikṣu*) are Buddhist monks, followers of Śākyamuni. Monks and nuns who describe themselves as 'Śākya' in dedicatory inscriptions may or may not have been practitioners of Mahāyāna, but whether or not this is so is to be deduced for each individual case, taking into account the context and the nature of the object dedicated. Mahāyāna affiliation is not intrinsic to the term. The perceived relation to Mahāyāna has been overstated in the literature, the staunchest proponent being Schopen 2005. See Cousins' critique (2003) and Schopen's response in the reprint edition of his article (2005: 244–6). The entry in the recent *Princeton Dictionary of Buddhism* gives a balanced definition: 'in its most general sense the term refers to any Buddhist monk' (Buswell and Lopez 2014: 741).

14 Tsukamoto 1996. Part I (II): Amar. 12.2; 14; 31; 45.1; 46.5; 50; 77; 140.2; *dhañakaṭe mahacetiye*: 31; 20.7.

15 Tsukamoto 1996. Part I (II): Amar. 12.2: ... *[to] mahācetiye cetikiyānaṃ nikā(ya)sa parigrahe aparadāre dhamacakaṃ de(ya)dhaṃ [maṃ ṭh]āpita.*

16 Tsukamoto 1996. Part I (II): Jagg. 1.6 *bhagavato budhasa mahācetiyapuvādare āyakhaṃbhe*; 3.6, idem.

17 First Apsidal Temple inscription E (*EI* 20: 21–2).

18 Tsukamoto 1996. Part I (II): Kesanapalli 16.4. The inscription is fragmentary and therefore difficult. In line two is the phrase *bahusutiyānaṃ mūlavasivihāracetik[e].*

19 For the inscription, see Nakanishi and von Hinüber 2014: 31–3 (I.8) and pl. 2. For pictures of Kanaganahalli see www.luczanits.net (accessed 23 June 2016). For the ASI report, see Poonacha 2011.

20 For the inscription see Nakanishi and von Hinüber 2014: 30–1 (I.7); for the relief, see Poonacha 2011: pls LX B, CIX B.

21 *deyadhama payapato*: Nakanishi and von Hinüber 2014: 73–4 (II.6.1, 2). For the inscription on the slab at the northern Āyaka, see *MASI* 106: pl. 138.2 (p. 490); for the Buddhapāda see ibid.: pl. 21A (p. 133) and fig. 16 (line drawings, p. 69).

22 Nakanishi and von Hinüber 2014: 49–50 (II.2.15). For *puphagahani*, an architectural term 'which does not seem to occur elsewhere', except once at Amaravati, see ibid. 44–5. The meaning is not clear to me.

23 Nakanishi and von Hinüber 2014: 106–7 (IV.8), *dhañakaḍikāya pavayitāya aya mitāya....*

24 For the vocabulary of *stūpas* in Sri Lanka, see Paranavitana 1946: 1, n. 1; Silva 1988: 11; 2007: 464.

25 I leave out here the 'Svayambhu Mahācaitya' in Kathmandu, because there is no evidence for its name in the earliest period, and it may have come to be called *Mahācaitya* much later. As for the Great Stūpa at Bodnath, it is called *Mahācaitya* in Tibetan sources (see Dowman 1973). Further research is needed on these terms in the Kathmandu valley in the Newar and Tibetan traditions (and in the Newar, Tibetan and Himalayan traditions in general).

26 Jayawickrama 1971; Berkwitz 2007. For vernacular histories like the many *tamnan* of north Thailand and Nepalese texts like the *Svayaṃbhū-purāṇa* see Skilling 2005: 272–3.

27 For the history and literature of the Great Thūpa see Mudiyanse 2002. Arunasiri 2002 is mainly a digest of materials from the *Mahāvaṃsa*.

28 For another reading, see Karunaratne 1984: no. 80.

29 Regnal dates from de Silva 2005: 739.

30 *Anavataptagāthā*: for the versions see Salomon 2008: § 1.2; for the

Turfan manuscripts, see references in Chung and Schmidt 2008: 350.

31 I cite Salomon's translation without the brackets, but retaining the question marks, '[?]', which express his doubts about a reading or translation.

32 The Turfan manuscript is fragmentary; the verse is incomplete but is sufficiently preserved to be coherent. The exact nature of the parasol is not clear to me: Salomon translates 'the middle umbrella'.

33 For the dates of the Gandhari scroll and other versions of the *Anavatapta-gāthā* see Salomon 2008: 11–13.

34 The passage is difficult and warrants further research because there is no narrative context and no exegetical or other development of the subject. The rule at *Śrīghanācāra* § 39, which refers to gain received at the birth and awakening festivals may be relevant: *jāti-saṃbodhyādimahodbhavaś ceti yo'yaṃ daśaprakārī lābhaḥ sa saṃmukhībhūtānāṃ prāpnoti* (Singh 1983: 85.16 [trans. p. 178]; Derrett 1983: 49–50).

35 The Sanskrit would be *mahāsthāna*, but I do not know if this term is attested for a group of four sites, as it is for the group of eight great sites, the *aṣṭamahāsthāna*, also described as events, great miracles or prodigies, *aṣṭa-mahā-pratihārya*. For these see Parimoo 2010. For some Siamese liturgies in Pali (which themselves do not use the term), see Skilling 2010b and Skilling and Santi 2010. Cf. also the *Mahāsāṃghika-vinaya* preserved in Chinese, cited in Rhi 2005: 169.

36 Lévi 1932: 82–3, § LVII; Kudo 2004: 178–80,§ 62. I follow generally Kudo's version, guided by his annotations.

37 For these, especially in Tibetan tradition, see Skorupski 2001.

38 Bagchi 1941: 223–35 (repr. 1982: 138–53); Nakamura 1980 (with further references). There are several cognate texts on the theme; the lists are similar but not quite identical.

39 The Tibetan word *chöten*, written *mchod rten*, means a 'support or receptacle (*rten*) for veneration or offering (*mchod*)'. In the 'official' translation vocabulary established at the end of the 8th century CE, it can stand for either *stūpa* or *caitya*, without distinguishing between them.

40 *Li yul lung bstan pa*: Emmerick 1967: 4–5 translates 'eight great *stūpas*'.

41 *Candraprabha-avadāna*: Cowell and Neil 1886: 326.22ff.

42 Aranābhī = Rtsibs kyi lte ba: *Saṃghabhedavastu*: Sanskrit in Gnoli 1977: 161.11; Tibetan in *'Dul ba gzhi*, Derge, *'dul ba*, *nga*, 75b1: *mahān stūpaḥ pratiṣṭhāpitaḥ / mchod rten chen po brtsigs so.*

43 D 915, *Sgo bzang po zhes bya ba'i gzungs*, *Gzungs 'dus*, *E*, 255a1, *'di skad bdag gis thos pa dus gcig na | bcom ldan 'das byang chub kyi shing drung na byang chub kyi snying po'i mchod rten chen po na | dge slong stong nyis brgya lnga bcu'i dge slong gi dge 'dun chen po 'di lta ste |...*

44 For *śrāvaka-stūpa* (Tib. *nyan thos kyi mchod rten*) see Pagel 2007: 372–3 and 373, n. 1 (from Guṇaprabha's *Vinayasūtra*); ibid.: 374, n. 7, with reference to *Vinayasūtra* and *Vinaya-uttaragrantha*.

45 *Mahākarmavibhaṅga*: Lévi 1932: 82–3, § LVII; 84, § LVIII; Kudo 2004: 178–80, § 62; 180–1, § 63.

46 *Kūṭāgāra-sūtra*: Tseng 2010, I: 11–95.

47 *Saddharmapuṇḍarīka*: e.g. Kern and Nanjio 1908–12: 414, penult.

48 *Ratnamegha-sūtra* at *Śikṣāsamuccaya* in Bendall [1897–1902]: 313.12, 348.4, 349.4. The term occurs several times in tandem with 'image of the Buddha': see e.g. *'Phags pa Dkon mchog sprin ces bya ba theg pa chen po'i mdo*, in *Bka' 'gyur las khol du phyung ba'i nges don dang snying po'i mdo bcas pa bzugs so*, I: 262 (Chengdu, 2010), penult, *de bzhin gshegs pa'i mchod rten dag dang*, *de bzhin gshegs pa'i sku gzugs*; also: 291.13; 292.16; 403.10; 409.9; 433.3.

49 *Pūrṇaparipṛcchā*, Derge 189b5, *de bzhin gshegs pa rnams kyi mchod rten la mchod par byed pas.*

50 *Bodhisatvapiṭaka* and *Ratnarāśi*, examples as cited in Śāntideva's 'Compendium of Training' (*Śikṣāsamuccaya*): see Bendall [1897–1902]: *Bodhisattvapiṭaka* at 311.13, 17; *Ratnarāśi-sūtra* at 56.13, 312.9, 11, 17, 19, 20.

51 Ch. 16 of the *Bodhisatvabhūmi*: Wogihara 1971: 231ff.

52 Tsukamoto 1996. Part I (III): Kanheri 14: *tasyaiva paramamuner agryaśrāvakasy' ārya-śāradvatīputrasya caitya.*

53 Schopen 2014: 367–8. For the *Vinaya Kṣudrakavastu* narrative of Śāriputra's Nirvāṇa, relics, *stūpa* and festivals, see Roth 1980: 183–5; Schopen [1994] 2004: 296–310 (n. 38, p. 324, refers to earlier summaries by Rockhill and La Vallée Poussin in addition to that of Roth).

54 Pali of the root verses in Jayawickrama 1977: 51–3; Pali of the Commentary in Hardy 1901: 156–65; English translation of the verses in Ireland 1996 and Horner 1974: 71–5 (with excerpts from the Commentary); of the Commentary in Masefield 1989: 234–48.

55 See Skilling 2003, especially 290–2.

56 *śarīra-stūpa/sku gdung gi mchod rten* and *dhātu-stūpa/ring bsrel gyi mchod rten* respectively: see Ejima *et al.* 1985–93: 973 and 525, respectively, for their occurrence in the 'White Lotus of the True Dharma'. The 'Giant Jeweled Stūpa' (*mahāratnastūpa*, *rin po che'i mchod rten chen po*, references at ibid. 813–14) refers only to the *stūpa* of the past Buddha Prabhūtaratna. For the 'Concept of the Stūpa in the Lotus Sūtra', see Tsukamoto 2007: 109–23.

57 Translation after Rotman 2008: 329 (with slight modification). For hair and nail relics, see Strong 2004: 72–84.

58 See Prakong Nimanhaemind 2012.

59 For *stūpas* 'raised for monks' see Schopen [1994] 2004: 305–6.

60 For Mahindu Seya see Disanayaka 1987: 23; for Ambasthale, see ibid.: 19, fig. 1. I do not think there is any epigraphic or other evidence to confirm the identification of the *stūpas* with Mahinda's relic. Relic caskets were found during excavations at Mahindu Seya (ibid.: 33, fig. 2; 90, fig. 2), but they were not inscribed.

61 For the many roles of relics, see Skilling forthcoming a.

62 For the Pali version, see *Dīgha Nikāya* Sutta no. 32, one of the great apotropaic texts used for healing and exorcism. There are Sanskrit, Tibetan and Chinese versions.

63 *Mahāparinibbānasutta*, *Dīgha Nikāya* no. 16, 163.30. *Mahāparinirvāṇa-sūtra* (ed. Waldschmidt 1950–1) §49.14–21 is different and does not have the circumambulation by 500 monks.

64 *Caityapradakṣiṇa-gāthā*: Cook 1997: 216–31.

65 Similar verses are recited to this day in Thailand, in merit-making and consecration (*buddhābhiseka*) ceremonies.

66 *Prasenajit-paripṛcchā* or *Prasenajit-gāthā*: for Sanskrit and Tibetan, see Tseng 2010, I: no. 6; English translation of excerpt from Tibetan in Cook 1997: 388–90.

67 For early centres and their art, see Lamotte 1958: 441–57, 'L'ancienne école de sculpture de l'Inde centrale'.

Chapter 3
Money and the Monuments: Coins of the Sada Dynasty of the Coastal Andhra Region

Shailendra Bhandare

The region of the Krishna–Godavari delta, drained by those two major rivers and their several tributaries, is one of the most fertile parts of peninsular India. It is no wonder, therefore, that it produced a large agricultural surplus and emerged as a zone of considerable economic activity. A good survey of pre-historic, proto-historic and Early Historic settlements in the region has been provided by Shimada in his study of the Amaravati *stūpa* (Shimada 2013: 128–31). Around this core area lining the banks of the Krishna River, a number of sites of archaeological interest lay along the river's tributaries and along the maritime coast of Andhra Pradesh (ibid.: Appendix B).

The chief site of interest in the region has, of course, been Amaravati and its key monument – the famous Buddhist 'Great Stupa'. However, one of the major problems of the study of Amaravati is that it tends to place excessive emphasis on the monument itself and to focus mainly on sculptural remains from the site in an art-historical perspective. Right from its earliest 'discovery' by Colin Mackenzie through to the local *zamindar*'s vandalizing it for building material in the late 18th–early 19th centuries, much scholarly attention has been paid to the monument in regards to what the *stūpa* looked like, what its phases of construction and chronology were and who its political patrons were. By and large this obsession appears to have spilled over to other sites in the region as well. As rightly lamented by H. Sarkar (Sarkar 1987: 631–2; Shimada 2013: 23):

> When sites like Amarāvatī, Bhaṭṭiprolu or Sālihundam were excavated our emphasis had been on individual buildings or groups of sculptures and we had only a vague idea about the social and economic dynamics operating behind the rise and decline of a township or settlement. We excavated Amarāvatī not as a suburb of Dhānyakaṭaka or Dharanikota but as a mere Buddhist establishment or a number of them. A proper approach should have been to study the entire area as an organic whole. … We focused all our attention on the Buddhist Stūpas as they yielded fine examples of architecture and sculptural art. The fact that they formed part of a larger social and economic fabric was completely lost sight of.

In an attempt to remedy this to a degree, this chapter shifts the emphasis from the monuments and sculpture to contemporary objects (coins) which were shared by all the sites in the region, and which no doubt sustained the monuments from an economic perspective. Monumental architecture needs artisans and craftsmen and they need to be paid. Although we do not know exactly what the mode of payment might have been, it is reasonable to assume that at least some transactions must have been with coins. After all, they are found – both as stray finds and in archaeological contexts – at many sites in the region. This chapter will focus on one series, issued under the Sada dynasty, which is regionally specific to the region of the lower Krishna valley and to coastal Andhra Pradesh in general. These coins are characterized by a shared numismatic vocabulary – they are broadly of the same type, same metal and many bear Brahmi legends which indicate their issuing authority. However, I will not make this an essentially numismatic essay; I will rather focus on the history of their discovery and their appearance in the numismatic literature and offer for comment salient points that contextualize the coins in broader historical themes like chronology. I will also argue for a reappraisal of previously published aspects of some of the coins, such as their legends.

The beginning of coinage in the lower Krishna valley

'Monetization' was a phenomenon not unknown in the lower Krishna valley by the time the region was teeming with Buddhist activity. By far the chronologically earliest coins ever to be discovered in the Amaravati region are the punch-marked coins. Two hoards are well known to numismatists – the Singavaram hoard and the Amaravati hoard. The contents of these hoards, although generically described as 'punch-marked' coins, vary significantly. The Singavaram hoard was brought to scholarly notice in 1936 (Aravamuthan 1938). It apparently consisted of about 60,000 silver coins. Each of them had four marks, which is a type commonly ascribed to the pre-Mauryan horizon and attributed to the 'period of the sixteen Mahajanapadas'. These are thus believed to be issues of 'Andhra Janapada' (Rajgor 2001: 23–6) and dated to approximately the 4th–3rd centuries BCE. A group of 90 coins from this hoard were republished by Puljal and Reddy (2005) after they managed to track them down in the reserve collections of Government Museum, Chennai.

The Amaravati hoard was published in detail by P.L. Gupta (Gupta 1963). It was discovered 'about 20 yards away from the Stupa site and 15 yards to the north of the Travelers' Bungalow, in a Government land' on 3 August 1953 in an earthen pot buried at a depth of about 8–10 feet (2.5–3.0m) from the surface level. The pot contained punch-marked coins estimated to weigh about 60lb (27.215kg). On actual weighing, they were found to be 2,333 *tolas* (around 27kg) comprising 7,668 coins. These coins belong to the 'imperial' Karshapana series, widely considered to be the monetary apparatus of the Magadha–Maurya Empire (Gupta and Hardaker 1985: 1–2), and consequently dated to approximately the 3rd–2nd centuries BCE.

The Sadas: predecessors of the Sātavāhanas in coastal Andhra

The dynastic history of the Krishna–Godavari delta region after the Mauryan period is discussed by Shimada (2013: 39–48). The sites of the Krishna delta are generally associated with the Sātavāhanas and the Ikṣvākus. However, the Sātavāhanas were preceded in coastal Andhra by rulers with names ending in '-Sada'. They are therefore conveniently identified as the 'Sadas of coastal Andhra'. Their coins have been chiefly reported from the Krishna and Godavari Districts, from sites as various as Gudivada, Amaravati, Dharanikota, Bapatla, Chebrolu and Vaddamanu.

The coins of the Sadas have been known for a long while, but it took almost a century to arrive at their correct attribution. The general type of these coins consists of, on the obverse, a lion, standing majestically in profile, mostly facing right, but on some coins to the left. He is usually accompanied by a symbol in front of his mouth, frequently a 'tree-in-railing' symbol. On the reverse these coins have an 'arched hill' symbol, often enclosed in a rectangular border, sometimes accompanied by crescent. However, on many coins the reverse is found obliterated. Sir Walter Elliot described some of these in his publications (Elliot [1886] 1976: 152b). Rapson was the first to make a note of the specimens held in the British Museum (Rapson 1908: 10–11: pl. 3, 33–46, GP-2 and GP-3), which came from the collections of Elliot, Alexander Cunningham and Robert Sewell, who had collected them from sites dotted across the Krishna and Godavari Districts. On one small lead coin, he also read the legend '…*(gha)sadasa*'. This was by far the earliest recorded mention of a name ending in '-Sada'.

At the outset, it must be said that Rapson's treatment of these coins is rather unusual and this contributed to a great degree to their incorrect attribution. For understandable reasons he identified them as 'Andhradeśa' coins. He categorized them into two classes by their 'fabrics', and further grouped them by type and weight (ibid.: lxxi). This is against the grain of the normal numismatic treatment, where one places primacy on the type, not the 'fabric'. Why Rapson employed such a method of classification for this category of coins is puzzling and the fact he did not define these classificatory 'fabrics' doesn't help the researcher either!

Rapson considered the geographic label 'Andhra' to mean a dynastic appellation too. He therefore tried to attribute coins of both 'fabrics' to the rulers of the 'Andhra' or Sātavāhana dynasty. He grouped 23 coins of 'Fabric B' as of 'lion' type under the category 'name uncertain', because they 'are either uninscribed or have coin-legends so fragmentary that their decipherment must for the present remain uncertain'. However, he did restore the truncated Brahmi legend seen on some of them as '…*saka sa[da]sa*' and offered a speculation that these could be attributed to Madhariputa Siri Sakasena, an ephemeral 'Andhra' monarch (ibid.: lxxv). Further to these, two large 'lion'-type lead coins, originally collected by Walter Elliot 'from Chittala in Yernagudem Talook Godavari district', were listed by Rapson in the 'Andhradeśa' category, but under a different heading, after reading the truncated inscription on one of them as '…*vira*' (ibid.: 2, pl. 1, item 4). Lastly, he noticed two more 'lion'-type coins bearing legends which 'might well contain the title and name of Pulumavi' but hesitated to attribute them conclusively owing to the truncated nature of the inscriptions (ibid.: lxxv–lxxvi). The small lead coin with the '…*(gha)sadasa*' legend was tentatively ascribed by Rapson to the Sātavāhana ruler 'Meghasvati', and the animal on it hesitantly described as a horse (ibid.: lxxvii).

The 'Andhra' attribution of Rapson made a lasting impact on the identification of these coins. Rama Rao published similar coins from Amaravati (Rama Rao 1942: 92) and Dharanikota (Rama Rao 1961: 39) but attributed them to the Sātavāhanas. A coin bearing the legend 'Sivamaka Sada' was reported from Chebrolu (Hanumantha Rao 1966). This ruler is mentioned in one of the Amaravati inscriptions (Shimada 2013: 41); however, the inscription had already been identified as belonging to Siva Siri Sātakaṇi, a Sātavāhana king, by Rapson (1908: lii) on the basis of a strange linguistic logic. I.K. Sarma attributed the British Museum's 'lion'-type coins to the Sātavāhana ruler Vāsiṭhiputa Siri Puḷumāvi. In addition to the British Museum coins, the Dharanikota coin published earlier by

Rama Rao was attributed by Sarma to Vāsiṭhiputa Sātakaṇi, as was another very large lead coin, weighing 39g, found at Mukhalingam and reported in *IAR* 1957–8 (Sarma 1980b: 240).

D. Raja Reddy and P. Suryanarayan Reddy (Reddy and Reddy 1985) were the first to distinguish the 'lion'-type coins as separate from the Sātavāhana or 'Andhra' dynasty. They listed a further 11 coins in their monograph with legends ending in '-Sada', most of them collected as stray finds at Amaravati and Dharanikota. The names recorded on these coins include Maha Sada, Siri Sada, Siva Sada and Sivamaka Sada. After an inscription of a 'Maharaja Siri Sada', reported from Guntupalli (Srinivasan 1971–3), which records him as a member of the 'Mahāmeghavāhana' family, these coins were identified as 'Mahāmeghavāhana' coins by Reddy and Reddy (hence the name of their monograph). The dynastic name 'Mahāmeghavāhana' was indeed not new – Khāravela, the 1st-century BCE king of Kaliṅga, well known from his Hathigumpha inscription (Jayaswal 1927), was known to have used it. Based on this link, Reddy and Reddy suggested that the rulers who struck these coins must have shared an ancestry with Khāravela (Reddy and Reddy 1985: 2–5).

Around the same time that Reddy and Reddy published their monograph, the Birla Archaeological and Cultural Research Institute (BACRI) of Hyderabad conducted excavations at Vaddamanu, to the east of Amaravati, in four seasons between 1981 and 1985. These excavations yielded coins with legends ending in '-Sada' in archaeological context, which were published in detail by Kasturi Bai (1986; 1987). The names Maha Sada, Asaka Sada and Sivamaka Sada were noticed on the coins and it was apparent that the suffix 'Sada' indeed had dynastic connotation. Accordingly, Kasturi Bai called them the coins of the 'Sada dynasty'. A total of 47 inscribed and 40 uninscribed 'lion'-type coins were found at Vaddamanu. Kasturi Bai reattributed the British Museum coins with truncated legends published by Rapson (see above) to Asaka Sada and Sivamaka Sada in light of the new finds at Vaddamanu (1986: 19) and offered a view that 'Maharaja Siri Sada' of the Guntupalli inscription might have been the same as 'Maha Sada' of the coins found at Vaddamanu. This view was later also advocated by A.M. Shastri, who contended that '*Maha*' (= 'great') was a title Siri Sada adopted after he became the 'Lord of the *Kalinga-Mahiṣaka* Country' as indicated in the Guntupalli inscription (Shastri 1993).

The excavators of Vaddamanu, however, took the stratigraphy of their finds too literally and proposed the existence of three rulers named Sivamaka Sada, namely Sivamaka Sada I, II and III, judging from their stratigraphic placement of their coins. The chronology they proposed was to regard Maha Sada as the earliest ruler, followed by Sivamaka Sada I and Asaka Sada, who were succeeded by Sivamaka Sada II, then an unidentified ruler and, lastly, Sivamaka Sada III (Kasturi Bai 1986: 16–19). This sequence is based on the stratigraphic locations of the coins bearing the legends of these rulers, but as the coins came from trenches situated in different localities it will not be until the stratigraphic evidence has been conflated that they can be correlated to one another in an 'exact' chronological fashion. It is not, therefore, reasonable to infer that there was more than one ruler named 'Sivamaka Sada'.

The Sadas finally arrived on the numismatic scene of Amaravati with the publications of archaeologist P.R.K. Prasad (Prasad 1993a; 1999b). He consolidated previous reports of these coins, such as those by Reddy and Reddy and by the excavators of Vaddamanu. In addition, he noted one more coin of Asaka Sada from the collection of the Archaeological Museum at Amaravati (Prasad 1993b), most of the contents of which are made up of excavated finds from that site. Here he offered a view that 'Asaka Sada' of the coins might have been named 'Asoka Sada', in memory of the great king of the same name. He identified him with a ruler named 'Dhammarañа Asoka Siri' mentioned in an inscription found on a slab from Sālihundam. He noted the presence of several Sada coins in the collection of the State Archaeology Museum in Hyderabad and pleaded for a detailed study in order to ascertain the existence of more issuing entities.

Prasad also offered a scheme for the chronological placement of individual Sada kings. According to him, the Siri Sada mentioned in the Guntupalli inscription should be regarded as the progenitor of the dynasty, although he did consider the possibility that Siri Sada and Maha Sada were the same individual. He further proposed the order of succession in the Sada dynasty as Siri Sada > Mahā Sada > Asaka Sada > Siva Sada > Sivamaka Sada. He contended that the dynasty must have ended with Sivamaka Sada, whose coins show similarities to those issued in the same type by Vāsiṭhiputa Siri Puḷumāvi. Another numismatic marker he employed to corroborate this dynastic succession are some Sada coins which are countermarked with a '*nandipada*' symbol. Prasad contended that the countermark must have been applied by the Sātavāhanas when they took over from the Sadas. In addition to the lead coins, Prasad published a hoard of small, uninscribed copper coins found at Amaravati (Prasad 1999a). Most of these coins had a 'standing lion with curved and uplifted tail to left facing a tree-in-railing' on the obverse, while the majority had a *svastika* on the reverse. A few were also noticed with other symbols, such as a *nandyavarta*, a wheel and a '*śrīvatsa*' symbol. In spite of the obvious similarity of the contents of the obverse motif with Sada coins, Prasad placed a greater emphasis on the 'crude' style of manufacture of these small, uninscribed copper pieces, which led him to comment that 'no doubt the present series of the hoard are archaic' (1999b: 321). He therefore opted to place them chronologically before the Sadas, commenting that the Sadas might have copied the design motif from these uninscribed coins. However, it is difficult to agree with him, particularly in light of the fact that several similarly uninscribed coins are also found in lead (see below) and they are undoubtedly Sada issues of a lesser denomination. It is more plausible, therefore, to regard the uninscribed copper coins as Sada issues, particularly considering the strong typological link of employing the same 'lion'-type and having the same overall design as the lead fractional pieces. Most likely, they represented copper equivalents of the small lead denomination.

Notwithstanding the Vaddamanu finds and Prasad's contributions, Sada coins continued to be published as

'Sātavāhana' issues. In 1998 I.K. Sarma published the findings of a small excavation he had undertaken at Amaravati in 1973–5. Here, 'lion'-type lead coins were recovered from Period II (2 coins) and Period III (37 coins). These are clearly Sada issues and should have been recognized as such but Sarma identified them, as before, as Sātavāhana coins. Not all are illustrated, but nos 3, 5, 6, 7 and 8 shown on plate 4 (Sarma 1998) are most certainly Sada issues. Most of the larger coins are in a poor condition; they have no readable legends and cannot be attributed to specific rulers. The smaller coins appear to be uninscribed fractional Sada issues. The most recent notice of Sada coins in an excavated context comes from M. Veerender and G. Kamalakar of BACRI (Veerender and Kamalakar 2010: 29), who published a preliminary report on the excavations conducted in 1992–4 at Garapadu, located in Peddakurapadu Mandala of Guntur District, Andhra Pradesh. No illustrations are supplied.

According to Prasad's dynastic scheme, five Sada rulers are known from inscriptions and coins. To these, we may add one more. The coin on which Rapson read the legend '*...(gha)sadasa*' can also be identified as a Sada issue, particularly because it has a legend that ends with the genitive form of 'Sada', much like other Sada issues. Rapson had attributed this coin to the Sātavāhana ruler Meghasvati (see above), but the legend on this coin can be restored as '*... ya Sadasa*'. In all probability therefore the issuer of this coin is another Sada ruler whose name was (Vija?)ya Sada.

In this context it is useful to examine some lead coins obtained from Ghantasala, published by I.K. Sarma (2000: 185–90). These have on the obverse a lion standing, facing left, with tail curled on the back, fairly similar to that seen on most Sada coins. Some show traces of a Brahmi legend in exergue around the lion. Sarma has proposed reading it as 'Maharaja Vijayadeva...' and suggests identifying this ruler with Vijaya Deva Varman of the Śalankāyana dynasty that succeeded the Ikṣvākus in the coastal Andhra region in the late 3rd or the early 4th century CE. However, as the lion on these coins is overwhelmingly similar to that on the Sada coins, it seems unlikely that they are separated by nearly two centuries. Even more interesting is the reverse motif on these coins – they show a two-mast ship exactly like the one seen on Sātavāhana issues of Vāsiṭhiputa Siri Puḷumāvi (Rapson 1908: 22–3) and Siri Yaña Sātakaṇi (Mirashi 1941). This feature, too, gives a mid 1st- to mid 2nd-century CE context for the coins. It is plausible therefore to regard 'Maharaja Vijayadeva' to be a Sada or Sada-affiliated ruler, who ruled the Krishna delta region sometime in the 2nd century CE, perhaps as a viceroy of the Sātavāhanas.

A fascinating insight into how Sada coins might be deployed as markers of cultural connectivity between the 'Buddhist' worlds of the Indian subcontinent was offered by Walburg (2005: 373–6), who published a lead coin excavated at the monastery of Tissamaharama in Sri Lanka. This coin, ostensibly of 'lion' type, bears a truncated legend which identifies it as an issue of a '*mahārathi*', a feudatory title well known from several inscriptions in the Deccan. The lion is closely modelled on the lion seen on many Sada coins but on the reverse the coin bears a symbol (a *svastika* standard in railing) which is entirely Sri Lankan in its employment. It is certain that this is a locally issued Sri Lankan coin, but the type, the style and script employed and the overall 'fabric' and design are all informed by contemporary coins from the delta regions of Andhra. Walburg also mentions one more coin bearing very similar designs, found at Kantarodai and published by Codrington, which he considers to be a fraction of the Tissamaharama coin (Walburg 2005: 375). The Buddhist connections between Andhra Pradesh and Sri Lanka have been discussed by Padma and Holt (2008) and Walburg's coins fit in with the context neatly.

Chronological considerations

As indicated by Prasad (1999a: 334), it is almost certain that Sivamaka Sada was the last Sada ruler in the region of Amaravati–Dharanikota. His successor was the Sātavāhana ruler Vāsiṭhiputa Siri Puḷumāvi, as is evident from a number of observations. Numismatically, the regiospecific coins (i.e. those coins peculiar to a particular area) of Vāsiṭhiputa Siri Puḷumāvi are the direct type successors of Sivamaka Sada's coins. The coins in the British Museum published by Rapson are a classic example of such type succession. They retain the Sada lion in its entire splendour, but conspicuously substitute the arched hill motif with Sada affinity on the reverse with an 'Ujjain' symbol, which has Sātavāhana affiliations. The tree-in-railing in front of the lion on Sada coins has been omitted on the Sātavāhana coin. Epigraphic evidence also points to such a succession of authority at Amaravati. Excavations at several sites in the lower Krishna–Godavari valleys have amply demonstrated the complete lack of any traces of Sātavāhana rule before Vāsiṭhiputa Siri Puḷumāvi, thus making it clear that it was during his reign that the region was brought under Sātavāhana control, taking over from the preceding dynasty of the Sadas.

The chronological considerations of this dynastic interface are unfortunately not clear. The inscription of Vāsiṭhiputa Siri Puḷumāvi at Amaravati has lost its chronological detail of regnal year, and that of Sivamaka Sada is too fragmentary to indicate one. Other inscriptions say that Vāsiṭhiputa Siri Puḷumāvi reigned for 35 years, while the *Puranas* assign him a rule of 28 years. I have argued for the dates of Gotamīputa Siri Sātakaṇi to be *c.* 60–85 CE (Bhandare 1999: 168–78). If this is the case, we can regard the accession of Vāsiṭhiputa Siri Puḷumāvi as taking place after that date.

An epigraphical clue that helps ascertain the date of conquest of the lower Krishna valley lies in Vāsiṭhiputa Siri Puḷumāvi's inscription at Nasik (Senart 1905–6: no. 2). This is dated in his 19th regnal year, which would correspond to 104 CE if we consider Puḷumāvi to have succeeded Gotamīputa Siri Sātakaṇi *c.* 85 CE. The epithet accorded to Puḷumāvi here is *dakhiṇāpathésara* (Skt *dakshiṇāpathéshwara*), meaning 'the Lord of the Deccan'. Such a lofty epithet could be applied to him only after his conquests, which can be dated *c.* 85–103 CE. It is reasonable therefore to assume that the Sātavāhanas succeeded the Sadas around 100 CE.

Based on this chronological surmise, the Sada ruler Sivamaka can be dated to the same epoch. Prasad has argued on linguistic evidence that Siva Sada was the father of Sivamaka (1999b: 334). The second chronological marker, for the inception of the Sada dynasty, may be decided by the palaeography of the inscriptions of Maha Sada and Siri Sada, which exhibit an earlier, simpler form of the script than that seen in the case of the inscription bearing Sivamaka Sada's name. The link between Siri Sada and Khāravela, the 1st-century BCE king of Kaliṅga, is clear because they use the same familial term '*Mahāmeghavāhana*' for them. It is reasonable therefore to regard Siri Sada, the first of the Sada dynasty, to be a close successor of Khāravela. Shimada, discussing this epigraphic context (Shimada 2013: 57), suggests an inception date for the Sadas of around 40–20 BCE. Working within these parameters, we get the following chronology for the Sadas:

Siri Sada	*c.* 20 BCE–10 CE
Maha Sada	*c.* 10–30 CE
(Vija?)ya Sada	*c.* 30–40 CE
Asaka Sada	*c.* 40–65 CE
Siva Sada	*c.* 65–75 CE
Sivamaka Sada	*c.* 75–100 CE

It may be seen that a relatively shorter period has been proposed for (Vija?)ya Sada and Siva Sada than the other kings. This is because not many coins of these rulers are known, which suggests they probably had short reigns. The kings with most numerous coins known are Asaka Sada and Sivamaka Sada, hence the broader span of years proposed for their rule.

A word may be said here about Prasad's contention that the coins counterstruck with a *nandipada* symbol should be regarded as a marker for dynastic succession between the Sadas and the Sātavāhanas. As will be shown below, the counterstriking appears not to have been confined to Sada coins alone – even Sātavāhana issues are known with a *nandipada* countermark. It is more reasonable, therefore, to see the countermarking as a process that happened later, perhaps in late 2nd–early 3rd century CE, to revalidate older coins already in circulation. The reasons behind such revalidation can be numerous – and dynastic succession can indeed be one of them, though available data suggest this was certainly not the Sada–Sātavāhana interface. A plausible guess would be the Sātavāhana–Ikṣvāku interface, but other more mundane reasons such as the reintroduction of older coins into circulation because of an episode of paucity of metal to make new ones should also be considered.

Sada coins: reattribution and commentary

With this backdrop, I will now turn to some coins. A number of Sada coins are listed below. In each case I give a numismatic description of the coin and add further commentary if necessary. Most are from the British Museum's collection. After the initial publication of Rapson, who regarded them as 'Andhra' (or Sātavāhana) coins, it is time that they are now accorded their correct attribution as 'Sada' issues.

1. Coin with the title 'Aira' (lead, 36.2g; BM no. 1886,0505.7; ex-Walter Elliot) (Fig. 29)

- Obv.: a lion in profile, facing to left; truncated; Brahmi legend '*airasa (raño)*...' above.
- Rev.: obliterated.

Notes: Rapson (1908: lxxiv–lxxv; also 2, n. 4, pl. 1) suggests this coin bore 'a name ending in *–vira*' but postulates that it cannot be attributed to any known member of the 'Andhra' dynasty. He also considers it to be a uniface coin and as such of an 'early date' and therefore rules out its attribution to the Ikṣvāku ruler Śrī Vīra Puruṣadatta.

The legend in fact is '*airasa (raño)*...' and there is nothing to suggest that it was struck only on one side. As many 'lion'-type coins listed by Rapson and indeed hereunder show, it is quite common for these coins to have an obliterated reverse. The palaeography of the visible letters appears to be early. The positioning of the letters also suggests that it begins with the visible word rather than ending with it.

'Aira' as a title is known from a number of inscriptions in the coastal Andhra region or the *Kalinga-Mahiṣaka* country of yore. It is appended to the name of King Khāravela in the Hathigumpha inscription (Jayaswal 1927: 221) of the Udayagiri monastic cave complex. In the same complex cave no. 9, or 'Manchapuri cave', has an inscription of a king named 'Kudepasiri' who sports this title (Sircar 1965: 221–2). Most importantly, it was also held by Maha Sada in the Velpuru inscription (Sircar 1957: 82–6). The exact meaning of this title has eluded scholars, but Sircar suggests it means 'noble', deriving it from the Sanskrit '*ārya*'. The occurrence of this title on the coin undoubtedly indicates that its issuer was either a Sada or related to other kings in the region where the Sadas flourished and claimed a kinship and/or ancestry by the use of similar titles. It would not be implausible to take it as an issue of Maha Sada, because it weighs close to his coins unearthed at Vaddamanu (see below) and he is known to have used the title.

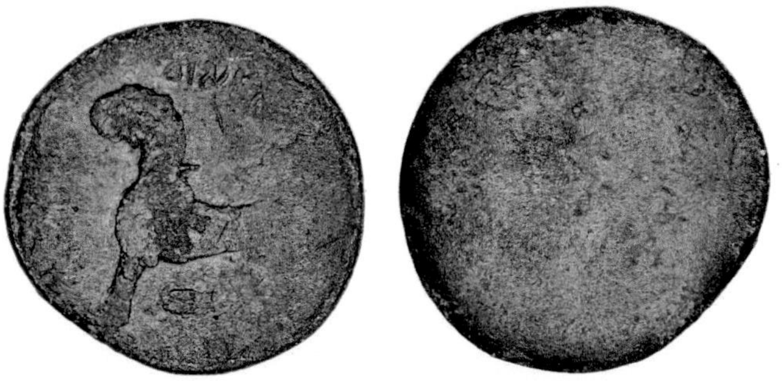

Figure 29 Coin with the title 'Aira', lead, 36.2g, British Museum, 1886,0505.7

2. Coin of Siri Sada (lead, 3.7g; Reddy and Reddy 1985: 14, no. 9; collection of Dr T. Devendra Rao, New Hampshire/Hyderabad) (Fig. 30)

- Obv.: lion standing facing right, traces of a symbol in its front; Brahmi legend '...*Siri Sadasa*' above.
- Rev.: three-arched hill enclosed in a double rectangle.

Note: Reddy and Reddy 1985 describe the material as copper, but on physical examination it was found to be of lead.

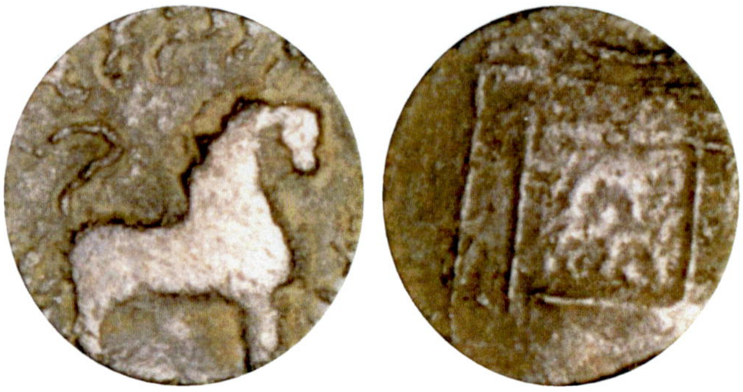

Figure 30 Coin of Siri Sada, lead, 3.7g, collection of Dr T. Devendra Rao, New Hampshire/Hyderabad

3. Coins of Maha Sada

Example 1 (lead, 35.5g; Vaddamanu excavations, no. 1165, C 7.2 VDM III; (Fig. 31)

- Obv.: lion in profile standing facing right, tree-in-railing to right; Brahmi legend '...*ño Siri Maha Sadasa*' above.
- Rev.: obliterated.

Example 2 (lead, 7.21g; Reddy and Reddy 1985: 9, no. 1; collection of Dr T. Devendra Rao, New Hampshire/ Hyderabad) (Fig. 32)

- Obv.: lion standing facing left with curved tail; Brahmi legend '*Raño Siri Maha Sadasa*' above.
- Rev.: six-arched hill with dots in each arch, enclosed in a double rectangle.

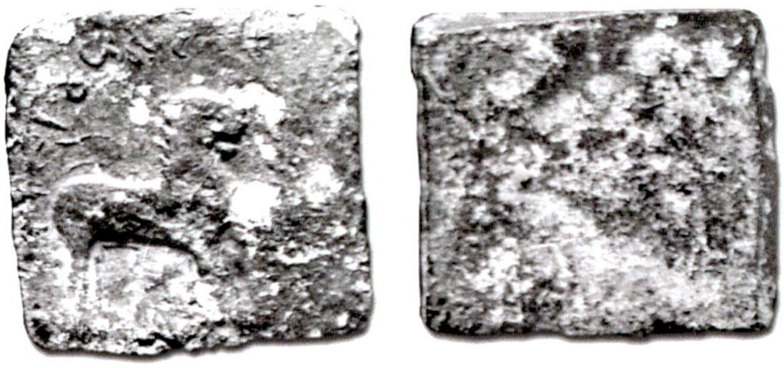

Figure 31 Coin of Maha Sada, lead, 35.5g, Vaddamanu

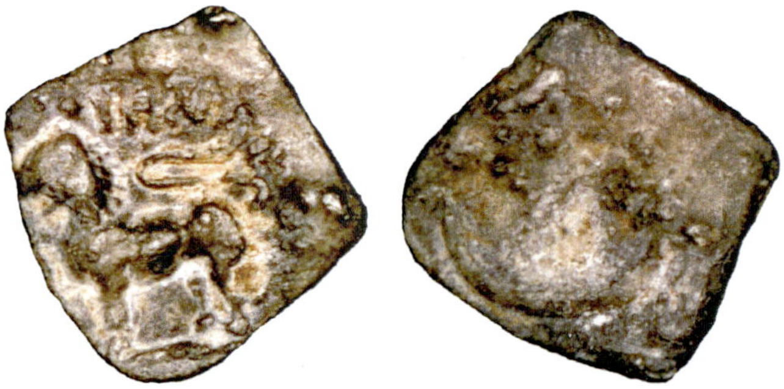

Figure 32 Coin of Maha Sada, lead, 7.21g, collection of Dr T. Devendra Rao, New Hampshire/Hyderabad

4. Coin of (Vija?)ya Sada

Example 1 (lead, 1.63g; BM no. 1908,0902.27; ex-Pearse) (Fig. 33)

- Obv.: lion standing facing left; Brahmi legend '...*ya Sadasa*' above.
- Rev.: obliterated.

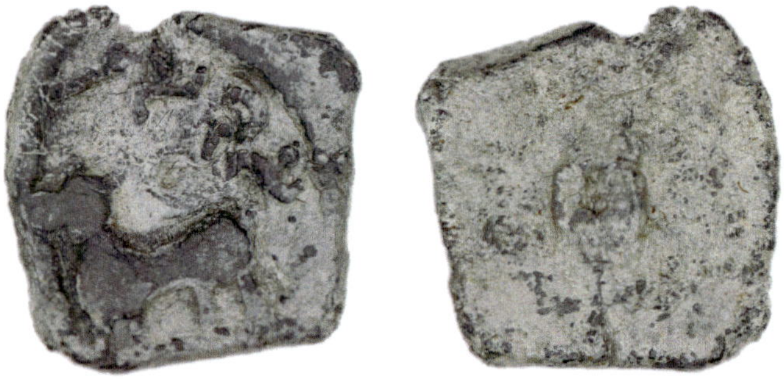

Figure 33 Coin of [Vija?]ya Sada, lead, 1.63g, British Museum, 1908,0902.27

5. Coins of Asaka Sada (Figs 34–7)

Example 1 (lead, 9.9g; BM no. 1908,0912.3; Rapson 1908: 10, no. G.P. 2; ex-Pearse) (Fig. 34)

- Obv.: lion standing majestically facing right; Brahmi legend '...*(A)sakasadasa*' above.
- Rev.: part of rectangular border and a crescent visible.

Example 2 (lead, weight not recorded; BM no. 1908,0912.4; Rapson 1908: 10, no. G.P. 3; ex-Pearse) (Fig. 35)

- Obv.: lion standing majestically facing right, a tree-in-railing in its front; Brahmi legend '...*kasadasa*' above.
- Rev.: part of rectangular border and a crescent visible.

Example 3 (lead, 7.7g; collection of K.K. Maheshwari, Mumbai) (Fig. 36)

- Obv.: lion standing majestically facing right on a double-lined platform, tree-in-railing to right; Brahmi legend '...*ri Asa(ka)*...' visible in top left corner.
- Rev.: six-arched hill, with a dot in each arch, enclosed in a double rectangular border.

Note: the coin was reportedly obtained at Hyderabad.

Example 4 (lead, weight not available; Prasad 1993a: 55, nos 2 and 3) (Fig. 37)

- Obv.: lion standing facing right, Brahmi legend '...*(Si)ri Asaka Sadasa*' above.
- Rev.: six-arched hill, with a dot in each arch, enclosed in a double rectangular border; wavy lines below, outside the border.

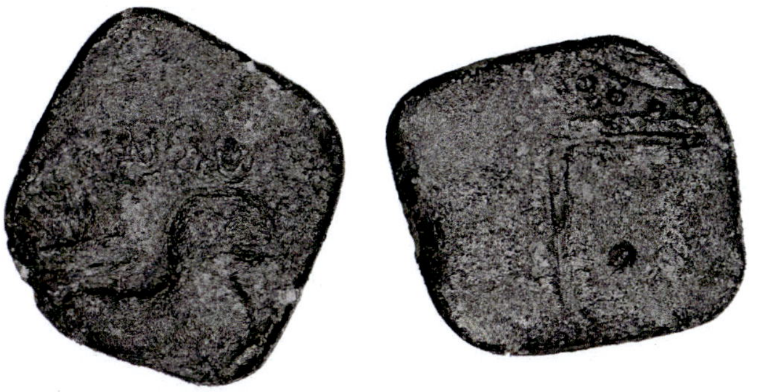

Figure 34 Coin of Asaka Sada, lead, 9.9g, British Museum, 1908,0912.3

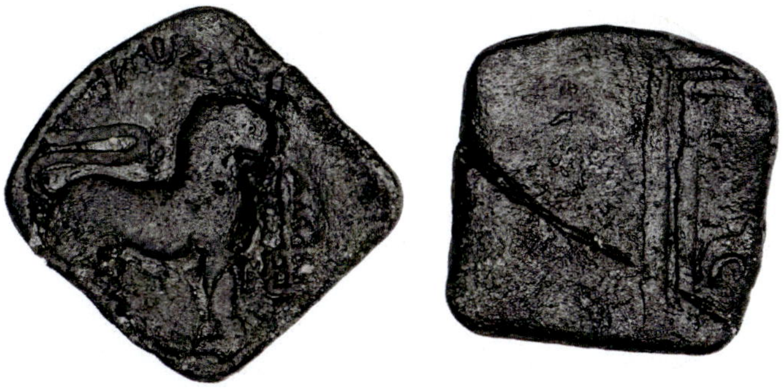

Figure 35 Coin of Asaka Sada, lead, weight not recorded, British Museum, 1908,0912.4

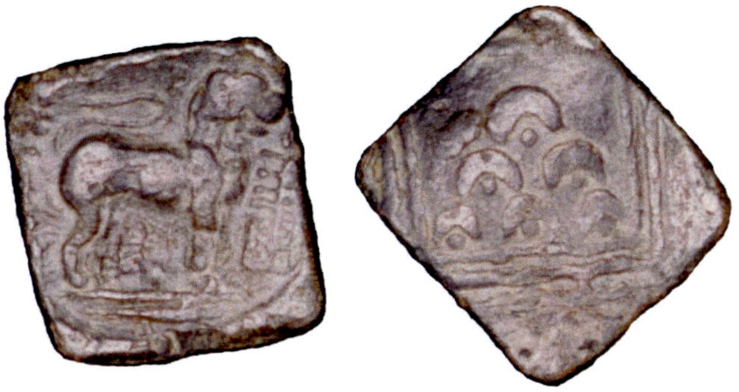

Figure 36 Coin of Asaka Sada, lead, 7.7g, collection of K.K. Maheshwari, Mumbai

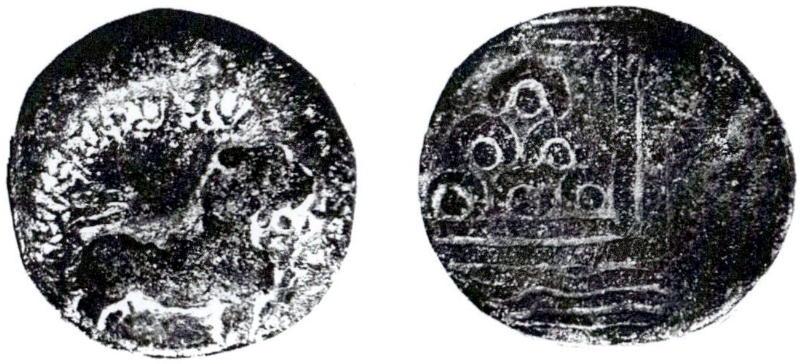

Figure 37 Coin of Asaka Sada, lead, weight not available

6. Coin of Siva Sada (lead, 4.4g; Reddy and Reddy 1985: 11, no. 4; collection of Dr T. Devendra Rao, New Hampshire/Hyderabad) (Fig. 38)

- Obv.: lion facing right, Brahmi legend '...*ño Siva Sa(da)sa*' above.
- Rev.: six-arched hill, surmounted by crescent and a wavy line below, enclosed in a border of double rectangle with a frill in between.

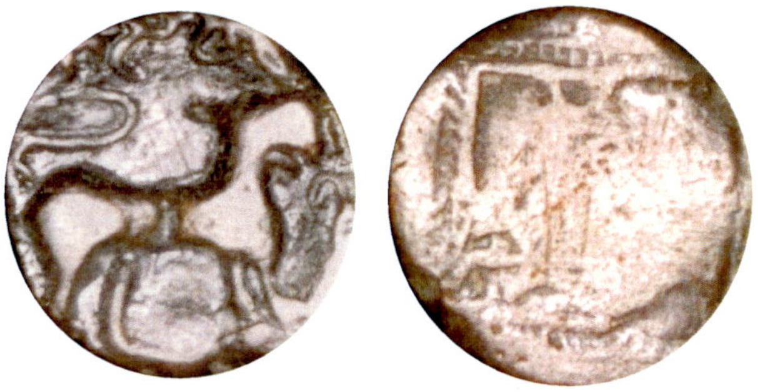

Figure 38 Coin of Siva Sada, lead, 4.4g, collection of Dr T. Devendra Rao, New Hampshire/Hyderabad

7. Coins of Sivamaka Sada

Example 1 (lead, 12.03g; Vaddamanu excavations, no. 1408, R7.3, VDM IV) (Fig. 39)

- Obv.: lion standing facing to right, tree-in-railing to right; Brahmi legend '...*(ño) Siri Sivamaka Sada*...' above.
- Rev.: traces of double rectangle and crescent.

Example 2 (lead, 15.08g; Vaddamanu excavations, no. 1407, D5.3 VDM II) (Fig. 40)

- Obv.: lion standing in profile facing right and a *Dharmachakra* or wheel-standard in its front, both on two-lined platform; Brahmi legend '...*Sivamaka Sadasa*' from 11 o'clock to 5 o'clock.
- Rev.: six-arched hill with a dot in each arch, surmounted by a crescent, enclosed within a double rectangular border.

Note: the device of a wheel standard in front of the lion definitely alludes to a Buddhist context.

Example 3 (lead, 7.55g; BM no. 1905,1007.55; Rapson 1908: 53, no. 205; ex-Sewell) (Fig. 41)

- Obv.: lion seated on its hind legs, facing; Brahmi legend '*Raño Siri Sivama[ka Sa]dasa*'.
- Rev.: indistinct, but appears to be a 'grain' shape between two vertical lines, all executed with rows of dots.

Note: this rather impressive coin was relegated to the category of 'uninscribed or of uncertain attribution' by Rapson. Perhaps before its cleaning and conservation the legend was invisible to Rapson but it is quite clear on the coin now. Although the top ends of the letters are truncated beyond the visible field, the legend can be assuredly reconstructed as indicated above.

The type of the coin is remarkable for showing the seated lion in its frontal view much like it would be depicted sitting on a pillar capital. If the depictions on drum slabs from the Amaravati *stūpa* (Shimada 2013: pls 21 and 61) are taken to be realistic, we see such pillars with seated lions adorning the entrance vestibules of the monument, as seen in different reconstructions of the *stūpa* (ibid.: 13–15).

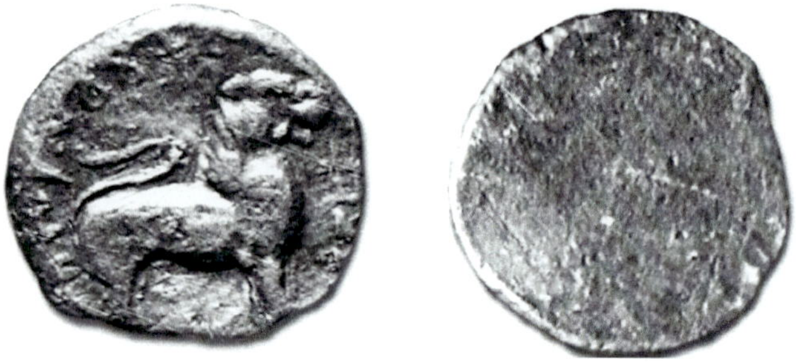

Figure 39 Coin of Sivamaka Sada, lead, 12.03g, Vaddamanu

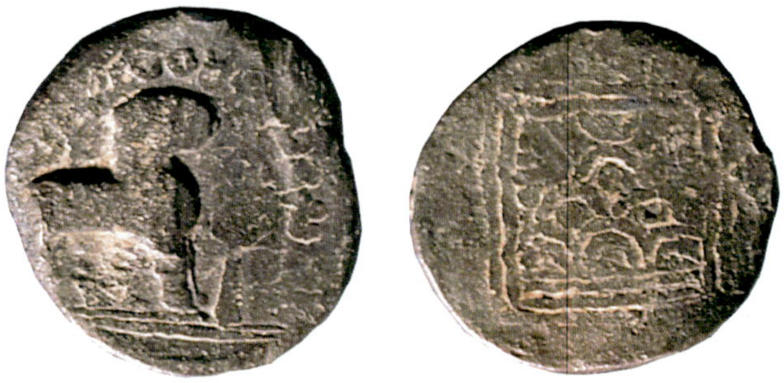

Figure 40 Coin of Sivamaka Sada, lead, 15.08g, Vaddamanu

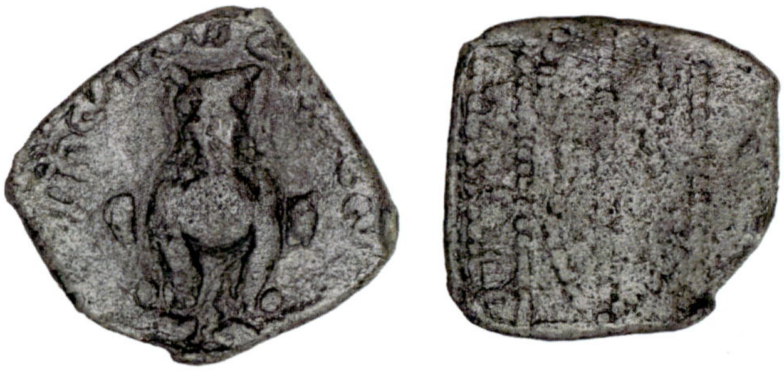

Figure 41 Coin of Sivamaka Sada, lead, 7.55g, British Museum, 1905,1007.55

8. Uninscribed fractional Sada coins

Example 1 (lead, 5.5g; Rapson 1908: 12, no. 44; BM no. 1905,1007.2; ex- Sewell) (Fig. 42)

- Obv.: lion standing facing to right.
- Rev.: obliterated.

Example 2 (lead, 2.87g; Rapson 1908: 53, no. 206; BM no. 1908,0912.26; ex- Sewell) (Fig. 43)

- Obv.: lion standing facing to right.
- Rev.: obliterated.

Example 3 (lead, 1.6g; Reddy and Reddy 1985: 14, no. 10; collection of Dr T. Devendra Rao, New Hampshire/ Hyderabad) (Fig. 44)

- Obv.: lion standing facing right, a round object to right.
- Rev.: six-arched hill with a dot in each arch.

Example 4 (lead, 3.2g; collection of Dr T. Devendra Rao, New Hampshire/Hyderabad) (Fig. 45)

- Obv.: lion standing facing left, on a platform; tree-in-railing to left and *nandipada* symbol above.
- Rev.: blank.

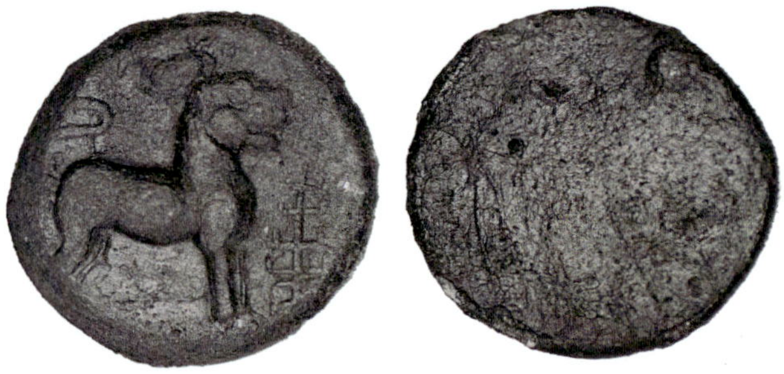

Figure 42 Uninscribed Sada coin, lead, 5.5g, British Museum, 1905,1007.2

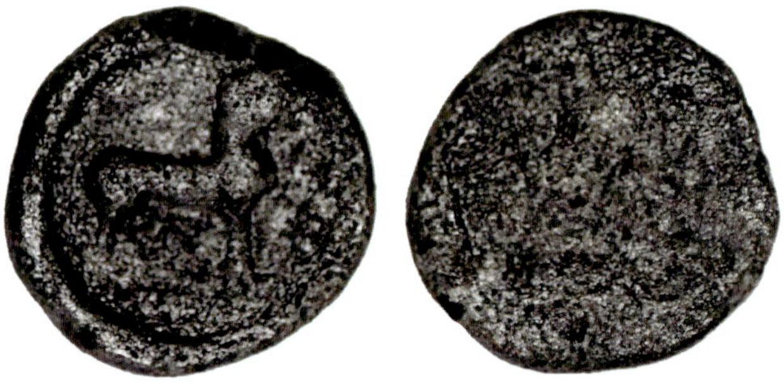

Figure 43 Uninscribed Sada coin, lead, 2.87g, British Museum, 1908,0912.26

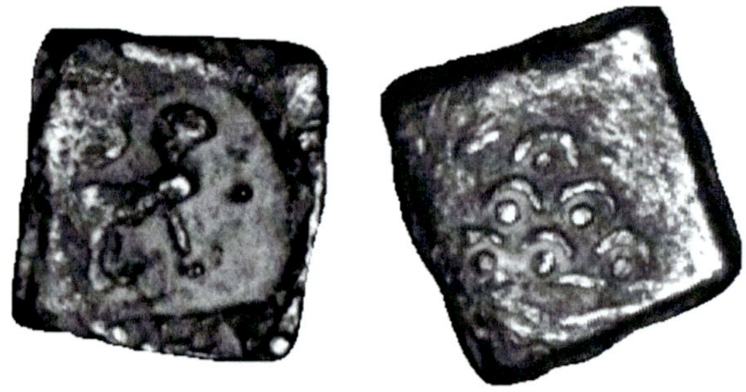

Figure 44 Uninscribed Sada coin, lead, 1.6g, collection of Dr T. Devendra Rao, New Hampshire/Hyderabad

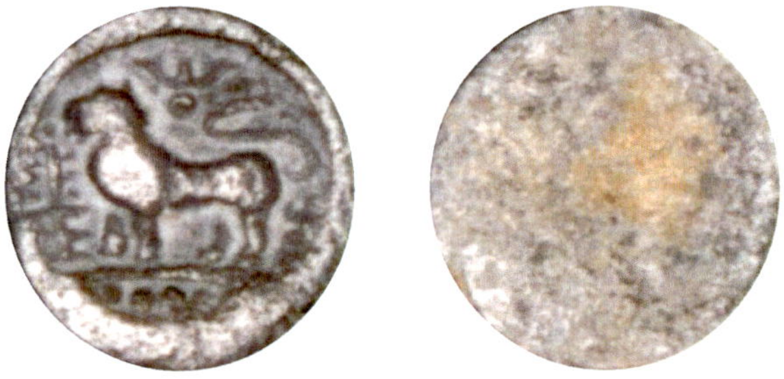

Figure 45 Uninscribed Sada coin, lead, 3.2g, collection of Dr T. Devendra Rao, New Hampshire/Hyderabad)

9. Coins of Siri Pulumāvi in 'lion' type

Example 1 (lead, 8.72g; Rapson 1908: 24, no. G.P. 2; BM no. 1908,0912.17) (Fig. 46)

- Obv.: lion standing in profile, facing right; Brahmi legend '…*Samisa Siri*…'.
- Rev.: Ujjain symbol.

Example 2 (lead, 7.2g; Rapson 1908: 24, no. G.P. 3; BM no. 1908,0912.18) (Fig. 47)

- Obv.: lion standing in profile, facing right; Brahmi legend '…*Siri Pulu*…'.
- Rev.: Ujjain symbol.

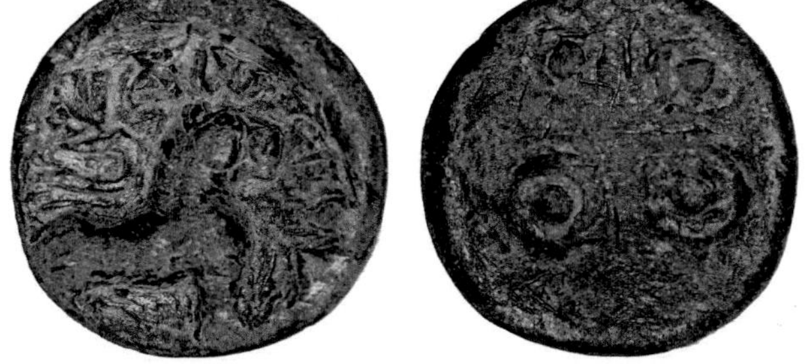

Figure 46 Coin of Siri Pulumāvi in 'lion' type, lead, 8.72g, British Museum, 1908.0912.17

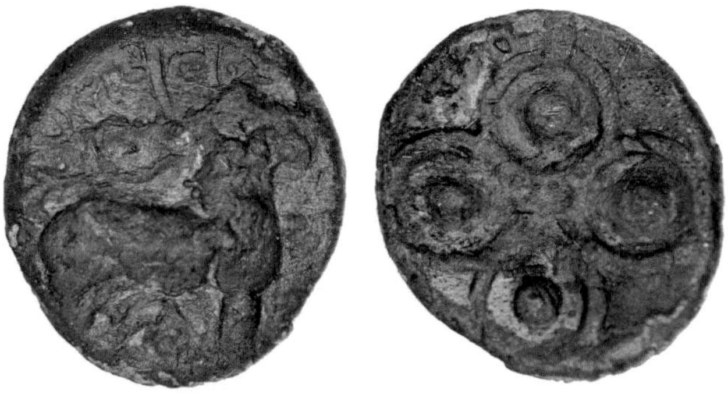

Figure 47 Coin of Siri Pulumāvi in 'lion' type, lead, 7.2g, British Museum, 1908,0912.18

10. Countermarked coins

Example 1 (lead, 11.5g; BM no. 1922,0817.10; ex-E.D. Puzey, Esq.) (Fig. 48)

- Obv.: lion standing profile to right, *nandipada* symbol countermarked on front legs.
- Rev.: blank.

Example 2 (lead, 10.2g; BM no. 1922,0817.15; ex-E.D. Puzey, Esq.) (Fig. 49)

- Obv.: lion standing profile to left, *nandipada* symbol countermarked on its face.
- Rev.: blank.

Example 3 (lead, weight not recorded; BM no.1905,1007.47) (Fig. 50)

- Obv.: horse facing left, countermarked twice with *nandipada* symbol; Brahmi legend '*Raño Gotamipu(ta)...*' around.
- Rev.: traces of Ujjain symbol.

Example 4 (lead, weight not recorded; BM no. 1922,0817.14) (Fig. 51)

- Obv.: six-arched hill surmounted by crescent in centre, deeply countermarked by a *nandipada* symbol; Brahmi legend '*...ri Yaña Satakani...*' around.
- Rev.: traces of Ujjain symbol.

Note: the last two coins in this group are of the Sātavāhana ruler Gotamiputa Siri Yaña Sātakani. The presence of *nandipada* countermarks demonstrates that this was not done by the Sātavāhanas when they succeeded the Sadas.

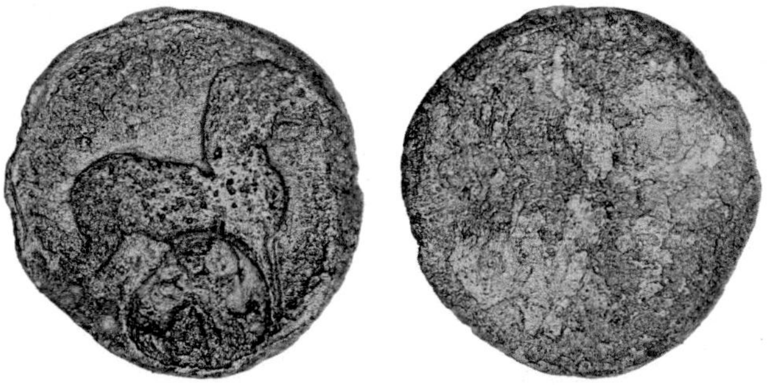

Figure 48 Countermarked coin, lead, 11.5g, British Museum, 1922,0817.10

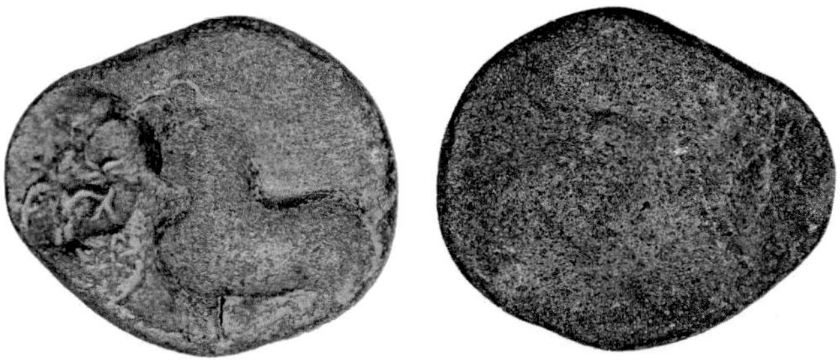

Figure 49 Countermarked coin, lead, 10.2g, British Museum, 1922,0817.15

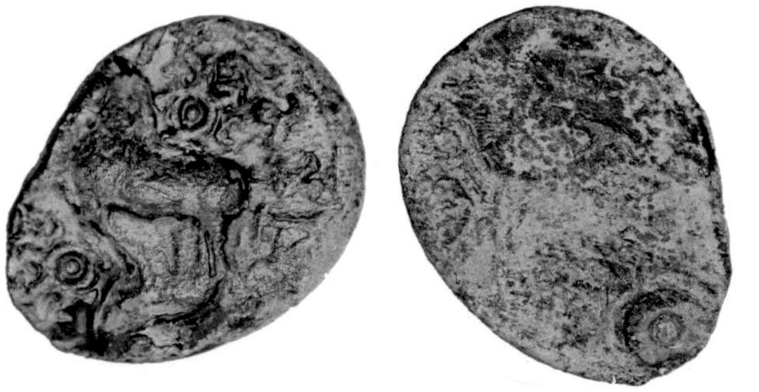

Figure 50 Countermarked coin, lead, weight not recorded, British Museum, 1905,1007.47

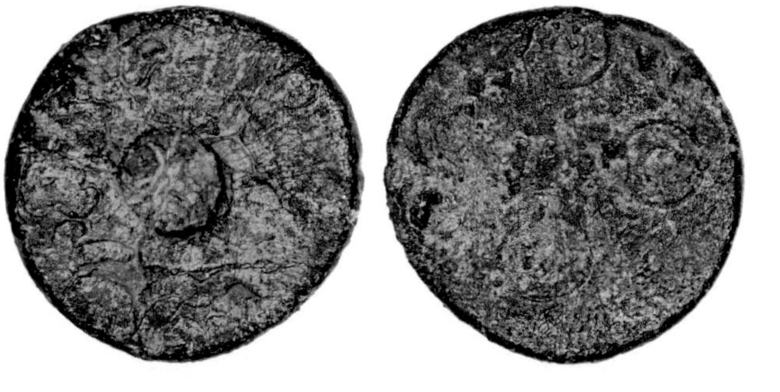

Figure 51 Countermarked coin, lead, weight not recorded, British Museum, 1922,0817.14

Chapter 4
Buddhist Narratives and Amaravati

Monika Zin

The role of the Amaravati school of sculpture in the development of Buddhist narrative representations is difficult to overestimate. This is well known with regard to later art, since Amaravati and the later centre of Nagarjunakonda substantially influenced the 5th-century CE Ajanta paintings. But it is also becoming apparent, albeit slowly, that the iconography from Andhra must have had an impact on the art of northern India in earlier times too (Zin forthcoming a and b). Comparisons with contemporary Gandhara demonstrate that the influences were from Andhra to Gandhara rather than vice versa. The relief art of Andhra is old, dating back to at least the beginning of the 1st century BCE, and the earliest specimens are in many ways comparable with Bharhut.

This long tradition is presumably why the Andhra artists, with the experience of generations, could create a better 'visual language' than can be observed in Gandhara. They could, for example, represent young girls differently (with tiny breasts, narrow face and childish wisps of hair) from the mature women in the same relief: a remarkable achievement.[1] The territory of the so-called Andhra art is huge, greater than today's Andhra Pradesh, and so far more than 50 developed Buddhist centres with *stūpa*s and monasteries have been excavated. There is certainly plenty still unfound: the newest excavations at Kanaganahalli (Gulbarga District, Karnataka), with a *stūpa* decorated with 60 uniform relief slabs nearly 3m in height, and at Phanigiri (Nalgonda District, Telangana), with the most elegant *toraṇa* gate of the entire region, show that the soil of Andhra still holds potential for future revelations (Skilling 2008; Poonacha 2011). The diversity of artistic production in the Buddhist centres of this vast territory – certainly mirroring the communities supporting them – was wide: some of the reliefs are of a superior and sophisticated character, some are archaically unpretentious, others that seem archaic are rather rough and primitive, apparently being not old but somewhat provincial. Interestingly, in many centres no narrative representations have been discovered. Were the representations there on perishable materials, like paintings on wood? Or perhaps not every monastic community was interested in pictorial representations?

The place that we now call Amaravati was the biggest centre of artistic production and was certainly of great artistic impetus. The Buddhist *area sacra* was located on the outskirts of the city of Dhāñyakaṭaka, the capital of the kingdom. The kings, whether of the Sada or Sātavāhana dynasty, who were not Buddhist themselves, supported Buddhism and wanted to create a gorgeous Buddhist site in their metropolitan district, so that it would be an important destination for pilgrims and for wandering merchants, who were traditionally of the Buddhist faith.

What we encounter in the reliefs from Amaravati is a sort of 'court art', a sublime style, with well-designed forms and compositions and painstakingly elaborated details – surely expensive and unquestionably reflecting the luxurious life of the upper class, rich, and engaged in the vibrant trade with many parts of India and the wider world, including Rome.

The reliefs illustrate scenes from the life story of the Buddha, or his previous lives, the *jātaka*s. The exact purpose of the representations is not quite apparent: at first sight the reliefs simply display aesthetically faultless pictures that

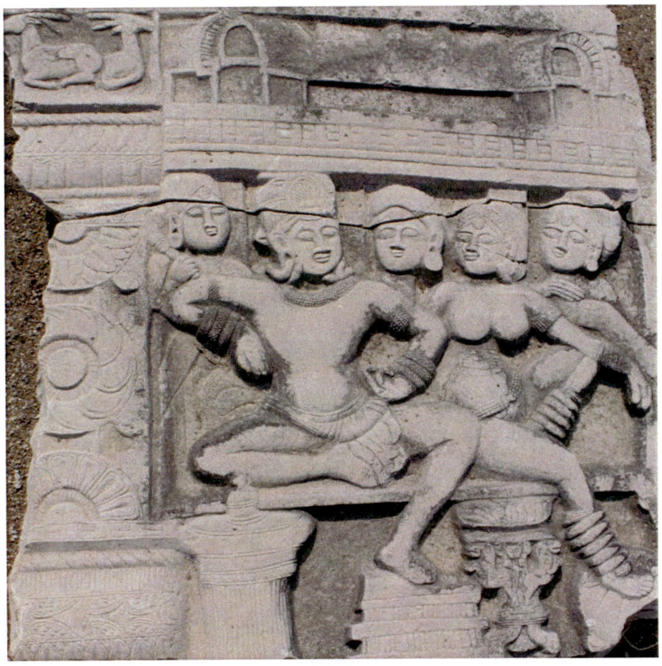

Figure 52 Portrait of Chimukha Sātavāhana, upper drum slab (detail), Kanaganahalli, *c.* 1st century BCE/CE (photograph: Maiko Nakanishi)

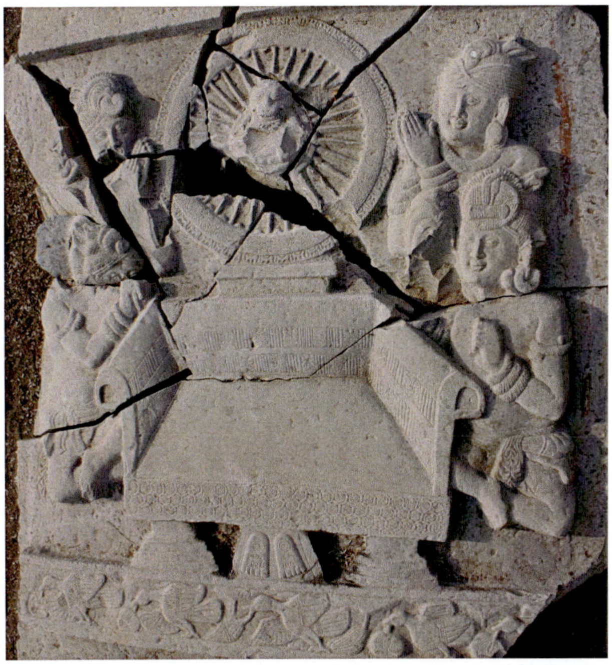

Figure 53 *Dharma* wheel, throne and devotees, upper drum slab (detail), Kanaganahalli, *c.* 1st century CE (photograph: Maiko Nakanishi)

might evoke religious experience and the will to praise the glory of the Buddha. But after a second's reflection they make clear, by the care with which the scenes were selected, arranged and ordered, that their intentions went further – perhaps to provide the basis for meditation. In any case, the reliefs, unlike the chronologically arranged reliefs in Gandhara, force the viewer not just to see the images but to become engaged in the thoughts that they provoke (Zin forthcoming a and c).

The art of Andhra had a venerable tradition on which it could rely, but this does not mean that Mediterranean influences are not to be found; as a matter of fact we see them quite often. Was it 'fashionable', perhaps, or indicative of high status to make use of western motifs? In Kanaganahalli, among the usual scenes from the life story of the Buddha and the *jātakas*, there are also representations of 'historical' kings. One, the founder of the dynasty, Chimukha Sātavāhana, is shown with an obviously Roman small chair (**Fig. 52**),[2] an elegant and probably prestigious object with rampant lions as supporting legs and decoration which imitates acanthus leaves. The question of whether the images of Aśoka and the kings of the Sātavāhana dynasty were intended to be understood as 'historical portraits' rather than indications of auspicious 'royal protection' must, however, remain open for the time being.

Roman elements were incorporated in the narrative art not because Andhra lacked its own visual form (which often seems to have been the reason in Gandhara) but to refine the existing one. The reused motifs could take on religious meaning, like the '*dharma* wheels' symbolizing the Buddha's teaching, which are represented in Kanaganahalli (and nowhere else) with lion heads on the hub (**Fig. 53**).[3] The form is certainly taken from the Roman ornamentation of the wagons, or rather from depictions of them, but the significance was fresh, since the Buddha, as everybody knew, preached with the lion-voice.

The iconography of the sleeping queen Māyā with the future Buddha becoming embodied as an elephant was invented in the 2nd century BCE and widely used, appearing also in Kanaganahalli.[4] But in Amaravati, around 70 CE, a new pictorial model was applied that was apparently taken from Roman art. Māyā – one of the best examples can be seen in the British Museum (**Fig. 54**)[5] – begins at this time to be depicted as lying asleep with her arms held above her head, on a very peculiar object no longer recognizable as a

Figure 54 Māyā's conception, drum slab (detail), Amaravati, *c.* 1st–2nd century CE, British Museum, 1880,0709.44

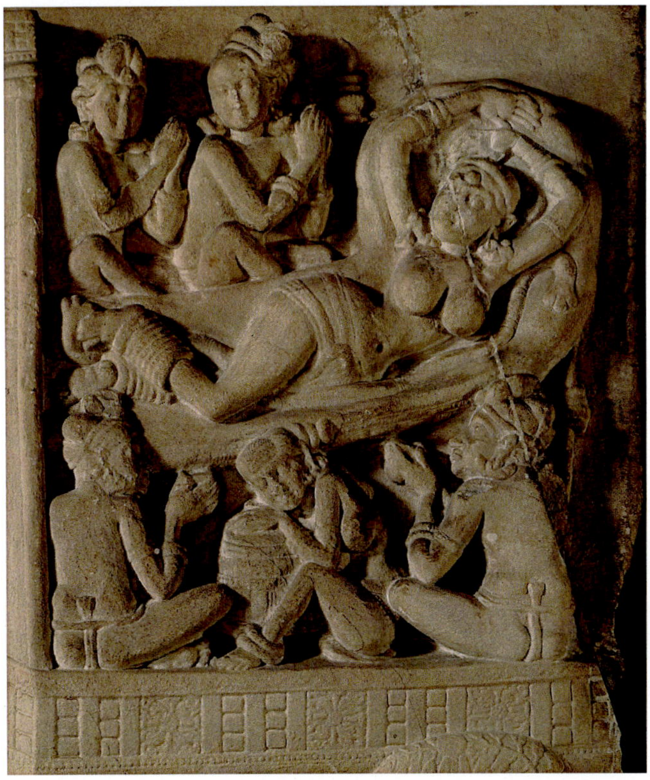

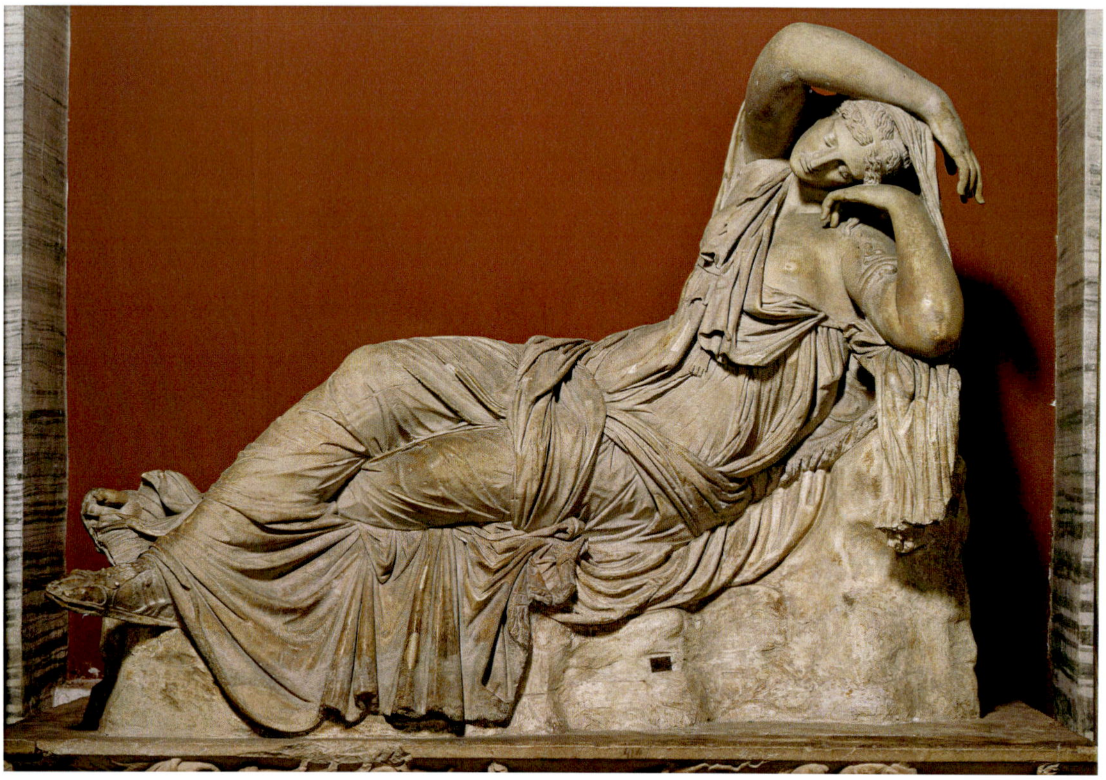

Figure 55 *Sleeping Ariadne*, 2nd century CE, Vatican, Museo Pio-Clementino

bed and covered in the fur of a lion whose paws are visible near her left arm and feet. This is no doubt an intentional visual echo of Ariadne sleeping on the rock (**Fig. 55**),[6] representations of which were popular at that time (the narrative of Ariadne abandoned by Theseus on the island of Naxos was a favourite one, as seen in the paintings in Pompeii: McNally 1985: 177; Zin 2015a). This model was also repeated on small objects which could be taken to India.[7] Additionally, it might well be that there were western influences on both the composition of the scenes and the way bodies were represented, with muscles visible, a feature atypical of Indian art.[8]

The *mahācaitya* of Amaravati, for the terminology of which see Peter Skilling's essay in this volume (Chapter 2), was so large that it never completely disappeared; the first excavations were as early as the 18th century. It must have been the aesthetic of the reliefs – anatomically properly depicted bodies, readable compositions and bright marble-like stone – that fascinated British researchers educated in classical Mediterranean art. We cannot say that the reliefs were not explored, but they were not sufficiently scrutinized, and thus many misunderstandings have survived, especially about their contents, and many questions remain open. The re-examination of the reliefs is necessary, particularly with regard both to new findings at Kanaganahalli and to the literary and art-historical research.

In broad terms, the literary tradition of the Amaravati reliefs is not known. A relief in the British Museum provides one example (**Fig. 56**).[9] The narrative is well known across the Buddhist world: it is the story of King Śibi. The king is seated on the throne in the left section of the three-part composition, and on the palm of his left hand sits a dove. The bird came to Śibi asking for help and the king cut off flesh from his own body – depicted in the middle section – in exchange for the bird, rather than allowing it to be killed. Behind the king we see a man with scales, checking the weights of the dove and the flesh. The person jumping in the right-hand section wearing a peculiar crown is the god Indra, going back to heaven: the story is that it was Indra who disguised himself as a dove as a test of the righteousness of King Śibi. The story of Śibi and the dove is well known, but this is not the story represented in the relief.

In the Śibi narrative it is the falcon who is chasing the dove and he demands it from the king as his own prey; this is how the narrative is often depicted, for example on the relief from Gandhara in the British Museum.[10] In our Amaravati relief, however, the falcon is not depicted: a point recognized by Sivaramamurti.[11] At Amaravati the reason for the king's cutting of his own flesh is not the demand of the falcon but rather that of the bird-catcher. The hunter, indicated by a long-handled net often held across the shoulder, appears in most of the Andhra representations of the narrative, but never the falcon; in **Figure 56** he is shown kneeling at the side of the king. Only in better preserved examples (**Fig. 57**)[12] does it become apparent how the net would have been understood at the time, but even in a small, unclear depiction its visual message should have been comprehensible for everyone who knew the story. The narrative is known from Andhra in at least 26 other examples, and – as a crucial demonstration of the continuity of the tradition – it also appears in a painting in Ajanta of the late 5th century.[13] This story of the king and the bird-catcher is thus not the story of Śibi, but that of King Sarvaṃdada, of which the earliest literary version is known today only from Kashmir and the 11th century.[14] The reliefs from Andhra demonstrate that the story was already widely known nearly a millennium earlier – but this literary basis has not survived. This is important as an illustration of a fact

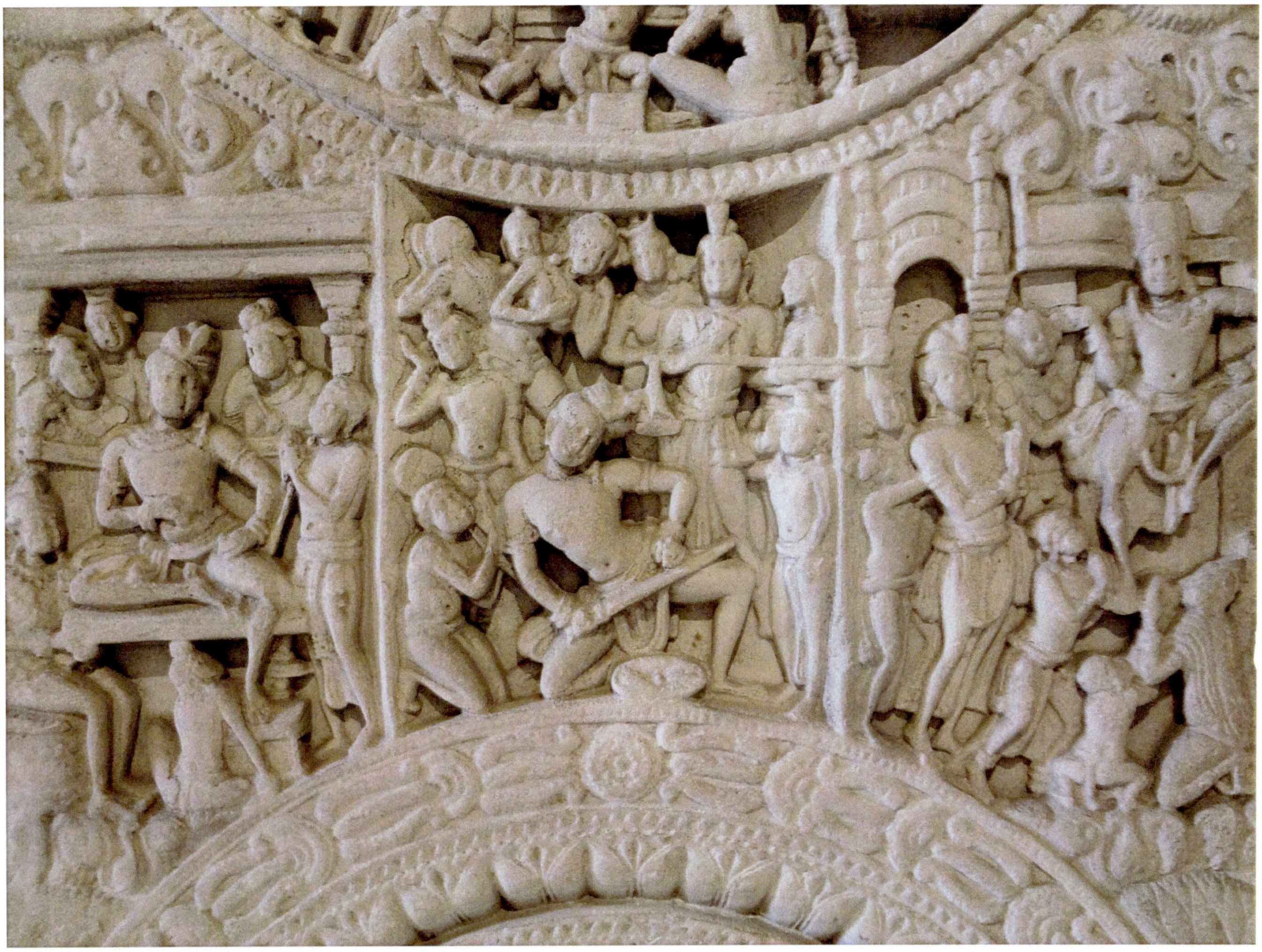

Figure 56 Sarvaṃdada *jātaka*, rail pillar (detail), Amaravati, *c.* 3rd century CE, British Museum, 1880,0709.14

that art historians would rather not believe but which is perfectly well known to Buddhologists: the scriptures of the Buddhism of Andhra are utterly lost. In some rare cases, as in the story of the king with the dove and the bird-catcher, the stories survived by chance, but in very many they did not. We can recognize several narratives, like the popular *jātaka*s or events from the life story of the Buddha, because of their similarities with representations in other parts of India or in commonly known literary traditions: they are explained – confidently, if not reliably – in the publications of the British Museum (Barrett 1954a; Knox 1992). However, many representations are not recognizable because the stories are, in fact, missing. This is what makes the explanation of the Amaravati reliefs so difficult and it is connected with another fact – namely, that many of the reliefs have been incorrectly explained, mostly by means of sources in Pali, which, as is confirmed by recent research, were not the literary tradition of Andhra.

For the time being it appears that the most reliable information on which to base an explanation of the reliefs is offered by the reliefs themselves; the developed nature of their visual language can help. All the details must be taken seriously for this reason, in addition to the fact that the reliefs not only illustrate the Buddhist narratives but reveal the everyday lives of the elite at the time.

Let us look at one example, the representation on the middle part of an Amaravati rail pillar in the British

Figure 57 Sarvaṃdada *jātaka*, fragment, Nagarjunakonda, *c.* 3rd century CE, Archaeological Museum, Nagarjunakonda, no. 802, reserved collection (photograph: Wojtek Oczkowski)

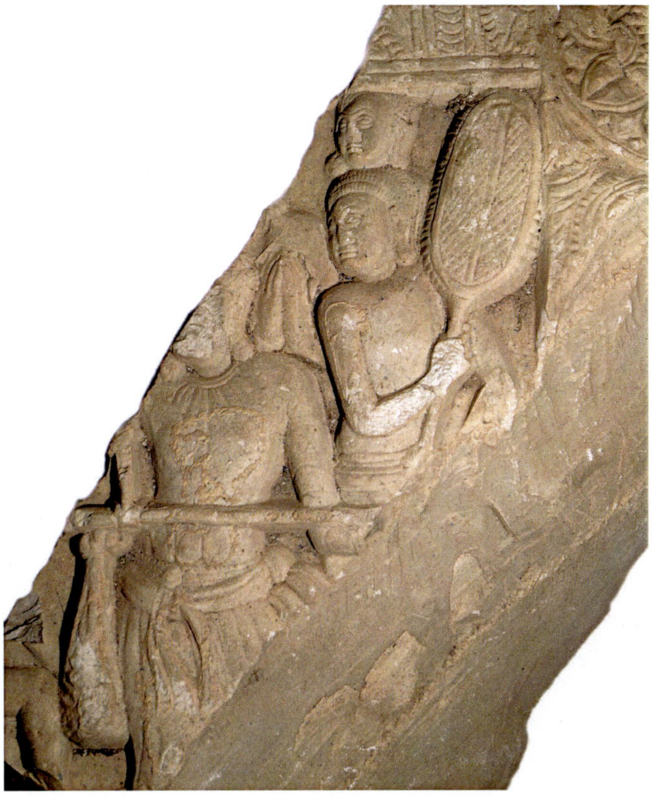

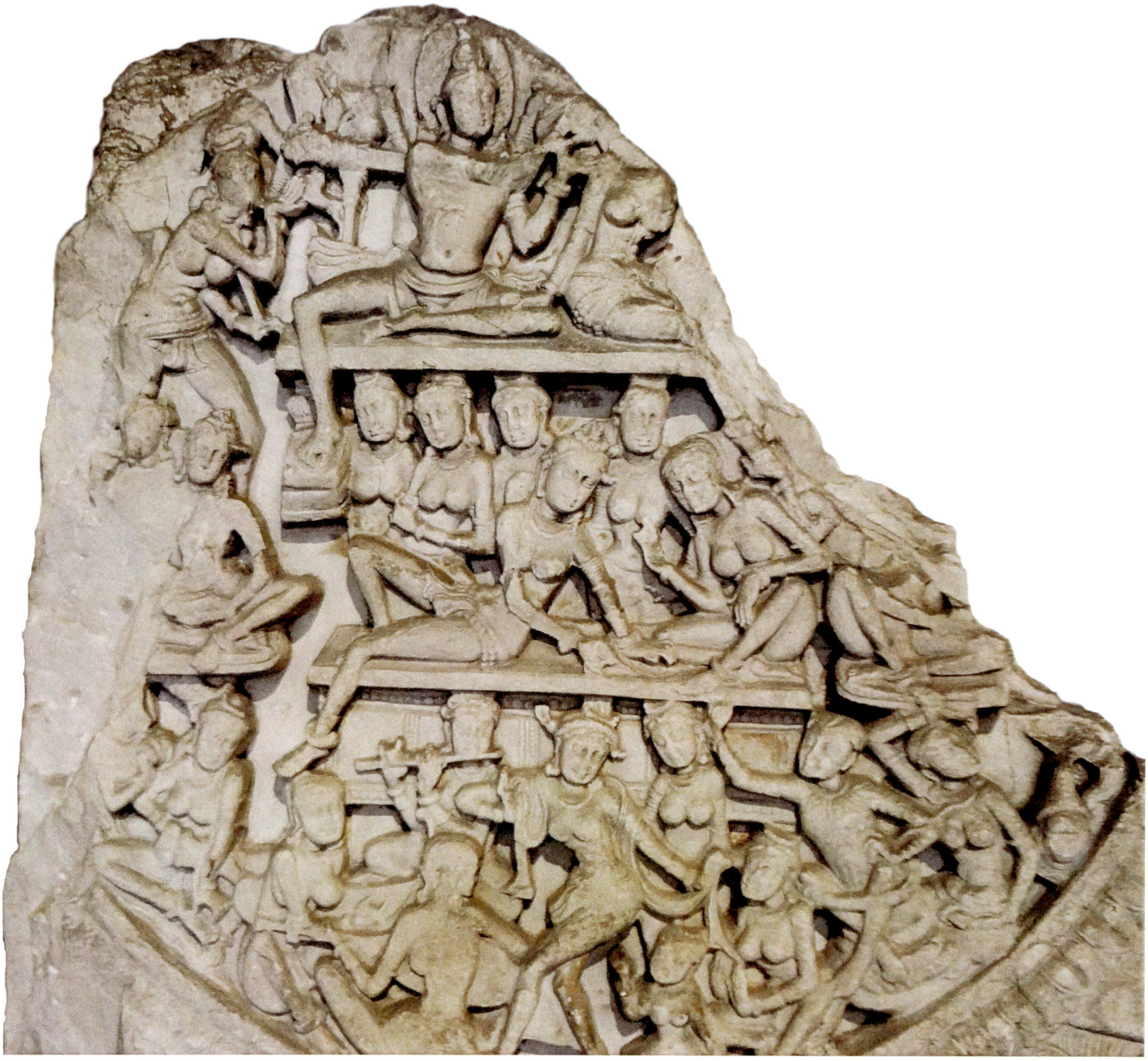

Figure 58 Unidentified scene, rail pillar (detail), Amaravati, c. 3rd century CE, British Museum, 1880,0709.17

Museum (**Fig. 58**).[15] We are at the court: the king and the queen sit on their wide joint throne, with the backrest tastefully decorated in the form of the head of a sea-monster (*makara*) and a rampant lion. The queen's hand rests coquettishly on the king's leg despite the fact that she turns away her face, which the king tries to touch. From the viewer's left-hand side a female guard (*prātihārī*) approaches, apparently with the message that somebody is waiting at the door.[16] Below we see the court ladies enjoying themselves; the fine-looking women are all beautifully clad and are decorated with rich body ornaments and elegant headgear. On the bench, or perhaps a chest, sit two ladies. One is drawing or writing something with a long stick and the other comments on it with a raised index finger (**Fig. 59**). Women below make music; one is dancing. The instruments of the ensemble comprise cymbals, a drum, a bow-shaped *vīṇā*,[17] a transverse flute and a stringed instrument in the form of a mandolin (its name was probably *vallakī*).[18] All are so accurately depicted that it is possible to use them for music archaeology. The drum, for instance, with resonating body in form of a sandglass, has strings round the drumhead, held by a cord the loop of which the musician holds with the thumb of the left hand. By pulling the cord, the musician can change the tension of the skin and thus the sound of the instrument; it is possible that what we see here is the instrument called the 'little string-drum' (*tantrīpaṭahika*).[19]

The portrayal of such details in the reliefs, although they are part of a composition dominated by the narrative, is realistic: we can be sure that these are faithful representations delivering insights into daily life because we can compare them with images from other parts of India and with literary works. In our relief, for example, there is a figure of a small man, the only man apart from the king in the entire depiction. He is sitting on a round stool behind the dancer and lifting his right arm (**Fig. 60**), apparently giving the king his views on the dancing performance below or perhaps about the visitor who is being announced by the *prātihārī*. It is possible to recognize the appearance and characteristics of this man from other reliefs (**Fig. 61**):[20] he is holding a bent stick in the middle and his hair falls in waves

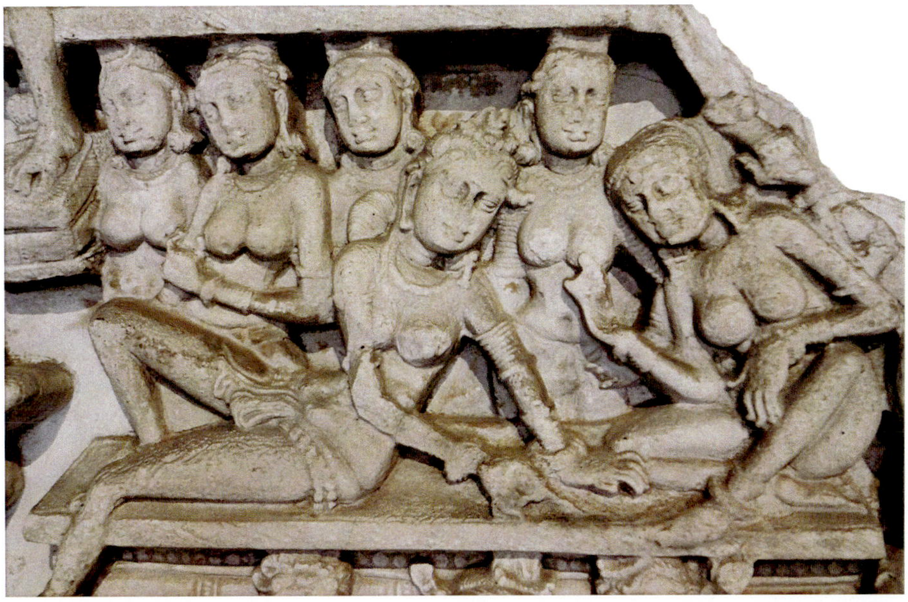

Figure 59 Courtly ladies (detail of Fig. 58)

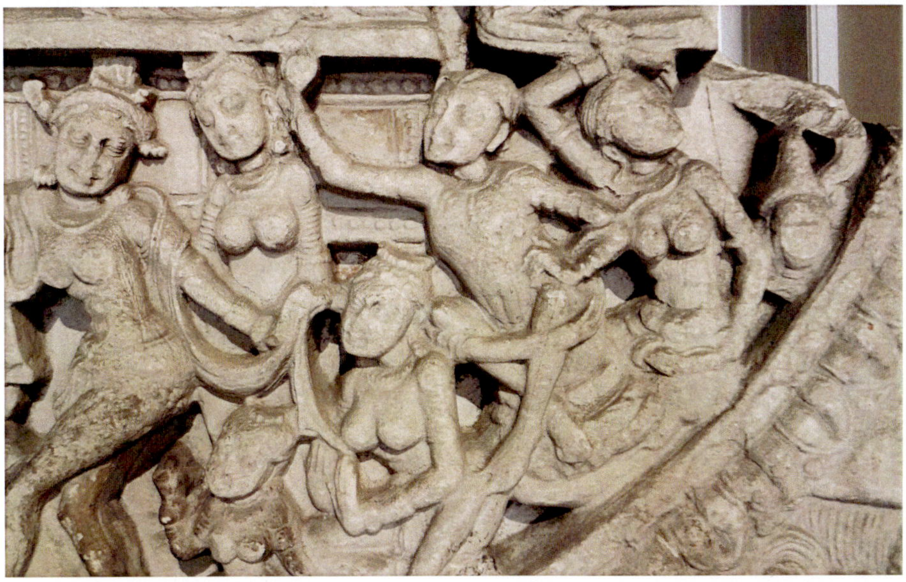

Figure 60 Jester (detail of Fig. 58)

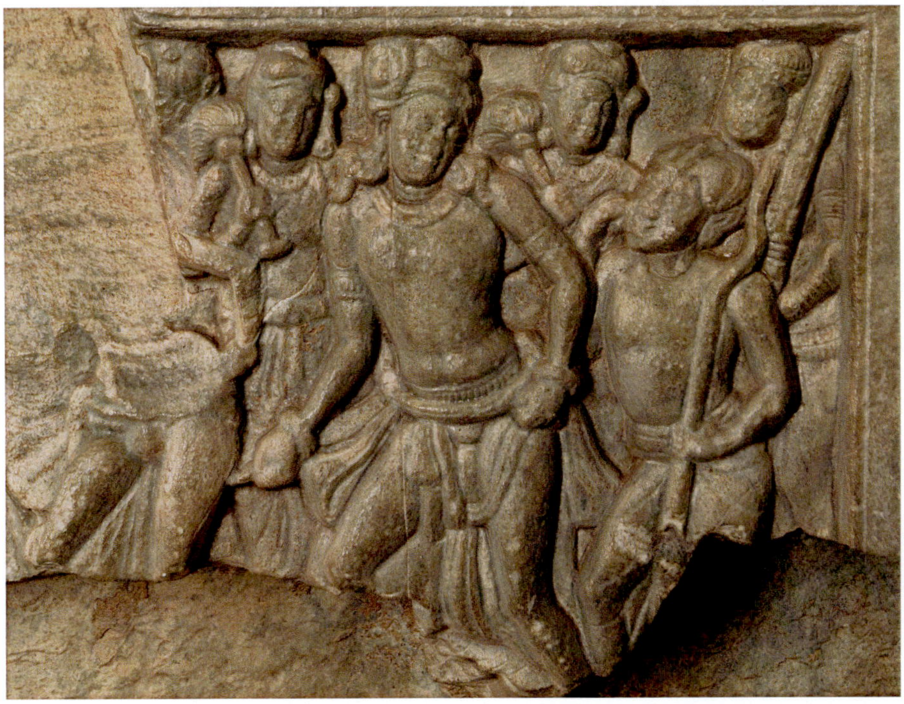

Figure 61 Jester, Nagarjunakonda, *c.* 3rd century CE, Archaeological Museum, Nagarjunakonda, no. 36 (photograph: Wojtek Oczkowski)

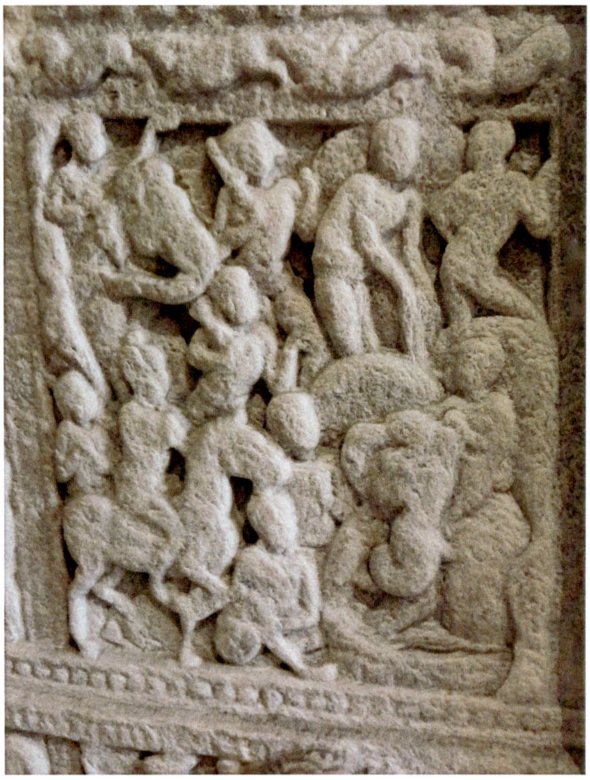

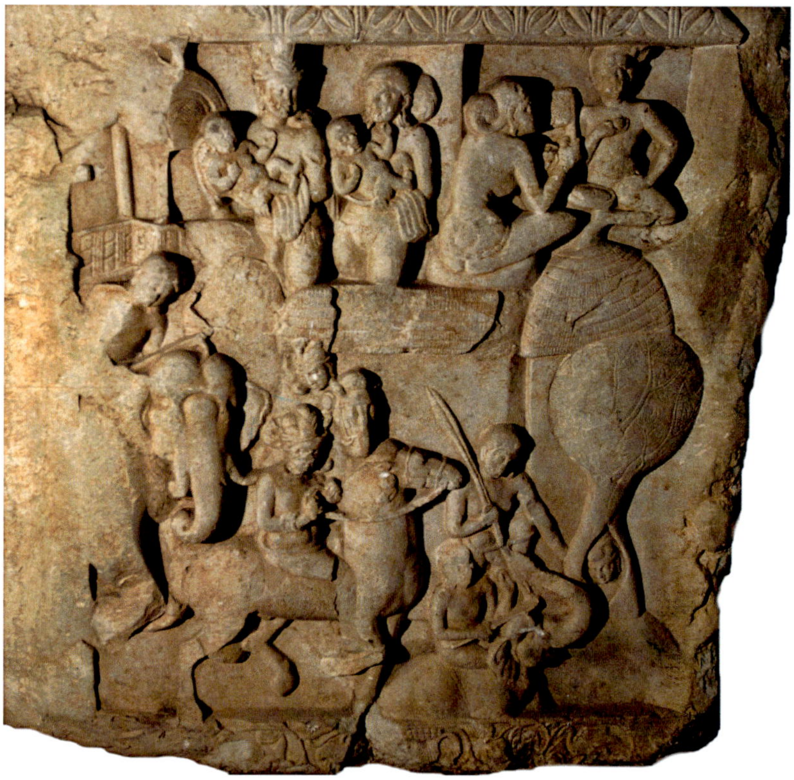

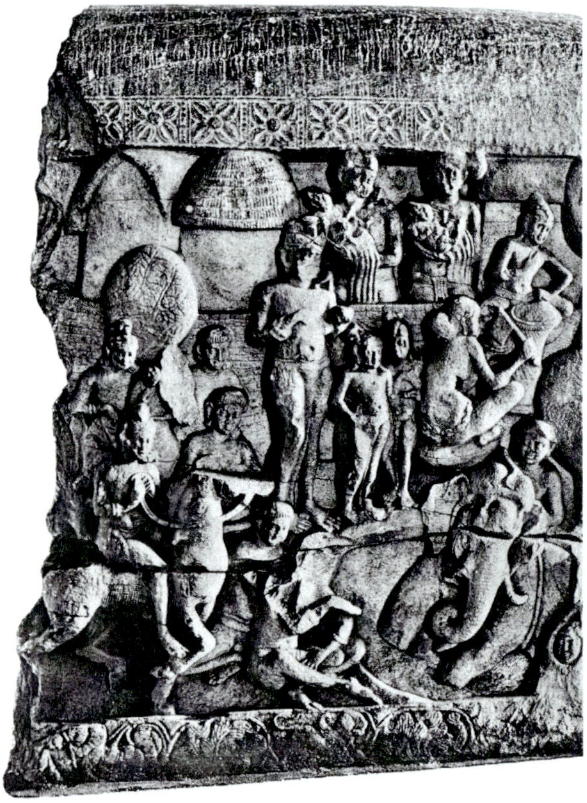

Figure 62 (above left) Unidentified scene, drum slab (detail), Amaravati, *c.* 3rd century CE, British Museum, 1880,0709.72

Figure 63 (above right) Unidentified scene, rail coping (detail), Amaravati, late 1st to early 2nd century CE, Archaeological Museum Amaravati, no. 433, reserved collection (photograph: Wojtek Oczkowski)

Figure 64 (left) Unidentified scene, rail coping (detail), Amaravati, *c.* 1st–2nd century CE, Government Museum, Chennai, no. 58

to the front and to both sides of his head. This is none other than the court jester. His appearance corresponds closely with descriptions of the jester in theatrical performance, the *vidūṣaka*, given by the *Nāṭyaśāstra*, an early treatise on theatre and allied arts (Zin 1998; 2015b; 2015c). The *vidūṣaka* should carry the staff, called 'the bent one' (*kuṭila* or *kuṭilaka*), which is often likened to the snake, in his left hand. The three sets of waves of hair on his head in the relief correspond well with the description in the *Nāṭyaśāstra* which talks about the 'crow's foot' (*kāka-pada*) on the top of *vidūṣaka*'s head. In the Ajanta paintings and in paintings in Kucha on the northern Silk Road (Arlt and Hiyama 2015), the *kāka-pada* takes the form of round tufts of hair often decorated with flowers or beads. The theatre character of the *vidūṣaka* was probably taken from life, and this is likely to have included his main characteristics: his position at the court, his close relationship with the king and his gluttony and ignorance of school knowledge, which in itself evokes jocularity since the *vidūṣaka* in theatre is a Brahmin who should practise abstinence and erudition. In narrative representations the jester is often shown in stories about people joining the monasteries, a decision that he does not welcome kindly.[21]

All details of the representation must be taken seriously since they may carry information important for understanding the narratives. Also noteworthy in terms of help in reading them are the methods used by the sculptors: the reliefs placed in the friezes, for instance, often have rows of running animals at the bottom (sometimes there are herdsmen among them or the animals are depicted inside tendrils): the direction in which the animals move indicates the succession of the scenes, right to left or left to right. The minute detail in the masterfully elaborated reliefs should also not make us forget that the narrative depictions in Amaravati are repetitions: they would need to be similar to others so that they would be recognizable at first glance. For the researcher these repetitions are a blessing because not only do they indicate which topics were popular but, more importantly, when one of the representations contains conclusive iconographical elements it facilitates identification of all repetitions. Unfortunately, as discussed above, the stories of Andhra Buddhism are gone, so identifications are not always possible, even when several representations of the same topic are preserved and the reliefs are of the highest artistic quality and provide excellent details.[22]

The comparisons are still of great importance, however, at least for avoiding false explanations in the case of less readable examples, such as the tiny scenes covering the *stūpa*s on the slabs such as **Figure 62**. These are representations of the representations. Such miniature scenes, only a couple of centimetres high, when they are not illustrations of well-known topics, are readable only by comparison with the 'full-size' reliefs (**Figs 62–4**).[23] A tiny representation on a *stūpa* slab in the British Museum, for example, can be identified as a scene of a king or prince whose court is being attacked by a group of armed soldiers (**Fig. 65**).[24] This can be compared to a larger example in Chennai with a more detailed depiction (**Fig. 66**),[25] such as

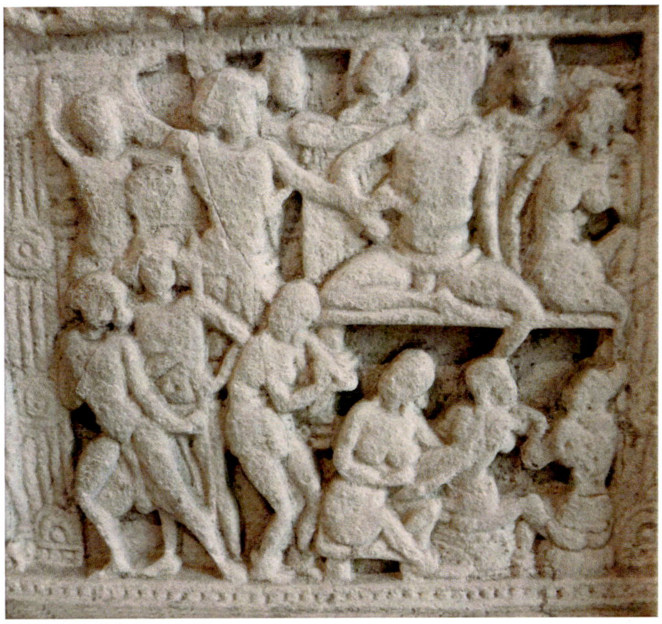

Figure 65 Unidentified scene, drum slab (detail), Amaravati, *c.* 3rd century CE, British Museum, 1880,0709.69

the jester holding his 'bent one' stick above his head, the tufts of hair making the 'crow's foot' visible, while one of the soldiers tries to strangle him and the terrified female musicians below. Unfortunately nothing can be said about the content of the scene.[26] To assist future research, however, it is important to offer detailed observations on each scene, since such observations are crucial for the explanation of the Buddhist narratives at Amaravati.

The organization of the scenes, the order in which they are placed and the way in which the composition highlights the 'key' element are all very important, since the reliefs are not only precisely executed but also designed with masterful premeditation. The representations – even in horizontal succession – were apparently not intended to be looked at simply in passing: the compositions are too sophisticated for that. The middle scene often plays the role of the axial centre, and the scenes at the sides are placed symmetrically

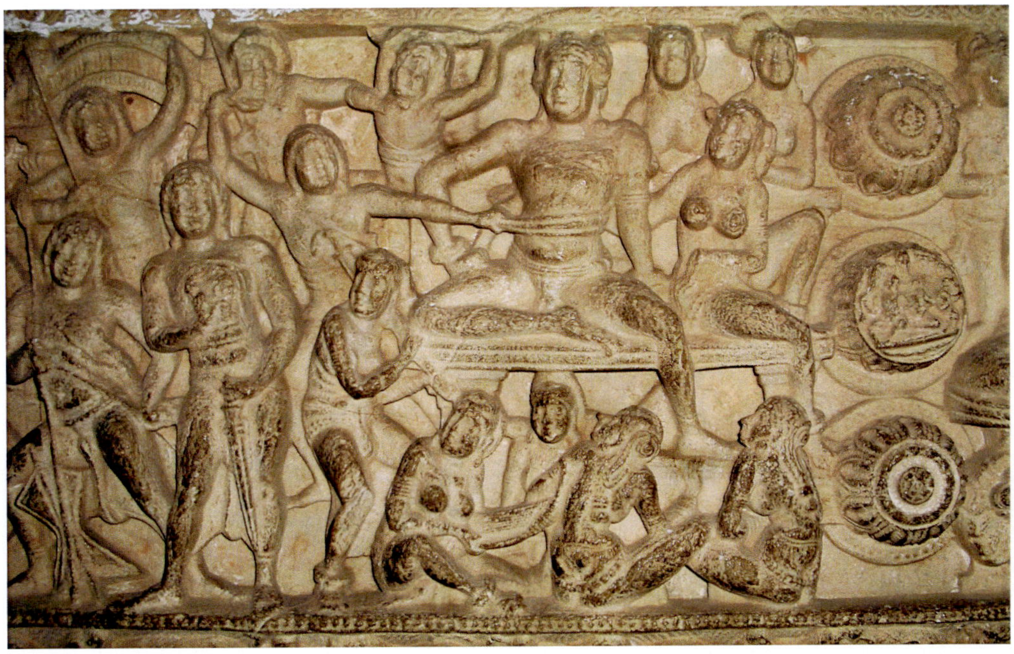

Figure 66 Unidentified scene, drum frieze (detail), Amaravati, *c.* 3rd century CE, Government Museum, Chennai, no. 105

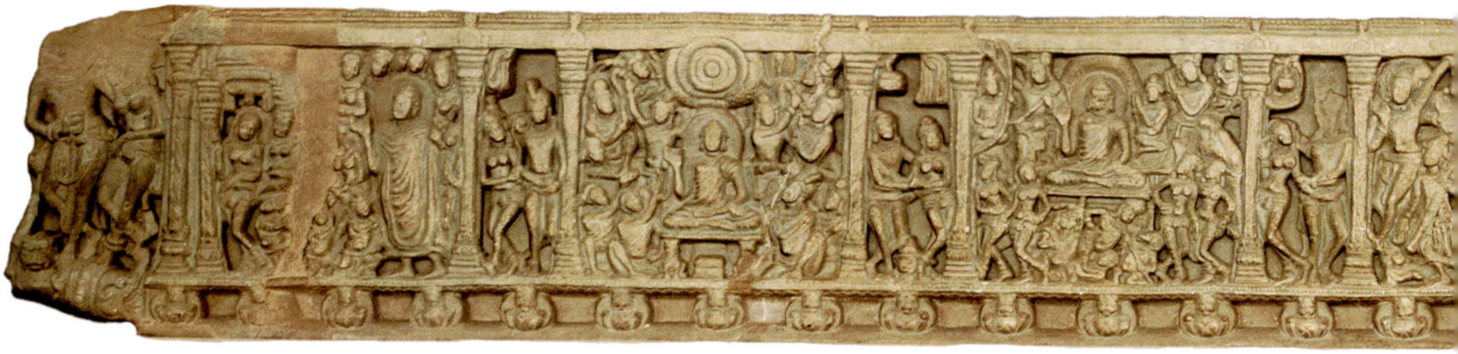

Figure 67 Seven scenes from the life of the Buddha, drum frieze, Nagarjunakonda, *c.* late 3rd century CE, Archaeological Museum, Nagarjuakonda, no. 45 (photograph: Wojtek Oczkowski)

to it; it is necessary to view the entire piece to recognize the nuance of such well-planned arrangements. A relief from Nagarjunakonda with seven scenes from the life of the Buddha (**Fig. 67**),[27] for example, has the scenes arranged symmetrically with the scene of Bodhisatva's departure from Kapilavastu, the turning point of his life, at the centre of the frieze. A standing woman at each end of the frieze (Māyā on the right end and the mother of Rāhula on the left) also shows a mirroring relationship to the woman of the other end.

Unfortunately, in many friezes, we do not see the entire composition of the scenes as they are damaged. In the case of the frieze in the British Museum (**Fig. 68**),[28] however, it is possible to see the entire scene since its missing left portion has survived and is kept in Chennai (**Fig. 69**).[29] The narrow frieze underneath the narrative scenes, above the lion heads, shows animals running to the left and displays *makaras* on both ends, at the right side facing the left, on the left facing the right (**Figs 70–1**), indicating the ends of the composition and thus confirming that nothing is missing. The break in the frieze splits the middle image, which represents the ascension of the turban to heaven. The episode takes place shortly after the future Buddha had left Kapilavastu: in an act of self-ordination he has cut off his hair together with the turban and thrown it away, but the gods were there at once, taking the hair with the turban to heaven.[30] It is unfortunate that the splitting up of this portion of the frieze separates the two deities often represented in the ascension scenes, originally two arch-enemies but here united in their devotion to the Buddha: the cobra-deity (*nāga*) is in London, the winged Garuḍa in Chennai.

Therefore, the ascension of the turban constitutes the very centre of the composition. The frieze as it would be, if the pieces were reunited, consists of nine compartments separated by dividing elements in the shape of three lotus rosettes placed one above the other. From right to left, as it was seen by visitors walking round the *stūpa*, each scene can be described as follows.

1. The final scene from the *Vidhurapaṇḍitajātaka* in which the wise minister Vidhura is preaching to the cobra deities.

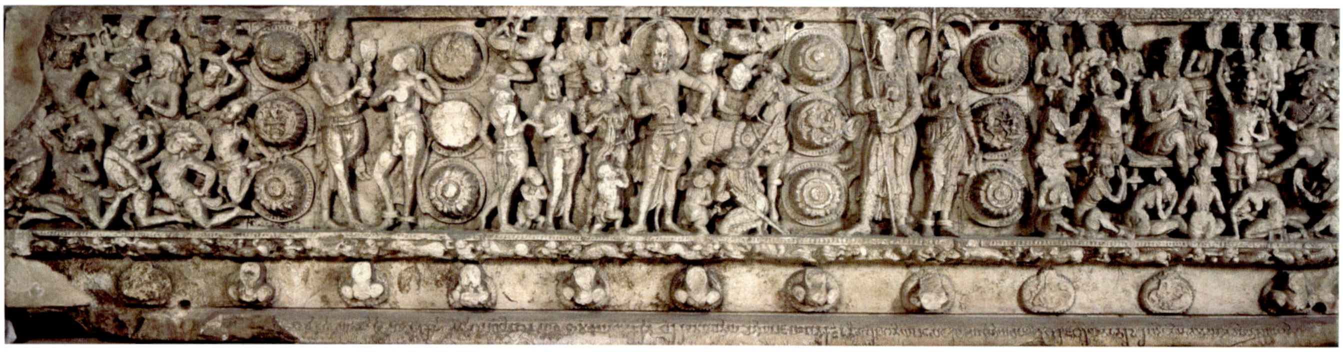

Figure 68 Unidentified scenes, drum frieze (fragment: right side), Amaravati, *c.* 3rd century CE, British Museum, 1880,0709.77

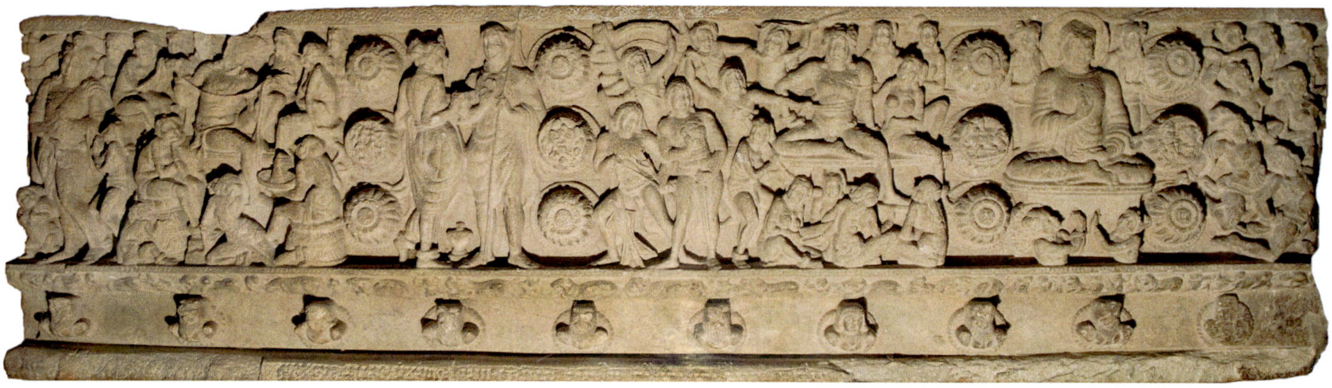

Figure 69 Unidentified scenes, drum frieze (fragment: left side), Amaravati, *c.* 3rd century CE, Government Museum, Chennai, no. 105 (photograph: Wojtek Oczkowski)

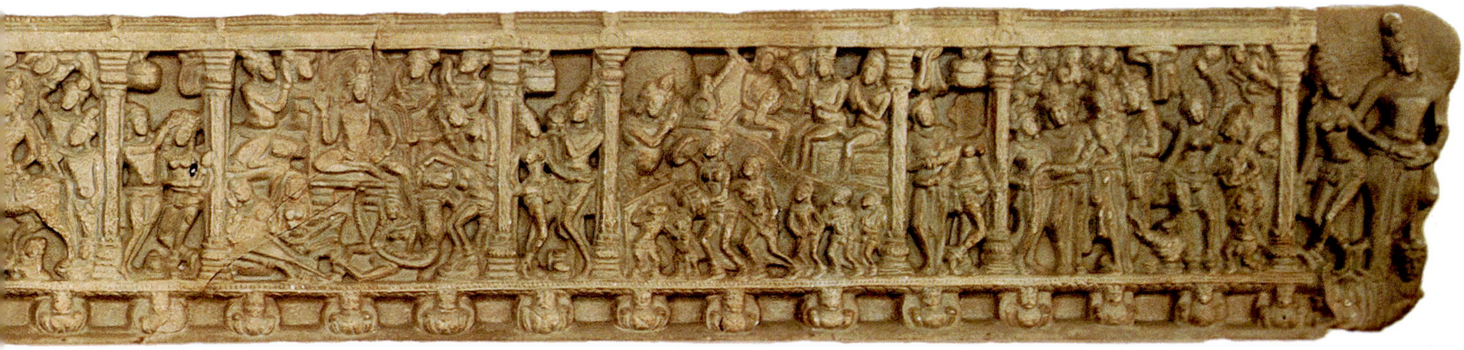

2. A couple dressed in 'northern' clothing (the man is wearing legwarmers and pointed cap and is holding a spear) (cf. **Fig. 73**).
3. The scene of Siddhārtha sending his horse and groom back home and exchanging princely clothes for the simple dress of the loner (the dwarves present in the scene must be those who were taking the horse out of the city).
4. A couple – a man holding a mirror in front of the lady who is fixing her earring.
5. The scene of the gods raising the prince's turban to heaven.
6. The Buddha on a throne preaching to the cobra deities emerging from the ground.
7. An unidentified scene, showing a king or a prince attacked by armed men (cf. **Fig. 66**).
8. A couple – a man with a spear and a lady whose look, from her mode of dress and from the goblet she is holding, is reminiscent of western sculpture.

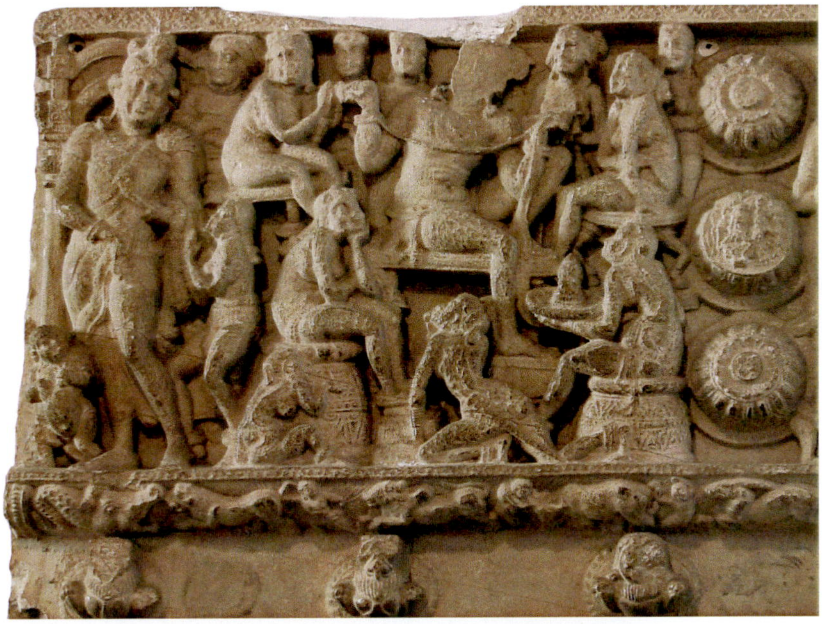

Figure 70 Left end of the frieze (detail of Fig. 69)

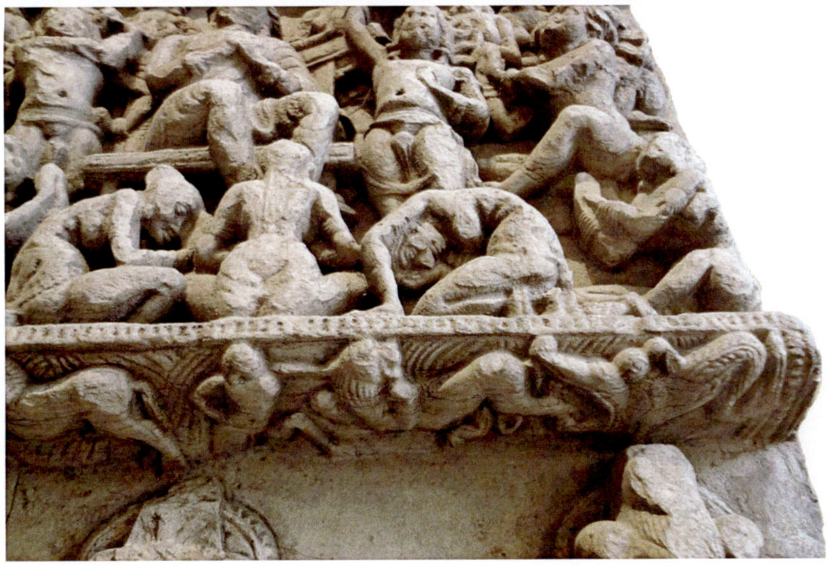

Figure 71 Right end of the frieze (detail of Fig. 68)

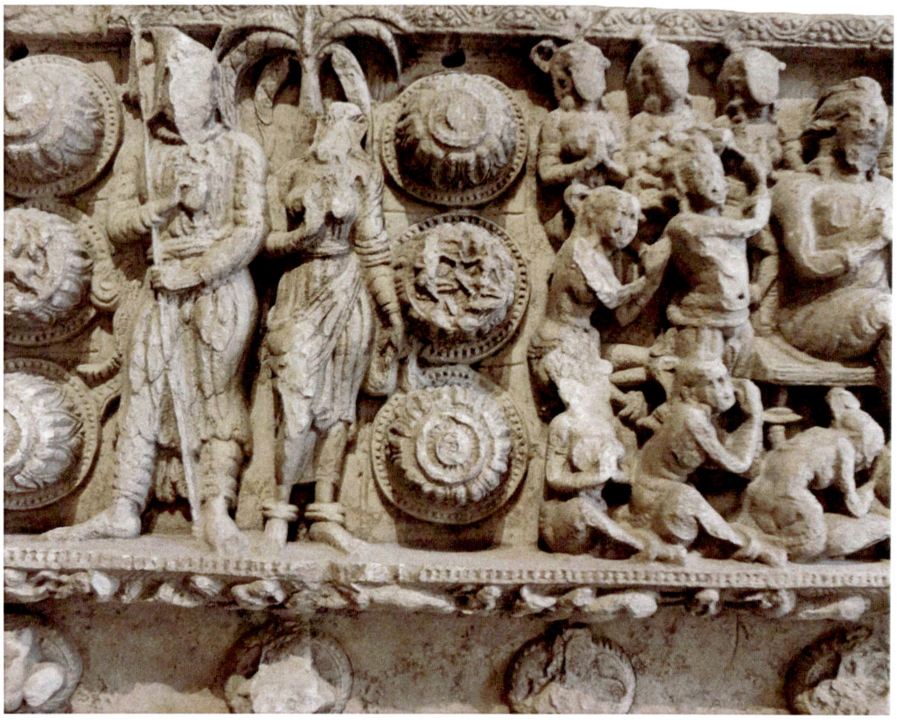

Figure 72 Narrative relief (undeciphered) depicted on rosette (detail of Fig. 68)

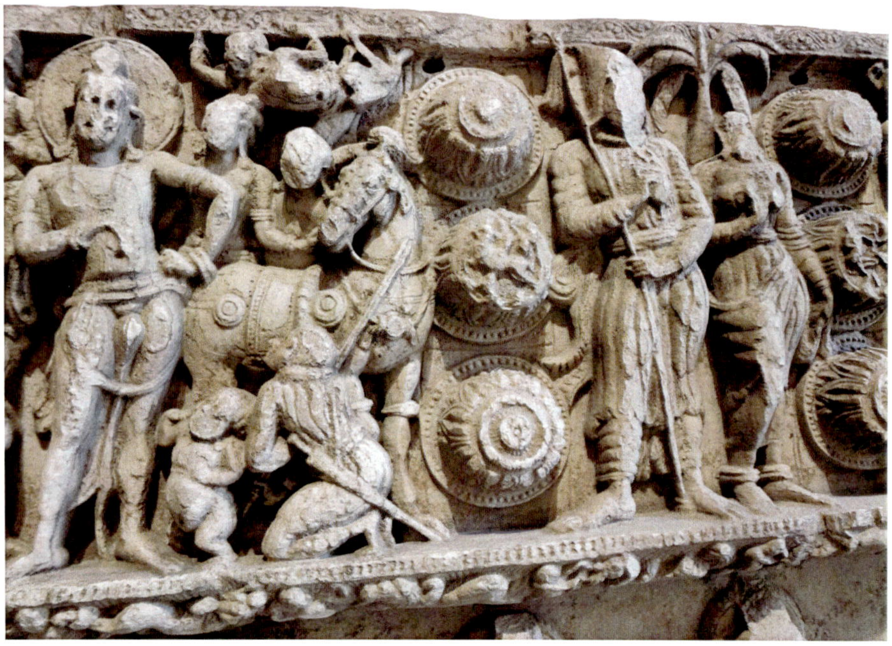

Figure 73 Great Departure depicted on rosette (detail of Fig. 68)

9. An unidentified scene,[31] showing a royal figure who holds cords (one of which is horizontal) in front of his chest and is surrounded by an assembly of ladies, and a man leaving the palace.[32]

The frieze thus consists of five broad narrative scenes, three narrow depictions of couples (typical scene-dividers at Amaravati) and instead of one such couple, a representation of the Buddha which, owing to the emerging *nāgas* (cobra deities), appears to be of a quasi-narrative character. In the narrative registers the *jātakas* or stories about contemporaries of the Buddha are mixed with scenes of the Buddha's life story. Out of five narrative scenes, only three can be explained given our present state of knowledge. The rest cannot. This frieze gives us the sort of insight typical in Amaravati research. We must accept that this evidence at least gives us the basis of future research and for this the credit must be given to the ancient artists. For further progress in Amaravati research, the visual language of ancient Andhran artists has to be fully studied, since we have to rely on the full range of pictorial messages that have survived from those times – these are the only primary source to identify the narratives in the sculpture.

Despite the difficulty of identifying some scenes, the axial symmetry of the composition of the middle scene apparently runs throughout the entire piece, as with the spears held by the men in both 'western'-looking couples, placed symmetrically to each other. The peculiar depiction of Vidhura at the right-hand end, facing outwards in three-quarter perspective (in other representations he is always shown full face), can also be explained by the left-hand end, where he faces left, that is, again, to the outside. A very intriguing scene is the one in which the Buddha replaces the couple, which in such a meticulously designed piece cannot be called a mistake. The Buddha is preaching to the cobra deities, just as Vidhura does. Siddhārtha's leaving Kapilavastu carries the same message as the scene at the left-hand end which, although it is not explained, surely illustrates a decision to leave worldly life behind. There are good reasons to believe that the piece *in toto* had a particular significance and carried a message which we do not recognize because we have not yet identified the stories. One last important factor must be mentioned: the frieze once contained eight more narrative representations, one on each of the middle rosettes of the vertical scene-dividing elements. The miniature pictures on the rosettes are almost completely lost but their narrative character is still observable (**Fig. 72**). In one case (**Fig. 73**) the possible connection with the following unit can be supposed: the rosette to the right of the farewell of the horse and the groom (i.e. the one before it) seems also to represent the horse, so it is apparently the *abhiniṣkramaṇa*, the departure of the Bodhisatva from Kapilavastu.

If the miniature depictions are as significant in the narrative as the bigger ones, it means the bigger ones were selected for their importance for the composition as a whole, or perhaps for their relationship with its overall message (for example, the leaving of Kapilavastu is actually much more important than sending the horse back home), and not merely to represent the story. It is clear from the reliefs – consummately beautiful and loaded with significant details, such as the enigmatic object on the tray in **Figure 70** – that the research is still very far from complete. The Amaravati reliefs tell stories in the most sublime way, their superb composition tantalizes the viewer with associative thinking whose meanings we often cannot read. But we need to hope that one day we will fully understand them.

Notes

1 See Kanaganahalli relief no. 56 showing the narrative of Vidhura (cf. Aramaki *et al.* 2011: 89; Poonacha 2011: pl. 79).

2 **Fig. 52**: illustrated in Aramaki *et al.* 2011: 90 (no. 58); Poonacha 2011: fig. 48A (drawing), pl. 60A; Zin 2012: fig. 10 (drawing). As for the inscription, see Nakanishi and von Hinüber 2014: 29 (I.4), pl. 1.

3 **Fig. 53**: illustrated in Aramaki *et al.* 2011: 63 (no. 1); Poonacha 2011: pl. 81; the inscription is not preserved; cf. Zin 2015a.

4 Aramaki *et al.* 2011: 64 (no. 3); Poonacha 2011: pl. 83B; Zin 2015a: fig. 10.

5 **Fig. 54**: BM no. 1880,0709.44; illustrated in Knox 1992, no. 61 (with references to earlier publications); Roy 1994: pls 66–70; Dehejia 1997: fig. 41; Schlingloff 2000/2013, II: 56 [9] (drawing); Zin 2015a: fig. 11.

6 **Fig. 55**: *Sleeping Ariadne*, the 2nd-century CE Roman replica of a Greek sculpture from the 2nd century BCE, Vatican, Galleria delle Statue, no. 548, cf. *LIMC*: Ariadne no. 118 (with references); McNally 1985: fig. 15; Köhn 1996: fig. 23.

7 Köhn 1996; Roman representations of Ariadne have not been discovered in India, but one – a metal piece of ornamentation on a *kline* – was found under a ship's cargo at the bottom of the Arabian Sea. In southern India Roman items were discovered at many sites; the Brahmapuri in Karnataka or Karur in Tamilnadu, at least, deserve a mention here.

8 E.g. the hoard of Roman bronzes discovered in Kolhapur (see De Puma 1991), which contains statues whose western style of representation of the body could have inspired imitation.

9 **Fig. 56**: BM no. 1880,0709.14. Illustrated in Knox 1992: no. 13 (with references to previous publications); Roy 1994: pl. 111; Sugimoto 2001: fig. 21.

10 BM, Asia, no. 1880,0709.39; illustrated in Zwalf 1996: pl. 5 and fig. 136 (with references).

11 Chennai Government Museum, no. 263; illustrated in Sivaramamurti 1942: 228–9 and pl. 28-1.

12 **Fig. 57**: Nagarjunakonda Archaeological Museum, no. 802 (depot).

13 Cf. Schlingloff 2000/2013, I: 231–2 (no. 48.1).

14 Kṣemendra, *Bodhisattvāvadānakalpalatā* 55 (Vaidya 1959, vol. 2: 334–6); the narrative is also retold in the later *Dvaviṃśyāvadānakathā*, cf. Schlingloff 2000/2013, I: 232.

15 **Fig. 58**: BM no. 1880,0709.17; illustrated in Knox 1992, no. 14 (with references to foregoing publications); Sugimoto 2001: fig. 3; Schlingloff 2000/2013, II: 52 [4] (drawing).

16 The medallion probably portrays a part of the narrative depicted on the pillar below, the story of the cobra deity Campaka, who was once captured by the snake catcher while he was meditating in his animal form. He wanted the privilege of being reborn as human and thus gaining the chance of entering *nirvāṇa* (right compartment), and he invited to his abode the human king who helped him from the captivity (left and central compartment). The representation of the narrative in Ajanta (cf. Schlingloff 2000/2013, I: 282 (no. 60)) includes the scene in which the wife of Campaka comes to the court of the human king to ask for help for her captive husband; this was probably the scene represented in the medallion.

17 See Zin 2004a: esp. 322–33, figs 3, 5–44.

18 See Zin 2004a: esp. 339–42, figs 3, 67–80, 83.

19 See Zin 2004a: 340, figs 80–2.

20 **Fig. 61**: Nagarjunakonda Archaeological Museum, no. 36; illustrated in Zin 2014: fig. 1, C1 and fig. 8 (with references).

21 The most beautiful of these representations is the painting on the veranda of cave XVII in Ajanta, showing a couple leaving their wealthy home to join the Buddhist order (cf. Schlingloff 2000/2013, I: 399–401 (no. 69)). The jester with his typical bent staff and hair tufts decorated with flowers (but also displaying some of the attributes of a Brahmin, the holy string *yajñopavīta* and the rosary) shows unmistakably by his gestures that he is protesting against his master and mistress's decision, while holding a bowl of sweets under his arm, apparently trying to protect them. A fragment of a painting from Ajanta has survived in the Museum of Fine Arts in Boston – cut off apparently due to the interesting tufty hair style of the person depicted. See Begley 1968. It was discovered that the fragment belongs to the narrative of Nanda in cave XVI in Ajanta (cf. Schlingloff 2000/2013, I: 415–25; no. 73(7)). It is the jester, who is trying to stop the monk bowing above Nanda shearing his head, i.e. preventing him from joining the monastery; there is a good illustration in Takata 1971: 11, fig. 4; cf. Zin 2015c.

22 E.g. in the case of the reliefs representing the scene including the parable about 'The man in the well', cf. Zin 2011.

23 **Fig. 62**: BM no. 1880,0709.72; illustrated in Knox 1992: no. 70 and 70c (with references to previous publications). **Fig. 63**: Amaravati Archaeological Museum, no. 433 (depot); illustrated in Parimoo 1995: fig. 12; Zin 2004b: fig. 12 (drawing); Gupta 2008: fig. 14(I)). **Fig. 64**: Chennai Government Museum, no. 58 (not on display and today broken and in a very bad state of preservation); illustrated in Burgess 1887: pl. 242.2 (drawing); Bachhofer 1929: pl. 127.2; Sivaramamurti 1942: pl. 46.2; Stern and Bénisti 1961: pl. 24b; Sivaramamurti 1979: fig. 17; Nagar 1993: C.P. 33; Parimoo 1995: fig. 11; Misra 2000: pl. 14-vi: Sugimoto 2001: fig. 12; Zin 2004b: fig. 11 (drawing).

24 **Fig. 65**: BM no. 1880,0709.69; illustrated in Knox 1992: no. 68 (with references to earlier publications).

25 **Fig. 66**: Chennai Government Museum, no. 105 (3rd register); illustrated in Burgess 1887: pl. 42.4; Sivaramamurti 1942: pl. 59.1; Stern and Bénisti 1961: pl. 45a; Parimoo 1982: fig. 119; Ramachandra Rao 1984: pl. 241; Stone 1994: fig. 70; Roy 1994: pl. 126; Zin 2004b: fig. 10 (drawing).

26 Sivaramamurti (1942: 251) explains the king as Siddhārtha and gives a caption (pl. 59.1c), 'Siddhartha lives in three pleasant palaces carefully guarded from the ills of life', whose nonsensical unhelpfulness can only be explained by his having had to rely on poor photography.

27 **Fig. 67**: Nagarjunakonda Archaeological Museum, no. 45. Unfortunately the relief was only seldom represented as an entire piece. Illustrated e.g. in Ramachandra Rao 1956: pl. 23 (1st

register); Ray 1965: figs 41–2; Ramachandra Rao 1984: pl. 390 (1st register); Stone 1994: fig. 209; Rama 1995: pl. 11a (3rd register).

28 **Fig. 68**: BM no. 1880,0709.77; illustrated in Knox 1992: no. 55 (with references to previous publications); Roy 1994: pls 124–5; Dehejia 1997: fig. 139.

29 **Fig. 69**: Chennai Government Museum, no. 105. For further references, see note 25.

30 Compare the representation with the same scene depicted on the Amaravati pillar in the BM (no. 1880,0709.46; illustrated in Knox 1992, no. 5). The scene was important and was often represented in art: perhaps it symbolized the beginning of the struggle for enlightenment on which everyone should embark. In Amaravati the ascension of the turban was often represented together with the ascension of the bowl which the Buddha received alongside last meal before the enlightenment; cf. Zin (forthcoming c).

31 The interpretations given hitherto of the scene, which is repeated several times in the reliefs in Andhra, do not, unfortunately, offer a solution; Longhurst (1938: 32) explained it as 'Siddhārtha and the mighty bow' and Sivaramamurti (1942: 251) as Siddhārta who 'holds three threads fondly, and ponders over them … The three cords may also signify *tanha*, *arati* and *rāga*, the three lusts personified as Māra's daughters, whom, as Buddha, the prince later overcame, but which now held him in their grasp'. We know these interpretations cannot be accepted simply because the person is not depicted with nimbus, i.e. it is not Siddhārtha.

32 It cannot be ruled out, though it is highly improbable, that it is one and the same man represented twice, since persons from the right scene are observing the man on the left; i.e. it appears to be one scene, not two successive ones.

Chapter 5
Reflections of Roman Art in Southern India

Elizabeth Rosen Stone

Amaravati, and its 3rd-century CE successor site, Nagarjunakonda, produced an art that is uniquely Indian. At the same time, they adapted and fully integrated certain artistic conventions which have been brought to India from elsewhere, frequently the classical world. The bustling narratives were essentially inherited from the traditions of Sanchi, and they contain the general requisite features of early Buddhist art, namely the tales of the current and past lives of Śākyamuni Buddha. At Amaravati, however, they attained a new life, apparently through the initiative of just a few artists, who experimented with both western spatial conventions and the use of individual western motifs. These innovations were, however, so thoroughly integrated into the style of the Amaravati school that their foreign origins were at first obscured.[1] I have addressed the subject of Roman influence in South Indian sculpture throughout my book on Nagarjunakonda (Stone 1994) and in three articles (Stone 2005; 2006; 2008), and Robert Brown (2004: 64–5) has been able to extend some of the arguments. My earlier works insisted on the adaptation of spatial convention, but western influence was even more pervasive than I first realized.[2]

In a 1981 article, Nagaswamy identified Roman trading sites in South India.[3] In his fascinating book, *Roman Karur*, Nagaswamy used evidence from both the Tamil literature and Roman archaeological finds from Karur to suggest that Romans had a hand in the actual carving of some of the spatially most interesting sculptures from Amaravati (Nagaswamy 1995: 105). Literary evidence, most notably the *Cilappatikāram* and the *Maṇimēkalai*, tells us of foreign imports, significantly Roman gold (mostly in the form of coins), wine (presumed from the numerous surviving *amphorae*) and lamps (Nagaswamy 1995: 96–7). But aside from the goods, he cites references to actual Romans (his interpretation of *yavana*) living in the region. The *Maṇimēkalai* refers to *yavana taccar*, which are variously interpreted as Roman sculptors or carpenters (Krishnaswami Aiyangar 1928, 159; Nagaswamy 1995: 98).[4] The *Cilappatikāram* has a reference to a colony of *yavanas* (*yavanar irukkai*) in Kāvēripumpattinam, the ancient Kaberis Emporium of Ptolemy. This is of significance, as much of the trade with the Roman world came through the ports of Alexandria and via the sea route to India as outlined in the *Periplus Maris Erythraei* (Casson 1989: 51–85). Although the *Periplus* is dated to the 1st century CE, goods continued to come into India until a much later time, perhaps through the 4th century, if not later.[5] Later references in the Tamil literature are less easy to substantiate but they deserve notice. They refer to *yavanas* who were skilled in the making of chests for jewellery as well as the building of chariots, which was amongst their skills (Nagaswamy 1995: 99–100). Despite literary references and inferences that some of the sculptures from Amaravati were done by actual Romans, Nagaswamy never actually compares the works from Amaravati with examples from the Roman world, but he certainly tempts us to do so.

Western evidence for the existence of Roman architecture in India appears on the Peutinger Map (*Tabula Peutingeriana*), a Roman road map or painted itinerary depicting Rome's conception of its own world in which India is included (Talbert 2010).[6] The original map was formerly

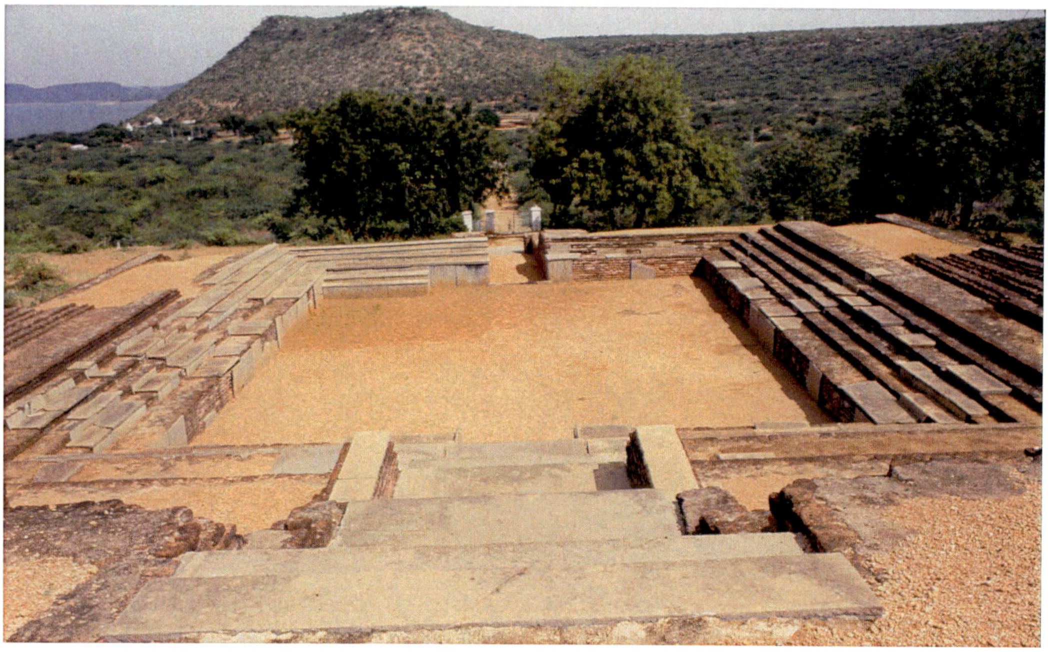

Figure 74 Assembly hall, Nagarjunakonda, c. 3rd century CE (photograph: Akira Shimada)

believed to have been drawn in the 4th or 5th century CE and is preserved in a medieval copy. Clearly depicted on the map is a building in highly schematized classical form with a rectangular plan and a peaked roof. It is labelled *templum augusti* (Temple of Augustus) and placed not far from the ancient site of Muziris on the Kerala coast. Traditionally this reference has been accepted as an actual Roman temple built on Indian soil by or for a colony of foreign traders (Cimino 1994; Sidebotham 2011: 191). That Muziris was a Roman trading centre is certain, but that the temple actually existed is still under discussion (Tomber 2008: 130, 148). Recent scholars have suggested that the structure was either built by a local chieftain for the Romans or there was an Indian temple which the Romans interpreted as their own (Ray 1998: 66, citing Metzler 1989).[7] Thus unless the temple to Augustus is actually found and excavated, we must leave this notion to the realm of 'plausible' but not 'proven'.[8]

There are more plausible reflections of Roman architecture in southern India. We begin with the great assembly hall (**Fig. 74**), probably the most conspicuous structure and the first thing one usually sees when visiting Nagarjunakonda. It is rather loosely referred to in the Indian literature as an 'amphitheatre' or 'stadium', although in the strictly Roman sense it is neither. Yet it resonates with almost all scholars of both India and the classical world as showing Roman influence. Constructed in the 3rd century CE, its basic form is rectangular with an enclosure measuring 16.46 × 17.42m; hence it is essentially square in form. Tiered galleries built of brick and encased with stone around the four sides provide seating for about 1,000 people.[9] This is similar to a construction method used in the Roman world from the 2nd century CE onwards (Boëthius and Ward-Perkins 1970: 245–63). Through the centre of the hall is a long staircase leading to the top of the structure (Varadpande 1973: 29 bottom). The ascent provides a magnificent view of the surrounding areas and sounds from the arena remain very clear at the top. Here one encounters the remains of a temple (Soundara Rajan 2006: 108 for ground plan) which housed a seated female deity, frequently referred to as Hāritī (Stone 1994: 18–19, figs 23–4). While this identification is still a matter of conjecture, it is supported by an inscription referring to an endowment given for the benefit of the Aparamahāvinaseliya sect of Buddhism (Sircar 1961–2: 210–11, Inscription III). Scholars have therefore suggested that the image is one of Hāritī, a popular Buddhist deity often shown seated.

To date we have been unable to find a direct parallel in India to this striking structure. In a previous publication however, I compared the structure to the 2nd-century BCE *bouleuterion* at Priene in western Turkey which is square in form and has similar steps for seating (Stone 1994: fig. 11).[10] A successor to it, which is closer in time to the structure at Nagarjunakonda, is the Roman Curia (Curia Julia) or senatorial assembly which was begun by Augustus in 44 BCE (Claridge 1998: 71). The interior of the hall is 25.2m long by 17.61m wide. Three broad steps could have fitted five rows of chairs or a total of 300 senators. There were many such assembly halls and any one of these could have been known to architects familiar with the Roman world. The only late Roman example of a rectangular structure of which I am currently aware is a 3rd-century CE rectangular 'arena' at Tyre in Lebanon – a structure whose exact function is unclear (Butcher 2003: 257–8).

M.L. Varadpande (1973), whose specialty is theatre architecture, treats the hall as if it is an amphitheatre despite the fact that it does not correspond in shape to the usual type of amphitheatre in the West. He considers the 'amphitheatre' and the temple above it as one unit (1973: 28–9), and boldly compares it to the semicircular Roman theatre-temple built by Pompey in 53 BCE. In the Roman example, one enters the temple of Venus by climbing the steps through the centre of the semicircular theatre (Hanson 1969: 45 and fig. 16). To the Romans the theatre was usually considered dishonourable, and so the purpose of the temple was to elevate the function of the compound. Varadpande implies that there is a parallelism between the Nagarjunakonda assembly hall and the theatre of Pompey. If the idea of juxtaposing a temple and a theatre did indeed

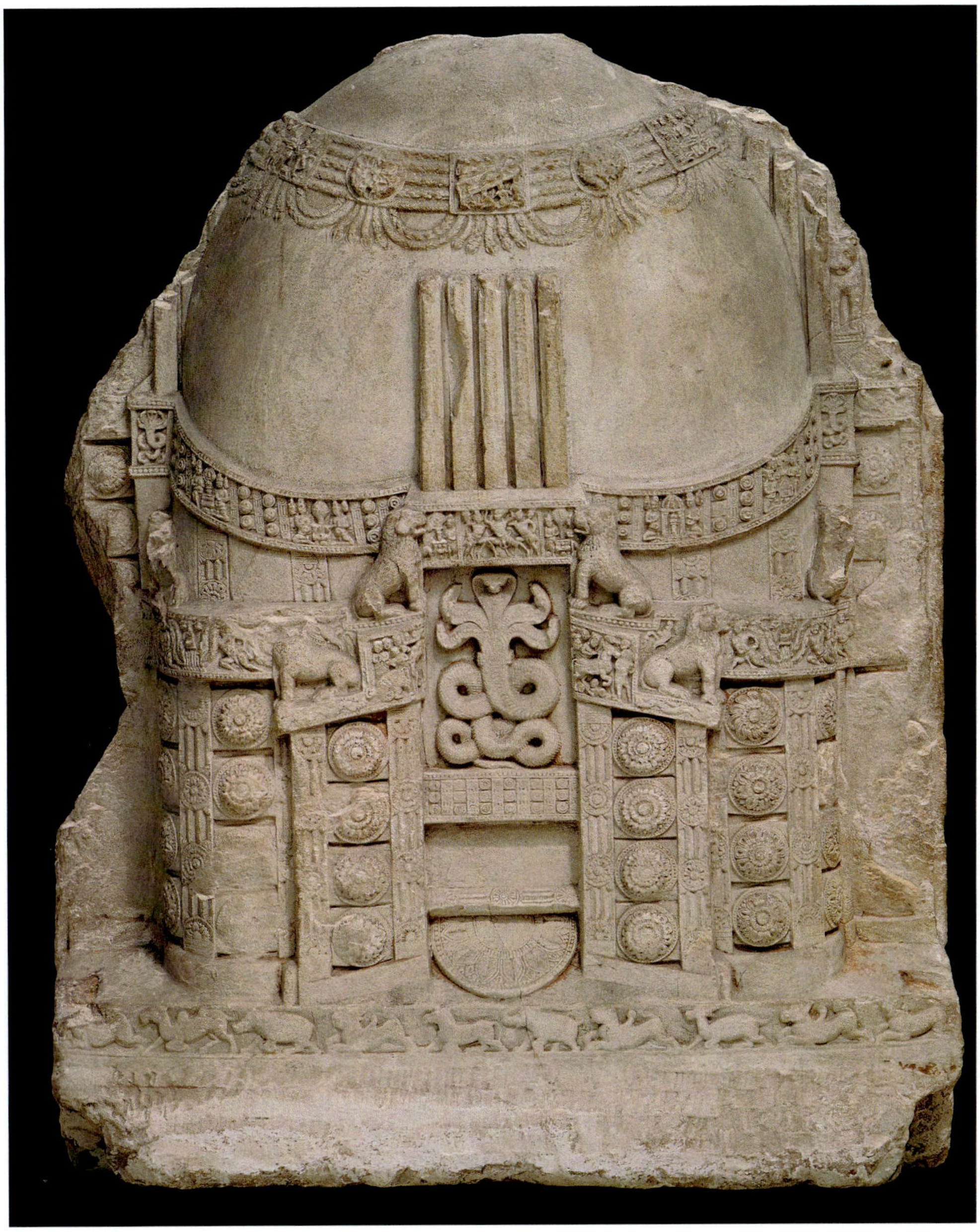

Figure 75 Drum slab depicting *stūpa* from the Amaravati *stūpa*, c. 3rd century CE, British Museum, 1880,0709.81

come from the Roman world, it seems completely compatible with the manner in which narrative was juxtaposed with the religious function of the *stūpa*. The idea, however, while conceptually satisfactory is less so visually. In almost every case, when we find Roman-looking structures or motifs they are used because there is a pre-existing Indian form or concept which can be adapted. Varadpande works on the assumption that the rectangular and circular forms are equally valid in India. Despite his emphasis on foreign sources (ibid.: 66), he illustrates rock-cut caves which were used for theatrical performances, thereby implying, but not directly stating, that the assembly hall had distant ancestors in the rock-cut theatres which were modified in light of foreign sources.

Roman coins should be an integral part of the study of South Indian art. Unlike the comparative study of architecture which implies the presence of foreign workers, the copying or adaptation of motifs from Roman coins could have been done by a talented Indian craftsman. But the study of Roman coins has its complications, for we cannot be certain as to how many of these coins were found in India. P.L. Gupta cites 18th- and 19th-century Indian records stating that the finds of gold coins were in a 'quantity amounting to five cooly-loads', and silver coins were 'some thousands, enough to fill five or six Madras measures' (Gupta 1965: 40), while Pliny's *Natural History* states that 'in no year does India absorb less than fifty million *sesterces* of our empire's wealth' (Pliny: 6.26.102). Despite these and several other literary references, we know of many of the coins solely from citations in archaeological reports. As gold coins are intrinsically valuable, many of them have been melted down or have disappeared into private collections. For those that have been published, frequently only the obverse containing a portrait of the emperor is shown. For our purposes it is the reverse of the coins which we find reflected on the sculptures of Andhra Pradesh. Thus, effectively unable to reconstruct what has been lost, we study coins from the same time periods as those known to have been found in India which are well documented in public collections. The validity of this method can be judged only by the number of comparisons we have been able to find. The fact is that there is only one case cited in this paper in which a coin was excavated in near

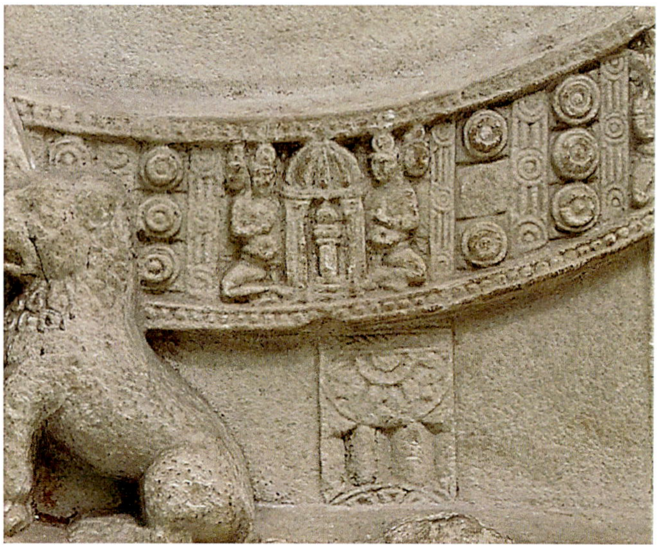

Figure 76 Domed shrine with worshippers, detail of Figure 75

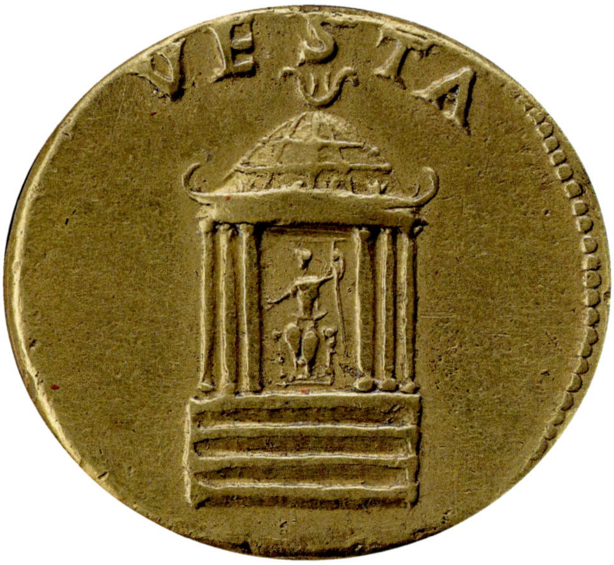

Figure 77 Temple of Vesta, reverse of *aureus* of Nero, 65–6 CE, British Museum, CGR88027

proximity to a sculpture which has clearly copied it. We were able to make this judgement because of the systematic excavations conducted at Site 6, Nagarjunakonda, but it is certain that many more would exist had all the archaeological and numismatic material been available to us.

While many of the Roman coins in India have been found in hoards, most of the sites in southern India have a few Roman coins. There is no doubt that artists looked at them, as they are accurately illustrated in Indian reliefs.[11] As we shall see, imagery on coins was used as source material for Indian sculptural art, and the coins served to transmit motifs derived from Roman sculpture, architecture and even painting.[12]

An Amaravati relief illustrates a *stūpa* decorated with miniature reliefs (**Fig. 75**). Most of the scenes illustrate well-known episodes from the life of the Buddha, but one is not familiar. On the illustrated drum frieze is the representation of a small, domed, pillared shrine flanked by worshippers (**Fig. 76**). Inside the shrine is a tall lamp on a columnar stand emitting flames.[13] While there are both earlier (Burgess 1887: pl. 45, 3; Srinivasan 1983: 17, fig. 7) and later pillared, domed shrines (Longhurst 1938: pl. 11-a; Sarkar 1960: pl. 46) represented in Andhra sculpture, this particular example is unique. The dome has an unusual ribbed structure and is seen in single-point perspective. Similar buildings with ribbed domed roofs are on Roman coins which illustrate the temple to Vesta, goddess of the hearth. These are known from the Republican period onwards (Cody 1973: pls 5.1, 6.3, 6.6; Tomeanko 1999: 177–83). An example of the simplest type belonging to the time of Nero (65 CE) has a statue inside the temple (**Fig. 77**). From the time of Vespasian (73 CE) we see additional figures added to the composition (**Fig. 78**). On a coin from the time of Caracalla (214 CE) an altar is placed in front of the temple and Caracalla is seen performing a sacrifice with onlookers present (**Fig. 79**). The reader may note that not one Roman coin I have cited is an exact prototype. However, all the coins have some elements which appear in the Amaravati shrine (**Fig. 76**), indicating that Roman numismatic imagery was well integrated into the art of South India.

Figure 78 Temple of Vesta, reverse of *aureus* of Vespasian, 73 CE, American Numismatic Society, no. 1944.100.39927

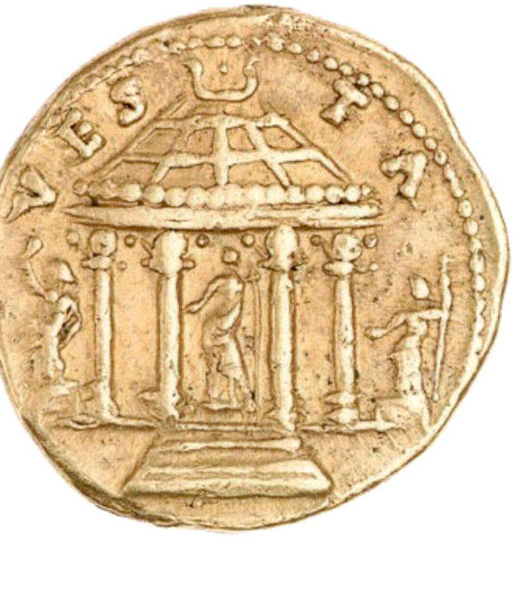

Figure 79 Caracalla sacrificing at the Temple of Vesta, reverse of *aureus* of Caracalla, 214 CE, British Museum, CGR89425

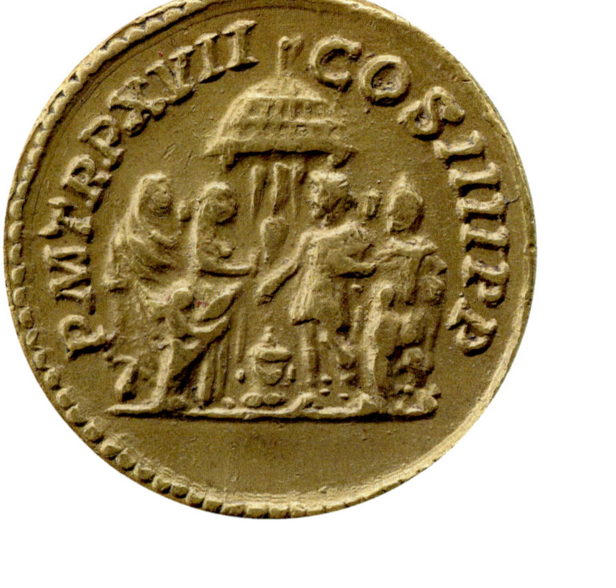

There is one detail of the Amaravati shrine (**Fig. 76**) which we have been unable to find in either the Roman repertory or that of southern India, and that is the tall lamp. Since lamps and burners are part of Buddhist ritual in Gandhara and throughout Buddhist Asia, it is interesting that they are not part of the South Indian repertory. Many of them have a dual function as both a lamp and a burner. On Gandharan narrative reliefs they are frequently placed in front of Buddha images at the base of the statue (Stone 2004: 91–2, figs 41–2). A fine seated Buddha image in the British Museum has a tall lamp, of the same type as the Amaravati example, placed in front of the image and being worshipped (**Fig. 80**). How then do we interpret this multiplicity of sources? Clearly images of Vestan temples appeared in many media and were therefore very much part of the visual culture of the Roman world. The artist of the Amaravati *stūpa* must also have seen images from Gandhara. Had Roman coins not been found in abundance in South India, we would be reluctant to make this comparison. But indeed they have been found. As far as the issue of the Gandharan illustration of the burner, we find that it is an outlier to our argument, and conclude that there are certainly other outside sources as well as internal developments.[14]

Scenes of the Great Departure which we find both at Amaravati (BM no. 1880,0709.112; illustrated in Knox 1992: 116, no. 57) and Nagarjunakonda may also be related to western sources. Hugo Buchthal (1943: 138–9) noted that the Great Departure, as depicted in Gandhara, is based upon the model of Roman imperial coins of the 2nd and 3rd centuries CE. Such coins represent the *adventus* or triumphal entry of the emperor into a town as well as for the *profectio* or departure, as seen on a coin of Trajan (112–14 CE) (**Fig. 81**). In a relief of the Great Departure from Nagarjunakonda (**Fig. 82**), there is indeed a reminiscence of the *profectio* as the diagonal lines of spears are transformed into the diagonal line of the umbrella held over the head of the Buddha. The Buddha and the emperor are flanked by the iconographically appropriate figures in front of and behind the horse, and there the similarity stops. The relief of the Great Departure comes from Site 6, Nagarjunakonda. In the vicinity of the *stūpa* was found a gold coin of Hadrian (117–38 CE) on horseback (**Fig. 83**).[15] If this coin had been found elsewhere we would not necessarily have made the association, but a Roman emperor with extended right arm in proximity of the Buddha sculpted on horseback in *abhaya mudrā* is certainly suggestive.

In books on Amaravati, the question of classical impact on narrative sculpture is usually glossed over. Roy (1994: I, 156) addresses the issue by quoting Sivaramamurti 1976 and accepts some of my own material. Huntington (1985: 176) discusses it briefly in the context of a survey book, while Ray (1983: 129) addresses the subject directly and concludes that the classical influence found in Andhra is inherited directly from Gandhara. Knox (1992) ignored the question and Barrett (1954a: 61) denied foreign influence with regard to the Buddha image. Sivaramamurti (1976: 8) was well aware that classical conventions were an integral part of Amaravati art. He used Renaissance paintings for his illustrations, as he did not have access to their classical sources (Sivaramamurti 1976: pls 24–6).

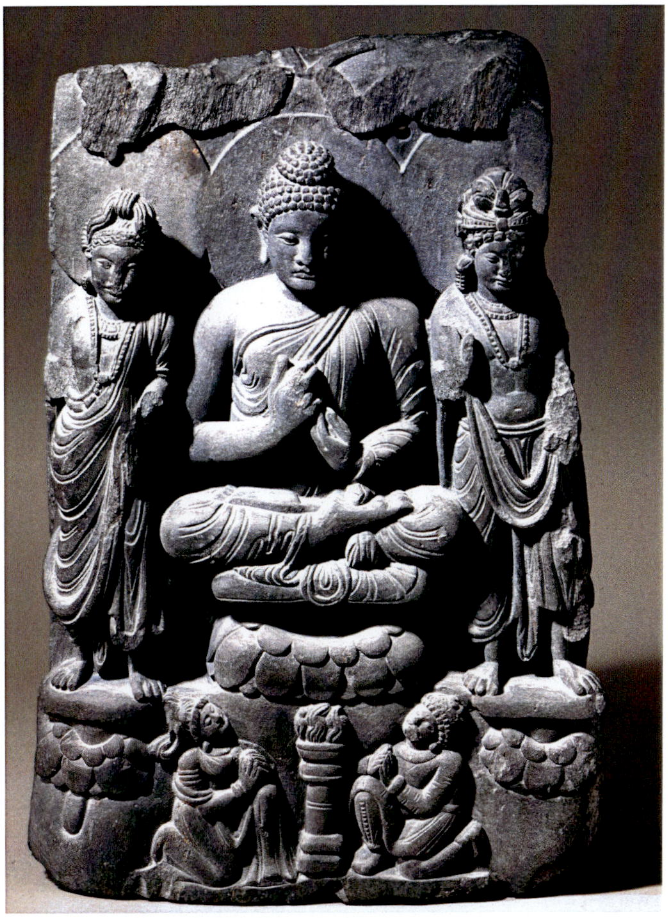

Figure 80 Preaching Buddha from Jamalgarhi, 2nd–3rd century CE, Gandhara, British Museum, 1887,0717.48

Many comparisons can be made, but in the compass of this article I will cite only two more. These concern the use of different postures on the sculptures. From the beginning of the high phase of Amaravati sculpture, the reliefs attain a greater sense of depth and the compositions are filled with people in dynamic poses. Many of these figures seem to be an adaptation from the Roman world. A relief on a pillar shows two female figures flanking a five-headed *nāga* (**Fig. 84**). The figures have been identified by Sivaramamurti as

Figure 81 *Profectio Augusti*, *aureus* of Trajan, 112–14 CE, American Numismatic Society, no. 1944.100.43617

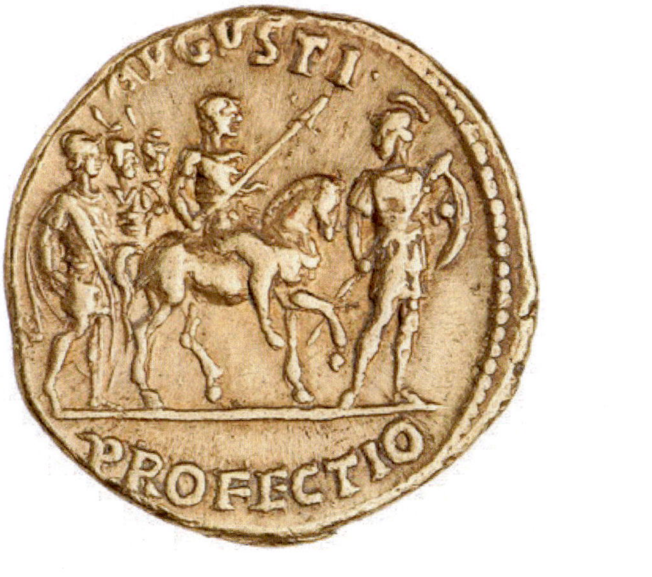

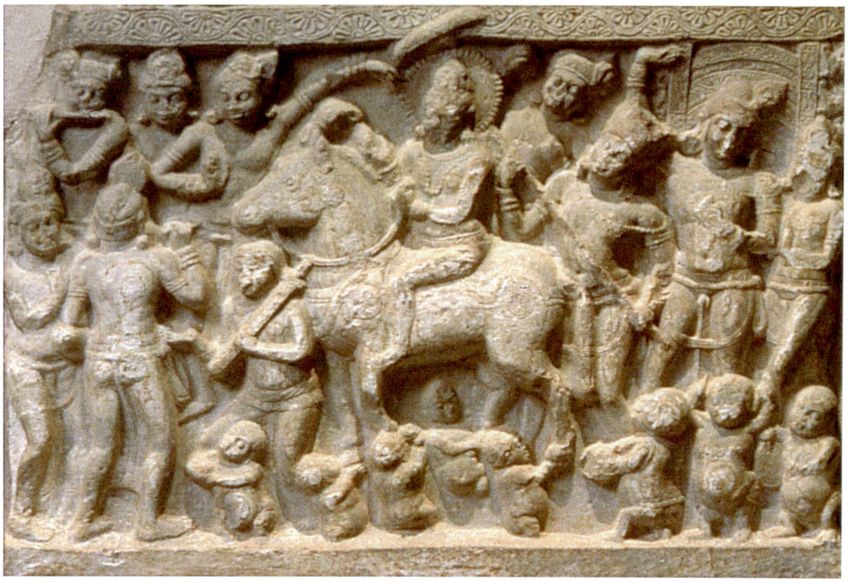

Figure 82 Great Departure of the Buddha, Nagarjunakonda, *c.* 3rd century CE, The Metropolitan Museum of Art, Fletcher Fund, 1928 (28.105)

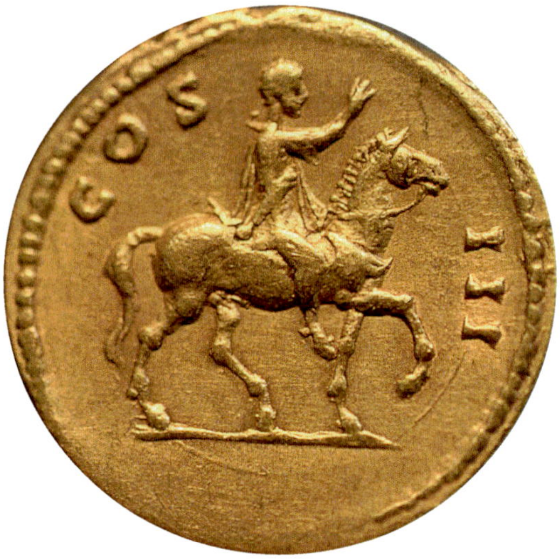

Figure 83 Hadrian bareheaded on horseback, reverse of *aureus* of Hadrian, 128–32 CE, American Numismatic Society, no. 1001.1.30102, from the former Huntington Collection

the earliest anthropomorphic form of the river goddess Gaṅgā (Sivaramamurti 1979: 3 and fig. 14). In each of their left hands they seem to be holding a plate or bowl. The source of this posture may well be Roman coins of Fides (**Fig. 85**), the personification of good faith and loyalty. She is represented on coins from the time of Vespasian (r. 69–79 CE) to the time of Constantine (r. 314–25 CE). There are many variants of the subject, but in the current example from the time of Antoninus Pius (139 CE), she is holding a bowl of fruit.[16] We certainly do not suggest that the Amaravati artist intended to represent Fides. He simply found the pose a good prototype for the Gaṅgā image.

The other coin I will discuss shows a figure which is repeated several times in Amaravati sculptures. In a relief of the Conversion of Nanda (**Fig. 86**), for example, we note on the lower left corner a female with a relaxed pose. One of her arms leans on the back of her chair. Could this not be an Indianized version of images of Salus, the Roman personification of wellbeing (**Fig. 87**), whose left arm leans on the back of her chair? A variant of the posture is repeated in the figure of Queen Māyā in both the British Museum (BM no. 1880,0709.5; illustrated in Knox 1992: 81, no. 25) and Government Museum, Chennai (**Fig. 88**) – versions of Śuddhodana's Visit to Queen Māyā. The above comparisons are just a small sample of the many available possibilities. While we might try to say that these comparisons are circumstantial, we must find some way to account for the increased number of poses and complex compositions in the art of Amaravati.

In three previous articles I have dealt with the use of spatial conventions in the art of southern India (Stone 2005, 2006, 2008). The comparisons we have shown are from both Roman painting and Roman sculpture. Many of the compositions are too complex to have been derived solely from coins so we will consider the possibility that Indian artists actually saw Roman paintings or even drawings. The most striking and literal example of the adaptation of a foreign composition is an unidentified battle scene from Nagarjunakonda (**Fig. 89**) belonging to the last quarter of the 3rd century CE.[17] The dominant figure is a man on horseback. The horse is in profile while the rider lifts his left arm up and back, exposing his chest to the viewer in three-quarter profile – a pose which has its roots in classical antiquity (cf. the Parthenon frieze). Two kneeling figures at the bottom of the composition beneath the horse have an ambiguous function. They may be read either as part of the

Figure 84 *Nāga* Mucalinda flanked by images of Gaṅgā, detail of a railing pillar from Amaravati, *c.* 2nd century CE, British Museum, 1880,0709.47

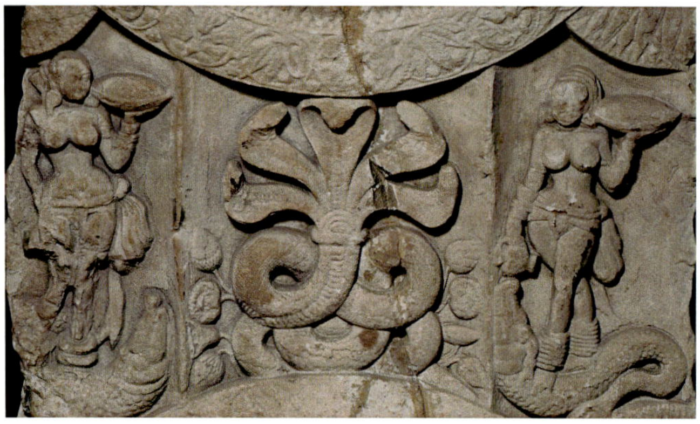

Figure 85 Fides, reverse of *sestertius* of Antoninus Pius, 139 CE, American Numismatic Society, no. 1995.11.172

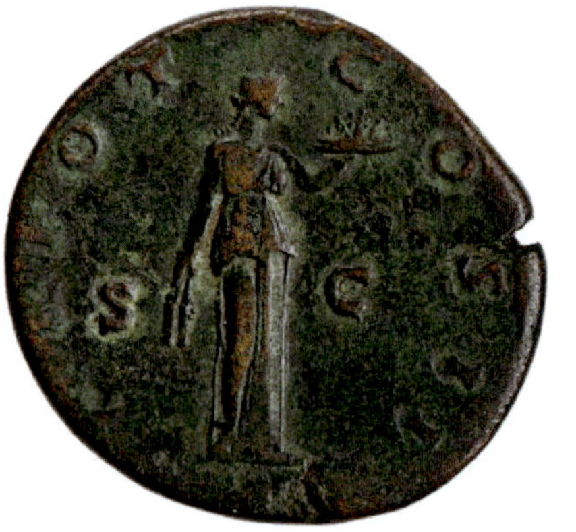

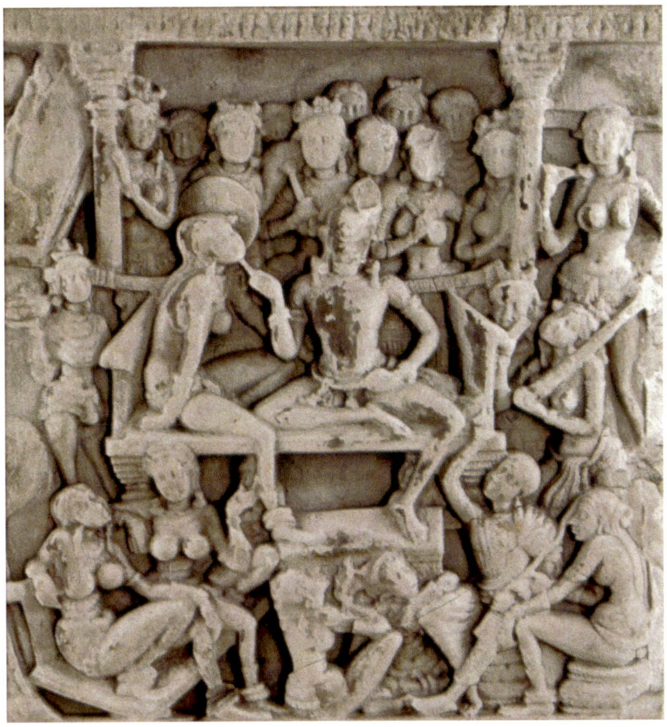

Figure 86 Conversion of Nanda, detail of railing coping from Amaravati, *c.* 3rd century CE, British Museum, 1880,0709.34

foreground, kneeling in supplication, or as under the rearing horse and about to be trampled. Most strikingly, in front of the horse is a man so foolhardy that his left leg is extended as if trying to kick the horse.

The Nagarjunakonda battle scene is based on a relief of Trajan riding against the Dacians (**Fig. 90**), part of the 'Great Trajanic Frieze' of around 110–17 CE and now placed in the Arch of Constantine.[18] At Nagarjunakonda the whole composition has been reversed. To facilitate our study, we have made a scan of the Nagarjunakonda relief which has been flipped from left to right (**Fig. 91**). This strongly suggests that images based upon the Trajanic relief were circulated in India and could be copied either directly or in reverse.[19] While making comparisons, we will refer to the reversed copy of the Nagarjunakonda relief as if it were the original. The dominant figure of the Trajanic relief is the emperor on his horse.[20] He is bare-headed, having left his helmet behind. His broken right arm is raised and a sharp diagonal to the lower right of the midpoint of the composition is suggested. It seems that Trajan originally carried a spear, and the direction of his action is towards a kneeling Dacian before the horse. The scene is clearly one of victory and defeat: the triumph of the emperor and the subjugation of his enemies. Visually, the left hand of the composition forms one group, the right hand another.

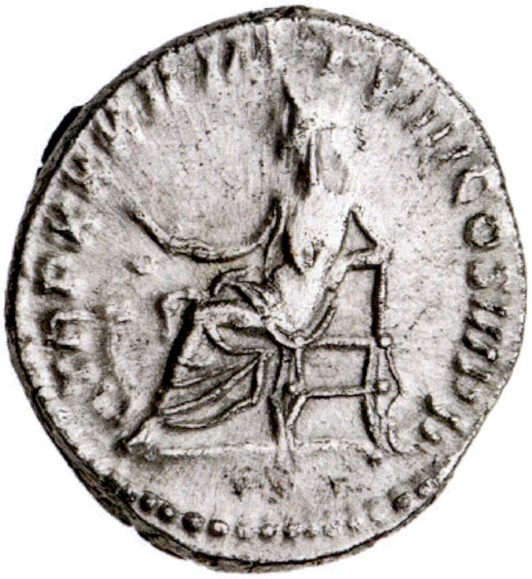

Figure 87 Salus, silver *denarius*, reverse of coin of Marcus Aurelius, 177–8 CE, American Numismatic Society, no. 1911.23.328

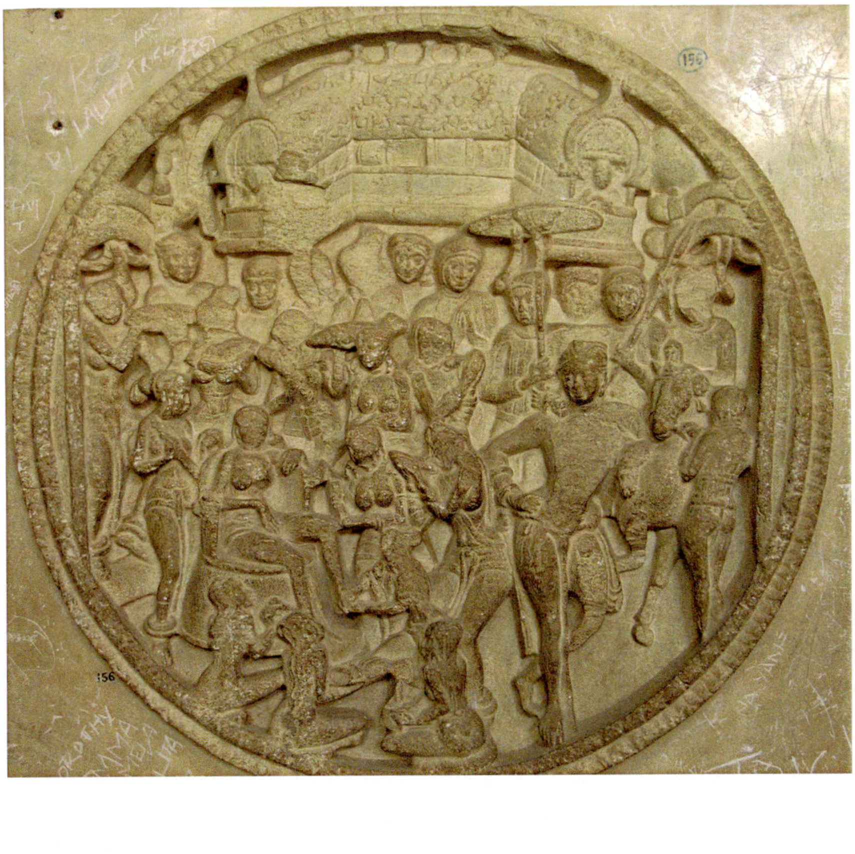

Figure 88 Śuddhodana's visit to Māyā, railing crossbar, Amaravati, *c.* 2nd century CE, Government Museum, Chennai (photograph: Christian Luczanits)

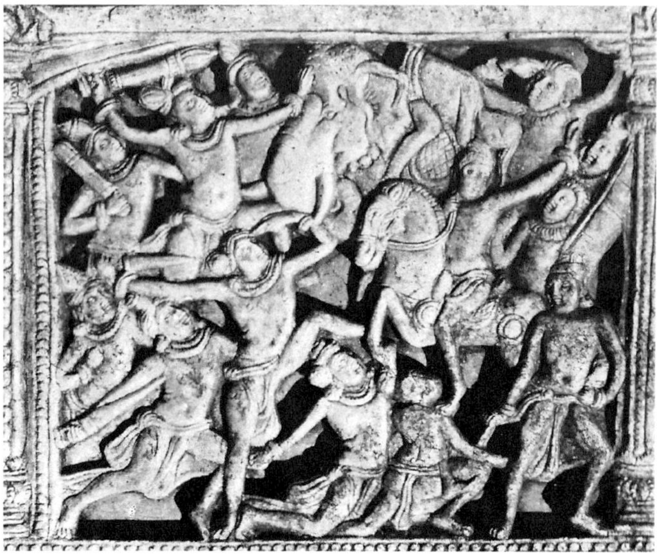

Figure 89 Battle scene, detail of an *āyaka* frieze, Site 2, *c.* late 3rd century CE, Archaeological Museum, Nagarjunakonda

Let us return to the Nagarjunakonda battle relief (**Fig. 91**). The main figure on the horse raises his right hand, which forms a diagonal leading towards the figure before the horse. Why the arm is raised in this manner is difficult to tell, but assuming this is a reverse copy of the relief of Trajan, the Nagarjunakonda artist clearly did not understand it for he did not include a spear. The Nagarjunakonda equestrian figure is not wearing the usual Indian turban, the equivalent perhaps of the un-helmeted Emperor, while the Nagarjunakonda 'enemy' does wear the usual Indian turban. With regard to the figure before the horse the error is comic. Instead of being in a pose of supplication he appears to be kicking the horse. While adapting the composition from the Roman prototype, the artist misunderstood the left foreleg of the horse and transplanted it to the man! The equivalent of the crouching Dacian, with one leg bent and the other extending behind him is rather clumsily represented by the two figures beneath the horse. Nevertheless, they are representations of supplication and submission, which is very much part of the Roman repertory. According to Richard Brilliant (1963: 189), motifs of submission and reverence went back to the beginning of imperial art and their use was broadened by the 3rd century CE to include both civil and military occasions.

The reader may realize that we are suggesting that the battle relief in South India, datable to the last quarter of the third century CE, has its source in a relief of the first quarter of the 2nd century CE. In fact, Roman images of victory compositions were disseminated throughout the Roman Empire for purposes of political propaganda and provided the source material for the Sassanian victory reliefs of Shāpūr I (r. 241–71 CE).[21] While the Sassanians used earlier Roman compositions to state that they were now victors over the Romans, we admit that we have absolutely no idea why the Andhra artists found such a composition suitable to copy in an Indian context. It is amusing to note that if we compare figure to figure, all the Romans have become Indians and it is only the composition which unmistakably survives. The artisans of Nagarjunakonda did not copy the Shāpūr reliefs, which are in Persian style, but certainly based their compositions on Roman copies of Roman originals. We know from our studies that Egypt was one of the sources for Roman imagery in Gandhara,[22] and we also know that there were Roman garrisons in Egypt. Could this imagery have been transported to India via Egypt? But the question is, 'In what form?'

In 1997, Peter J. Holliday published an article on Roman triumphal painting which opened up a new avenue of study. While there are in fact no surviving examples of Roman triumphal painting, he was able to reconstruct them through literary descriptions, wall paintings and reliefs. Surprisingly, he included in his discussion Andrea Mantegna's *The Triumphs of Caesar: Trumpeters, Bearers of Standards and Banners* (Canvas I) painted between 1484 and 1494,[23] which he convincingly demonstrates was a reasonable adaptation of ancient painting. From literary references, as well as surviving wall paintings and reliefs, we can begin to have some idea of what these paintings may have looked like in ancient times.

Roman triumphal paintings were intended to be carried in triumphal processions to commemorate victorious military campaigns, along with *spolia* including captured craftsmen and slaves, for the purpose of self-glorification and propaganda. The paintings were not all of one size and shape; those executed on large panels were called *tabulae*,

Figure 90 Trajan defeating the Dacians, 110–17 CE, Arch of Constantine, Rome

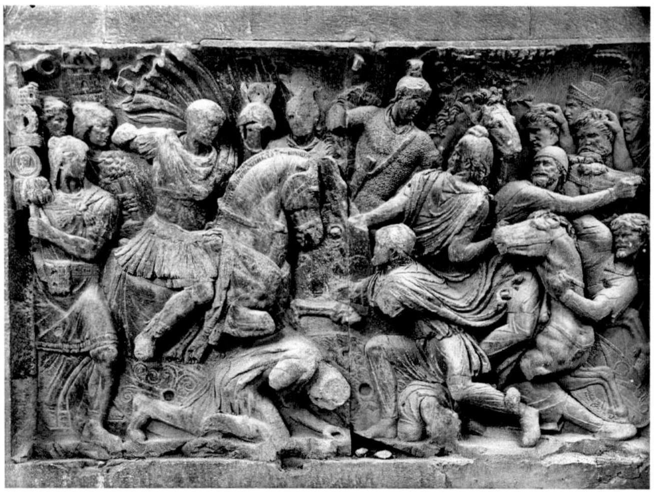

Figure 91 Reverse of Figure 89

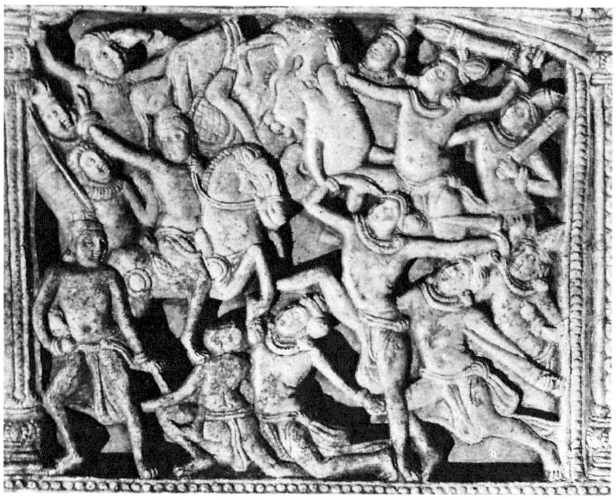

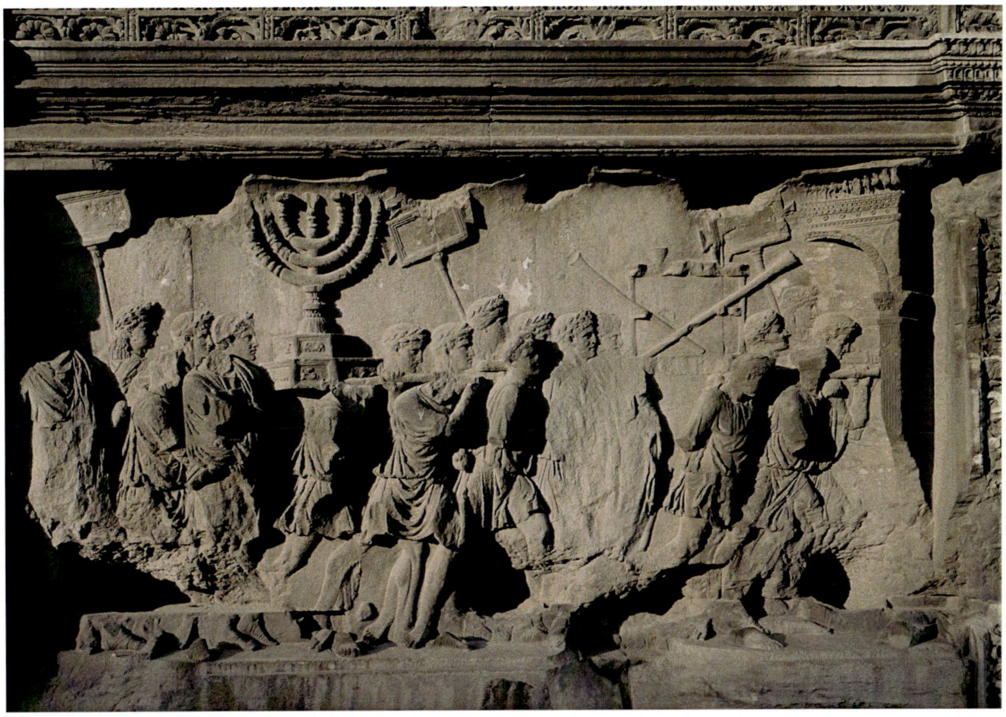

Figure 92 The triumph over Jerusalem, Arch of Titus, Rome, *c.* 90 CE

and could easily be carried in procession. Mantegna's interpretation of literary sources caused him to produce a painting with various scenes in horizontal rows. Accompanying these paintings were sign boards called *tituli*, intended to explain the pictures on display. Three of these are carried in the victory procession of the Triumph over Jerusalem on the Arch of Titus (*c.* 90 CE) in Rome (**Fig. 92**). Also carried in triumphal processions were various types of flags and standards.[24] An interesting example is found on an extremely damaged relief, published in a line drawing,[25] from Dura Europos, which shows a military standard near its centre. There appears to be fringes on the bottom, suggesting it is made of cloth. There are, in fact, two Nagarjunakonda reliefs from the latter part of the 3rd century CE which may illustrate Roman standards. We are reluctant to use the Latin terminology as we do not know what, if anything was painted on them. The first (**Fig. 93**) has a simple standard with a square top looking very much like the Dura Europos image. We do not know if it was intended to show pictures or writing. The second is on a magnificent *āyaka* frieze representing an episode from the Conversion of Nanda (**Fig. 94**). The standard in question is much more complex as the upper portion of it seems to have two parts. There is a flat board with alternating textures in horizontal rows. This seems to be partly covered with a cloth, which partially reveals the image beneath it. We believe that both these images are slightly misunderstood Roman standards or banners which may have been transported to India. A comparison of the Nagarjunakonda standards (**Figs 95a, 95c**) with that of Rome (**Fig. 95b**) leaves little doubt that they are related to each other. This, and similar objects, may have conveyed Roman triumphal painting to India.[26] Such paintings could account for many of the Roman features of Indian art which we now see in the art of southern India.

In this brief essay, I have dealt with several topics rather than developing one theme of the many reflections of Roman art in southern India. Any one of the comparisons which I have made, or which have been made by others, might seem like a coincidence. But there are too many

Figure 93 Dasaratha *jātaka*, dome slab, late 3rd century CE, Nagarjunakonda, Archaeological Museum, Nagarjunakonda (photograph: Akira Shimada)

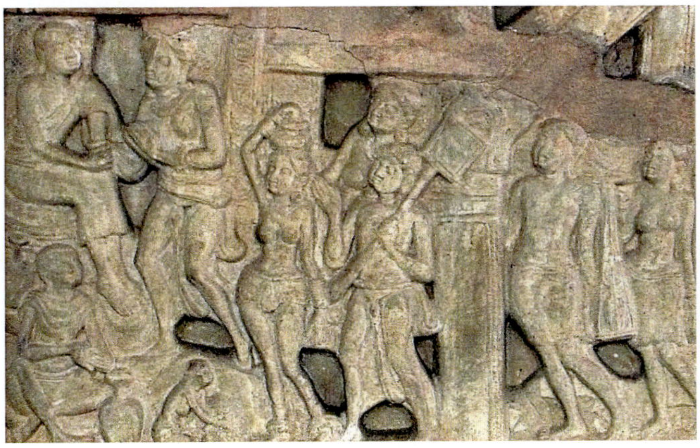

Figure 94 Scene from the Conversion of Nanda, late 3rd century CE, Archaeological Museum, Nagarjunakonda (photograph: John C. Huntington)

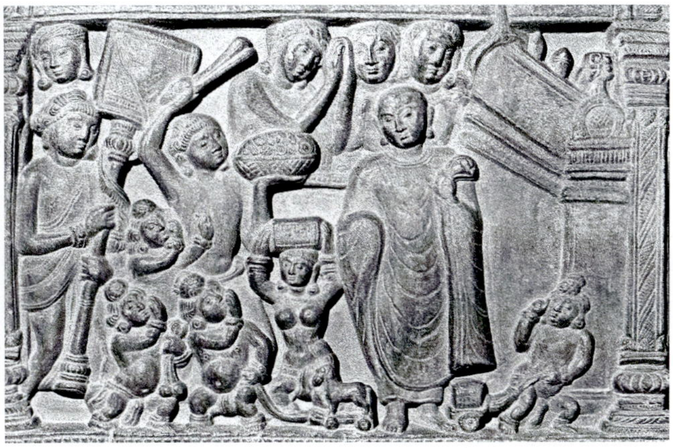

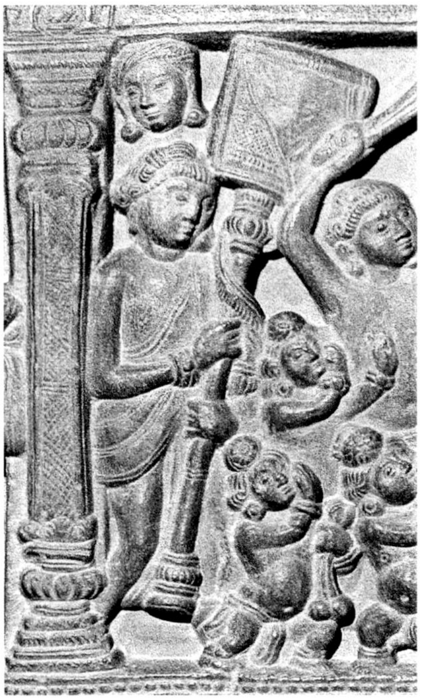

Figure 95a Standard (detail of Figure 94)

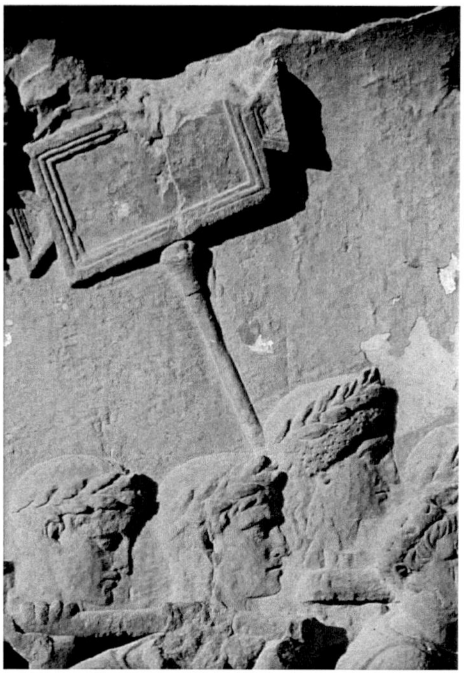

Figure 95b *Titulus* (detail of Figure 92)

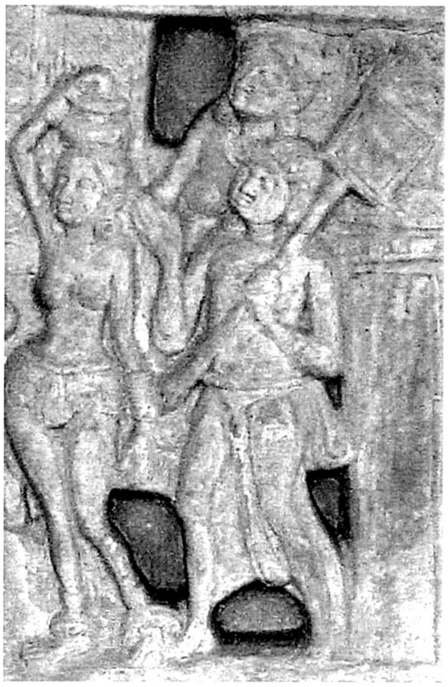

Figure 95c Standard (detail of Figure 93)

'coincidences' to ignore. With regard to the problem of the assembly hall, it was suggested by Varadpande that it might have evolved from an Indian prototype. My own thoughts about this are that it was modified under western influence. A study of motifs adopted from coins is much simpler. Roman coins were abundant in India and were often pierced to be used as jewellery. Highly skilled craftsmen, such as those of Andhra Pradesh, could easily choose a motif on a Roman coin and use it somewhere in the many complex compositions of Buddhist narrative. I have illustrated a few examples but there are many more.

The one problem which currently stands alone is the source of the battle scene from Site 2, Nagarjunakonda. It has no parallels in India, and has been referred to in literature many times as reflecting a Trajanic relief. But how could such a composition have been seen in India? Certainly we have no evidence that Roman sculpture was shipped to India. The only possibility is that it was derived from a scroll painting, which could have arrived in India via Roman Egypt. While we have touched upon the use of Roman triumphal painting as a possible means of transmission of the battle scene, there are many more sections of compositions in Andhra Pradesh which require study in this regard. Thus it is the confluence of all the individual reflections of Roman art in southern India which leads us to believe that this is a subject well worth pursuing.

Notes

1 Working across disciplines can be difficult, but I am grateful that both Richard Abdy and William E. Metcalf prevented me from publishing two 18th-century Roman 'Fantasy' coins! I thank Peter Holliday for his article on Roman triumphal painting, which greatly influenced my ideas on the transmission of Roman art to India, and for his encouragement, which gave me the strength to go ahead with this study. Similarly, I heartily thank both Christopher Lightfoot and Prudence Harper, who guided me to many unexpected references. Above all, Akira Shimada, through his own writings, as well as his careful work as an editor, has rekindled my interest in the complex problems of the art of Andhra Pradesh.

2 Those scholars most intimately connected with the archaeological material in Andhra Pradesh and Tamil Nadu are the greatest supporters of the theory of Roman influence. C. Sivaramamurti was formerly the Curator of the Archaeological Section of the Government Museum, Chennai (Sivaramamurti 1976); R. Nagaswamy was Director of the State Department of Archaeology in Tamil Nadu (Nagaswamy 1995) and V.V. Krishna Sastry was his counterpart in Andhra Pradesh (Krishna Sastry 1998). While Nagaswamy and Krishna Sastry built their theories on archaeological evidence, Sivaramamurti built his on style. Clearly, South Indian scholars have accepted the influence of Rome.

3 Vasavasamudram, not far from Mamallapuram, was occupied for a short period around the 3rd century CE; Karur, in Trichy District, which is identified as the capital of the Chera rulers during the Śangam age, showed a greater contact with Rome; Kodumanal seems to be a source for jewellery supplied to the Romans (Nagaswamy 1981: 337–9).

4 The 1928 edition of the *Māṇimēkalai* uses the term *yavana* carpenter (Krishnaswami Aiyangar 1928: 159).

5 A fascinating document, on a papyrus of the mid 2nd century CE, gives the terms of a loan agreement for a merchant to ship goods between Alexandria and Muziris, the great trading port in western India. It has been suggested that Muziris had a colony of foreigners who served as middlemen between their countrymen and local merchants (Casson 1989: 24). Further papyrological evidence cited by Manfred Raschke points to the fact that most of the papyri and ostraca mentioning Indian spices belong to the 3rd and 4th centuries CE (Raschke 1975: 244–5). An interesting fragment of an ostracon found in Egypt was written by an Indian merchant living in Egypt. According to Richard Salomon (1991: 731–3), the script on the inscription resembles the form of Prakrit used in the inscriptions of Amaravati and Nagarjunakonda.

6 While the map is frequently discussed, it is rarely accompanied by a photograph – a problem which has been solved by the creation of a new interactive website; see http://peutinger.atlantides.org/map-a/ (accessed 1 July 2016).

7 Amongst the many arguments referred to by Ray (1994: 66) is the suggestion by Metzler that the setting up of temples to Roman emperors was a diplomatic gesture by Indian chieftains.

8 A recent study of the Peutinger Map by Richard J.A. Talbert suggests that it was done about 300 CE by the Diocletian Tetrarchy as a testimony to Rome's glory (Talbert 2010: 133). As Rome was in the centre of the map, the implication is that all countries included were under Roman rule. While India was certainly never under Roman rule, its inclusion here may indicate that, directly or

indirectly, it was still a trading partner with Rome during the florescence of Nagarjunakonda as well as other late Andhra sites. It is also possible that its inclusion reflects an earlier period of Rome's glory. But whatever interpretation we may use for the existence of the Roman architecture, we are still left with the problem of lack of archaeological evidence.

9 In the centre of the quadrangle were the remains of a piece of stone whose function is unknown. Soundara Rajan (2006: 110) refers to this stone as a 'circular abacus'. It was originally constructed on the foot of the hill at Site 17, Nagarjunakonda. See map in Sarkar and Misra 1966: pl. 13. It originally overlooked the Krishna River, and was later transplanted to the eastern bank of Nagarjunasagar dam where it can be seen by visitors today. Even in its transplanted place, its acoustics are excellent.

10 Functionally, in the Greek world, the *bouleuterion* was intended for meetings of citizens, a function which would have no place in India, but if the *bouleuterion* was a source for the 'amphitheatre', it would be for form, not for function.

11 Contemporary punch-marked coins were illustrated at Bharhut in the scene of the Gift of Jetavaṇa Grove (Huntington 1985: 71, fig. 5.16). In Andhra Pradesh, similar square coins appear in the relief of Cakravartin and his Seven Jewels from Jaggayyapeta (ibid.: fig. 5.36). More importantly, there are round coins depicted on the memorial pillar to Cāṃtamūla I at Nagarjunakonda (Stone 1994: 34, fig. 54). The accompanying inscription on the pillar describes the king as 'giver of crores of gold' (Vogel 1930–1: 63–4, Pillar Inscription L).

12 M. Price wrote an insightful article on the relationship between Roman paintings and Roman coins (Price 1981: 69–75).

13 This image has been described by Knox (1992: 144) as the 'Worship of a pillar in a small domed building'.

14 Akira Shimada has pointed out to me the illustration of a Bactrian camel on an Amaravati relief (BM no. 1880,0709.52; illustrated in Knox 1992: 187, no. 104). It is clear that the artist of this small shrine did not know quite how to interpret the iconography using local imagery so he seems to have borrowed from Gandhara.

15 The available illustrations of the excavated coin are difficult to see (Ramachandran 1953: 30, fig. 36-1) so I illustrate another coin in the collection of the American Numismatic Society struck from the same die.

16 An imitation of a coin from the time of Antoninus Pius (147–8 CE) was found in the Tirukoillur hoard in Tamil Nadu (Krishnamurthy 1998: 149, no. 15, lower left).

17 The relief was part of an exhibition of Indian sculpture held in the United States in 1964. The catalogue suggests that the piece might represent the War of Relics (?) (Cleveland Museum of Art 1964: fig. 46).

18 We are fortunate to have obtained a photograph of the relief taken in the 1890s when the details were still crisp.

19 In connection with his studies on Ajanta painting, Walter Spink (2008: 41) has suggested that compositions might have been transferred to the walls from cloth paintings. We believe that a similar mode of transfer of images could also have applied to stone sculpture and the transfer could easily have been done in reverse. While we have literary evidence of cloth paintings from India, no early examples have survived from the subcontinent because of its wet climate. However, a magnificent fragmentary Kuṣān cloth painting in Gandharan style belonging to about the 2nd century CE was found in the Xinjiang province of China and preserved there, probably owing to its dry climate (Marshak 2006: 947–63). I thank Judith Lerner for this reference.

20 For an understanding of the Trajanic frieze, I have been aided by Leander-Touati (1987).

21 It is well known that victory compositions were also disseminated in Parthian territory, as the Romans defeated the Parthians. In turn, their successors the Sassanians were victorious over the Romans and used the same type of compositions of domination and supplication in reverse, with the Sassanian king in the position of domination. This is well documented in a series of victory reliefs of the second Sassanian king, Shāpūr I, who reigned 241–71 CE (Mackintosh 1973: 181–203). This is very shortly before the Nagarjunakonda 'victory' relief was created in Nagarjunakonda in the last quarter of the 3rd century CE. I thank Prudence O. Harper for the reference to the Mackintosh article.

22 The importance of the trade route from the Roman world through Alexandria and then to Gandhara is discussed in detail in Stone (2004).

23 Holliday 1997: 134, fig. 2.

24 Brilliant 1967: pl. 90a; Coarelli and Patterson 2008: pl. F.

25 Butcher 2003: 400, fig. 189.

26 While we are suggesting that Roman triumphal painting may have been a means of transmission between Rome and India, we are not the first to do so. In 1929 Albert Ippel wrote a small book on this very subject. The comparisons in the plates are fascinating, but the text is so completely ahistorical that the book was completely ignored (Ippel 1929).

Chapter 6
Mahinda's Visit to Amaravati?: Narrative Connections between Buddhist Communities in Andhra and Sri Lanka

Catherine Becker

For better or worse, Ananda Coomaraswamy's pronouncement in 1908 that 'Sinhalese art is essentially Indian', has served as a starting point for discussions of connections between the art of India and Sri Lanka (1908: v). This comment has a troubling effect, tying South Asian art to nationalist politics – with 'Sinhalese' and 'Indian' posited as distinct and ahistorical categories even if the art that corresponds to these political entities is 'essentially' the same – and also encouraging Sinhala nationalist responses that seek to tease out uniquely 'Sinhalese' characteristics of the art from the island nation. Nevertheless, Coomaraswamy's remark recognizes a long history of artistic impulses that appear in both South India and Sri Lanka. For example, a comparison of sculpture produced in the early centuries CE for Buddhist sites along the Krishna River valley in Andhra Pradesh and the sculptural remains associated with the Buddhist communities in Sri Lanka reveals numerous similarities. Juxtaposing a 2nd- to 3rd- century CE standing Buddha image from Amaravati in Andhra (**Fig. 96**) with a 5th- to 6th-century CE standing Buddha now in the Archaeological Museum in Anuradhapura (**Fig. 97**) demonstrates a shared understanding of a Buddha's perfected body and features. Both sculptures render the Buddha with a somewhat athletic build that is only partially visible beneath robes which fall over the Buddha's body in distinctive curving folds. Similarly, the appearance of common motifs in Andhra and Anuradhapura, such as the use of moonstones to mark the thresholds of religious structures, provides evidence of a shared understanding of the adornment of sacred spaces between these regions. Moreover, as Osmund Bopearachchi has observed, a number of limestone objects seemingly imported from Andhra – or, more tantalizingly, perhaps carved in Sri Lanka by a crew of sculptors from Andhra – were found during excavations of the Bodhighara near the Jetavanarama *stūpa* in Anuradhapura, further attesting to close connections between the Buddhist communities in these regions (Bopearachchi 2008). In his careful study (1990) of the extant remains of Sri Lanka's early Buddhist sculpture, Ulrich von Schroeder also explored some of the artistic connections between Andhra and Sri Lanka; Sree Padma and John Clifford Holt state that von Schroeder's evidence reveals 'striking stylistic affinities reinforcing the view that Sinhalese artists modeled their work on Andhra prototypes' (Padma and Holt 2008: 119). While this is a more precise statement than Coomaraswamy's claim one hundred years earlier, the underlying assumption remains essentially the same: that art from India served as inspiration for works produced in Sri Lanka. Perhaps our discussions of connections between these two regions within South Asia remain too focused on looking for the origins of artistic expression in one country or the other.

In an attempt to expand our approach to the obvious links between Buddhist communities in Andhra and Sri Lanka, I propose that we shift our tactics from tracing stylistic similarities, the shared use of specific motifs or the movement of objects from one region to another – although these are important modes of inquiry that should continue to be considered – and instead investigate shared narrative strategies between these two regions. This is a challenging

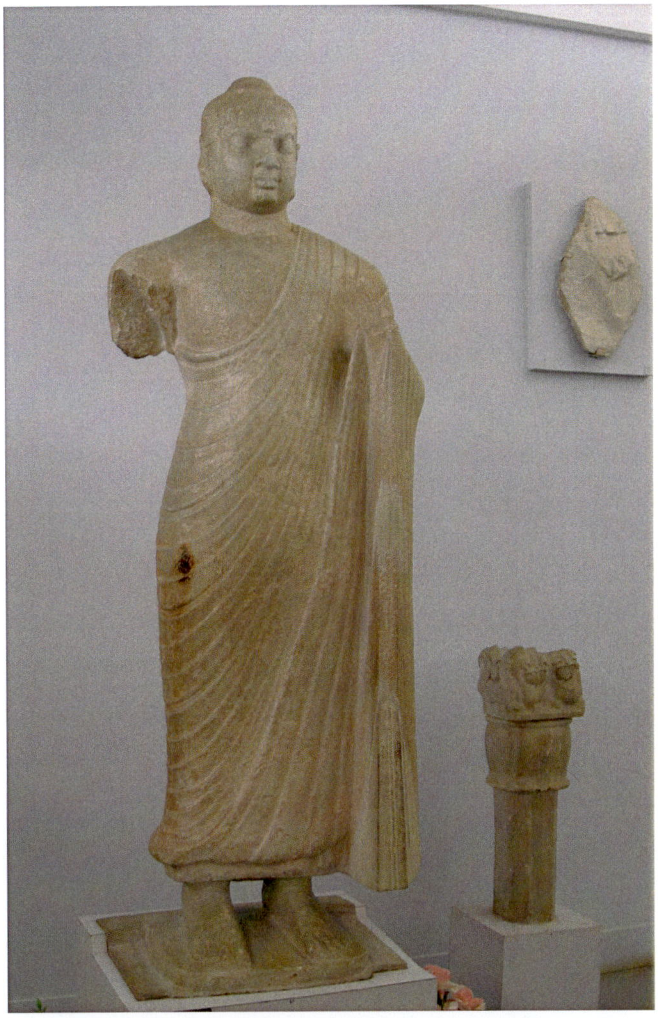

Figure 96 Standing Buddha, Amaravati, 2nd–3rd century CE, Archaeological Museum, Amaravati, acc. no. 16

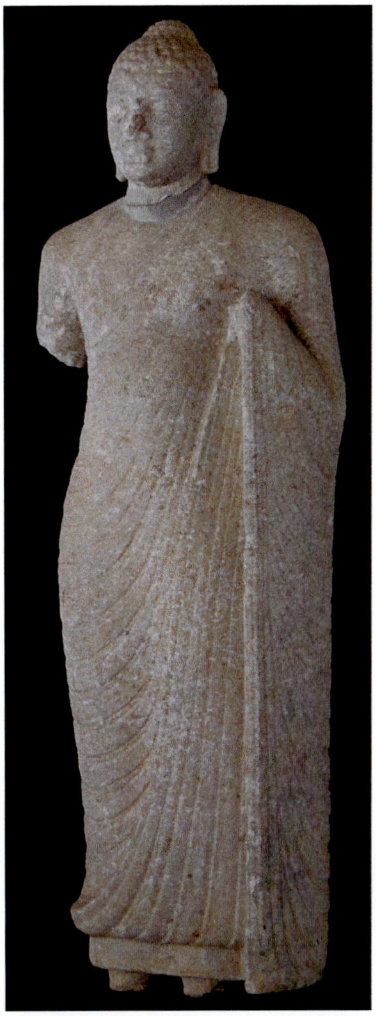

Figure 97 Standing Buddha, Chunnakam, 5th–6th century CE, Archaeological Museum, Anuradhapura (photograph: Françis Ory)

proposition, as the sculptural remains from Buddhist sites along Andhra's Krishna River valley in the 2nd and 3rd centuries CE feature an abundance of narratives carved in stone, while the contemporaneous and often later remains from Sri Lanka lack such a profusion of sculptural narratives. Nevertheless, such a comparison of narrative proclivities is possible as Sri Lanka boasts a robust literary tradition in the form of the Pali *vaṃsa* texts. The earliest of these, the *Dīpavaṃsa* and the *Mahāvaṃsa*, are often consulted as historical accounts of the founding of Sri Lanka, but they are also clearly polemical texts detailing the royal patronage of the Mahāvihāra in Anuradhapura. As something of an experiment, I juxtapose these two story-telling traditions – that is to say, narrative sculpture from Andhra and key passages from Sri Lanka's *Mahāvaṃsa* – in order to explore the rhetorical strategies employed in both sources to advance claims for unique and authentic Buddhist homelands in regions that are temporally and geographically remote from the life of the historical Buddha. Although the *Mahāvaṃsa* helps to clarify unidentified relief sculptures from Amaravati and Phanigiri, there seems to be little benefit in assuming that these select sculptural remains from Andhra actually depict the *Mahāvaṃsa* or, provocatively, that such sculptural narratives might have inspired the Pali chronicles. The impulse to seek a single source for such ideas suggests that 'Andhra' and 'Lanka' were fixed and distinct categories. In contrast, I see value in understanding how Buddhist communities in neighbouring regions employed similar strategies to justify the creation of new monasteries, encourage lay devotion and legitimize their relic caches. Noticing these parallels in how Buddhists in Andhra and Sri Lanka conceptualized the role of storytelling allows us to understand linkages between these communities without insisting on unidirectional models of cultural borrowing, which often seem content to determine the origin of a style, motif or concept without exploring how these artistic linkages might testify to meaningful and thoughtful gestures. This essay, which I hope to complement with future publications, concludes by proposing some new directions for the study of artistic and cultural interaction among the Buddhist communities in Andhra and Sri Lanka.

An unidentified relief sculpture from Amaravati

The primary impetus for this investigation is an enigmatic damaged sculptural fragment that once adorned the railing of the main *stūpa* at Amaravati and is now housed in the British Museum (**Fig. 98**). Akira Shimada has convincingly dated this limestone coping fragment to the second half of the 1st century CE (Shimada 2013: 99). At first glance the events depicted are not immediately clear, although the activity of the humans throughout the composition suggests

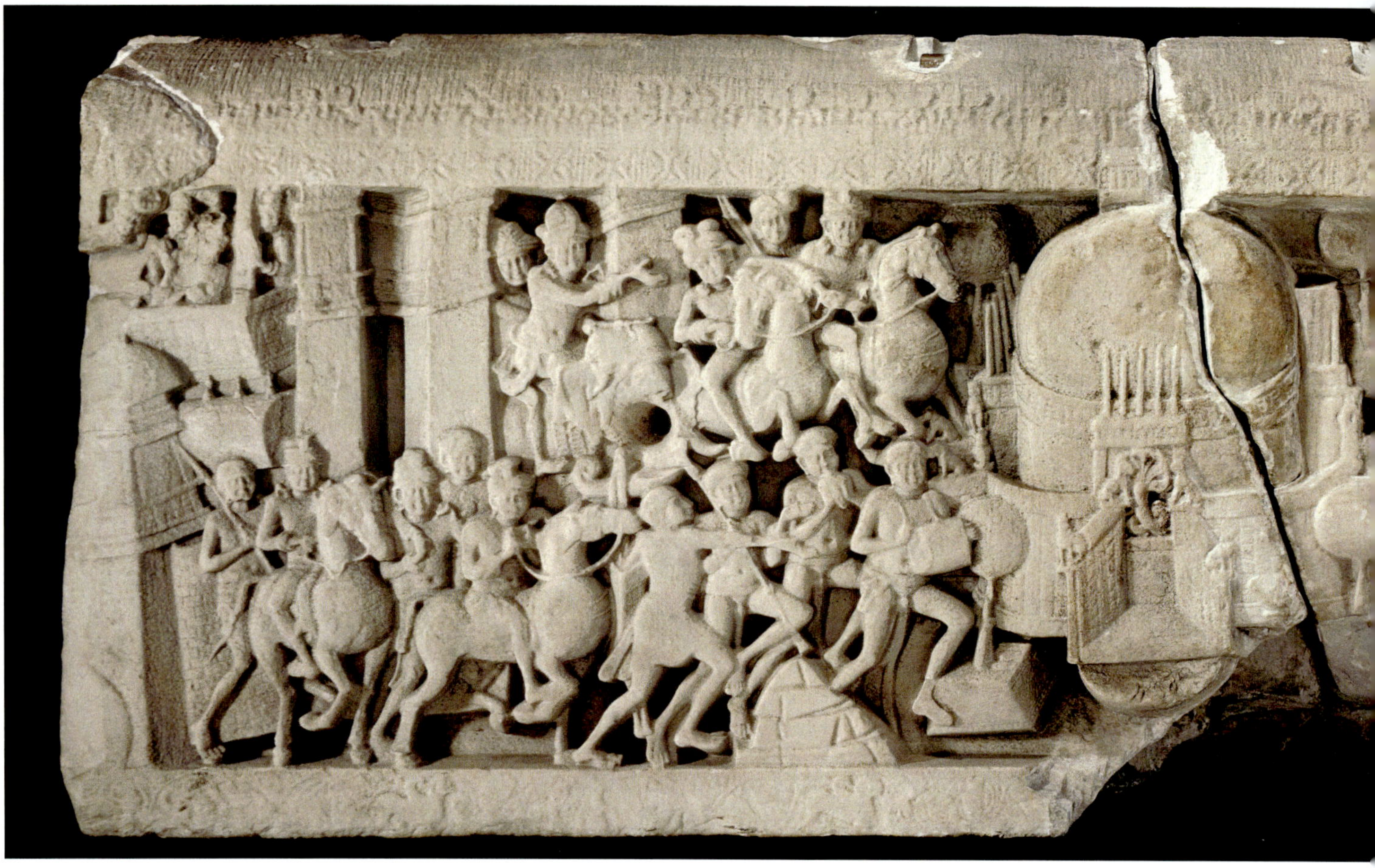

Figure 98 Railing coping fragment, Amaravati, c. 1st–2nd centuries CE, British Museum, 1880,0709.19–20

the unfolding of a continuous narrative, with figures repeated to convey action across time and space. Moving from left to right, the viewer encounters five scenes. The action begins with a flurry of movement, as a procession of figures that has assembled outside a city wall rushes towards the viewer's right. In the foreground, some figures ride on horseback while others undertake their journey on foot. Clasping spears and swords, our figures seem ready to subdue an enemy or pounce on a wild animal. The vanguard includes a man pounding a drum suspended from his neck while nearby his compatriot puffs out his cheeks to blow into a conch shell – perhaps inviting the viewer to imagine the cacophony of thrumming hooves mingled with steady drumbeats and the resounding call of the conch. The deeply carved legs of the horses and men – jutting out at odd angles – create vivid and varied juxtapositions of light and dark, a sort of visual cacophony that conveys the energetic movement of this throng. The musicians in the foreground also step over a rocky formation, which, in the visual shorthand of Andhra's sculptors, usually indicates mountainous terrain, suggesting that a journey into the countryside is under way. Directly above the procession of musicians and armed troops additional figures appear on horseback. Two figures astride an elephant emerge from a gate in the city's wall. The presence of the elephant suggests a royal entourage, perhaps storming out of the town for a battle, a hunt or a ceremonial display of royal pomp.[1] As our gaze follows the charging figures to the right, we encounter the second scene and experience a sudden pause in the action, as a *stūpa* fills the vertical expanse of this frieze. I analyse this *stūpa* more fully below, but in presenting a sudden visual shift – from active bustling human figures to a still architectural space – the *stūpa* most immediately functions to arrest the motion of the royal entourage and to prepare the viewer for another vignette in this visual narrative.

The action on the coping fragment resumes to the viewer's right of the *stūpa*, with three additional scenes. A crowd of people has assembled around a levitating figure in monastic robes. He faces out towards the viewer – although damage to the stone has obliterated his face – and raises his open-palmed right hand at a slight angle in a gesture that suggests explication.[2] Surrounding this hovering figure, men in turbans clasp their hands together in respect while five monks adopt similarly reverent gestures. The sculptor not only employed subtle hierarchical scale to emphasize the importance of the levitating figure in this crowd, but also carved a deep trough of negative space around the figure to help the viewer understand that the figure is surrounded by air. The toes of the floating figure point downwards to indicate that they are dangling freely rather than supporting the weight of the standing body. These toes also hover above the head of a seated man, whose gesture of reverence seems directed to the levitating figure while his seated position links him to a larger group of seated men to the viewer's right. This seated man appears to serve as a visual pivot guiding the viewer to the next vignette, which features the turbaned men now seated and listening to a seated figure in monastic robes, behind whom four monks have gathered. All the figures sit directly on the ground; two trees nearby

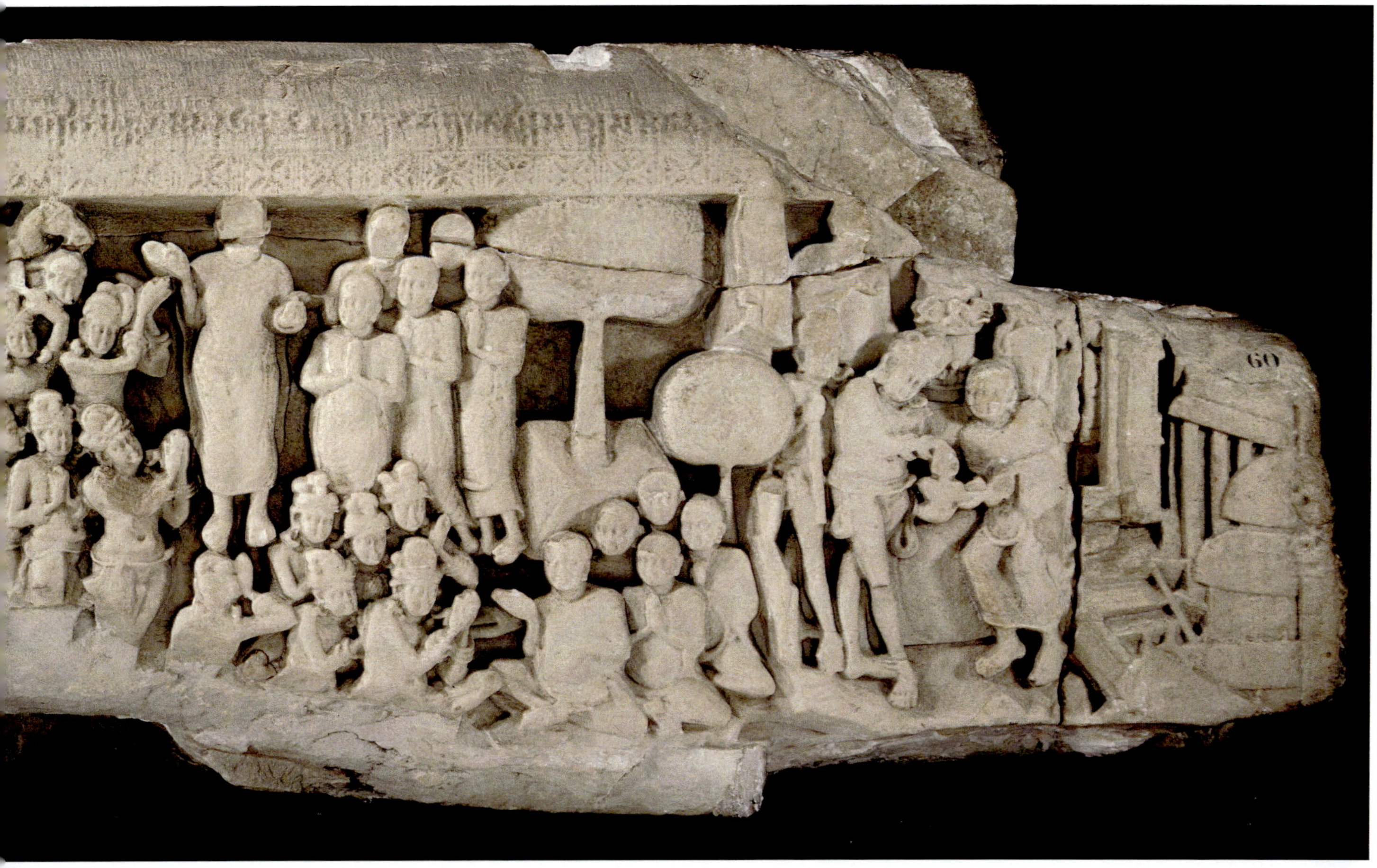

indicate that this teaching scene unfolds in a grove of trees. Furthest to the viewer's right, the fifth and final scene is the most damaged portion of the coping frieze. The events have shifted from the grove to a small complex of buildings, with a staircase, the rounded roofline of a hall and a pillared structure still visible at the far right edge of the relief. In the foreground a royal or elite figure, wearing a turban and jewels, leans forward with a water pot and pours water on the hands of a figure in monastic robes, presumably to ratify the exchange of the gift of the buildings behind these figures.

Although the sculptors of this railing coping from Amaravati crafted an animated series of events, scholars have yet to agree on a plausible interpretation for the narrative depicted here. Phillipe Stern and Mireille Bénisti, perhaps noting the dominance of the *stūpa* within the larger composition, refer to it simply as a scene of adoration to a *stūpa* (Stern and Bénisti 1957: 375–80). Douglas Barrett hazards an interpretation that this fragment represents the Buddha's visit to Kapilavastu and King Śuddhodana's encounter with his newly enlightened son (Barrett 1954a: 67). Yet Barrett seems not entirely convinced by his own interpretation and remarks that 'if this interpretation is correct, it is noteworthy that the Buddha is trice represented without a halo' (ibid.). Indeed, the absence of halos throughout the composition prevents the easy identification of any figure as the Buddha. Aside from the monastic robes, these figures also lack other obvious marks of a Buddha.

A detail of a frieze from Nagarjunakonda helps to elucidate the Buddha's iconography as often represented in Andhra (**Fig. 99**). This panel, depicting an episode from the story of the conversion of Nanda, features the Buddha seated on a throne and displaying the standard iconography of an enlightened being: cranial protuberance; *ūrṇā*, the flaming tuft of hair between the Buddha's eyes; elongated earlobes; and snail shells curls. The sculptor of this panel has also carefully rendered the Buddha's followers. The monks adopt a variety of gestures and poses: some clasp their hands in a

Figure 99 A gathering of monks (detail of a drum frieze), Nagarjunakonda, *c.* 3rd century CE, Archaeological Museum, Nagarjunakonda, acc. no. 3

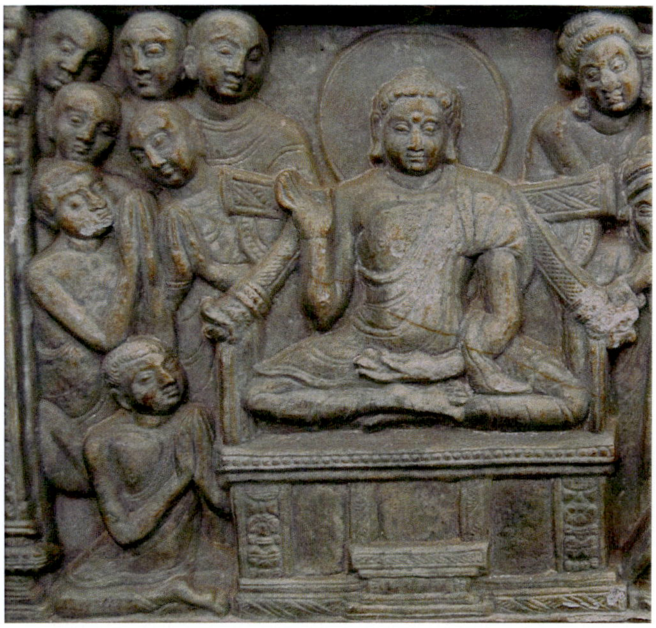

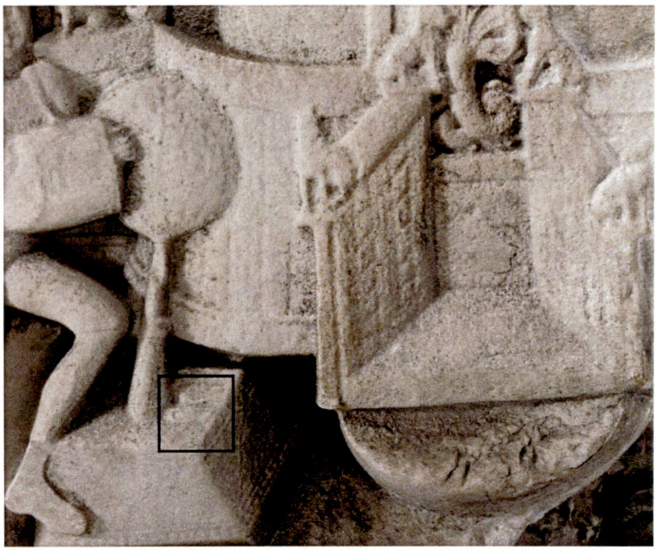

Figure 100 Footprints (detail of Figure 98)

gesture of veneration and gaze adoringly at the Buddha while others turn as if to chat with their neighbours. Close examination reveals that the monks even have varying degrees of stubble on their heads, some appear to be entirely bald while others are rendered with a hairline to suggest that a few days' growth of hair has emerged. The monks in the Nagarjunakonda relief resemble the robe-clad figures in the coping relief from Amaravati. Barrett's interpretation of the three largest and most prominent of these monastic figures – presumably it is the same figure that appears levitating, teaching and receiving a royal offering – as the Buddha is unwarranted. Rather than an event from the life of the Buddha, this railing frieze seems to depict an episode involving members of the monastic community, with one monk cast in the role of a miracle-performing teacher.

Reading the *Mahāvaṃsa* alongside the Amaravati railing frieze

If we set aside Barrett's assumption that the scene depicts the Buddha but understand it rather as chronicling the activities of a monk, then this becomes a tale of royal and monastic interaction and the subsequent founding of a monastery. In fact, some of the events depicted here roughly correspond to descriptions of Mahinda's transmission of Buddhism to Sri Lanka during the reign of Aśoka. This story, known from texts such as the *Dīpavaṃsa*, the *Mahāvaṃsa* and the considerably later *Thūpavaṃsa*,[3] describes Mahinda as rising up in the air with an entourage of monks in order to journey from India to the pleasant Missaka Mountain, near Anuradhapura (Geiger and Bode 1912: 89–90). According to the *Mahāvaṃsa* version of these events, at the moment of Mahinda's arrival King Devānampiyatissa had just left the palace with his own entourage of hunters and begun the journey to Missaka Mountain, perhaps paralleled in the frieze by the small rocky mound in the foreground. Although initially afraid when they first encountered Mahinda and his fellow monks, the king and his hunting party soon laid down their weapons, and Mahinda, after ascertaining that the king was sufficiently intelligent, preached to him (Geiger and Bode 1912: 93). The *Mahāvaṃsa* then details some anxiety on the part of the king about properly hosting the monks, particularly regarding where the monks might reside. The elephant stalls were cleaned and adorned with canopies, but upon reflection were deemed too small for the monks. Finally, Mahāmegha-park was identified as the right location. The king, 'taking a splendid vase, … poured water (in token) of giving, over the hand of the *thera* Mahinda with the words: "This Mahāmegha-park do I give to the brotherhood." As the water fell on the ground, the great earth quaked. And the protector of the earth asked the (*thera*): "Wherefore does the earth quake?' And he replied: "Because the doctrine is (from henceforth) founded in the island"' (Geiger and Bode 1912: 99). Thus the first monastery in Sri Lanka was purportedly inaugurated.

While sculptors in Andhra and, indeed, everywhere were necessarily selective in their choice of the key episodes from the larger narratives they depicted, the text of the *Mahāvaṃsa* contains a great deal of information that is not visible on this frieze. Rather than understand the relief as a rendering of the *Mahāvaṃsa*, I propose that we see a functional similarity between these two narratives, in that both attempt to record the founding of a monastery or the bringing of the dharma to a new region, specifically at the hands of miracle-performing monks with the ability to charm gifts of land from willing royal patrons. Just as the *Mahāvaṃsa* positions Devānaṃpiyatissa as an ideal Buddhist ruler, so too this relief sculpture seems to depict a generous elite patron.

Delving further into the *Mahāvaṃsa*'s account of Mahinda's interactions with King Devānaṃpiyatissa reveals the monk to be something like a savvy property developer, helping the king to see the potential of his realm to be physically transformed into a Buddhist kingdom. After the founding of the *vihāra* at the Mahāmegha-park, the king and Mahinda surveyed the surrounding landscape, with Mahinda prophesizing where the various structures in the monastic complex will be located. The king responded to Mahinda's prophecies by sprinkling flowers, or, in one case, planting a mango pit that miraculously sprouted and grew into a fruiting tree. Eventually, the king and Mahinda came to the spot within the royal park where the text tells us 'the Great thūpa (afterwards) stood' (Geiger and Bode 1912: 101). After the dharmic duo offered flowers, the earth quaked and Mahinda proclaimed, 'This place, O great king, which has been visited by four Buddhas, is worthy of a *thūpa*, to be a blessing and happiness to beings' (ibid.). This is not so much a prophecy as a revelation, in which Mahinda demonstrates that the island has long been a sacred space, visited not only by our historical Buddha, but also by Buddhas of the past. Mahinda brings the dharma to the island of Sri Lanka, but, of course, it was always already there. With the assistance of his royal patron, Mahinda reveals that the physical manifestations of the dharma will soon be restored.

Returning to the frieze, the *Mahāvaṃsa* might also help to clarify the presence of the *stūpa* in the middle of a narrative about the foundation of a monastery. The *stūpa*, which initially seems to interrupt the narrative, was especially puzzling to Barrett, who notes, seemingly as an aside, 'The presence of the stupa is difficult to explain' (Barrett 1954a: 67). Keeping some of the details of the *Mahāvaṃsa* in mind, we might notice that four trees punctuate the periphery of the *stūpa*. Could these visually refer to the visitation at this site of four past Buddhas? The trunk of one of these trees in the foreground includes a base, reminding us that this tree is maintained through human intervention. Careful examination also reveals a pair of tiny footprints just visible on this base (**Fig. 100**). These footprints suggest not only the traces of a Buddha's presence, but also that those traces contribute to this site's status as worthy of veneration. While textual storytelling traditions can employ vivid descriptions to convey concepts like flashbacks, temporal progression or prognostication, visual storytelling must rely on other tools. Moreover, visual imagery has some unique advantages in this context. For example, while Mahinda strolls around with King Devānaṃpiyatissa narrating events that occurred in the past or identifying sites that will be built in the future, a visual representation of a site can convey the simultaneity of past and present in a manner that is not entirely possible in oral or textual narratives. Here the *stūpa*, with its four trees and footprints, visually marks a sacred space that collapses past and present, as the past presence of four Buddhas might mark this site's long sacred history and inspire present and future acts of devotion, such as the building of a new *stūpa*.

The importance of local relic veneration in text and image

The *Mahāvaṃsa* is concerned not only with the past presence of Buddhas on the island but with the construction of new sacred spaces where the Buddha – in the form of relics – will be present. Not long after Mahinda and his monks were comfortably ensconced in the Mahāmegha-park, it became apparent that they required a retreat for the rainy season, which the king dutifully provided. Then, after the rainy season, Mahinda complained to the king, 'Long is the time, O lord of men, since we have seen the Saṃbuddha. We lived a life without a master. There is nothing here for us to worship' (Geiger and Bode 1912: 116). And so Mahinda, noting the absence of the Buddha and the desire to establish a nearby location where the Buddha might be venerated, set in motion the construction of a *stūpa* on Missaka Mountain with willing and lavish patronage from the king. As the building of a new *stūpa* requires a cache of relics, the monk Sumana was deputized to fly to Pāṭaliputra to collect from Aśoka the right collar bone relic to be placed within the *stūpa*. Shortly upon their arrival in Sri Lanka, the relics performed the 'Twin Miracles', by which 'the whole land of Laṅkā' was 'illumined and flooded again and again' (ibid.: 120). Eventually, a branch of the bodhi tree was also brought to the island and planted within the Mahāmegha-park, where a range of miracles appeared. Obviously the miraculous events described within the text are not depicted on what remains of this frieze. Rather, both the frieze and the text frame the founding of a new Buddhist community in similar ways. For example, this frieze also gives prominence both to a *stūpa* and to a large tree in the midst of a story of royal conversion and the gifting of a monastic residence. Both sources also seem concerned with the proper number of monks for the establishment of a new community. Kevin Trainor, in his analysis of both the *Dipavaṃsa* and the *Mahāvaṃsa*, notes that five monks is the minimum required

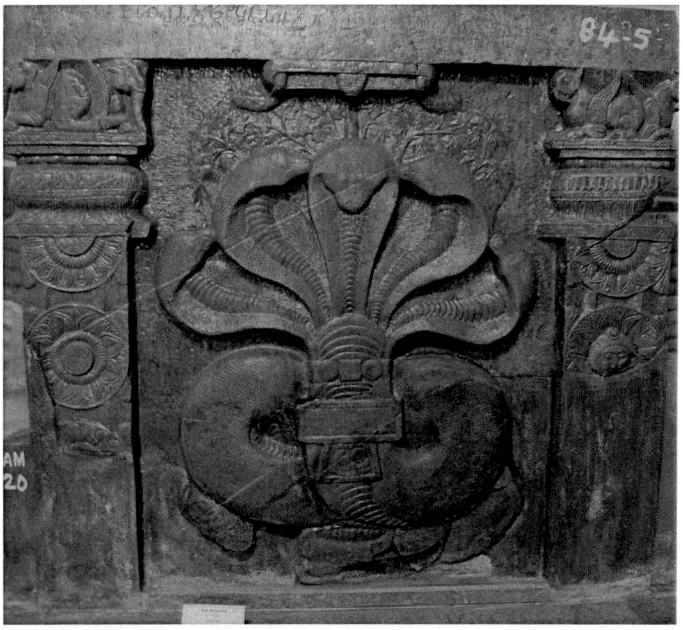

Figure 101 Relief sculpture with polycephalous *nāga*, Dhulikatta *stūpa*, c. 2nd–1st century BCE, Amaravati Museum and Interpretation Centre, acc. no. 20

for the founding of a new monastery (1997: 84–5). Assemblies of monks in the coping frieze twice appear in groups of at least five. Although the exact miracles described in the *Mahāvaṃsa* as signalling momentous and auspicious events – the quaking of the earth, for instance – are not discernible in the relief sculpture, one of these monks clearly has the ability to levitate, which is certainly a miraculous power.

The precise appearance of the *stūpa*, which as I noted above is the most prominent element of this frieze's composition, requires additional consideration. Complete with projecting *āyaka* platforms surmounted by pillars, a railing with lions guarding the gateways, and a semi-circular moonstone in front of the central gateway, this *stūpa* greatly resembles what I have elsewhere described as an Andhra-style *stūpa* (Becker 2015: 40–3). The five pillars, in particular, are a regional feature that appears at sites throughout Andhra. We might also note the presence of the tiny five-headed *nāga* within the gateway of this *stūpa*. *Nāga*s are abundant in the sculptural remains from Andhra, not only in the form of the large-scale depictions of serpents that adorned the drums of *stūpa*s, such as a theriomorphic *nāga* from the *stūpa* at Dhulikatta (**Fig. 101**), but also as participants in narratives and represented as devotees on figural representations of *stūpa*s. The multi-headed *nāga* also seems to have been a potent figure in the Buddhist imaginary in Sri Lanka, as suggested by the appearance of relief sculptures of multi-headed serpents adorning *stūpa*s in Anuradhapura.[4] The inclusion of *nāga*s on *stūpa*s suggests that these creatures function as both guardians and devotees. The *Mahāvaṃsa* relates how *nāga*s recovered a cache of the Buddha's relics, which they venerated in their own *stūpa* (Geiger and Bode 1912: 210–11). As the *nāga*s fiercely guarded their portions of the Buddha's relics, Aśoka left this relic deposit undisturbed when undertaking his miraculous relic redistribution campaign. This is also the very portion of relics that, according to the *Mahāvaṃsa*, was predestined to be enshrined within the massive *stūpa* built by

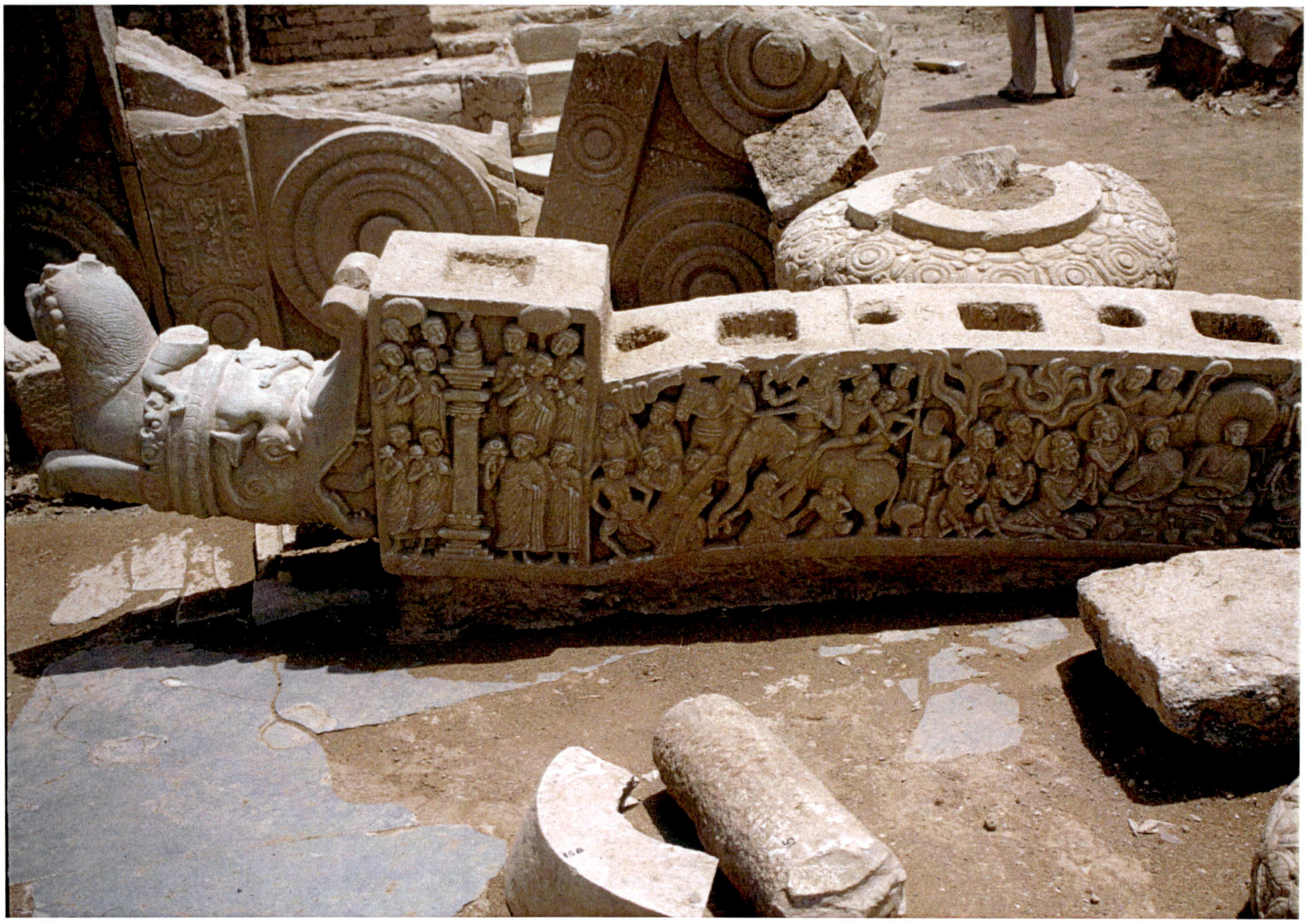

Figure 102 Gateway lintel, Phanigiri, *c.* late 3rd century CE

the repentant King Duṭṭagāmaṇī for the Mahāvihāra in Anuradhapura (Strong 2004: ch. 6). Or might those relics have had a different destination?

The site of Phanigiri in Nalgonda District, formerly part of Andhra Pradesh and now included within the borders of Telangana, reveals another sculptural narrative that has resisted easy interpretation and might be productively juxtaposed with the *Mahāvaṃsa*'s account of the bringing of the Rāmagrāma relics to Sri Lanka. When it was excavated in 2003, Phanigiri revealed spectacular limestone sculptures, including a damaged frieze from a gateway lintel (**Fig. 102**). To our left, a scene of monks venerating a relic casket is attached to larger narrative scene (**Fig. 103**). To the right of the monastic assembly appears a king mounted on an elephant and accompanied by musicians. This procession moves towards the left, as if the royal entourage were heading towards the monks and the reliquary. Moving further to the right, we encounter a damaged depiction of a narrative. Seated celestial beings, their status indicated by their halos, clasp their hands together in respect and pay homage to a seated monk, who raises his hand in a gesture of explication. An odd scene appears directly above this monk's head (**Fig. 104**). A blocky pattern, again used to indicate mountainous terrain, suggests we are looking at a location distinct from the scenes below. Two monks confront two *nāgas* – one massive with five heads and the other a single-headed serpent. One of the monks fearlessly raises a hand towards one of the serpents, as if to arrest the creature's

Figure 103 Monks venerating a reliquary, gateway lintel (detail), Phanigiri

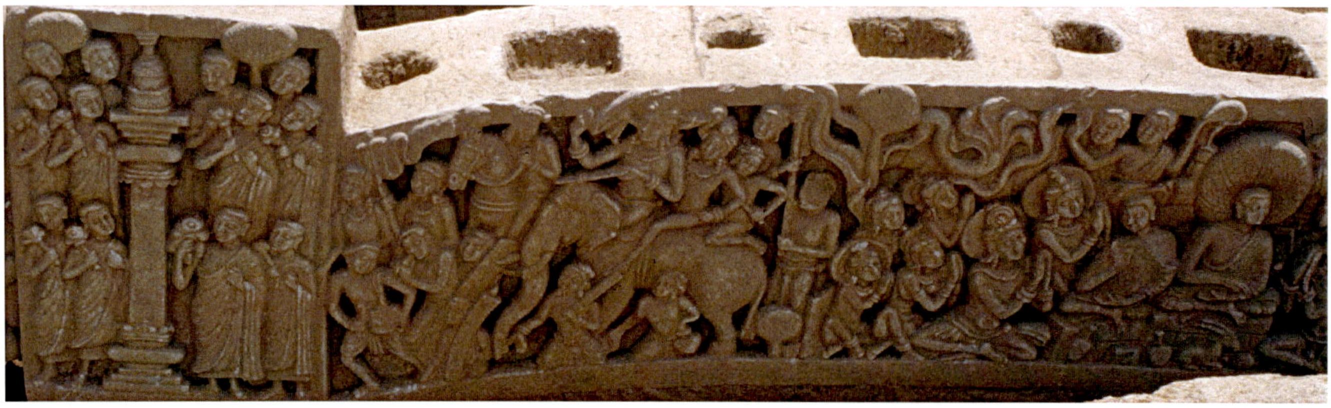

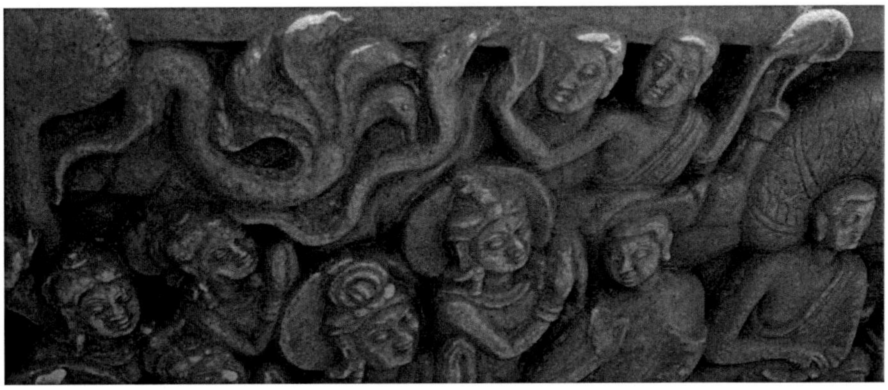

Figure 104 Monks confronting *nāgas*, gateway lintel (detail), Phanigiri

motion. The monk's other arm is peculiar indeed – the arm itself is slender and elongated. Moreover, the hand is not readily visible. I have puzzled over this scene since I first encountered it shortly after its excavation. The *Mahāvaṃsa* provides a possible parallel.

We now skip ahead to a later episode in the text. The great King Duṭṭhagāmaṇī violently quelled the armies of Elāra and attempted to atone for his bloody battles by promulgating the dharma and undertaking massive building campaigns, including the construction of a splendid *stūpa* associated with the Mahāvihāra in Anuradhapura. Once the king had an elaborate relic-chamber constructed, the monk Sonuttara was dispatched to India to recover the relics from the Rāmagrāma *stūpa*, fulfilling the Buddha's deathbed promise that these relics were predestined for the Great Thūpa in Sri Lanka. Despite this prophecy, the monk Sonuttara found upon his arrival that the *nāgas* were unwilling to part with their precious relic treasure. The *nāga*-king's nephew swallowed the relic urn and withdrew to Mount Sineru. Meanwhile the *nāga*-king, overly confident that the relics would never be discovered in his nephew's belly, promised Sonuttara that if he could find the relics, he could have them. At which point, the monk 'standing on that very spot, created a (long) slender arm, and stretching the hand straight-way down the throat of the nephew he took the urn with the relics, and crying: "Stay, *nāga*!" he plunged into the earth and rose up (out of it) in his cell' (Geiger and Bode 1912: 214). Sonuttara simultaneously addressed the *nāga*-king and miraculously used his elastic arm to snatch the relics. This stretchy-arm skill also seems to be employed by one of the monks in the relief from Phanigiri. The monk raises one hand to repel flying serpents while the other arm is attenuated and the hand obscured. While the monk's arm disappears into an indecipherable, possibly zoomorphic, form,[5] could we see a parallel here between the monk Sonuttara's recovery of the *nāgas*' relics and this monk's encounter with *nāgas*? At the very least, we see a monk actively confronting *nāgas* within a larger sculptural context that clearly celebrates the arrival and veneration of relics.

Returning once again to the coping frieze from Amaravati and the *stūpa* that dominates the composition of this scene, perhaps we might understand the inclusion of the *nāga* in this gateway to serve as a sort of label – a marker for the presence of a portion of the *nāga*'s cache of the Buddha's relics.[6] The choice to depict a recognizably Andhra-type *stūpa* in the midst of this narrative of royal conversion, when considered alongside the Phanigiri relief of monks tussling with *nāgas* and venerating relics, raises some important questions. Does the depiction of an Andhra-style *stūpa* with a *nāga* suggest that the Buddhist community at Amaravati imagined Andhra to be the home to a portion of this mythical cache of relics?[7] Or perhaps the coping frieze from Amaravati suggests that Buddhists in Andhra had their own version of Mahinda bringing Buddhism to Andhra. In truth, I am reluctant to propose that the relief sculptures from Andhra depict the *Mahāvaṃsa*, which has become so central to a Buddhist national identity in contemporary Sri Lanka. Rather, by noting parallels between these reliefs and tales of the legendary introduction of Buddhism to Sri Lanka, we might understand the text and image to have similar functions. Just as the Pali chronicles employ multiple strategies for legitimizing and localizing Buddhism in Sri Lanka, so too the British Museum frieze seems to depict a similar tale of legitimization and localization – with respect not to Sri Lanka but to Andhra.

Conclusions and future directions

As I noted at the start of this essay, the artistic connections between Buddhist communities in Andhra and Sri Lanka have long been recognized in the form of stylistic parallels, the common use of specific motifs and examples of sculpture imported from Andhra. Moreover, inscriptional evidence reveals that monks from Sri Lanka resided at Nagarjunakonda during the 3rd and 4th centuries CE (Khare 1962) and that in the 14th century a powerful monk in Sri Lanka donated funds for the restoration of an image house near the Amaravati *stūpa* (Paranavitana 1935). In discussing the Nagarjunakonda inscriptions, Gregory Schopen notes some similarities with the *Dīpavaṃsa*, specifically the appearance of the word *dhātuvara* in both sources. Schopen argues that both regions shared a similar conception that 'relics are characterized by – full of – exactly the same spiritual forces and faculties that characterize, and, in fact, constitute and animate the living Buddha' (Schopen 1997: 154).

While Andhra lacks the sort of textual sources associated with the establishment of Buddhism in Sri Lanka, as Schopen's work has indicated, there are more parallels to be uncovered between these two regions, particularly with respect to the use of stories, relics and *stūpas* to shape and localize Buddhist communities. If done with care, it might be productive to place text and image alongside each other to trace a more nuanced understanding of the artistic and intellectual exchanges between the Buddhist communities in

Andhra and Sri Lanka. Yet, given the abundance of evidence of shared artistic practices and conceptual elements within some of the Buddhist communities in Andhra and Sri Lanka, a number of questions remain unanswered. Why, for example, does Andhra experience such an efflorescence of narrative sculptures while so few narrative reliefs appear at the monastic sites in Anuradhapura? How might the appearance of similar motifs at sites in Andhra and Sri Lanka reflect deliberate attempts to forge and advertise affiliations between distinct Buddhist communities in these regions? Exploring these and a host of other questions may allow us to move beyond the tendency to look for the origins of styles and motifs and to think meaningfully about more dynamic artistic relationships between Andhra and Sri Lanka.

Notes

1 In his exploration of the close relationship between Indian rulers and elephants, Thomas Trautmann has noted the diverse roles elephants played in expressing royal power. Although their foremost role was for warfare, elephants also appeared in many other royal contexts (2015: 51).

2 This gesture, which appears frequently in sculpture from Andhra's Buddhist sites, would seem to be a variant of *abhaya mudrā*, which generally features an open palm facing outwards and upright with all five fingers held straight. Here the figure's fingers are straight, but the hand turns slightly to the side as if to share something with the audience.

3 Although the *Dīpavaṃsa* and the *Mahāvaṃsa* purport to document events from before the Common Era, scholarly consensus seems to date these texts to the 4th or 5th centuries CE (Padma and Holt 2008: 120).

4 Some of these reliefs of *nāgas* from Sri Lanka have been published by Ulrich von Schroeder (1990). We might also note that the moonstone that marks the threshold of this *stūpa*'s gateway is a motif that appears in Sri Lanka, often with elaborate sculptural adornment.

5 In personal correspondence, Monika Zin interprets this form at the end of the monk's left arm as a bird. Indeed, a tiny eye appears to be visible and perhaps two legs. However, the relationship between the monk and this creature remains unclear.

6 Monika Zin has also examined the links between the Rāmagrāma story in the *Mahāvaṃsa*, relief sculptures in South India and the appearance at Kanaganahalli of a relief of a *stūpa* labelled in an inscription as the Rāmagrāma *stūpa*. Noting parallels, Zin also wonders 'if such stories were an invention of the Ceylonese chronicle or if they were perhaps known in Andhra before' (Zin forthcoming d: 8).

7 Zin similarly remarks on the presence of '*nāgas* at the entrances to stūpa enclosures in Andhra, as if they were guarding the precious relics; they tempt us to imagine that they are guarding a portion of the eighth share of the relics from Rāmagrāma' (Zin forthcoming d: 11).

Chapter 7
A Third-Century CE Nagarjunakonda Relief and Other Sculpture from Andhra Pradesh in the Victoria and Albert Museum

Nick Barnard

Despite having one of the largest collections of South Asian art outside India, the Victoria and Albert Museum (V&A) in South Kensington, London, does not hold any sculptures from Amaravati itself. It does, however, have a very small but interesting group of sculptures from the surrounding region, including one relief from the related site at Nagarjunakonda, some 100km west of Amaravati, higher up the River Krishna or Kistna. In addition, a small group of plaster casts in the V&A has recently been identified with some of the Amaravati sculptures now in the British Museum. This chapter will introduce these still relatively unstudied pieces of sculptures in the V&A collection and highlight their importance.

A Buddha relief from Nagarjunakonda

In 1936, E.H. Hunt (1874–1952), F.R.C.S., a retired surgeon and medical officer, presented the V&A with a group of six objects. Hunt, after completing his education at Harrow and Balliol College, Oxford, had gone to India in 1903 as medical officer to the state railways of the Nizam of Hyderabad.[1] He remained in this work, alongside a private practice, until he returned to England in 1932. Having developed interests in archaeology, anthropology and other subjects in India, he published papers on cairn burials as well as on medical subjects such as 'The regulation of body temperature in extremes of dry heat' (Hunt 1912; 1924). The objects he gave consist of a sword with a Deccani mount, four ceramics from prehistoric burial sites at Raigir and a small limestone slab carved with a figure of the Buddha, which is described by Kenneth de Burgh Codrington and P. Wright, in the 1936 V&A acquisition papers relating to these objects, as 'from Amaravati' (**Fig. 105**).[2] Among Hunt's gifts, the Buddha figure was considered 'by far the most

Figure 105 Mucalinda Buddha, mid 3rd century CE, probably Nagarjunakonda, Victoria and Albert Museum, IM.81-1936, given by E.H. Hunt Esq., F.R.C.S.

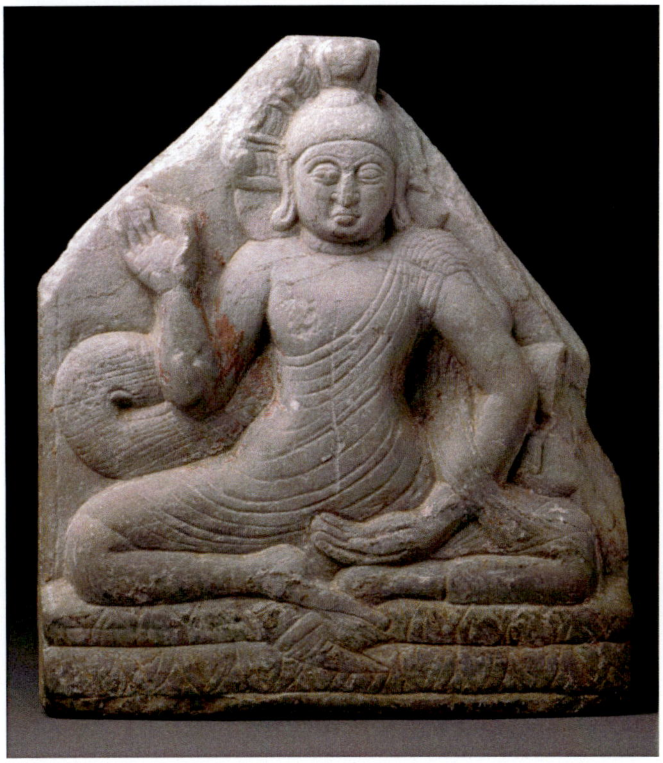

important object', partly because it was believed to come from Amaravati and the V&A had nothing from that site.[3] It was subsequently reattributed to Nagarjunakonda, but, as such, it remains unique in the V&A's collection.

The sculpture shows the Buddha being protected from a violent storm by the *nāgarāja* or serpent king Mucalinda, an event which occurred after the Buddha's enlightenment. The Mucalinda theme is also represented elsewhere at Nagarjunakonda. In this relief, the coils of the snake can be seen behind the Buddha on his right and in fragmentary condition on his left, as can the multiple heads of the great snake, which form a protective canopy behind the Buddha's head. Mucalinda's heads were either seven or nine in number, though because of damage it is now not possible to be absolutely certain how many were depicted here. The top, central head, which is the only complete one, shows traces of facial features. The scales of the snakes are represented by cross-hatching. The Buddha's *uṣṇīṣa* is small. The curls on his head are very lightly incised, and the treatment of his hair has been likened to a cap (Stone 1994: 53). Lotus petals are incised in fairly rudimentary form on the base. The posture and arrangement of the figure, cross-legged with the feet, which cross over each other, overlapping the lotus throne below, is seen quite commonly at Nagarjunakonda although it appears also on drum pilasters from Amaravati. The figure's left hand is, perhaps, disproportionately large. The figure is carved in very low relief and the object is small in size, measuring 165mm high by 146mm wide by 30mm deep.[4]

A note in the V&A register records that the sculpture was purchased by Mr Hunt from a dealer in Hyderabad, though it does not say when. No further information on its earlier history survives and the reattribution to Nagarjunakonda, which may have been made by the time the Museum's registered description was written in 1936, must have been on stylistic grounds.[5] It is described there as 'Nagarjunikoṇḍa, Andra Pradesh [*sic*]. Amaravati Style (Late Phase), mid-3rd century A.D.'. The timing of the acquisition, which Hunt must have made before returning to England in 1932, seems entirely consistent with the discovery of Nagarjunakonda in the 1920s and its excavation, which continued until 1931. Although the remote site was discovered in 1920 by an Andhra school teacher, assisted by villagers (Stone 1994: 1), it only came to the official notice of the Archaeological Survey of India in 1925 (Longhurst 1931: 115). In July 1926 interest in the site was stimulated after Jouveau-Dubreuil of the Pondicherry College investigated it and removed two beautiful reliefs from the *stūpa*, then called Site 4 (later known as Site 6), as M.H. Kuraishi reported after his trial excavation for the Archaeological Survey of India in 1926–7 before the major excavations by Longhurst in 1927–31 took place (Kuraishi 1930: 160). Kuraishi commented that the *mahācaitya*, or principal *stūpa*, had already been 'excavated by some treasure-seekers or amateur archaeologists before its existence became known to the officers of the Archaeological Department' (ibid.: 156–7). Indeed, it is tempting to wonder if the Hyderabad dealer might have acquired the sculpture from among pieces removed before Nagarjunakonda received official involvement and government approval for conservation.

Elizabeth Rosen Stone suggested on stylistic grounds that the V&A Buddha figure might be one of the later works that came from Site 6 (originally Site 4) at Nagarjunakonda, using the numbering system employed by H. Sarkar in his work on Buddhist architecture (Sarkar 1966), which departs from earlier systems (Stone 1994: 3, 27, 52–3). Stone also notes the removal of 'several sculptures' from Site 6 before Nagarjunakonda's preservation order (ibid.: 27–8). Along with several other sites, Site 6 was characterized by having a *stūpa* and a monastery and no *caitya-grihas* with *stūpa* or Buddha image (Sarkar 1966: 79).[6] The *stūpa*, which has a diameter of over 15 metres, was constructed in the form of a wheel with eight spokes and, like Amaravati, had four *āyaka* platforms at the cardinal points. Sarkar comments on the paucity of sculpture at Site 6 but Stone suggests that the site may have furnished some of the figures removed from Nagarjunakonda at an early date and compares the V&A figure with two 'crude, corpulent Buddha' figures from Site 6 carved on the *āyaka* pillars, which acted as altars at the four cardinal points of each *stūpa*. Stone describes the Buddha type represented by those two as 'an overweight, full-bellied, full-chested type whose hair is placed upon his head as if it were a tight fitting cap' (Stone 1994: 52–3). She is somewhat scathing about the V&A figure, characterizing it as 'very crude', and states that it bears the same 'full breasts and pot belly' as a Buddha figure from Site 6, while the 'cap-like coiffure and crudely cut open staring eyes' are similar to another, related Buddha figure. Although much of this seems valid, especially concerning the cap-like hair, the small scale of the carving in the V&A should be borne in mind with regard to its quality. There are also differences between the figures of the Buddhas in these reliefs: the V&A figure appears not corpulent but slender, albeit with a widening at the hips. The right foot and arm of the V&A figure are also gracefully depicted, though the left hand is over large and the left foot very sketchily carved. A similar treatment of the eyes, which on the V&A figure have very pronounced lids, can be seen in many reliefs from Nagarjunakonda. Chronologically, Stone mentions the 'long building history' of Site 6 but discusses the V&A relief with others in the context of the reign of Vīrapuruṣadatta, second of the four identified Nagarjunakonda kings, whose regnal dates she gives as '*c*. AD 240–50–*c*. AD 265–75' (ibid.: 7, 52–3, 57, 66). This agrees with the dating of the sculpture in the V&A records to the mid 3rd century.

What is perhaps more distinctive about the V&A figure than the features described above, however, is its severe expression and gloomy mien. This resembles some of the Nagarjunakonda sculptures but is very different from the Amaravati figures. Although the feature is particularly prominent in the V&A Buddha, figures from Nagarjunakonda with a similarly downcast or serious expression can be seen on some of the sculptures described as 'beams' by Longhurst, as well as in other pieces, suggesting that there may be other ways in which comparisons could be built up with other figures from the site (Longhurst 1931: pl. 51; Ramachandra Rao 2001: pl. 46). The arrangement of the feet of the V&A figure has numerous parallels at Nagarjunakonda (including the two Buddhas from the *āyaka* pillars at Site 6), and may be another starting point.

Although Stone's comments about the figure are very useful and her arguments definitely plausible, it may never be possible to be quite certain from which site at Nagarjunakonda the figure came. In 1961 the entire valley was flooded by a dam, creating one of the largest artificial lakes in the world, which limits the information available today despite the extensive investigative and rescue archaeology carried out from 1954 to 1960 (Ramachandra Rao 2001: xi, 47; Sarkar and Misra 2006: 3–5). Given the lack of detailed provenance information it is not even absolutely certain that the figure came from Nagarjunakonda, although its style and the date at which it came on the market do seem to favour that site. It is also not known what context on a structure the relief may have come from, although some part of an *āyaka* structure such as a pillar or beam seems a possibility. However, comparison with Buddha figures on the surviving fragments preserved in the Nagarjunakonda Archaeological Museum suggests that despite a broad stylistic similarity it is not possible to make any very close match between the V&A figure and specific examples shown on fragments from known sites, although there are points of similarity with numerous sculptures. Its very shallow relief in comparison to many of the architectural pieces and its small size as well as its relatively crude carving could also suggest that the Buddha figure was a votive offering, rather than an architectural piece, albeit probably from Nagarjunakonda.[7]

Sculptures collected by Robert Sewell

This relief, however, was not the first sculpture from the region to come into the collection, and we must now turn to a group of later sculptures sold to the Museum in 1913–14 by none other than Robert Sewell of the Indian Civil Service, who excavated the Amaravati *stūpa* in 1877. As his report on the Amaravati Tope explains, Sewell was stationed in 1875 in the Kistna District with its headquarters at Bezwada (now Vijayawada), 'once the capital city of the small kingdom of Veṇgi, and afterwards one of the chief towns of the Eastern Chalukyas', 27km east from Amaravati (Sewell 1880: 7). Sewell commented that 'in the neighbourhood almost every village has especial relics of the past'. In 1876 he was granted Rs.1000 by the Government of India to explore Amaravati, Bezwada, Uṇḍavilli and other places. After illness followed by a posting to another district he returned to the Kistna District early in 1878 before being invalided home. It seems very possible that the sculptures he later sold to the V&A were discovered in this period, 1876–9, when he was exploring the Kistna District and its antiquities.

The group of objects sold to the Museum were described in some detail by Sewell, who was by this time a member of the council of the Royal Asiatic Society. The objects purchased included three limestone sculptures from Guntur District, Andhra Pradesh, as well as a bronze figure of Maitreya from the Krishna River delta (Krishna or Guntur District), a number of specimens of prehistoric pottery and ironwork, mostly from Bellary District, as well as glazed tiles from Vijayanagar and terracotta Buddhist votive tablets from Burma. The stone sculptures were, Sewell wrote, 'from a deserted village in a forest tract in the Pālnād Taluqā, Kistna District … near the S. bank of the Krishnā River'.[8]

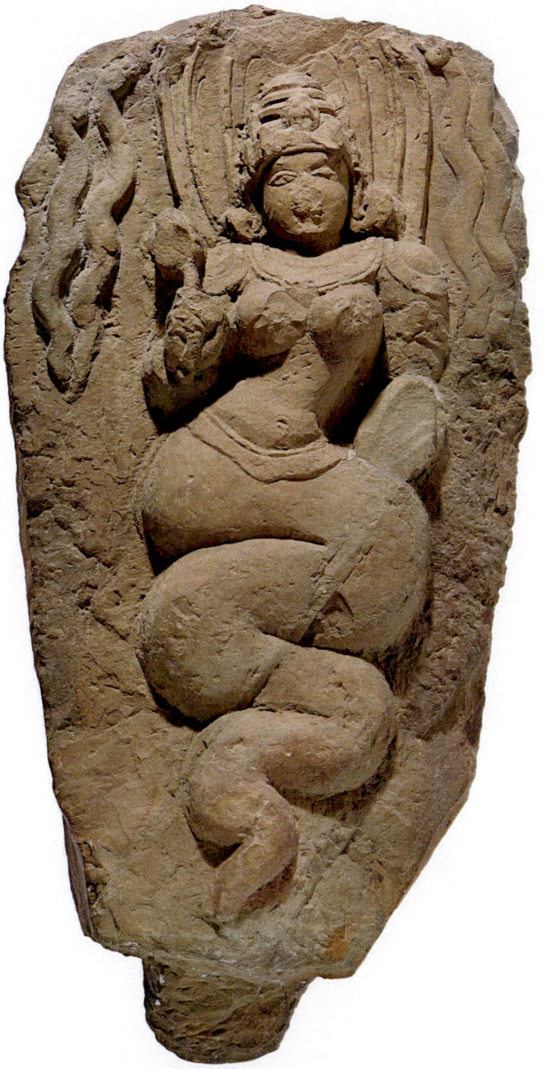

Figure 106 ***Nāgakal*, possibly 7th–9th century CE, former Pālnād Tāluk, now part of Guntur District, Andhra Pradesh, Victoria and Albert Museum, IM.309-1913**

Administrative boundary changes transferred this taluk to the newly created Guntur District in 1904 and further changes took place in the 1970s and 1980s. In 1908 the *Imperial Gazetteer of India* described Pālnād Tāluk 'in the extreme west of Guntūr District … lying between 16° 10' and 16° 44' N. and 79° 14' and 80° E.' as 'a more or less elevated tract, intersected by numerous mountain torrents and almost surrounded by low outliers from the Eastern Ghāts. Bounded on the north and west by the Kistna River, which is here both narrow and swift, and fringed on the south and east by hills and jungles, it is a somewhat inaccessible spot' (Government of India 1908: 371). Sewell commented that 'the style of the sculptured figures has something of the vivacity of the Buddhist period, which ceased in that tract between the 7th and 12th century A.D.'.[9]

Enthusiastic about these important objects, but unable to buy them all at once owing to lack of funds, the Museum made its first purchase a relief of a *nāgakal* or serpent stone, bearing a relief of a *nāginī* or snake goddess, associated with fertility (**Fig. 106**). *Nāgakal*s are traditionally set beneath certain trees or near to a water source. This well-rendered example, which is 760mm high, depicts a *nāginī* with three superimposed cobra hoods behind her head and a pair of

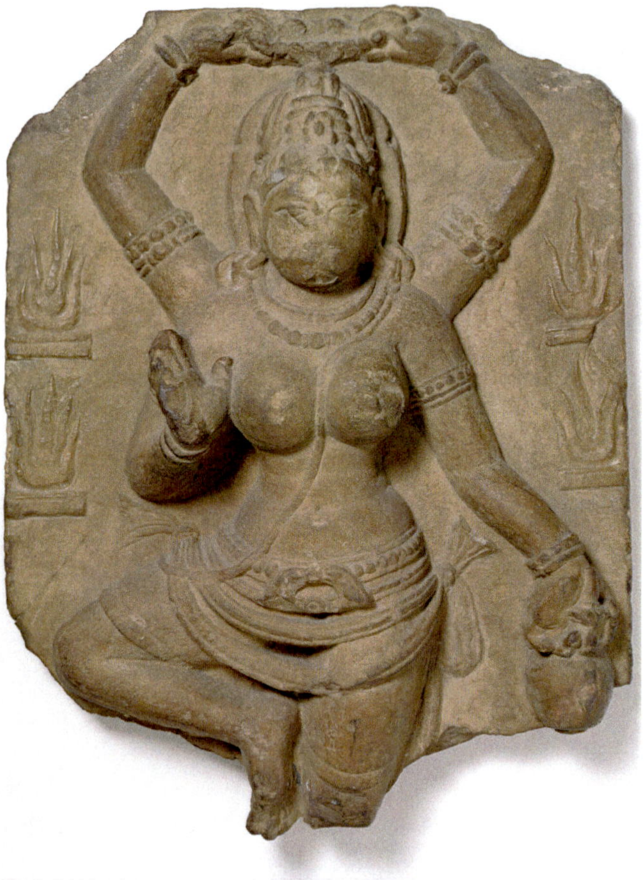

Figure 107 Pārvatī, possibly 8th century CE, former Pālnād Tāluk, now part of Guntur District, Andhra Pradesh, Victoria and Albert Museum, IM.298-1914

smaller snakes on each side of her. *Nāginī* figures often appear to carry weapons, but she seems to hold a lotus bud in her right hand while her left hand is too damaged to identify the gesture. She wears a crown and other jewellery. Her expression, despite damage to the face, appears gentle and compassionate. The V&A curator, C. Stanley Clarke, who became the Deputy Keeper of the Indian Department, described this as a 'Beautifully sculptured Nāginī figure, which although weathered and damaged (chipped and flaked) is in wonderfully good condition for Museum purposes'.[10] Priced at £20, this was by far the most expensive of the entire group and compared to only £6 and £5 respectively for the very fine, though smaller and incomplete, reliefs depicting Pārvatī and Śiva, which were purchased along with the remainder in 1914. It was recorded in early Museum records as 'anterior to 6th century', later amended to 'early medieval', though it may be difficult to date precisely.[11]

Of the three stone sculptures bought from Sewell in 1914 along with the remainder of the pieces offered, it is a beautiful figure of Pārvatī carrying out austerities that has attracted most attention in recent years (**Fig. 107**), appearing in 2007 in a V&A-led exhibition in Spain, *La escultura in los templos indios: el arte de la devoción*, curated by John Guy, as well as in his book *Indian Temple Sculpture* (Guy 2007a: 100; 2007b: 142–3). The relief (439 × 330mm) depicts Pārvatī 'performing extreme austerities in order to win the favour of her Lord Shiva in a subject known as Tapasvini Parvati' and 'demonstrating her own advanced mastery of yogic skills' (Guy 2007a: 100). She is standing in a yogic posture on one leg, with two of her arms above her head holding a string of *rudrākṣa* beads. In her lower left hand, as John Guy explains, she holds a holy water bottle, while the lower right hand is in *abhaya-mudrā*, the gesture of bestowing fearlessness. Guy adds that the presence of four burning pyres indicates she is performing her austerities in a cremation ground, one of Śiva's favoured locations (ibid.). However, the presence of four fires also recalls the *pañcatapas* or *pañcāgni* or 'five fires', a practice in which ascetics expose themselves 'to four fires in the four quarters, sitting amidst them, and to the sun overhead as a fifth fire', an ordeal which Pārvatī carried out from childhood while practising austerities (Liebert 1986: 210). The figure is very elegantly depicted and beautifully balanced. Guy observes that it probably came from the exterior of the sanctuary of a Śaiva temple and, in agreement with earlier scholars, ascribes it to the 8th century CE, Eastern Cāḷukya period (Guy 2007a: 100), although a 9th- to 10th-century dating had been temporarily proposed (Guy 2007b: 142–3).[12]

Although in fragmentary condition, a dancing figure of the god Śiva from the same group and, presumably, the same temple as the Pārvatī was clearly another sculpture of very fine quality (**Fig. 108**). The fragment measures 240 × 323mm. As Śiva performs the *tāṇḍava* or cosmic dance, the

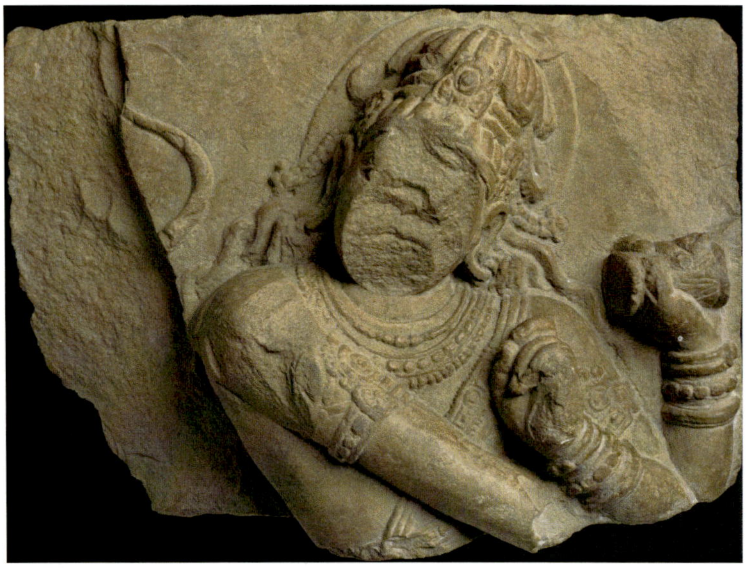

Figure 108 Śiva, possibly 8th century CE, former Palnad Taluk, now part of Guntur District, Andhra Pradesh, Victoria and Albert Museum, IM.299-1914

figure is richly imbued with motion, visible in the swinging head ornaments with strings of pearls and the movement of the hair locks. The strong diagonals of the figure's head and limbs further accentuate the dramatic motion, yet such details as survive of the hands and head also suggest a sensitively rendered image. Śiva holds a *ḍamaru* or small drum in his upper or rear left hand while his lower, front left hand may be in *kaṭaka-hasta-mudrā*, in which the fingers and thumb form a ring. The surviving part of the front right arm shows that it was in *gaja-hasta-mudrā*, thrown out in front of the torso to resemble an elephant's trunk. It seems probable that the elegantly tapering, curved object on the figure's right is part of the prong of Śiva's *triśūla* or trident, as suggested in the V&A register. Its position serves well to balance the dancing figure and emphasize its motion. Like an image of dancing Śiva in the Elephanta caves, which were begun in the 6th century CE, the pose of the body is reversed in comparison to the classic form of the later, well-known Naṭarāja bronze icons of Tamil Nadu, which reached their zenith in the Cola period, as the right hand, instead of the left, is in *gaja-hasta*, whereas in the classic images the front right hand would be in *abhaya-mudrā*. The *ḍamaru* drum is also held in his left upper hand rather than the right, as in a pose called *kālmāṟi-āḍiya-tāṇḍava* or 'dancing with the leg reversed' (Liebert 1986: 120). The figure was described in the Museum register as Śiva Bhairava in the 'lalitani' dancing pose. Sadly the rear right hand has not survived.

The Śiva and Pārvatī figures may be compared to Buddhist sculptures of the later-period Amaravati school in the British Museum, published by Douglas Barrett and Robert Knox, for some of which affinities have been noted with Pallava art and with the early Cāḷukyan dynasty sculpture at Pattadakal, Karnataka from the 8th century (BM nos 1880,0709.59, 1880,0709.61, 1880,0709.68, 1880,0709.125–128; Barrett 1954b: 43–4; Knox 1992: 215–22). The area of the Vengī kingdom, where these sculptures were found, came under a branch of the Cāḷukya family called the Eastern Cāḷukyas from the 7th century CE, although hostility later developed. Of the British Museum group, the V&A figures resemble more closely the Bodhisattvas Avalokiteśvara and Mañjuśrī, attributed to approximately the 8th century CE, and to a lesser extent the 9th-century CE Bodhisattva Cundā, in their proportions than the attenuated Bodhisattva Vajrapāṇi of the early 8th century, and they share the rounded faces of both the earlier Bodhisattva sculptures and the long, almond-shaped eyes of the Avalokiteśvara figure, as well as the narrow, oval halo, which is seen in most of the group and elsewhere in Cāḷukya and other sculpture (BM nos 1880,0709.59, 1880,0709.125–127; Knox 1992: 215–20).

A fragmentary image of *tāṇḍava* Śiva survives at the Mogalrajapuram Cave II, Vijayawada, probably dating to the late 7th to 8th century (Soundara Rajan 1981: 41, 248–52, pls CXV-B, CXVI). Unlike the V&A sculpture, this figure had at least six arms, recalling several early reliefs depicting the dancing Śiva with six or multiple arms on the caves at Badami, Aihole and Ellora, as well as Śiva as Andhakāsuravadhamūrti at Elephanta (ibid.: pls IX, XL-B, XLIII, LXXXVIII-B, XXXIII). At Mogalrajapuram it is the front left arm (proper) instead of the right arm of the

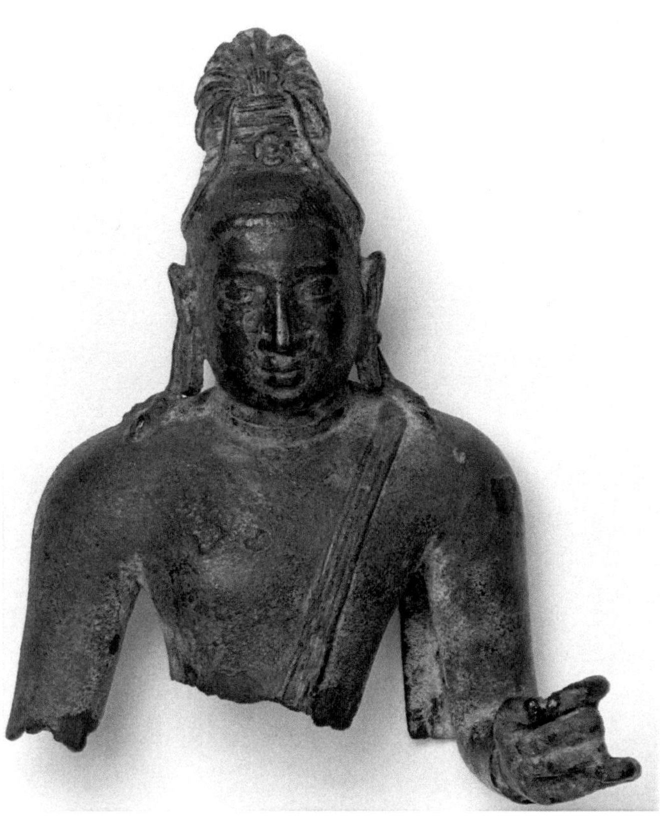

Figure 109 Bodhisattva Avalokiteśvara, copper alloy, *c.* 6th–7th century CE, Krishna River delta, Victoria and Albert Museum, IM.300-1914

V&A figure that crosses the body, presumably to form the *gaja-hasta* posture. The Mogalrajapuram figure's pose is striking, with the left leg lifted high and folded almost horizontally across the body and its powerful angular and very attenuated character contrasts with the more graceful physiognomy of the surviving part of the relief of Śiva at the V&A and its companion figure of Pārvatī, whose more rounded, fuller form is treated in a more naturalistic way than the Mogalrajapuram Śiva. The Mogalrajapuram figure has more in common with Pallava and Early Western Cāḷukya sculpture of the 7th–8th century, and it seems likely that the V&A figures are a little later, possibly dating from later in the 8th century or even into the 9th century. Perhaps more similar in shape to the V&A piece, despite its rather distant location, is the fluid figure of the dancing Śiva from Tirupparankunram (Madurai) dating to 773 CE, whose right hand gesture resembles the V&A Śiva's front left hand, although again the hands are reversed (Lippe 1978: 270). Another, minor point of comparison is the treatment of the hair and its ornaments in a Noḷamba Umā-Maheśvara from Hemavati from around the 9th century CE (Huntington 1985: 339), by which time figures of more similar proportions and general aspect had emerged. Even allowing for a slightly later dating of the V&A's sculptures than the Mogalrajapuram Śiva, the figure remains a good and reasonably early representation of the dancing Śiva from eastern Andhra Pradesh.

The earliest in date of Sewell's four sculptures from Andhra Pradesh is a very fine bronze head and upper body of a bodhisattva (150mm high), and Stanley Clarke recognized that this was a 'Very important piece' (**Fig. 109**).[13] Sewell, who had written an article on Buddhist

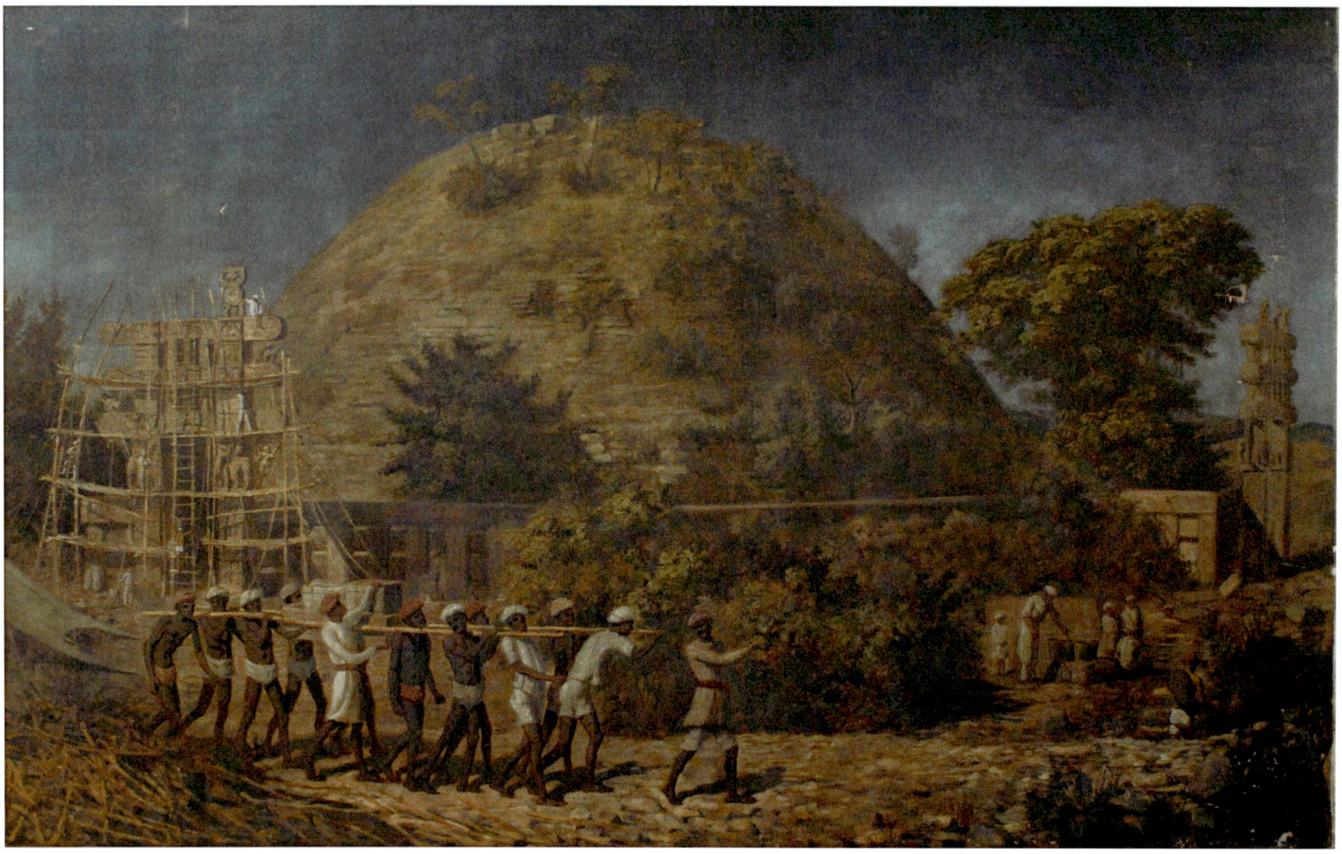

Figure 110 *The Sanchi Tope*, unknown artist, oil on canvas, India, 1870–4, Victoria and Albert Museum, 09200(IS)

bronzes of the same period for the *Journal of the Royal Asiatic Society*, reported for the V&A acquisition papers that 'The figure was found in the bed of an irrigation canal in the Kistna River delta' and dated it as probably 'not later than AD 650'.[14] John Guy, who dates the bronze to around the 6th century CE, has discussed its similarity to a Sri Lankan example found in Thailand and other examples found in south-east Asia, and it may be an interesting indicator of the spread of the style of the Amaravati area to a much wider region (Guy 2014: 36–7). As the piece has been fully published (Guy 2000: 105–6; 2014: 36–7), it is not necessary to discuss it at length here.

Plaster casts of Amaravati sculptures

There is one further way in which the collection relates to Amaravati. The V&A, which was called the South Kensington Museum until 1899, was set up in the 1850s primarily to spread the knowledge of good design and art. To this end the Museum was heavily involved in using representations of architecture and sculpture at an early stage. It thus became a pioneer in the use of photographs and plaster casts, as well as housing what became the National Art Library.

At the Paris Universal Exhibition of 1867, five frames containing photographs by W. Griggs of the Amaravati marbles then in the India Museum (London) and now in the British Museum, as well as two frames of photographs of Sanchi, arranged by James Fergusson, were shown with around 260 other photographs of Indian architecture. These appeared in the section entitled 'History of Labour before 1800', in the Fine Arts Division of the British Section. The photographs included restorations of the *stūpa* rail as far as this was possible. The photographs of Amaravati and Sanchi must have been those used in Fergusson's seminal work *Tree and Serpent Worship*, published in 1868, which extensively discusses Amaravati as well as Sanchi and includes 37 photographs by W. Griggs of the Amaravati sculptures (Fergusson 1868). In accordance with the importance given to this subject, the South Kensington Museum purchased no fewer than four copies of *Tree and Serpent Worship* in 1869.[15] As well as the bound copies of the book, the Museum was presented with a complete unbound set of Griggs' photographs for the book by Forbes Watson of the India Museum.[16] Lieutenant Waterhouse's photographs of Sanchi and Griggs' photographs of the Amaravati sculptures were also shown with others of Indian architecture, selected and arranged by Fergusson, at the Vienna Universal Exhibition of 1873 (Watson 1873: 22).

The collection and use of photographs and plaster casts fits in with a practice, of which the South Kensington Museum was at the forefront, of using reproductions and images to show art and architecture. In 1867 the Museum's director, Sir Henry Cole, had brought about an International Convention for Promoting the Universal Reproductions of Works of Art, which gave a great impetus to the collecting of casts by the late 1860s and 1870s (Bilbey and Trusted 2010: 466). A plaster cast of the entire eastern *toraṇa* of the Great Stūpa at Sanchi was acquired by the Museum in 1870, having been made in 1869–70 under the direction of Lieutenant Henry Hardy Cole, son of the Museum's director. The process of making the casts is shown in a large oil painting (2740 × 1840mm) by an unknown artist (**Fig. 110**). The cast of the gateway was shown in the London International Exhibition of 1871, where it reportedly 'claimed the attention

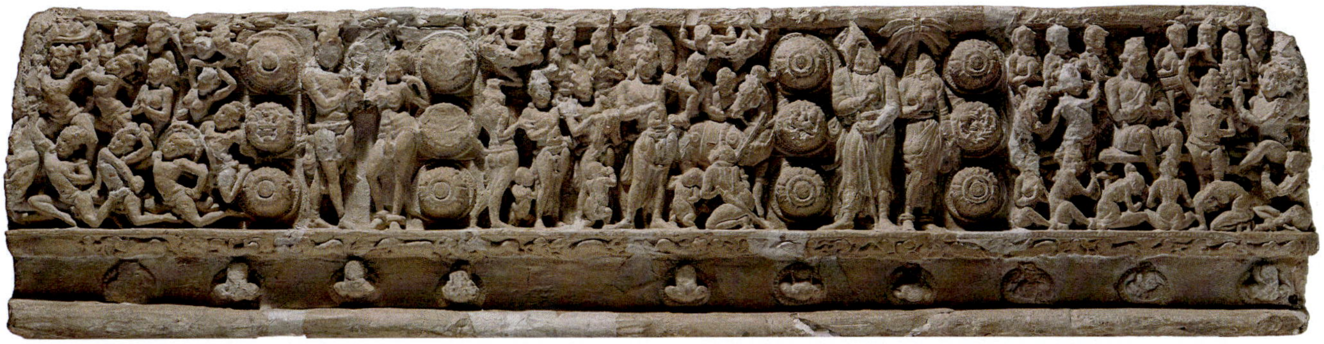

Figure 111 Plaster cast of a portion of drum frieze from Amaravati, London, probably 1850–60, Victoria and Albert Museum, IS.77-2016

and interest of both archaeologists and architects' (Cole 1872: 3). It was then displayed in the South Kensington Museum in a new architecture gallery, opened in 1873, with plaster casts of international architectural monuments. These included large casts of numerous European buildings as well as a cast of the central structure of the Diwan-i Khas of Akbar from Fatehpur Sikri and numerous other plaster casts of Indian monuments in Fatehpur Sikri and Delhi made for the museum by Henry Hardy Cole in 1870–1 (Cole 1872: 4; Pollen 1874: 71–92; Bilbey and Trusted 2010: 467). The South Kensington Museum also sought to obtain illustrations of architectural monuments of all countries, including India, at a time of awakened interest 'for Indian monuments of antiquity' (Cole 1872: 1–2). Henry Hardy Cole argued that a student of architecture should acquire knowledge of the Indian modes of building and decoration, as an important part of the history of world architecture, and could learn much from studying reproductions in his own country; and that Indian museums should show these too (ibid.: 8–9). Photography was seen as complementing the plaster casts in the representation of architecture: it was arranged for Charles Shepherd, of Bourne and Shepherd, to come to the Qutb Minar 'to form a collateral series of illustrations to the casts exhibited at the South Kensington Museum', published in Cole's book on the subject (ibid.: 5). The plaster cast of the Sanchi gateway is sadly no longer extant, though a small number of plaster casts of reliefs from the *stūpas* at Sanchi remain in the collection.

It was not perhaps widely known until now that in the V&A's collection there are at least nine plaster casts of the Amaravati sculptures. Their identity had been lost but it has recently been possible to identify them with their originals in the British Museum. Perhaps the earliest of the Amaravati plaster casts in the V&A to have been made is a drum frieze panel, probably dating to before 1860 when the British Museum purchased the original (BM nos 1860,0712.1, 1880,0709.77; Knox 1992: 114–15) (**Fig. 111**). As Fergusson recounted, before he became familiar with Amaravati sculpture, he was shown the relief by a sculptor, Monti, who was looking after it in Great Marlborough Street (Fergusson 1868: 205, n. 1; 1873: 223, n. 1). Struck with its great beauty, Fergusson had three casts made. Two, presented to the Crystal Palace and the Asiatic Society, were destroyed in a fire in December 1866, but the third, given to the India Museum, survived and is presumably the one now preserved in the V&A.[17] Fergusson later saw the original relief in the British Museum, one of whose officers had been told about it while having his hair cut by a barber in Great Marlborough Street and had bought it for the museum.

The casts also include the outer face of a railing crossbar in the form of a lotus medallion, the original being also in the British Museum (BM no. 1880,0709.13; Knox 1992: 87–8) (**Fig. 112**). The V&A turns out to have an almost complete representation of the inner and outer surfaces of a railing pillar in the British Museum, with casts of five out of a possible six sections identifiable with corresponding parts of the original (BM no. 1880,0709.7; Knox 1992: 58–9) (**Figs 113–18**). Three casts show the inner face and two the outer face, though no cast of the surviving fluted area in the central part of the latter appears to be extant. A plaster cast of part of another pillar also survives (BM no. 1880,0709.47) (Knox 1992: 57) (**Fig. 119**). It is not always clear how the existing casts were selected, or whether more may once have existed.

It is not known when all the Amaravati casts were made but, other than the first one discussed above, it seems likely it was some time in the late 19th century when this practice was at its peak.[18] Increasing criticism from the mid 1890s culminated in the decision in 1908 not to acquire further architectural casts for display in the V&A's galleries (Bilbey

Figure 112 Plaster cast of the outer face of a railing crossbar from Amaravati, London, probably 1880, Victoria and Albert Museum, REPRO.1880-39

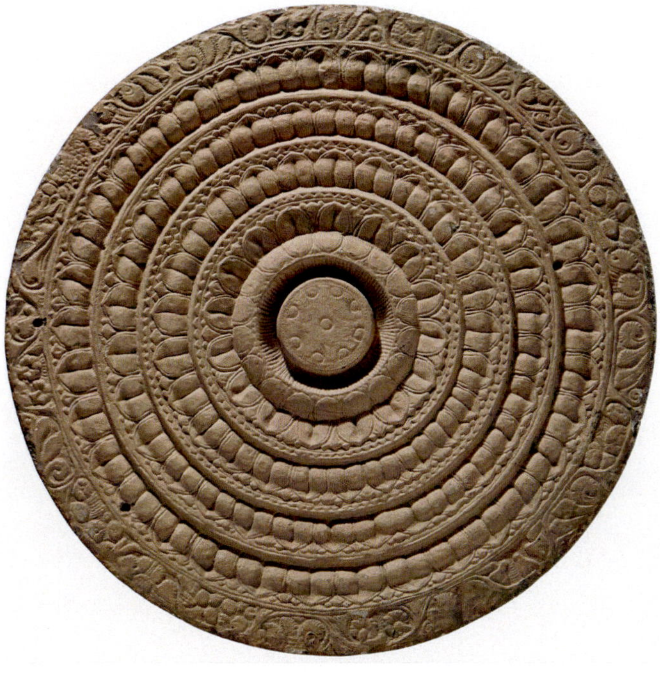

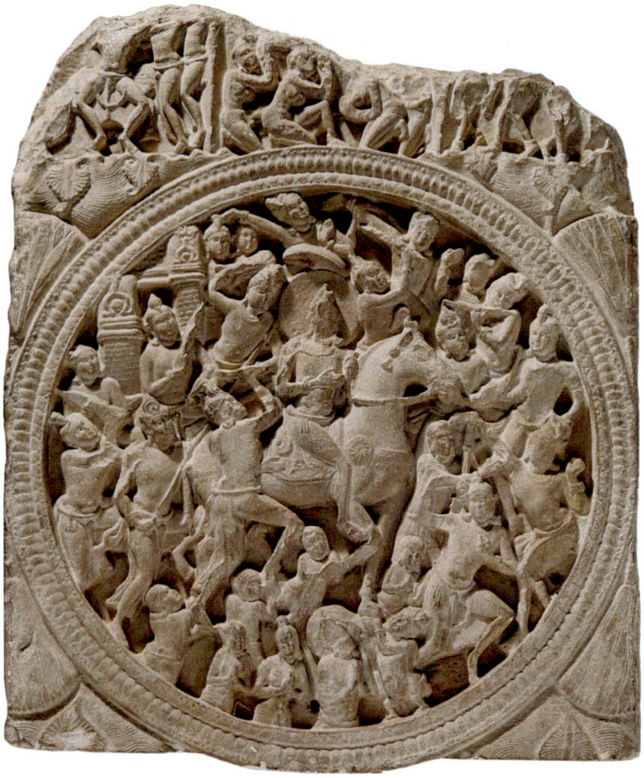

Figure 113 Plaster cast of the central roundel and part of the upper fluted area of the inner face of a railing pillar from Amaravati, London, possibly 1870–80, Victoria and Albert Museum, IS.78-2016

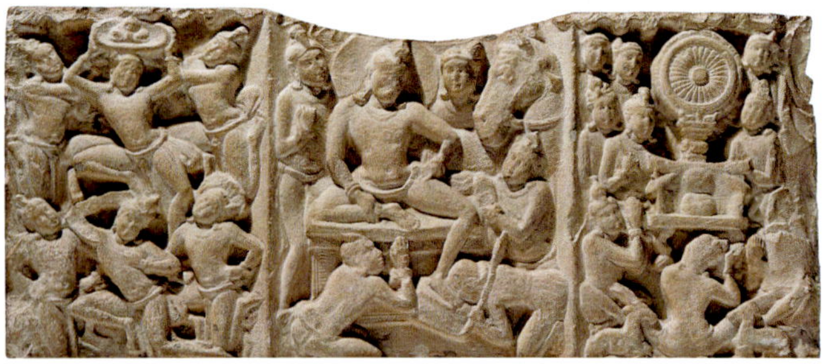

Figure 114 Plaster cast of the lower fluted area of the inner face of a railing pillar from Amaravati, London, possibly 1870–80, Victoria and Albert Museum, IS.79-2016

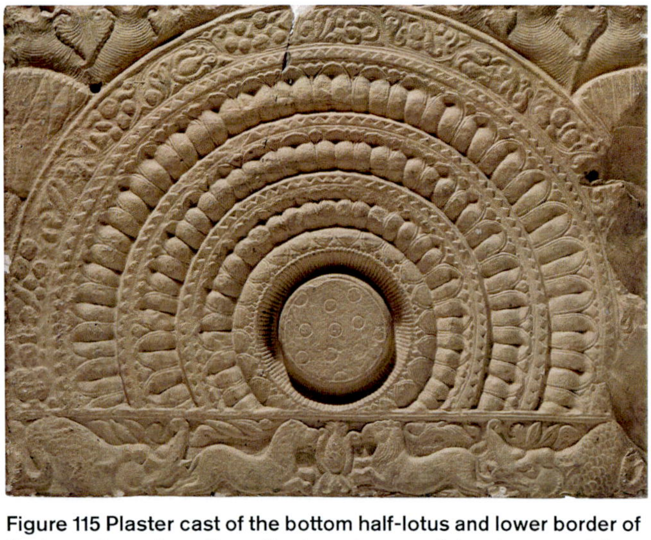

Figure 115 Plaster cast of the bottom half-lotus and lower border of the inner face of a railing pillar from Amaravati, London, possibly 1870–80, Victoria and Albert Museum, IS.80-2016

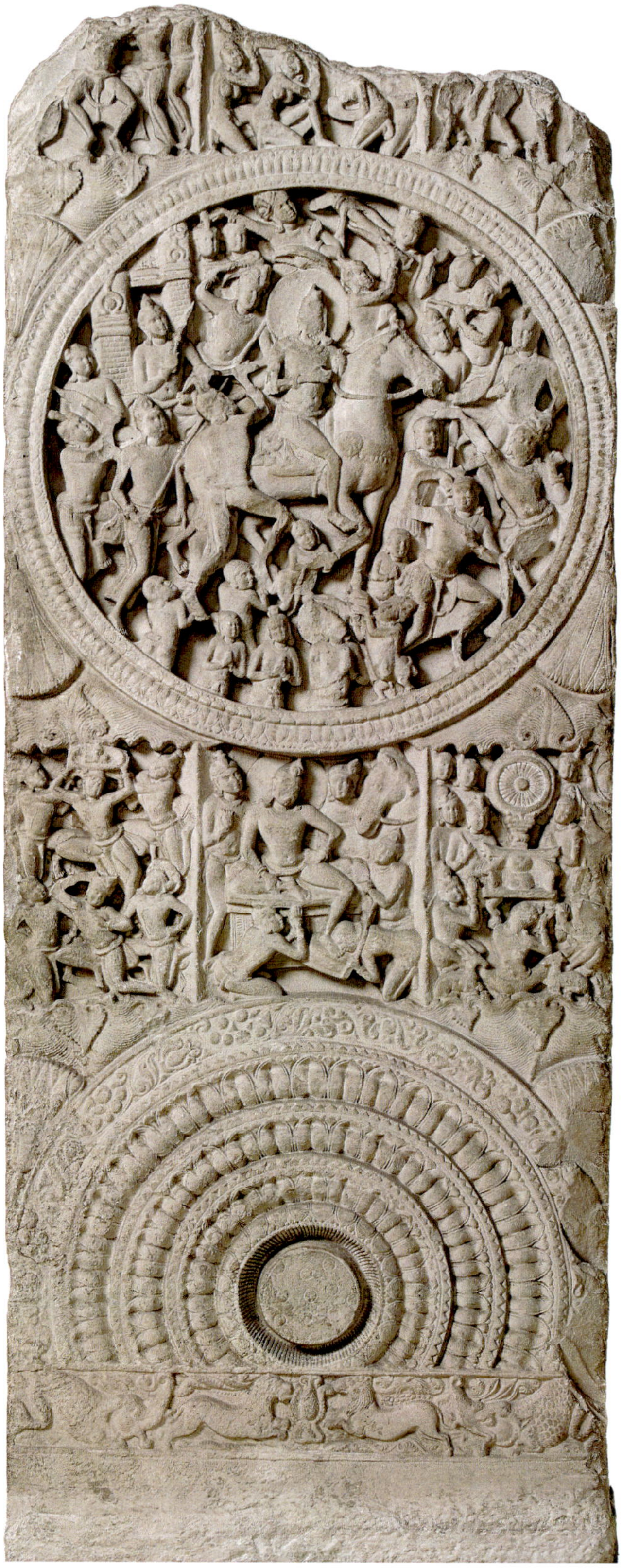

Figure 116 Inner face of a railing pillar, Amaravati, *c.* 3rd century CE, British Museum, 1880,0709.7

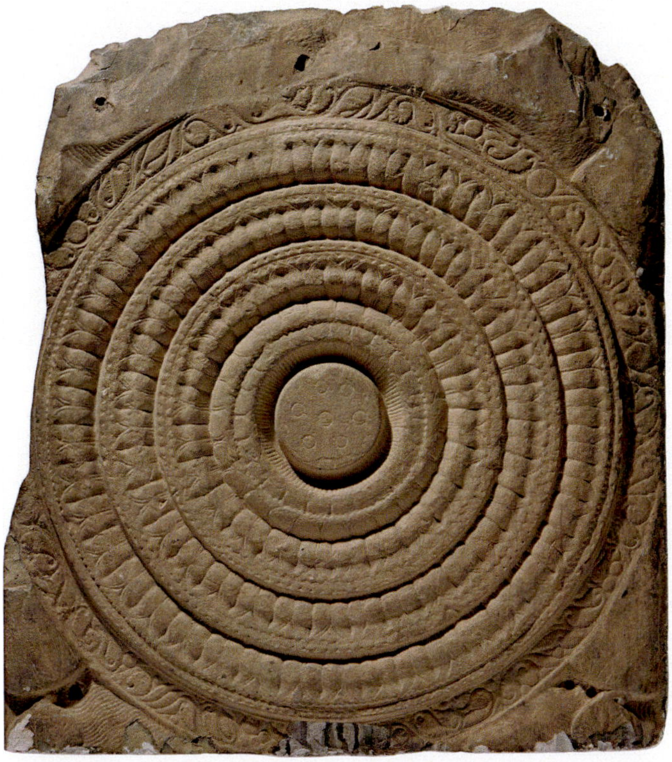

Figure 117 Plaster cast of the central roundel of the outer face of a railing pillar from Amaravati, London, possibly 1870–80, Victoria and Albert Museum, IS.81-2016

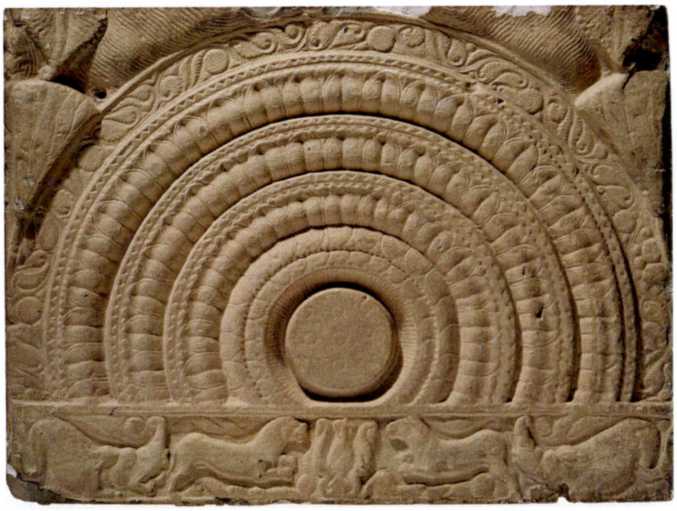

Figure 118 Plaster cast of the bottom half-lotus and lower border of the outer face of a railing pillar from Amaravati, London, possibly 1870–80, Victoria and Albert Museum, IS.82-2016

and Trusted 2010: 468–71).[19] When might the originals have been available for casts to be made? The 'Elliott marbles' were sent to London from Madras in 1859 but were stored at a wharf on arrival and did not enter the India Museum until 1861 (Desmond 1982: 93). They were photographed between 1866 and 1868 for *Tree and Serpent Worship* but were put in storage until 1874, when they were moved to the India Museum's new galleries in South Kensington, just across the road from the V&A's current building. The new India Museum galleries opened in summer 1875 and the Amaravati marbles 'enjoyed the distinction of decorating the principal entrance in Exhibition Road', before being moved to the British Museum in 1880 (Desmond 1982: 113–15, 143, 170–1, 178–9). When the decision was taken in 1879 to disperse the India Museum's collections it was agreed that the South Kensington Museum would receive most of the objects 'provided the Amaravati and other ancient sculptures went to the British Museum to fill gaps in their archaeological collections, casts of them being retained at South Kensington' (Desmond 1982: 178).[20] One cast bears the date '1880' on the back (**Fig. 119**) and it was given by the Trustees of the British Museum to the South Kensington Museum on 7 September 1880 along with two other casts, including one shown here (see **Fig. 112**).[21] The other cast was Museum number REPRO.1880-40, which can probably be identified with a cast temporarily numbered TN.509-2011 (not shown here). Although the true origins of the remaining casts are not known, and they cannot be dated precisely, one possible explanation is that they might have been made just before the Amaravati marbles were moved from South Kensington to Bloomsbury. It is also possible that they were made earlier, perhaps between 1874 and 1879, when the originals were easily available and interest in displaying plaster casts of Indian architecture would have been at its highest following the revelation of the Sanchi gateway and Henry Hardy Cole's casts and the opening of the South Kensington Museum's new cast courts.

Conclusion

The V&A's collection, although lacking any sculpture from Amaravati itself, can form part of the discussion of this topic both through the interesting collection of later works from the Krishna River area of Andhra Pradesh and from the treatment of this and related subjects in its photographs, plaster casts and other media. The plaster casts may also provide a useful comparison with the originals preserved in the British Museum.

Notes

1 Royal College of Surgeons, *Plarr's Lives of the Fellows Online, Biographical Entry: Hunt, Edmund Henderson (1874–1952)*, http://livesonline.rcseng.ac.uk/biogs/E005071b.htm (accessed 5 July 2016).

Figure 119 Plaster cast of the upper part of the outer face of a railing pillar from Amaravati, London, probably 1880, Victoria and Albert Museum, REPRO.1880-41, formerly numbered IPN.1392

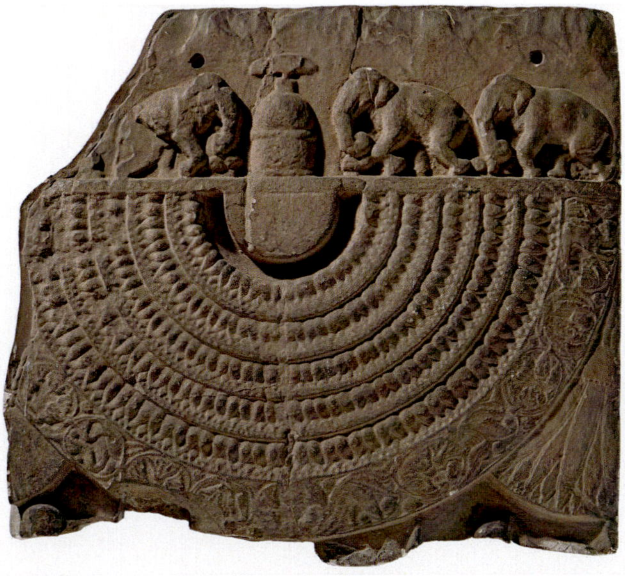

2 V&A registered papers, Hunt, E.H., MA/1/H3359, 36/4563.
3 P. Wright, V&A registered papers, Hunt, E.H., MA/1/H3359, 36/4563.
4 Traces of red paint on the figure were analysed by Raman microscopy and X-ray fluorescence to investigate whether this pigment could be original or if it was a more recent addition. No modern pigments were detected. Hematite was identified, a natural substance which has been in use since antiquity, but this is still in use today so no definite conclusions about the date of the pigment were possible. I am very grateful to Dr Lucia Burgio for her analysis and comments.
5 The entry for this object (museum no. IM.81-1936) in the 1936 V&A register was written by hand, but the text containing the attribution to Nagarjunakonda is typed on a piece of paper stuck on to the page. It is not possible to be certain when that was added, though it seems most likely to have been done soon afterwards.
6 Sarkar suggested that the prominence given to its large *stūpa*, along with the absence of a *maṇḍapa* or apsidal temples, may have been a characteristic of the Apara-mahāvina-seliya sect, who were predominant at Nagarjunakonda, or of the Caityakas (Sarkar 1966: 88).
7 I am very grateful to Mr Narsimham, curator of the ASI museum at Nagarjunakonda in March 2015, for his comments.
8 R. Sewell's Description of the objects, in V&A registered papers, Sewell, R., MA/1/S1227, 1913/1326M.
9 R. Sewell's Description of the objects, in V&A registered papers, Sewell, R., MA/1/S1227, 1913/1326M.
10 C. Stanley Clarke, Remarks on R. Sewell's Description of the objects, in V&A registered papers, Sewell, R., MA/1/S1227, 1913/1326M.
11 V&A register, 1913.
12 The entries in the V&A register for this object (museum no. IM.298-1914) and the following sculpture (IM.299-1914) gives their date as '8th century ?'
13 C. Stanley Clarke, Remarks on R. Sewell's Description of the objects, in V&A registered papers, Sewell, R., MA/1/S1227, 1913/1326M.
14 R. Sewell's Description of the objects, in V&A registered papers, Sewell, R., MA/1/S1227, 1913/1326M. Sewell's suggestion that the figure 'may be Jaina' was rejected and the figure tentatively identified as Maitreya. Later, the figure was for a period believed by John Irwin and others to be a Shaivite image, but it is now seen as a bodhisattva, possibly 'an early representation' of Avalokiteśvara (Guy 2014: 36–7).
15 V&A: Word and Image Department registers 65.069-125, 65.619-75, 65.676-732, 65.733-789.
16 V&A: Word and Image Department registers 67.480-536; and Library Receiving Room Diary volume 8 (1868–9), MA/34/8.
17 The India Museum's plaster casts were among over 19,000 objects transferred to the South Kensington Museum when the former's collections were dispersed in 1879. Most of these casts no longer survive and a lack of detail in the records of the time makes many of those that were listed impossible to identify individually.
18 Some of the casts have single figure numbers in an archaic hand incised on the back. The writing styles vary but appear to be of the 19th century. These casts are **Figures 113** ('4'), **114** ('3'), **115** ('2') and **118** ('N[?]2'), along with **Figure 119** ('1880'). The fact that the numeral '2' appears twice suggests that they are not part of a single sequence. The casts show a variety of different techniques and treatments on the backs but these do not appear to provide clues to dating them as they continued in use for a very long time. I am grateful to several colleagues and others for advice on these questions and for other help and information. While space does not permit me to mention them all I would particularly like to thank Charlotte Hubbard, Christopher Marsden, Nicholas Smith, Natalya Kusel, Robert Skelton, Graham Parlett, Divia Patel, Emma Rogers, Paul Gardner, Neil Carleton, Pamela Young and Marie de Lauzon. Any errors are of course my own.
19 After the V&A's Indian Section lost a large amount of space in the mid-1950s with the demolition of several galleries to enable the expansion of Imperial College, large numbers of objects including plaster casts such as the Sanchi gateway were de-accessioned. A large number of damaged casts were written off in 1964, other casts having already been de-accessioned in 1937.
20 India Office Records (IOR): L/E/2/88 Statistics & Commerce Dept. 13 Nov. 1879, item 5184. IOR: C/43 Council of India Minutes 11 Nov. 1879, f 319. See also Desmond 1982: 170, Willis 1997: 257 and IOR: L/E/2/84 Statistics & Commerce Dept. 30 Dec. 1879, item 5456.
21 V&A Register of Reproductions, vol. III, 1879–83.

Chapter 8
An Amaravati-School Pillar from the Collections of the Rijksmuseum, Amsterdam and the Tokyo National Museum: Style and Attribution

Anna A. Ślączka

Archaeological remains from Buddhist monuments in Andhra Pradesh often travelled a long way before reaching Europe or America, where they became part of a museum or a private collection. The paucity of information on provenance as a result of insufficient excavation reports or, at times, an unwillingness to reveal the circumstances of the discovery, has frequently led to an incorrect identification of Andhra pieces, with the majority being ascribed to Amaravati, the most renowned Andhran Buddhist site. This identification, in many cases, has been proved wrong.

The Rijksmuseum's collection of Indian art contains a pillar fragment 'in the Amaravati style' (AK-MAK-304; **Figs 120–2**). It was bought in 1955 by the Dutch Society of Friends of Asian Art (Vereniging van Vrienden der Aziatische Kunst, established 1918), whose collection is on long-term loan to the Rijksmuseum. It was long thought that the sculpture had come from Amaravati proper. However, in view of the recent scholarship on the early Buddhist sites of Andhra, I believe that this attribution should be reconsidered.

In the first part of this article I will therefore discuss the style and iconography of the fragment. I will then compare it with similar archaeological remains from Amaravati and related sites. On the basis of this comparison, and in view of its acquisition history, I will propose that the pillar does not come from Amaravati, but rather from Nagarjunakonda or one of the smaller sites that were close to the art of early Nagarjunakonda in style and date.

Description

The fragment in the Rijksmuseum (48cm high × 34cm wide × 17cm deep) amounts to five faces of what was originally an octagonal pillar, now missing the upper and lower parts of the shaft and split longitudinally. The faces are decorated with a heavy undulating garland supported by dwarf-like figures, the *gaṇas*. Its lower bends are adorned with lotus medallions carrying eight petals around a small centre, with five thick tassels or garland ends hanging below. There is

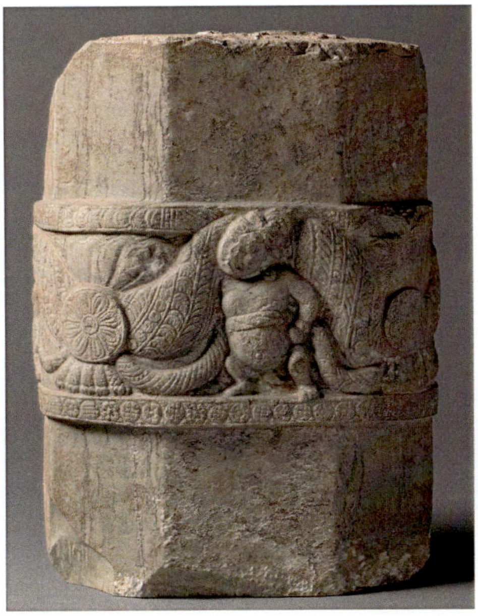

Figure 120 Pillar fragment, 3rd century CE, Amaravati school, Rijksmuseum, Amsterdam, no. AK-MAK-304

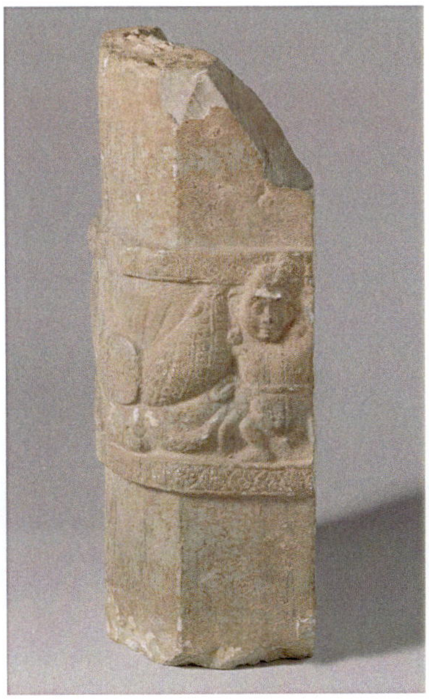

Figure 121 Right side of Figure 120

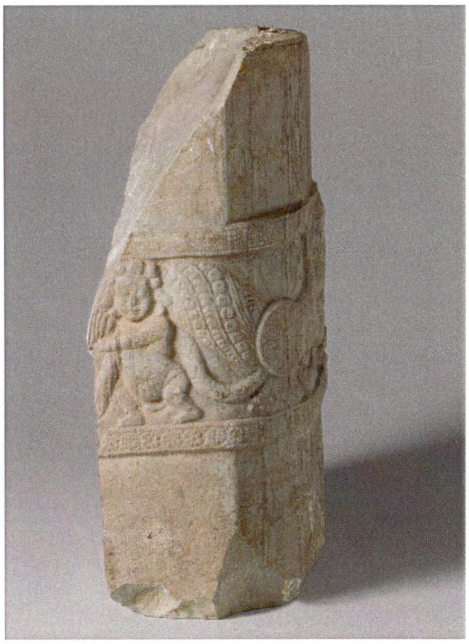

Figure 122 Left side of Figure 120

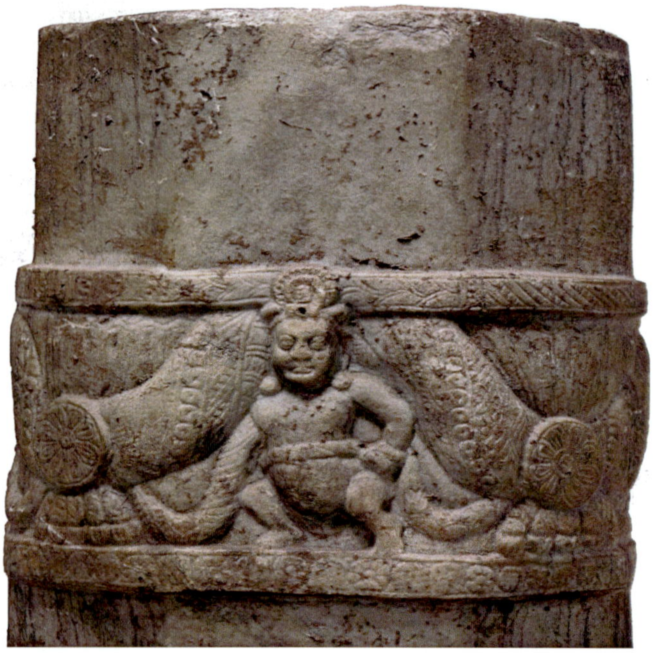

Figure 123 Pillar fragment, 3rd century CE, Tokyo National Museum, no. TC-739

also a second, thinner garland shown below the main one. The space above each medallion is filled with a motif resembling the cup-shaped calyx of a flower marked on top with a double undulating line. The frieze is framed above and below with a thin ornamental border. In contrast to numerous other cases of split-up pillars,[1] the missing 'back' has in this case survived and has been traced to the Tokyo National Museum (TC-739), where it has also been attributed to Amaravati (**Fig. 123**).[2]

The fragment in the Rijksmuseum, bearing three *gaṇa*s and two medallions, constitutes the larger part of the split-up pillar. The Tokyo fragment has one *gaṇa* flanked by two medallions. If joined together, the two parts would form a slightly asymmetric octagon of alternating larger (*c.* 16cm, carrying the *gaṇa*s) and smaller (*c.* 11cm, depicting the medallions) sides.[3] The parts seem to match pretty well, with no fragments missing, as demonstrated by one of the Rijksmuseum dwarves, whose severed left arm can be seen on the Tokyo fragment (**Fig. 124**).

The four *gaṇa*s constitute the most captivating part of the frieze, and their faces, with chubby cheeks and small pointed chin, are executed with great delicacy. They wear a little loincloth of the type known as *langoṭi*, the hem of which is visible just below the hips,[4] and all but one have a sash wrapped around the waist. Three *gaṇa*s have their hair gathered in a knot surrounded by a round frill, while one has large curls.[5] Further, they are adorned with round or flower-shaped earrings, bracelets (two dwarves) and upper-arm bracelets (one dwarf).

The pillar is carved from a greenish limestone. Its sculptured faces bear traces of pinkish coating, which in some areas has formed grain-like particles, perhaps representing the remains of paint.[6] It is a soft stone, prone to flaking and powdering, a characteristic of the so-called Palnad limestone that has been used in several Buddhist sites in Andhra and beyond.[7]

Comparison

The garland motif

Considering the style, decorative motifs and the material used, there can be no doubt that the pillar fragment belongs indeed to the so-called Amaravati school of art. But which among the numerous Andhran Buddhist sites would have produced it? There are more than 140 Early Historic sites (*c.* 300 BCE–300 CE; see Shimada 2013: 130 and Appendix B) in the entire Andhra region, many of them Buddhist, and new ones are still being discovered. Yet, in spite of a long search through published reports, catalogues and museums, I did not come across a pillar resembling the one discussed here.[8]

Although the motif of garland and garland-bearers is quite common in the art of Amaravati, it seems never otherwise to have been used on a pillar. In the early phase of Amaravati (*c.* 50–1 BCE) undulating garlands carried by *gaṇa*s decorated the inner face of a rail (*vedikā*) coping (**Fig. 125**).[9] These carvings, however, are rather shallow, and the hairstyle and postures of the dwarves are very different from those on the Rijksmuseum–Tokyo fragment. Besides, the execution of the garland is much more schematic and the area above the lower bends is filled with large half-lotuses seen from above, resembling those frequently depicted on rail pillars.

After the early period the garland-bearing dwarves seem to have been replaced by running youths, at least on large-scale sculptures (**Fig. 126**). The garland becomes now much more elaborate, with decorative horizontal bands, and the composition is more complex, showing the *horror vacui* characteristic of mature Amaravati art. Such friezes are found on larger fragments, such as the outer face of rail copings[10] or, in miniature, as decoration on rail copings of *stūpa*s depicted on drum slabs (**Fig. 127**). The miniature friezes of garland-bearers also adorn a number of the 3rd-century CE *stūpa* slabs from Nagarjunakonda and Gummadidurru.[11] All these friezes seem even more remote from the one on the pillar under discussion than those belonging to the first phase.

Figure 124 Ornamental frieze (the entire length) of Figure 122 (Rijksmuseum, AK-MAK-304) and Figure 123 (Tokyo National Museum, TC-739)

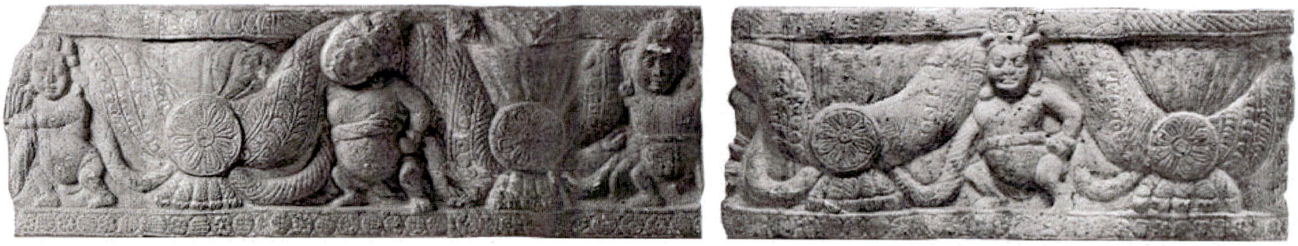

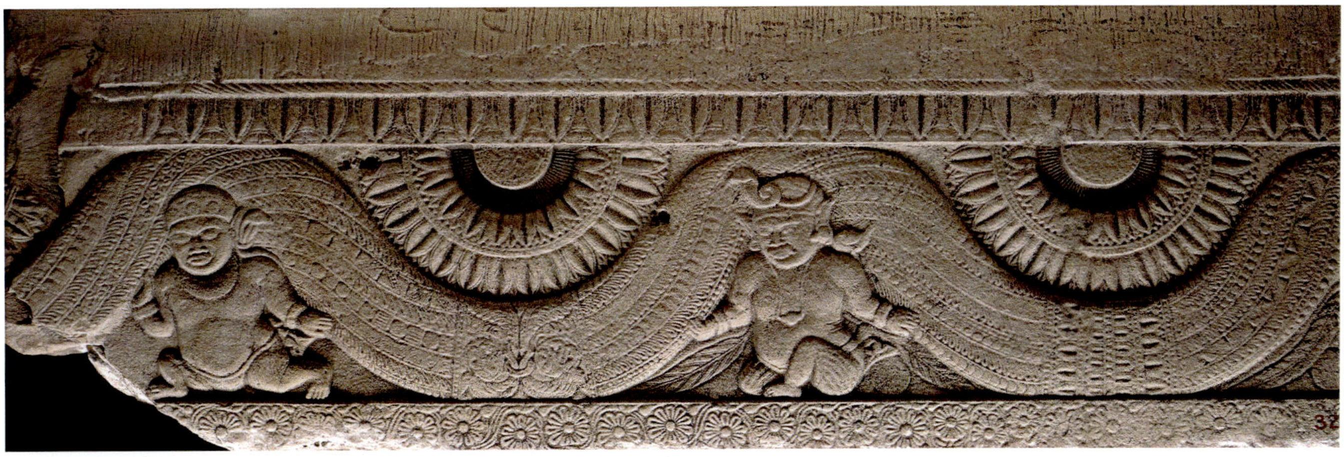

Figure 125 Rail coping, *c.* 1st century BCE, Amaravati, British Museum, 1880,0709.32

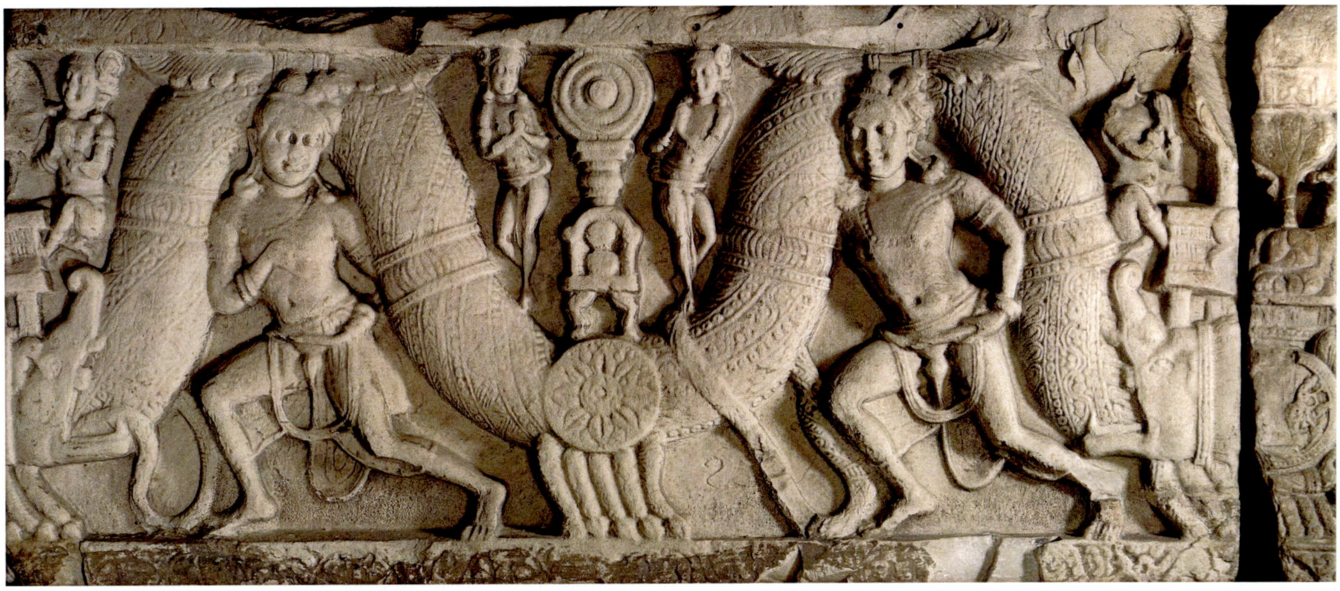

Figure 126 Miscellaneous fragment, 2nd–3rd century CE, Amaravati, British Museum, 1880,0709.29

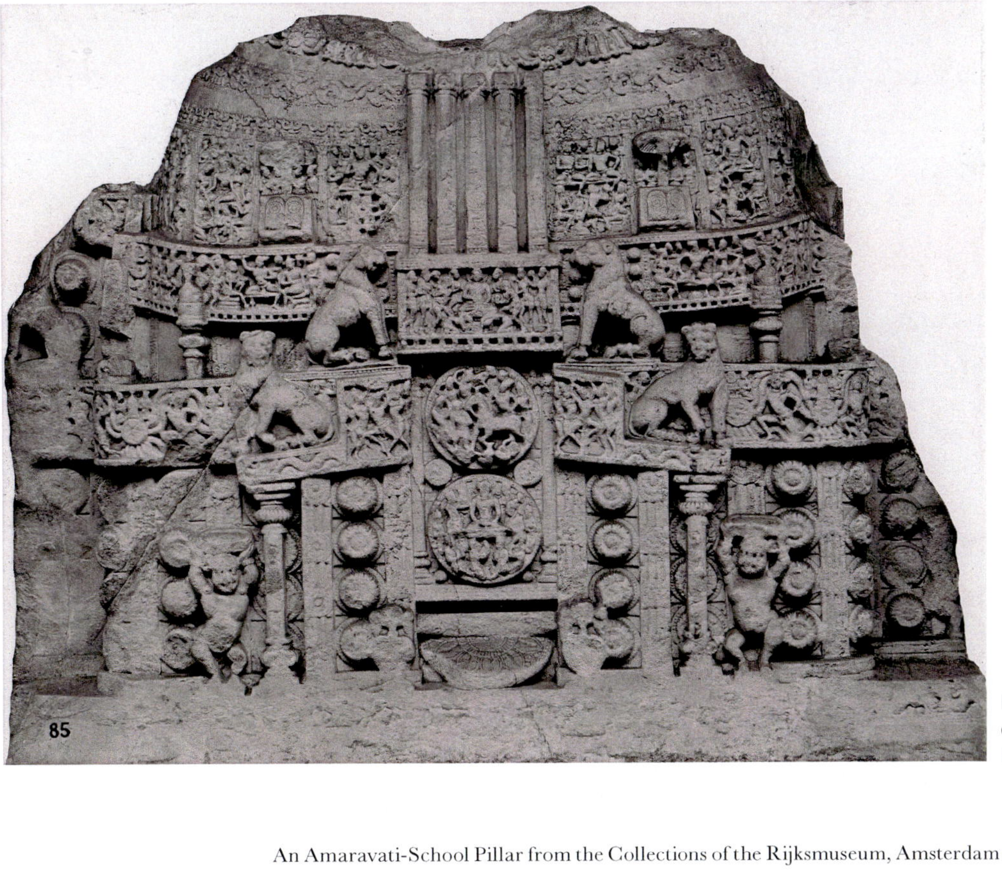

Figure 127 Drum slab, *c.* 3rd century CE, Amaravati, British Museum, 1880,0709.85

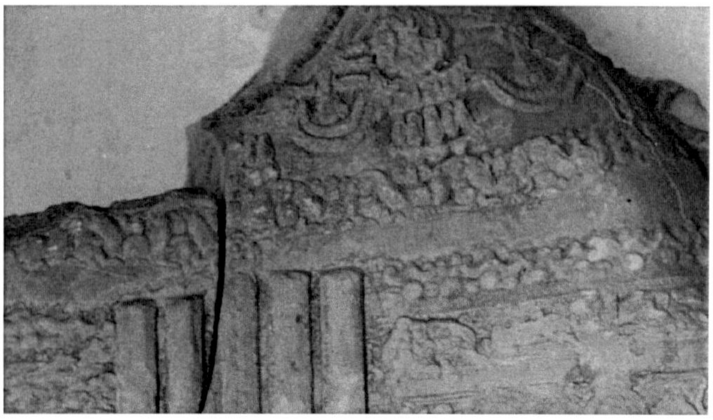

Figure 128 Drum slab from Nagarjunakonda (detail), *c.* 3rd century CE, present location unknown (photograph: J.E. van Lohuizen-de Leeuw)

And yet the *gaṇa*s did not disappear altogether after the early period. We see them, albeit in miniature sculpture, carrying the garland on the dome of *stūpa*s depicted on drum slabs, partly hidden behind the tops of the *āyaka* pillars (see **Fig. 127**, top of the dome slab). Interestingly, such friezes were never employed in the *actual* decoration of the dome, but it is of course possible that the sculptures have not survived. Admittedly, these carvings are so small and eroded that it is at times difficult to determine whether the tiny figures represent dwarves or 'youths'. In many cases, however, they seem to be genuine *gaṇa*s resembling those on our pillar. Other iconographical elements of the composition also recall our pillar frieze: the garlands are adorned with flat lotus medallions with hanging tassels and on some carvings a calyx-shaped motif fills the space above. On the other hand, the postures of the dwarves in miniature *stūpa* slabs are different from those on the Amsterdam–Tokyo pillar, as the former are running rather than standing. The garland appears neatly contained within the ornamental border, while on the Amsterdam–Tokyo pillar the garland overlaps the border. Unfortunately, the size of these carvings prevents a further comparison of details.[12] Again, very similar miniature friezes are seen on decorated drum slabs from Nagarjunakonda (**Fig. 128**).

Among these small friezes of dwarves bearing garlands, there is one that deserves special attention. It is part of the decoration of a miniature *stūpa* on a drum slab and is carved not on the *stūpa* dome but, uniquely, on a rail coping. This interesting sculpture does not come from Amaravati, but from Site 6 in Nagarjunakonda and has been dated by E.R. Stone (1994: 51–8 and fig. 124) to the reign of Vīrapuruṣadatta (238–62 CE).[13] Since Site 6 was amongst the first sites discovered in Nagarjunakonda, it was poorly documented. This sculpture's provenance is, however, confirmed by a photograph showing it *in situ* (**Figs 129–30**; the drum slab in question is seen in the centre). In contrast to the miniature friezes discussed earlier, the thick garland here hangs at a similar angle to the Amsterdam one and, as on 'our' pillar, is twisted in such a way that the strings fall vertically. Another, thinner garland is shown below and the lotus medallions have each eight petals and five tassels. Moreover, the heads of the figures overlap the upper decorative border. On the other hand, the motif above the medallions is not a cup-shaped calyx, but an open lotus flower, resembling those employed in early Amaravati art and, as in the previous examples, the headdress, ornaments and facial features cannot be seen in detail. In spite of this, the entire composition appears closer to that on the Rijksmuseum pillar than the miniature friezes from Amaravati.[14]

The ornamental border

Another element that might be of importance for determining the provenance of the Amsterdam–Tokyo pillar is the thin horizontal border above and below the garland-and-dwarves frieze. Remarkably, the decoration on the top is not the same over the entire length of the border. Zones of different motifs are separated by double (or triple) uprights with rows of beads in between. We can distinguish three different motifs divided over eight zones: leaves (overlapping in the fashion of fish-scales and marked with a double outline); half-moons or scoops marked with tiny horizontal grooves; and a twisted garland (see **Fig. 124**, where the

Figure 129 Site 6, Nagarjunakonda, *c.* 3rd century CE

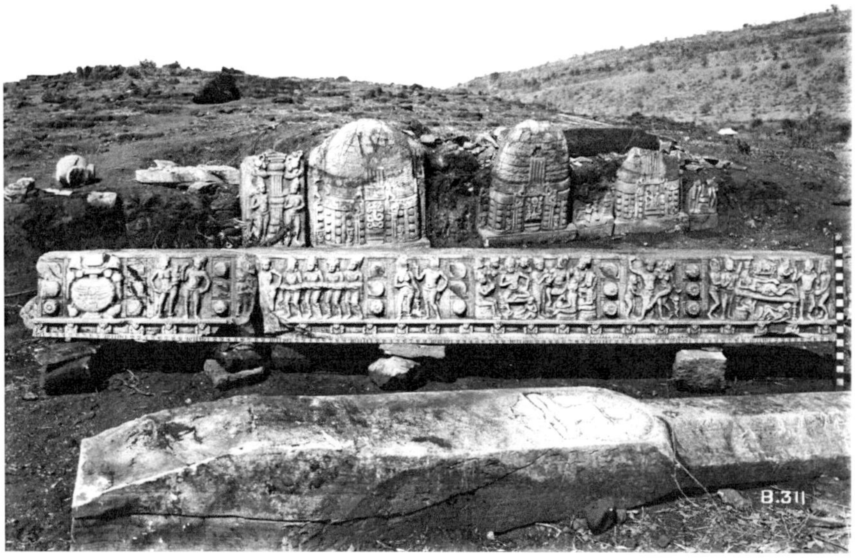

Figure 130 Drum slab from Site 6, *c.* 3rd century CE, Nagarjunakonda (detail), Archaeological Museum, Nagarjunakonda

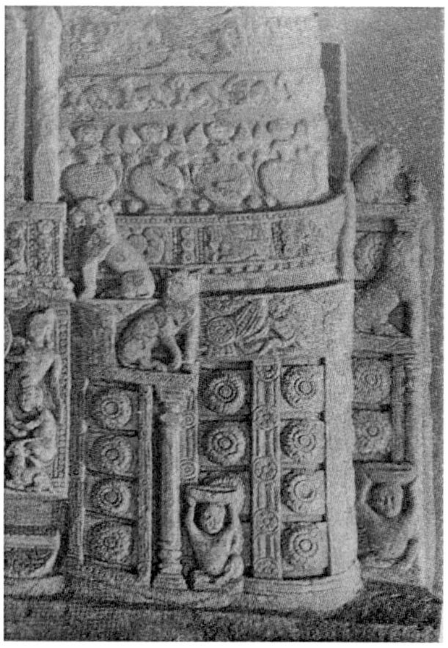

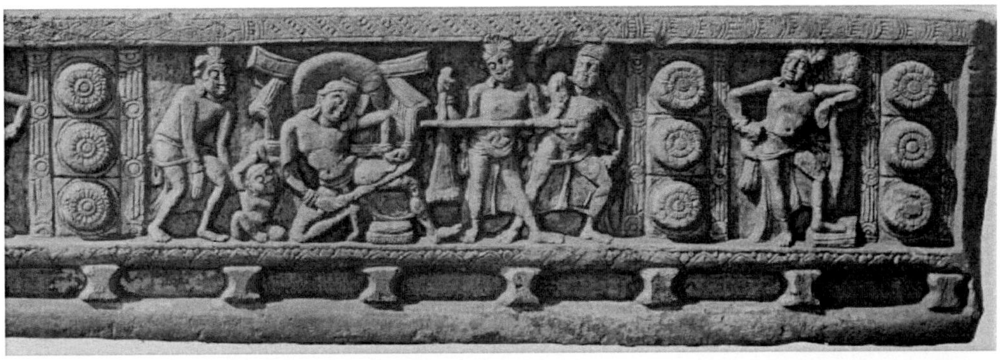

Figure 131 Śibi Jātaka (*āyaka* panel from Site 9), 3rd century CE, Nagarjunakonda, Archaeological Museum, Nagarjunakonda

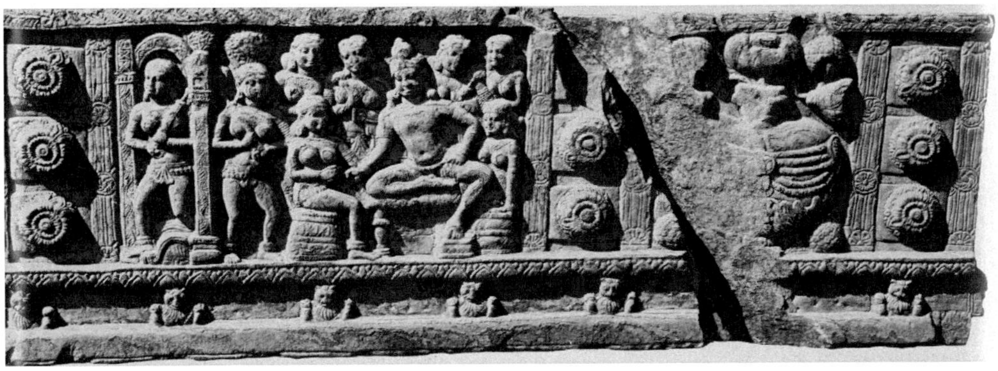

Figure 132 *Āyaka* panel from Site 9, 3rd century CE, Nagarjunakonda, Archaeological Museum, Nagarjunakonda

sequence is leaves, half-moons, garland, leaves, garland, half-moons, leaves, garland).

Contrary to what might be expected, ornamental borders of this type are not very common. The aforementioned decorative motifs can be seen on sculpture from later Amaravati, Nagarjunakonda and a number of smaller sites, but they are placed elsewhere, for instance on pilasters separating narrative scenes on drum friezes or on the 'necklace' that adorns the top of the *stūpa* domes depicted on drum slabs.[15] In ornamental horizontal bands, as a rule, a single pattern is used over the entire length. The only noteworthy exceptions are the *āyaka* panels from Site 9 in Nagarjunakonda where the upper ornamental border consists of a string of motifs, which are, moreover, similar to those on the Amsterdam–Tokyo pillar (**Fig. 131**). The border on the panels illustrating the Śibi Jātaka, for instance, has all three of the motifs noted above, that is the scale-like leaves marked with a double outline (albeit with three leaves instead of two); the 'oblique garland' (slightly more schematic here but also built up of rows of beads separated by two 'plain' strings); and the striated half-moons (here a mirror image of ours, curving in another direction). As on the pillar, the motifs are separated by vertical lines with dots or beads in between. The leaf pattern, which is the least common among the three, frequently consists of two leaves with the third one emerging from between them. Yet, on another panel from Site 9, it is built of only two leaves plaited in a similar way as on the Amsterdam frieze (**Fig. 132**).

The lower border consists of a row of small 'cornflowers' with four petals alternating with circles filled with chequered pattern. In this case, no identical or even similar border could be found, but such flowers and circles in combination with other motifs were rather popular during the 3rd century CE and seem especially frequent on sculpture from Nagarjunakonda.[16]

Acquisition: C.T. Loo and G. Jouveau-Dubreuil

As already noted, the pillar fragment entered the Rijksmuseum collection after it was bought by the Society of Friends of Asian Art in 1955. The Society's archive does not contain any information about the provenance except that the seller was the art gallery J.C. Moreau-Gobard in Paris.[17] It appears, however, that in 1934 both parts of the pillar had been owned by another Parisian art dealer, the renowned C.T. Loo (de Coral Rémusat 1934: pl. 74).[18] Interestingly, soon after the acquisition of the first fragment, the Society members learned about the existence of its counterpart and urged Moreau-Gobard to trace it. As a result, the sculpture was brought back to France and offered on sale to the society.[19] Yet the purchase was never finalized, probably owing to financial reasons.[20] After travelling a long and complicated journey – between 1977 and 1983 it was apparently on loan to the Denver Art Museum and in 1990 it suddenly appears in Sotheby's sale catalogue – the second part of the pillar eventually reached the Tokyo National Museum, where it still remains.[21]

C.T. Loo's supplier of Indian objects was the self-taught archaeologist and art historian Gabriel Jouveau-Dubreuil (1885–1945), author of several publications on Indian art. The two men met in Paris between 1922 and 1923, after which point Jouveau-Dubreuil returned to the French colony of Pondicherry in India as C.T. Loo's 'buying agent'.[22] Over the following years he shipped numerous sculptures to France, among them Pallava and Chola images from Tamil Nadu and several early Buddhist pieces from Andhra, which can now be seen in European and American collections. He also delivered sculptures from Andhra to the Government Museum in Madras (now Government Museum, Chennai).[23]

It is therefore quite possible that the Rijksmuseum pillar reached C.T. Loo via Jouveau-Dubreuil. With regard to this it is interesting to note that Jouveau-Dubreuil indeed visited Andhra in the period that is of interest to us, namely before 1934. In 1926 he even conducted a brief excavation of Nagarjunakonda's Site 6, from where he allegedly removed a number of sculptures.[24] As demonstrated earlier, at least one sculpture from this site is carved with the garland-and-dwarves motif, very similar to that on the Rijksmuseum pillar. Reliefs from Site 9 (**Figs 131–2**) also show strong similarity to the pillar in ornamental pattern, but this is only to be expected, for both sites belong to the so-called early Nagarjunakonda style and are close in date (Stone 1994: 52). No such similarity to reliefs from Amaravati is found.

Attribution and date

Although no identical pillar seems to exist, similar decorative patterns were used in Nagarjunakonda, particularly at Sites 6 and 9. The importance of ornamental motifs for the study of Andhran art was noted by Bénisti (1959: 218–22), who, indeed, classified the twisted garland, the cornflowers, the chequered pattern and the striated half-moons as typical for Nagarjunakonda. Stone (1994: 87) takes this further and ascribes an especially important role to the patterns bordering the narrative friezes. She observes that such decorative borders are as a rule specific to the find-site. The fact that an ornamental border resembling that on the Amsterdam–Tokyo pillar is found only on sculpture from Nagarjunakonda Site 9 therefore seems significant.

In view of the above, I believe that the previous attribution of the pillar to Amaravati is not convincing, but that there are instead good reasons to suppose that the fragment was collected from one of the earlier Nagarjunakonda structures, perhaps Site 6 or Site 9. It should be added that Gilberte de Coral Rémusat, in her 1934 article, implicitly considers the pillar, then in the collection of C.T. Loo, as being from Nagarjunakonda for she presents it as one of the examples of the influence of Nagarjunakonda on early Pallava style. She also states that she consulted Jouveau-Dubreuil about her article and one can assume that if he thought that the pillar came from elsewhere, he would have corrected her.

Of course, since no identical object has been found in Nagarjunakonda (or, indeed, anywhere else), the pillar could also have come from one of the smaller sites stylistically close to early Nagarjunakonda. Among sculptures donated to the Musée Guimet by Jouveau-Dubreuil and C.T. Loo there are a few from Gummadidurru, Ghantasala and Goli (the last site was also excavated by Jouveau-Dubreuil),[25] but it should be stressed that the identification of these and several other 'Andhra-school' sculptures is still a subject of discussion. Many sites have been disturbed quite early in time and are poorly documented – early explorers and scholars mention ancient pillars being used as boundary marks in villages or as building material in Hindu temples.[26] At the same time, Buddhist remains are still being discovered around Amaravati and Nagarjunakonda.

The fact that the pillar seems to belong to the early Nagarjunakonda style also has implications for its date. The piece has been variously dated: the 1st century CE by the Tokyo National Museum; '*circa* 2nd century' in the Sotheby's catalogue; the 2nd–3rd century CE in the article by de Coral Rémusat; and the 3rd century CE, as suggested by Vogel.[27] Considering that the drum slab from Site 6 (**Fig. 130**) and the *āyaka* panels illustrating the Śibi Jātaka from Site 9 (**Fig. 131**) have both been dated to *c.* 250 CE,[28] Vogel's suggestion seems the most plausible one. This rather late date is supported by the characteristic headdress of the dwarves, in which a hair knot is surrounded by a round frill. On two dwarves the frill has a pointed end, which is typical of sculptures post-dating the 2nd century CE.[29] The pillar could therefore have been made at some point during the reign of Vīrapuruṣadatta (r. 238–62 CE), whose period, moreover, is characterized by the combination of Amaravati and non-Amaravati elements in sculpture.[30]

We will probably never be sure where exactly the pillar came from, unless a similar sculpture is found somewhere.[31] Otherwise, the piece is too fragmentary, leaving very few elements for comparison. And yet this modest sculpture embodies a number of issues encountered by everyone who attempts to study Andhran art, and perhaps Indian art in general: poorly documented excavations and the following loss of the archaeological data; the advantages – these two fragments have survived, after all – but also the dangers of an art trade driven by the Western interest in Indian artefacts; and the need for well-documented acquisition history. I hope that in the future these two pieces can be joined, not only virtually as here, but in real life, even if just for a limited period of time.

Notes

1 For examples from Amaravati, see BM nos 1880.0709.63–65, 103 (illustrated in Knox 1992: nos 110–14).

2 http://www.tnm.jp/modules/r_exhibition/index.php?controller=item&id=3528&lang=en (accessed 8 July 2016).

3 The depth of the Rijksmuseum fragment is 17cm; the depth of the Tokyo fragment should be less than that (the Amsterdam fragment has three dwarves versus only one in Tokyo). The two fragments joined together would thus form a slightly 'flattened' octagon, with two dwarf-sides being the widest (those showing the 'complete' dwarves: the Tokyo one and the one opposite it on the Rijksmuseum fragment).

4 This detail was missed by Vogel (1955: 51), according to whom they only wear the sash. For the *langoṭi* worn 'with the end passing between the legs and tucked in behind', see K. Krishna Murthy (1977: 40). Dwarves dressed in the same way and with a similar hairstyle can, for instance, be seen on the Great Departure stele from Phanigiri (published, e.g., in Becker 2015: fig. 2.7), now in the Andhra Pradesh State Museum, Hyderabad (acc. no. 2002-270).

5 Such large, separate curls are not frequently depicted in Andhran sculpture, but can be seen, for instance, on the panel from Nagarjunakonda depicting the Buddha visited by Indra in the Cave of Indraśaila (Longhurst 1938: pl. 44 (b); also published in Stone 1994: fig. 218).

6 The pinkish layer is absent on damaged surfaces that show the core of the stone. A hypothesis, following an X-ray diffraction analysis of the accretions, that such reddish coatings represent relict paint was presented by A.P. Middleton (1992: 232) of the British Museum.

7 The stone is obtained exclusively in the plateau area around Palnad in Guntur District (Shimada 2013: 121).

8 In addition to the literature search, I conducted a brief fieldwork trip to museums and Buddhist sites in Andhra Pradesh (February 2015), when I visited, among others, Amaravati, Nagarjunakonda, Ghantasala, Bhattiprolu, Chebrolu, Guntupalli, Jaggayyapeta, Gummadidurru and Alluru. Unfortunately, I was not able to visit all the existing sites and some regional museums were closed for renovation. I was also not able to access the restricted collection of the Government Museum, Chennai. Still, none of the sculptural remains seen thus far matches the pillar.

9 The dates as given by Shimada (2013: 99). There is a disagreement among the authors about the dating of the Amaravati remains. Other dates for these early rail copings include: Sivaramamurti 1942: 27: 200–100 BCE; Barrett 1954a: 45–6: second quarter of the 2nd century CE; and Knox 1992: 89: 1st century BCE. For other examples see Gupta 2008: fig. xi and Shimada 2013: pl. 36.

10 Some of these reliefs seem to be genuine coping stones. See, e.g., Gupta 2008: fig. xiv (ii). Others, carved on one side only and lacking the mortise hole on the bottom, were categorized as 'miscellaneous pieces' by Barrett (1954a: 70) and Shimada (2013: 110) and as 'dome slab friezes' by Gupta (2008: pls 31–2), while Knox (1992: 98, 103) still speaks of them as 'rail copings'. Note that the 'miscellaneous fragment' reproduced here as **Fig. 126** has also been variously dated: 2nd century CE by Knox (1992: 103) and 3rd century CE on the British Museum website: http://www.britishmuseum.org/research/collection_online/collection_object_details.aspx?objectId=251195&partId=1&searchText=amaravati&page=1 (accessed 8 July 2016).

11 For examples from Amaravati, see BM nos 1880,0709.79, 1880,0709.80, 1880,0709.81, 1880,0709.83, 1880,0709.85, 1880,0709.87 (illustrated in Knox 1992: nos 72–77) and Gupta 2008: pls 20–4 and figs xxiii–xxv. For examples from Nagarjunakonda and Gummadidurru, see Stone 1994: figs 115, 143, 146–7) and Gupta 2008: fig. xxviii.

12 In spite of their size, it can be noticed that these miniature friezes are far from being identical. Sometimes there are two garlands of the same thickness and the space above the garland's lower bends is filled with different motifs. There are also considerable differences in the postures of dwarves. See, e.g., BM nos 1880,0709.69, 1880,0709.70, 1880,0709.72, 1880,0709.75, 1880,0709.79, 1880,0709.83, 1880,0709.85, 1880,0709.87, 1880,0709.120 (illustrated in Knox 1992: nos 68–72, 75–8) and Gupta 2008: pls 20–2, fig. xxiv; some of these friezes decorate the same miniature *stūpas* whose rail copings display carvings of youths carrying garlands (see **Fig. 127**). On only one relief do the dwarves seem to resemble those on the Amsterdam–Tokyo pillar. The calyx-shaped motif, however, is here replaced by a lion-head. Uniquely, the relief in question, which is a part of the decoration of a miniature *stūpa* depicted on a drum slab, is found to the side of the *āyaka* platform (it is perhaps meant as a decoration on the platform's side), and not on the top of the dome. The relief further differs from other such slabs in not showing any figures at the front of the railing, such as worshippers or dwarves holding large baskets or basins above their heads, and it would be interesting to study it in more depth (for illustration, see Stern and Bénisti 1961: pl. 44; the relief was dated to the 'fourth period' of Amaravati i.e. *c.* 200–50 CE by Sivaramamurti 1942: pl. 59.2).

13 According to the site numbering system in Sarkar 1966 and Stone 1994.

14 It should be added that the garland-and-*gaṇas* motif was employed also on sculptures from sites as far away as Ter in the present-day Maharashtra (see Shimada 2013: pl. 65). Ter was connected to the Amaravati area by trade routes and there must have been strong mutual influences in art.

15 For examples see, e.g., Barrett 1954a: pls xii, xviii and xxx (Amaravati); Longhurst 1938: pls ix c, xxx c, xliv a, xlix b and l a (Nagarjunakonda); and Stone 1994: fig. 123 (see the 'twisted garland' motif on the flaming pillar, Gummadidurru). The motifs were also employed on sculpture from other sites, such as the drum slab from Chandavaram at the Andhra Pradesh State Archaeological Museum (acc. no. 6650). The 'twisted garland' appears by far the most popular of the three motifs.

16 See, e.g., Ramachandran 1953: pl. 16; Bénisti 1959: fig. 30; Stone 1994: figs 119, 191, 229.

17 Moreau-Gobard himself refers to the piece as 'pilier d'Amaravati'. On the other hand, H.F.E. Visser, Curator of the Society's collection, refers to 'le fragment de Nagarjunkonda (?)'. See letters from Moreau-Gobard to Visser (undated, probably end 1954) and from Visser to Pierre Dupont (dated 24 January 1955) in the archives of the Society of Friends of Asian Art (VVAK) in the Rijksmuseum.

18 See de Coral Rémusat 1934: pl. 74. Both parts are depicted there, described as 'fragments de colonnette, style d'Amaravati, coll. C.T. Loo'; it is not clear from the article and the photographs whether the pillar was already split up.

19 It was apparently Mrs F.M. Minkenhof, herself a collector of Asian art and a member of the Society, who learned about the existence of the other part of the pillar and insisted on tracing it. The pillar happened then to be in the possession of an American private collector who had recently bought it from Switzerland. See letter from Jan Fontein to Jean-Philippe Vogel, dated 26 October 1955, in the Society's archives.

20 In the correspondence preserved in the Society's archives, Moreau-Gobard is described as a rather expensive art dealer; the price asked for the first fragment, 450,000 French francs, was considered very high indeed. See letter from H.F.E. Visser to Pierre Dupont, dated 24 January 1955. Eventually, the piece was bought thanks to external funding.

21 See Sotheby's 1990, lot 6: 'A limestone column fragment, Satvahana [sic] period, Andhra Pradesh, probably Nagarajunakonda, circa 2nd Century A.D. … Formerly on loan to the Denver Art Museum, 1977–1983'.

22 Delatour (1996: 37): 'Loo, grand promoteur de pièces archéologiques chinoises … s'intéressait depuis peu à l'art indien. Il était en quête d'un fournisseur avisé, capable d'évaluer et de garantir la qualité des objets. … C.T. Loo lui [Jouveau-Dubreuil] proposa de devenir son intermédiaire en Inde. Leur association fut brève – cinq ou six ans tout au plus –, mais elle porta sur quelques centaines de pièces…' See also Kaimal 2012: 7, 137–42.

23 For which he allegedly even received an affiliation there (ibid.: 138).

24 He removed them 'before this site was classified among the ancient monuments selected by the Madras Presidency for conservation' and just before the trial excavation of this site by Hamid Kuraishi (Dimand 1928: 238).

25 See Ramachandran 1929. For the sculptures at the Musée Guimet, see Okada 2000: 43, 51, 57, 75, 77. It should be added that although the published sculptures from Goli are not similar to the Rijksmuseum pillar in style and decorative patterns, this is not the case with Gummadidurru: one of the dwarves on the Rijksmuseum pillar smiles in a way typical of the Gummadidurru figures. Interestingly, according to Stone (1994: 51) some sculptures from Site 9 (e.g. some *āyaka* panels carved with a border resembling the one on the Amsterdam–Tokyo pillar) show stylistic affinities to Gummadidurru. Site 9 seems therefore a very likely source for the Rijksmuseum pillar.

26 See Sewell 1880: 10–11, 25–6; Rea 1894: 34.

27 http://www.tnm.jp/modules/r_exhibition/index.php?controller=item&id=3528&lang=en (accessed 8 July 2016); Sotheby's 1990; de Coral Rémusat 1934: 244; and Vogel 1955: 58. Vogel was explicitly asked by Visser to write an article about the pillar soon after its acquisition by the Society (see letter from Visser to Pierre Dupont, dated 28 January 1955 in the Society's archives). In his article Vogel refuted both Amaravati and Nagarjunakonda as plausible find-sites. His opinion, however, seems not to have been given much consideration for the pillar remained, until present, labelled 'Amaravati' in the Rijksmuseum files.

28 Stone (1994: 51–8) discusses at length the dating of various archaeological remains from both sites. According to her, some remains from Site 6, including the drum slab in question, and the remains from Site 9 date from the reign of Vīrapuruṣadatta (Virapurisadata, r. 238–62; ibid.: 6). She also states that the combination of Amaravati and non-Amaravati elements as seen on the drum slabs from Site 6 is indeed typical for the reign of this king. Interestingly, it is the same combination that we find on the Rijksmuseum pillar: the dwarves-and-garland motif, which was common also in the later Amaravati period, is here combined with the ornamental patterns typical for Nagarjunakonda. As for the specific *āyaka* panels from Site 9 carved with an ornamental band similar to that on our pillar (ibid.: figs 64 and 90–1), she places them, respectively, at the same time and shortly after the so-called 'memorial pillars' from the same site, which she dates to *c.* 240–50 CE.

29 The pointed frill (worn by two of the Rijksmuseum pillar dwarves) follows chronologically the round one (worn by the dwarf on the Tokyo fragment). In Amaravati proper it seems to be typical of the third-phase railing (200–50 CE or even later; see Shimada 2013:

100–2). In Nagarjunakonda it is already seen on sculpture from the earliest sites, such as Sites 6 and 9 (see Stone 1994: fig. 44) and it occurs also on sculpture from Gummadidurru (ibid.: fig. 245).

30 See n. 28 above. For the chronology of Andhra kings, see Stone 1994: 6.

31 It would also be desirable to consult the archives of C.T. Loo and G. Jouveau-Dubreuil which were, unfortunately, unavailable to me. Further, in light of new discoveries and more images being published, it would perhaps make sense to add to the wonderful research of Bénisti and Stone and compare and attempt to map the development of ornamental motifs, such as the garland and garland-bearers. On the other hand, it is doubtful if such study, even if certainly useful and necessary, would shed more light on the attribution of the pillar discussed here.

Chapter 9

Protective Goddesses in the Service of Buddhism: A Sculpture from Andhra in the British Museum

Michael Willis

The papers collected in this volume focus on the Buddhist sculptures from Amaravati, primarily those items now kept in the British Museum. Here I will deviate slightly from this theme and discuss a single piece that was acquired by the museum in 1955, some 75 years after the Amaravati collection arrived in 1880 (Willis 1997: 26). The sculpture I want to examine in this article is the upper part of a rectangular pillar that carries a large female figure on its front face (**Fig. 133**). As the illustration shows, the side of the pillar has the remains of two lenticular mortises. These show that this fragment was part of a *stūpa* railing. The back is rough, the sculpture having been broken away from its ground. The size indicates that the original railing to which it belonged was of substantial size, comparable in some ways to the famous Amaravati railing. This sculpture is not, however, from Amaravati. It is normally attributed to Goli – a site about 20km directly east of the lake of Nagarjunakonda – since Douglas Barrett first published the piece and suggested that Goli was the provenance (Barrett 1959: 102–4; Koezuka 1994: 11). There is, in fact, no direct evidence that the pillar is from Goli but it is, anyway, from the Andhra country.[1]

The full-bodied female figure is damaged and weather-worn. An overall impression of its original appearance is furnished, however, by a small bronze, also in the collection of the British Museum (**Fig. 134**). The bronze, like the sculpture, wears earrings, arm bands, wrist bands and necklaces that fall between the breasts. The arm band in the sculpture is decorated with a *makara* (a sea-creature). In both pieces, the hair is tied up with a band, the sculpture showing

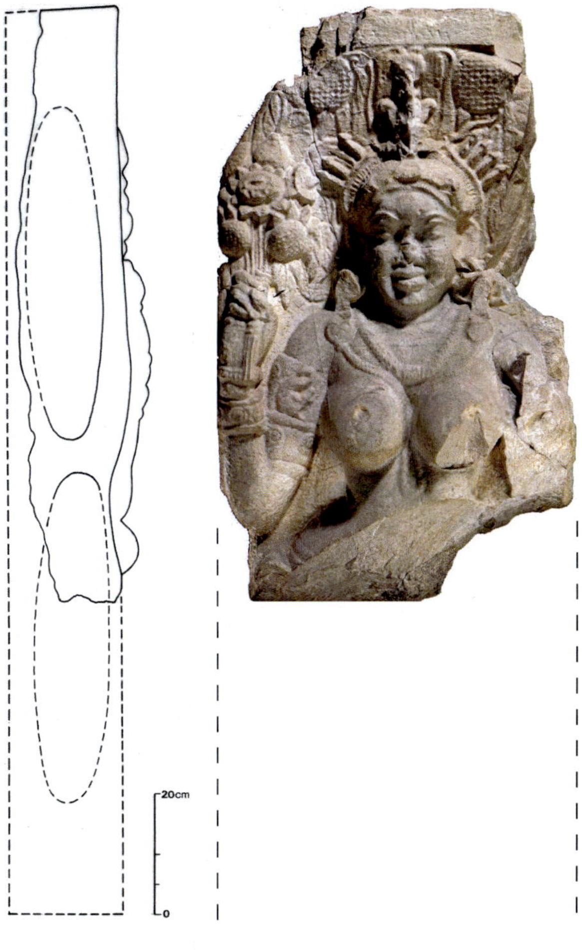

Figure 133 Railing pillar carved in sandstone with a standing female figure, *c.* 2nd century CE, British Museum, 1955,1017.1, donated by P. T. Brooke Sewell

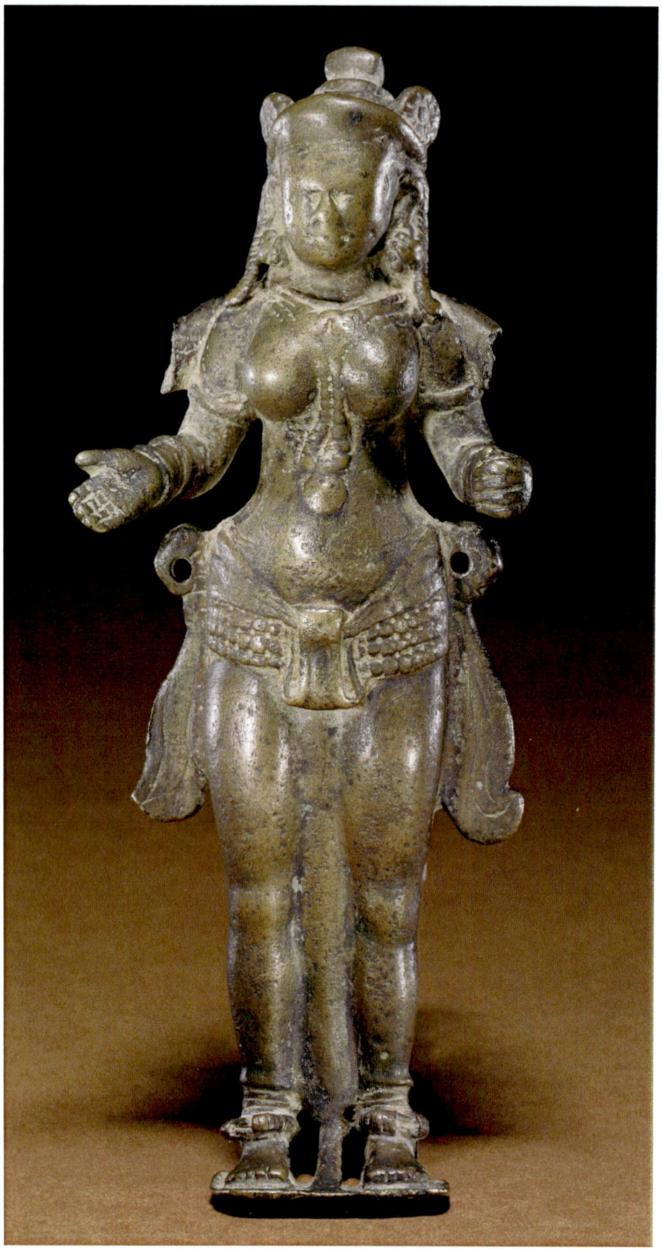

Figure 134 Standing female figure, once with four arms, flat cast in a copper alloy, *c*. 3rd to 4th century CE, British Museum, 1963,0215.1, Brooke Sewell Permanent Fund

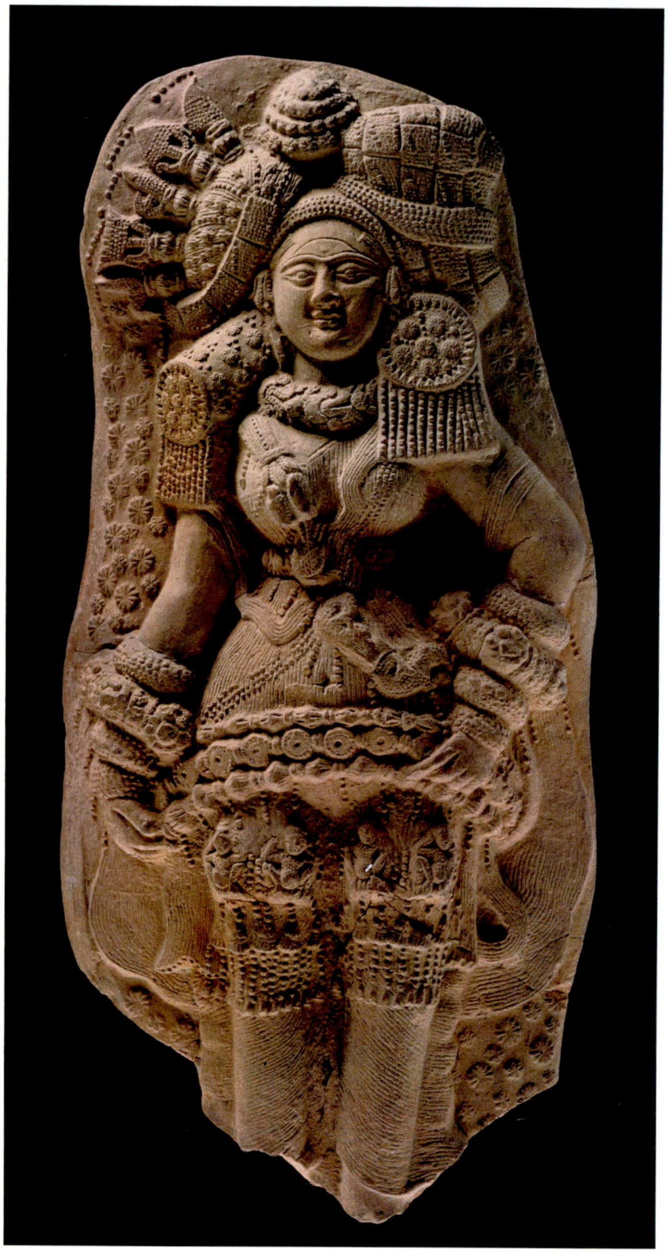

Figure 135 Terracotta plaque showing a standing goddess, *c*. 1st century BCE, Ashmolean Museum, University of Oxford, no. EAX 201

a prominent ornament or boss in the centre. This is a long-standing convention in Indian art, appearing first on the famous *yakṣī* (female fertility deity) from Didarganj in the museum at Patna.

The British Museum sculpture stands against a tree bearing fruit, a feature often found on Buddhist railings, those from Bharhut providing the best-known examples. Like the Bharhut sculptures also, the British Museum sculpture is inscribed, but only two damaged letters are visible, probably *ta* and *cha*. Given that identification labels are an early feature that dropped out of use in Andhra after the 1st century BCE, it seems likely that this is part of a donor's name. As a result, little of historical importance can be concluded from the inscription.

The figure holds lotus flowers and lotus pods in her raised hand. She has an unusually elaborate headdress that calls for attention. It consists of an incised band, crescent in shape, inserted into the hair. At the top, forming the centrepiece, are two *makara*-heads and a high finial. On either side, the band has projecting pins. These pins are of considerable importance because this iconographic feature is found in early terracottas.[2] The terracottas in question survive in great numbers, the most well-known example being in the Ashmolean at Oxford (**Fig. 135**). Noted for its elaborate ornament and fine detailing, this famous piece was discovered in 1883 in a riverbank at Tamluk, the ancient sea port of Tamralipti on the Bay of Bengal. Many others, as well as the moulds to make them, have been found at Candraketugarh, an archaeological site beside the Bidyadhari River about 35km north-east of Kolkatta (Haque 2001). Less well known is the fragment preserved in the Victoria and Albert Museum (V&A), London (**Fig. 136**). This specimen was acquired from Colonel D.H. Gordon with a provenance of Kauśambī (Gordon 1943).[3]

Two things can be concluded from a general survey of these terracotta figurines. The first is that there can be no

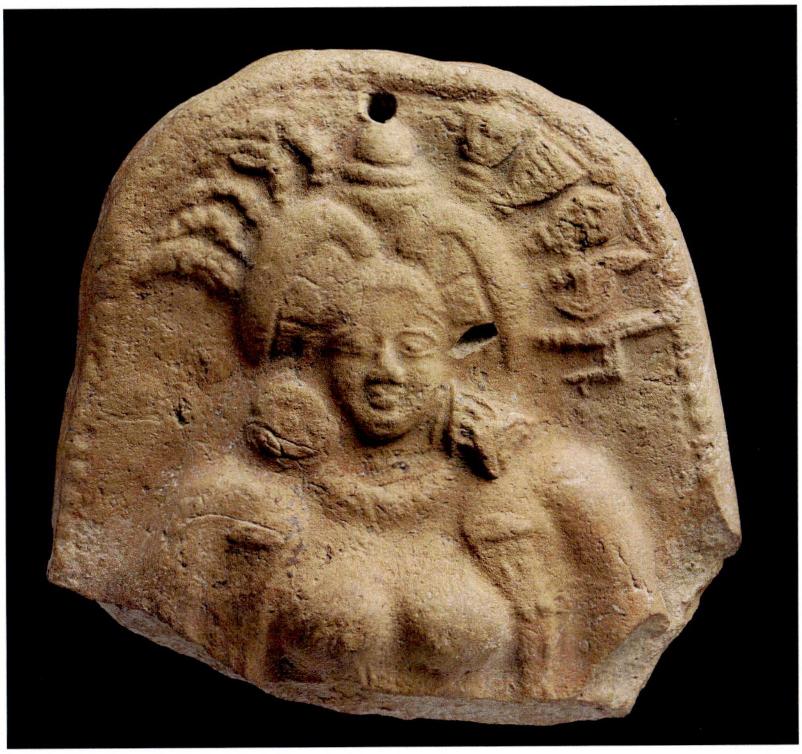

Figure 136 Terracotta plaque showing a goddess with rice fronds and ornamental pins in her hair, *c.* 1st century BCE, Victoria and Albert Museum, IS.57-1951

doubt that this is a representation of a goddess. The large number of plaques and their geographical spread show this deity was popular and worshipped over a wide area in the Gangetic plains of northern and eastern India. The hair in many examples – like the one in the V&A – carries fronds of rice, indicating that the goddess was connected with crops and fertility. A modern parallel can be found in Bijāsan Devī, the goddess of sprouting seeds, who is worshipped and presented with sprouts in the autumn before the winter crop is sown (**Fig. 137**). The sumptuous jewellery and the elaborate coiffure shown in the plaques also leave little doubt that this goddess was associated with wealth and prosperity, as one would expect of an agricultural deity.

Figure 137 Madanpur (Lalitput District), Jain goddess rededicated as Bijāsan Devī, shown after the autumn festival, main figure *c.* 11th century CE, with other fragments as old as the 8th century CE

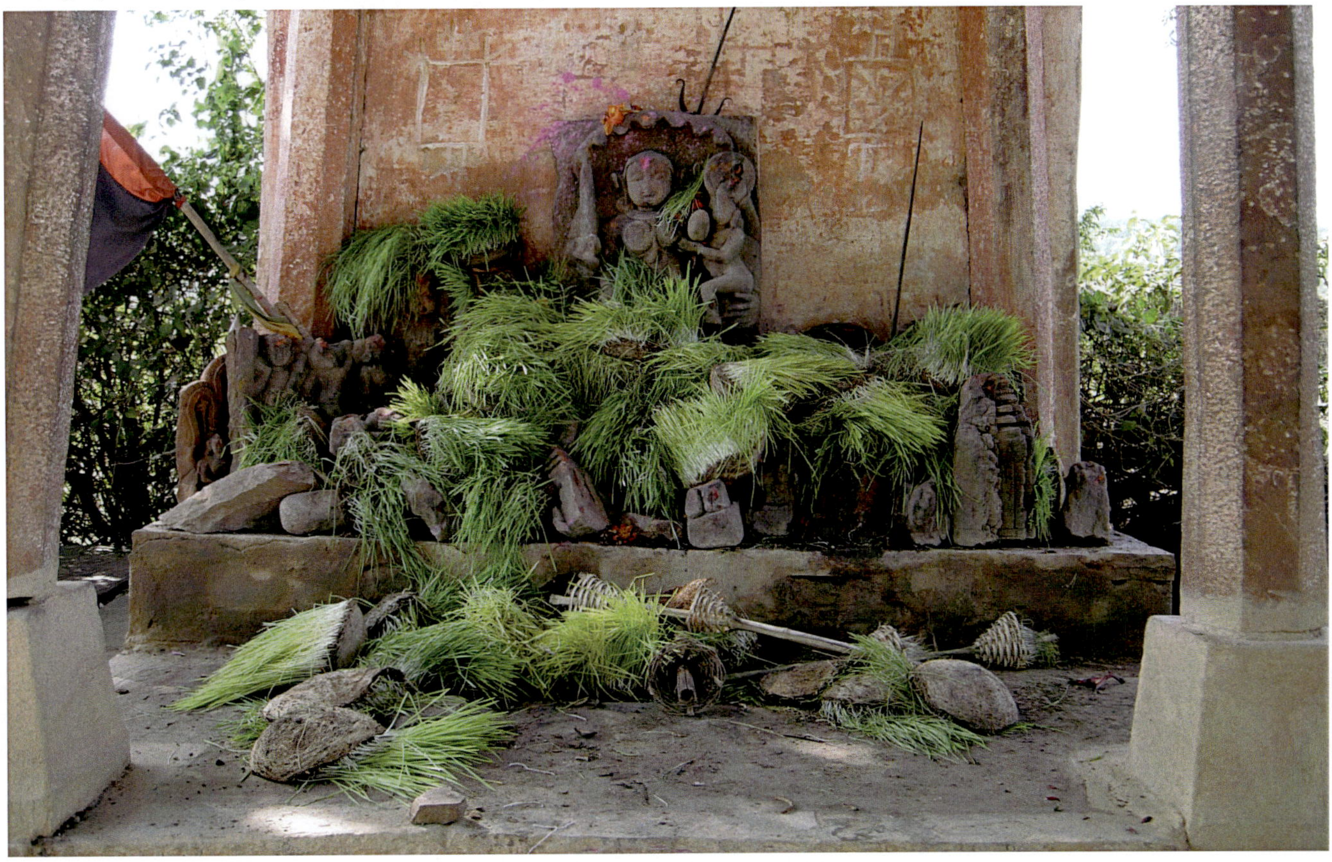

The main point that can be drawn from the terracotta plaques and British Museum pillar – at least from the perspective of the history of religions – is that they show how an independent goddess connected with agriculture and wealth was incorporated into the Buddhist framework. This is not exactly a new observation. The Bharhut railings are carved with a number of female figures and labelled. These labels give the name of the goddesses and demigoddesses (*yakṣī*) depicted. According to the readings provided by Lüders, they are as follows: *cadā yakhi* (= Candra); *sirimā devata* (= Śrīmatī); *yakhini sudasana* (= Sudarśanā); *culakokā devatā* (= little Kokā); and *mahakoka devata* (= great Kokā) (Lüders *et al.* 1963: 74–81).

What is apparent from this list, and what has been acknowledged at least since A.K. Coomaraswamy published his definitive study, *Yakṣas* (1928a; 1931), is that these goddesses are demigods external to Buddhism, and that they were brought into the service of the Buddhist faith to serve a protective purpose. This is confirmed especially by the appearance of the Four Great Kings – the guardians of the four directions – on the gateways from Bharhut (three of which are identified by inscriptions). As noted by Peter Skilling in his landmark article on protective literature, the *Āṭānāṭika sūtra* and *Mahāśitavana* feature the Four Great Kings, who express concern for monks, nuns, laymen and laywomen dwelling in remote places (Skilling 1992: 141). In other words, the Four Great Kings and the other demigods on the early Buddhist railings serve protective roles, creating, in Skilling's words, a *maṇḍala* or 'magic protective circle' (ibid.: 134, 163). As Skilling goes on to note in his discussion of the archaeological evidence, 'since Bharhut dates from about 100 B.C., and since the stone reliefs presuppose well-established (presumably oral) traditions as well as figurative prototypes, whether in wood or painted on cloth or other materials, we may say that the elements listed above go back to at least the second century B.C.' (Skilling 1992: 162).

The idea of vanished prototypes made of perishable material has enjoyed a long history in the study of early Indian art, and I will not deal with that historiography here. The only point I wish to make is that the British Museum pillar and the terracotta plaques provide the only physical evidence for the process and the 'figurative prototypes' long assumed. To put the matter another way, the idea that deities came from outside the religious core of Buddhism and were incorporated into early Buddhist cosmology is proven only by the British Museum sculpture and the terracotta plaques. The heart of the problem, of course, is that none of the non-Buddhist deities in early Buddhist art are known from non-Buddhist evidence. There seems no reason to doubt that serpent kings (*nāgarāja*) and demigoddesses (*yakṣī*, Prakrit *yakhi*) were part of the religious environment during and after the time of Asoka, if not long before. But such figures do not appear independently of – and prior to – the Buddhist context: it is only with the appearance of a strong Buddhist visual culture that the 'other' – the non-Buddhist – is at last articulated in substantial form. The imagery appears in the dialogue with Early Historic Buddhism and, we might add, under Buddhist control. And we, as later observers, are privy only to the end result. The British Museum pillar is thus a sculpture of considerable interest from the historical point of view. It is, as far as I am aware, the single example documenting how the process worked. The goddess in the terracotta plaques – whatever her name – was so widely worshipped that she found a natural resting place on a *stūpa* railing. Beyond her and her companions on the railings there were many others gods and goddesses: there was, outside the protective circle manufactured by the early Buddhists, a rich, diverse and potentially challenging world, filled with deities the myths, meanings and worship of which we can only guess. The British Museum pillar is the single point where these worlds actually meet.

Notes

1 See article by Anna A. Ślączka in this volume (Ch. 8) on the Rijksmuseum sculpture acquired at the same period and from the same source as the British Museum piece.

2 These terracottas have been studied by Naman Ahuja, to whom thanks are due for discussion around the themes presented here.

3 Gordon purchased in the market as well as collecting in the field, so his record of provenance, while reliable, is not absolutely so.

Chapter 10
Reviving the Lost Art of Amaravati: The Sriparvata Arama Project, India

Harsha Vardhan
(with supplementary remarks by Catherine Becker)

Introduction

The Sriparvata Arama is a theme park project aimed at recapturing the essence of the Buddhist heritage of the Telugu country and reviving the forgotten Amaravati school of art. The project, initiated in 2001 with the support of the Government of India and the State Government of Andhra Pradesh (now split into Telangana and Andhra Pradesh) has two goals: first, to provide ready reference to the grand sculpture of the Amaravati school of art; and, second, to offer an opportunity for the public to study the cultural positions of these architectural and artistic works in a context that recreates the original setting and space. This brief report aims at providing an overview of this ongoing project. As an artist who is participating in this project, I would also like to highlight a few of the challenges I encountered in developing the project and in achieving the above-mentioned goals.

Overview of the park

The Sriparvata project is taking place on the left bank of the Krishna River at Nagarjunasagar (ancient Vijayapurī, the capital of the Ikṣvāku dynasty) (**Fig. 138**). It is located 160km to the south-east of Hyderabad, the capital of Telangana, and 147km from Amaravati, the newly formed capital of Andhra Pradesh. The central monument in the 279 acres of the park is the *mahāstūpa*, built to commemorate the ancient Amaravati *stūpa*. The surrounding area of the *mahāstūpa* is divided into eight sectors, analogous to the eight-fold path of the Buddha.

Each of the sectors has a theme focusing on an important aspect of the Buddhist heritage of ancient Andhradeśa. The entrance plaza, for instance, is square in plan and has eight quadrants with four openings. All the eight quadrants are embellished with panels in relief sculpture depicting *aṣṭhamangala* symbols (eight auspicious objects), Buddhist

Figure 138 Aerial view of the Sriparvata Arama, Nagarjunasagar, 2014

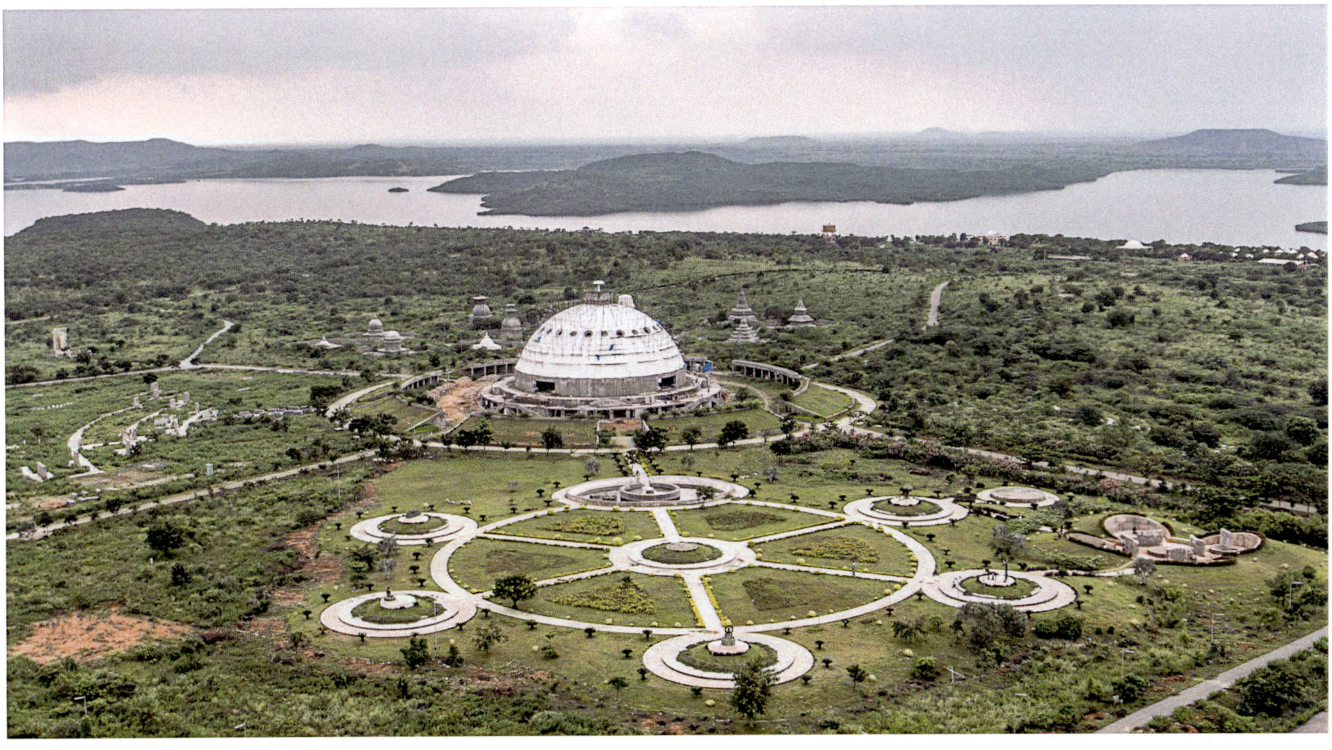

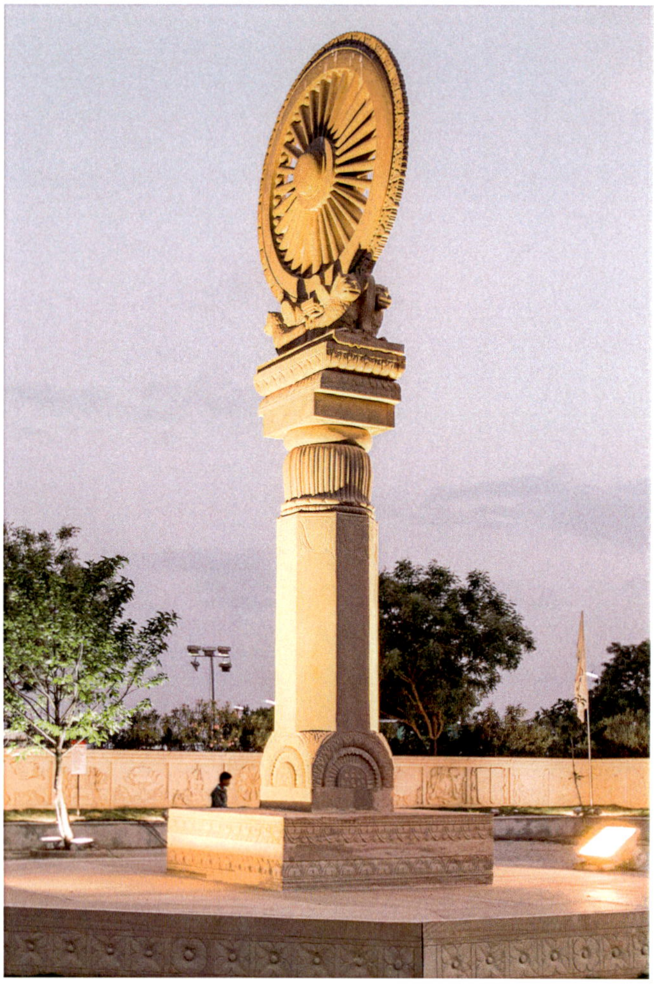

Figure 139 Dharma Chakra (Wheel of Law), the Sriparvata Arama, Nagarjunasagar, 2014

aniconic symbols and *mithunas* (amorous couples). At the centre of this plaza stands an octagonal column (*c.* 3.3m in height) that carries a *dharmacakra* (*c.* 1.8m in diameter) (**Fig. 139**). Another important sector is the Jātaka Park, which illustrates 40 stories of Buddha's former births in stone relief. They aim at depicting Bodhisattva's practice of ten perfections (*dadśa pāramitā*) to become the Buddha, such as *dāna* (generosity), *śīla* (moral discipline), *vīrya* (effort), *ksanti* (patience), *nekkhama* (renunciation), *metta* (loving kindness), *upekkha* (equanimity), *adhittana* (determination) and *prajnā* (wisdom).

The main *stūpa*

At the core of the Sriparvata Arama is the *mahāstūpa*, whose scale (21m in height and 42m in diameter) and design are based on the Amaravati *stūpa* (**Fig. 140**). It consists of a drum, a dome and *harmikā* with a *cchatra* (parasol) on its top. The drum and dome of the *stūpa* are encased with stone relief sculpture in sandstone, which resembles the original green limestone used in the Amaravati *stūpa*.

The drum slabs

The drum is *c.* 1.4m in height, and has four *āyaka* platforms (*c.* 1.8m in depth and 9.6m in width) at the cardinal directions. Each of the *āyaka* platforms is surmounted by five pillars (*c.* 4.2 m in height). These have square bases ornamented with lotus carvings, octagonal shafts and square capitals on top. As each pillar symbolizes one of the five important episodes of Buddha's life – Birth, Renunciation, Enlightenment, First Sermon and Extinction (*nirvāna*) – the capitals (*kudus*) of the pillars are adorned with symbols in bas-relief signifying these events – a white

Figure 140 The *Mahāstūpa* under construction, the Sriparvata Arama, Nagarjunasagar, 2016

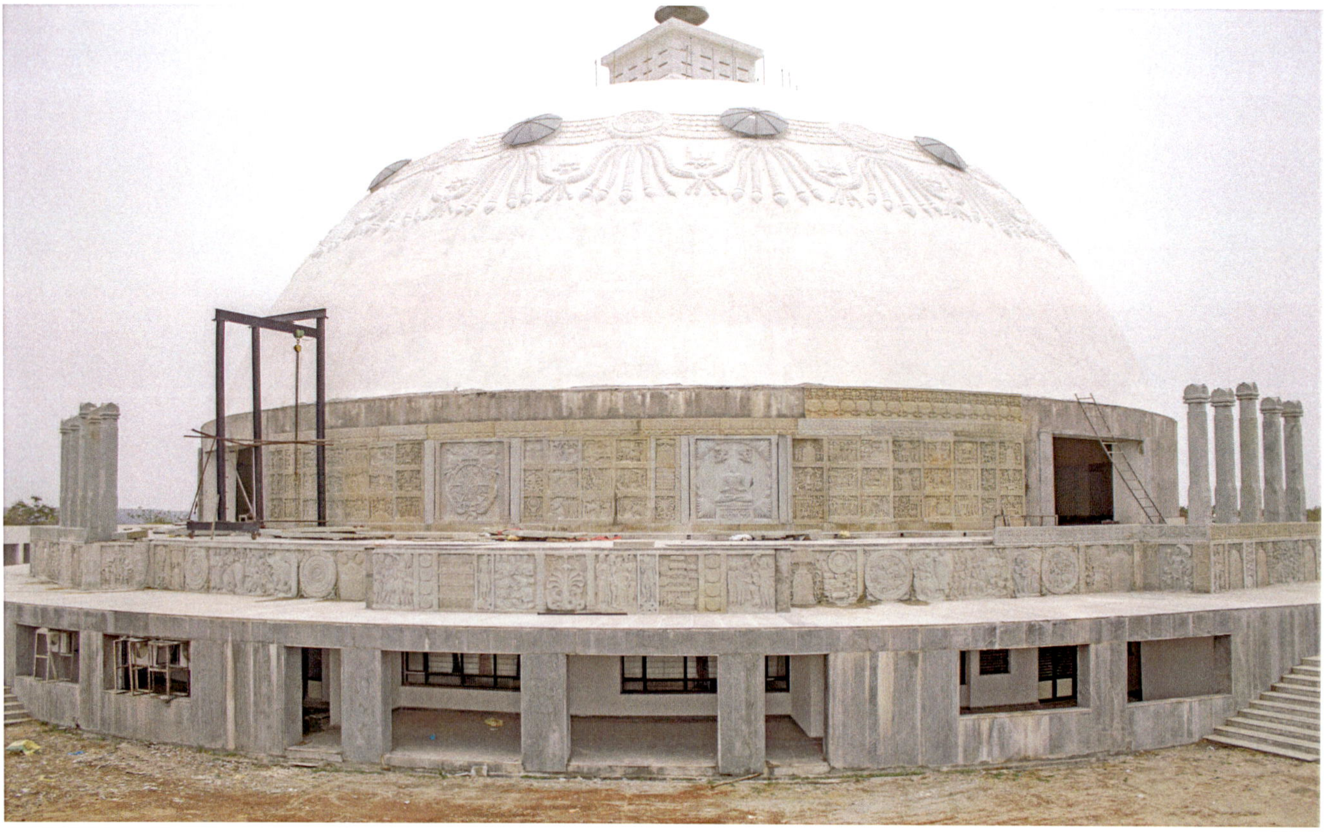

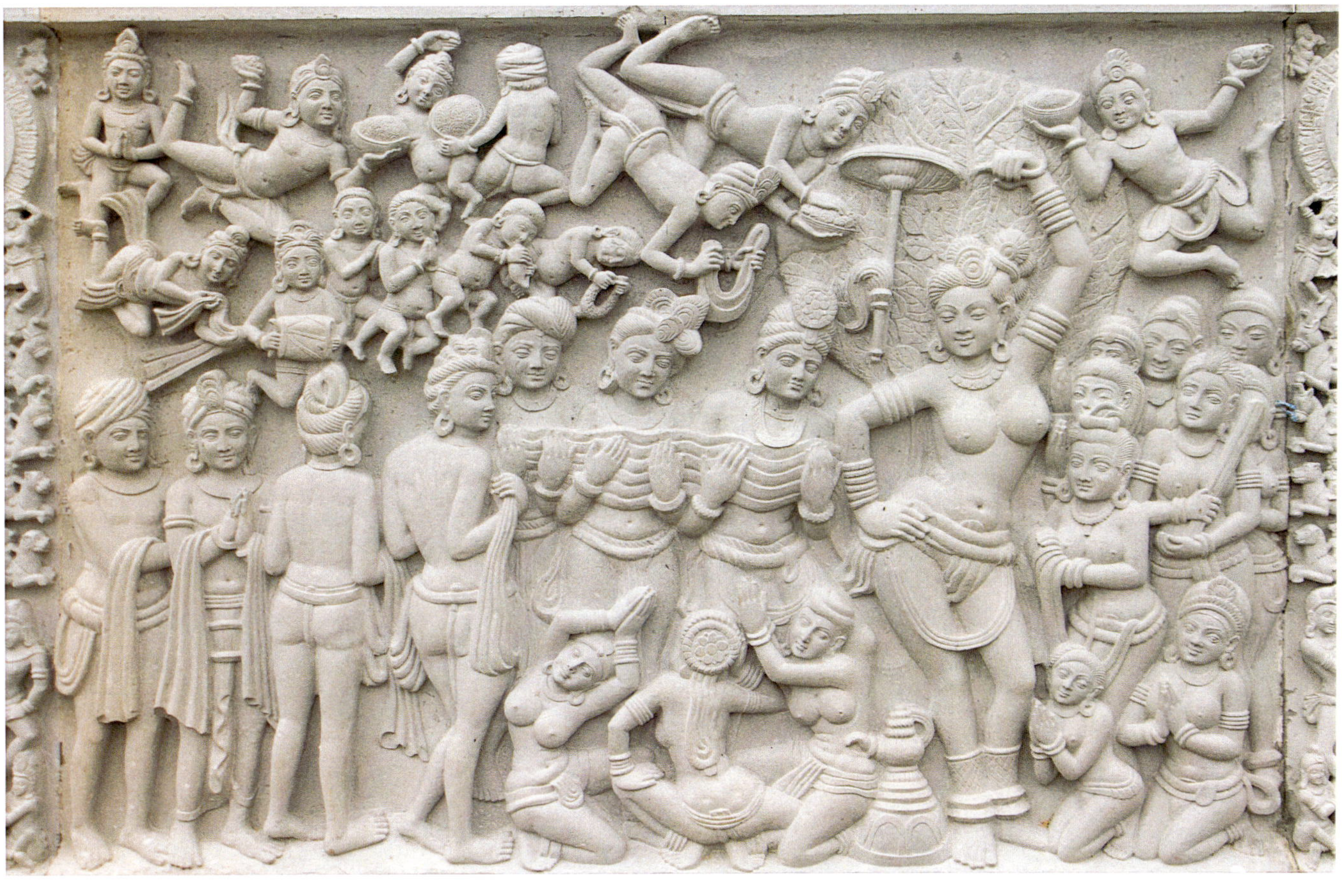

Figure 141 Drum slab depicting the Buddha's birth, the eastern *āyaka* platform of the *Mahāstūpa*, the Sriparvata Arama, Nagarjunasagar, 2015

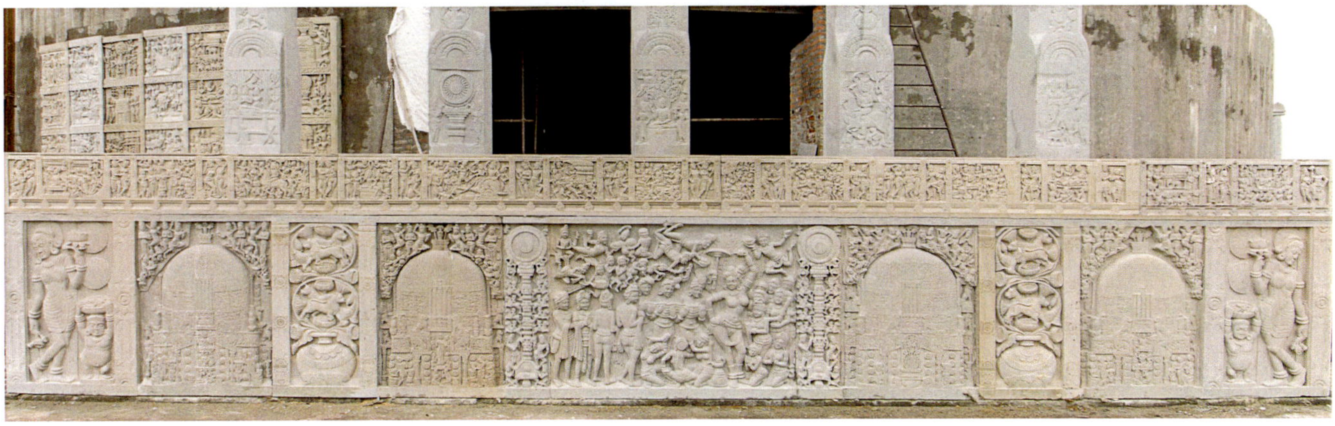

Figure 142 Eastern *āyaka* platform of the *Mahāstūpa*, the Sriparvata Arama, Nagarjunasagar, 2014

elephant (Birth), the horse Kanṭhaka with a parasol (Renunciation), a wheel (First Sermon), a bodhi tree (Enlightenment) and a *stūpa* (Extinction). Each of the four *āyaka* platforms, a distinct feature of Andhran *stūpa*, is decorated with a principal narrative panel (1.8m wide), which depicts one of the five important episodes of Buddha's life (**Fig. 141**). Both sides of the panels are decorated with slender pilasters and *stūpa* slabs (**Fig. 142**). At the ends of each side of the *āyaka* platforms a woman devotee is depicted as accepting flowers from a basket borne on the head of a dwarf. The projecting sides of the *āyaka* platforms are adorned with images of bodhisattvas in standing postures with pilasters on either side. Stairways attached to both sides of each *āyaka* platform are embellished with sculptural panels of Mucalinda *nāga*, the bodhi tree and a lady holding flowers (**Fig. 143**). The stairways also have panels depicting important Buddhist dignitaries, such as Faxian, Xuanzang, King Pulumāvi and Ācharya Nāgārjuna. The sections between the *āyaka* platforms and the stairways are embellished with slabs depicting the eight miracles performed by Buddha in his life. Each slab is 3.6m wide and is flanked by two roundels and *caitya* slabs on either ends. The other slabs embellishing these sections are symbolic signs of the Buddha, such as a wheel, a footprint, a pillar of fire, a throne with *svastika* etc.

The dome slabs

The dome (4.2m high from the top of the drum) rises vertically from the drum. At the bottom of the dome slabs is a plinth (0.3m high) with a rail pattern on it running through the entire circumference. The four entranceways, set at the cardinal points of the dome, afford access to the inner

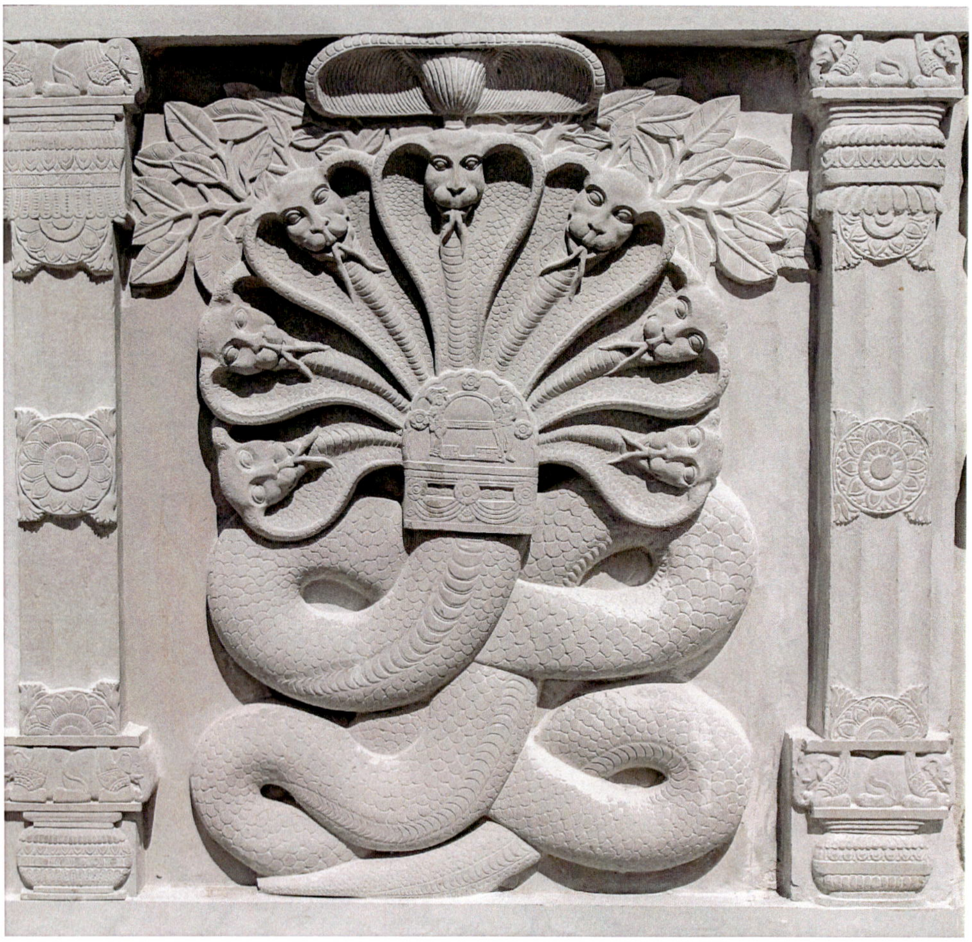

Figure 143 Drum slab depicting a seven-hooded Mucalinda *nāga*, south-west staircase of the *Mahāstūpa*, the Sriparvata Arama, Nagarjunasagar, 2015

sanctum of the *stūpa*. These entrances are to be encased with intricately carved door jambs. The dome wall is divided into four quadrants, each of which is *c.* 24m long at the bottom and is encased with *c.* 23 dome slabs. Each dome slab (*c.* 1m in width and 2.4m in height) is divided into three compartments by decorative bands. A vertical band on the right of each slab allows for a seamless join with the adjacent slabs. The themed dome slabs have been arranged in a chronological sequence of episodes from the Buddha's life, beginning with Birth and ending with *Mahāparinirvāṇa*.

Mention may be made here of a few of these important dome slabs in sequence. The top compartment of the first three-tiered dome slab depicts the Bodhisattva instructing the celestial beings in the palace; the central compartment has a group of flying *vidhyādharas* welcoming a bodhisattva; the last compartment has the descent of a bodhisattva in the form of a white elephant from Tuṣiṭa heaven. The adjacent slab, going in a clockwise direction (*pradakṣiṇa*), depicts the descent of the white elephant (top), Queen Māyā's conception (middle) and the Birth (lower). Other slabs depict the casting of Buddha's horoscope after his birth, the Great Renunciation and the transportation of Gautama's headdress to heaven. The second and fourth quadrants continue the narrative scenes of the Buddha's life and ministry from the conversion of Yasa by the Buddha until *Mahāparinirvāṇa* to the Formation of *sangha*. In addition, two special dome slabs depicting modern events such as the building of the Sriparvata Arama and its consecration, along with lifestyle traditions, are included in order to introduce a contemporaneous element to the *stūpa*. Sections above the dome slabs are adorned with a band of decorative panels depicting *pūrnagaṭha*, *triratna* and a lion procession; together they are 1.5m in height. This frieze band runs the entire circumference of the four dome quadrants, terminating evenly at the four entrance ways, which will be adorned with door jambs.

Figure 144 *Āyaka* frieze, Nagarjunakonda, Archaeological Museum, Nagarjunakonda, no. 5

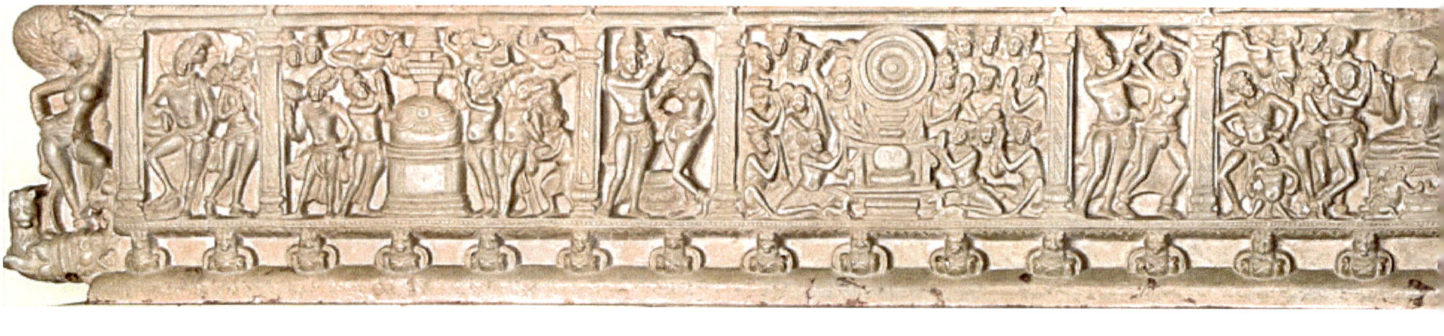

Designing the *Mahāstūpa*

Scope and arrangement

In order to decide the detailed design of the Sriparvata *Mahāstupa*, a creative workflow has been adopted. Inspiration for the reconstitution of the *stūpa* is drawn from the conjectural view sculpted on the *caitya* slabs of the Amaravati *stūpa*. The many drum slabs with different representations of the *caitya* present fresh viewpoints about the great *stūpa*'s architecture and art. Most challenging of all has been the selection of slabs for encasing the drum and dome of the *stūpa*. To look for the appropriate iconography to embellish these parts of the *stūpa*, Amaravati and Nagarjunakonda sculpture has been consulted as the primary sources, and relief sculpture from other sites of the south-east Deccan, such as Goli, Bhattiprolu and Jaggayyapeta in Andhra, Phanigiri in Telangana and Kanaganahalli in Karnataka, as the secondary sources.

Unfortunately, the slabs exhibited in museums are out of architectural context and provide insufficient clues for understanding their precise location on the *stūpa*. The late Dr B. Subrahmanyam thus developed the project based on his hypothesis that the slabs have no order other than one based purely on when they were donated. He also held the opinion that the veneering of the slabs took place in a clockwise direction on the drum. In order to obtain a clearer idea about the possible order of the slabs when they encased the Amaravati *stūpa*, the team visited the Kanaganahalli *stūpa*. Since the *stūpa* had been recently excavated and the sculptures remained at the site, this helped to decide the layout of the slabs on the *Mahāstūpa* at Sriparvata Arama.

The *āyaka* platforms of the Sriparvata *Mahāstūpa* are surmounted with narrative friezes containing the life events of Buddha in chronological order. The design of these friezes was decided on the basis of a cornice currently on display at the Archaeological Museum in Nagarjunakonda (**Fig. 144**). The cornice provides us with a good source of inspiration for the design of the drum frieze, showing important scenes from right to left, alternating with lively portrayals of *mithuna* couples in their affected moods. The team also learned that the *stūpa* at Kanaganahalli had simpler copings with rail patterns on the fringe of the drum. The design of the drum copings of the *Mahāstūpa*, excluding those on the *āyaka* platforms, follows this evidence. The five *āyaka* pillars on the platforms are designed with reference to a few preserved octagonal pillar fragments at Amaravati, Nagarjunakonda and Kanaganahalli, although the capitals on top of the *āyaka* pillars are based on imagination since there is little available evidence.

The dome slabs depicting the episodes of the Buddha's life are arranged in a chronological order, ranging from the Birth, through the Formation of the *sangha* to the Great Extinction. These episodes are distributed in the three-tiered slabs along the circumference of the *Mahāstūpa* on the dome in a clockwise direction. The dome also contains a few replicas of the three-tiered slabs from the Amaravati *stūpa* which contain the worship of *stūpa*, bodhi tree and an empty throne. The design of door jambs at the entrance to the *stūpa* dome came from the Buddhist cave temples, although both Amaravati and Nagarjunakonda *stūpa*s were solid at the core.

Carving process

Once the designs of each section of the *stūpa* have been decided, a dedicated team of artists sketches the individual slabs and traces them to create digital vectors. The artists work closely with scholars to make sure the narrative subjects stay authentic. If the original slabs consulted are damaged or insufficient, the artists recreate those parts with subjective feedback from the scholars. These complete drawings are then handed over to sculptors to initiate the sculpting work.

At the sculptors' workshop, the vector-line drawings provided by the artists are analysed and any necessary amendments made. The line drawings are then printed out on a sheet of poly vinyl flex in the actual size, and glued on to the top surface of the stone slabs using a mild adhesive. The outline is then chiselled on to the top surface of each slab by means of a pointed tool. The unwanted flat portions of the inner and outer areas of the outline are chiselled off (**Fig. 145**). Once the unnecessary portions of the slab have been removed to the desired depth, the carving of actual figures starts, with mildly rounded block forms. After this the contours of the figures are roughed out to bring out the volume in them. The later stages of carving involve shaping, fine carving and smoothing. Two skilled sculptors work for about three months to complete one drum slab. As for three-tiered dome slabs, three sculptors work on three compartments respectively and complete the carving in two to three months. Because of their large size and the fact that high relief requires the removal of a thick background, carving dome slabs is a time-consuming exercise (**Fig. 146**). In order to help the sculptors to understand the volume of the figures, replicas of some dome and drum slabs are made by using three-dimensional scanning as well.

At this stage a master sculptor ensures there is uniformity among all the sculptures and, where necessary, he himself carves the faces and more complex details. In this final stage,

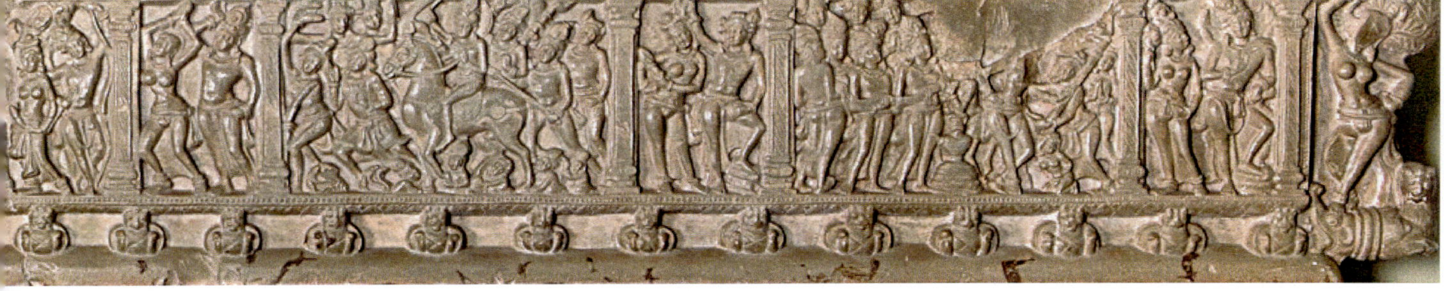

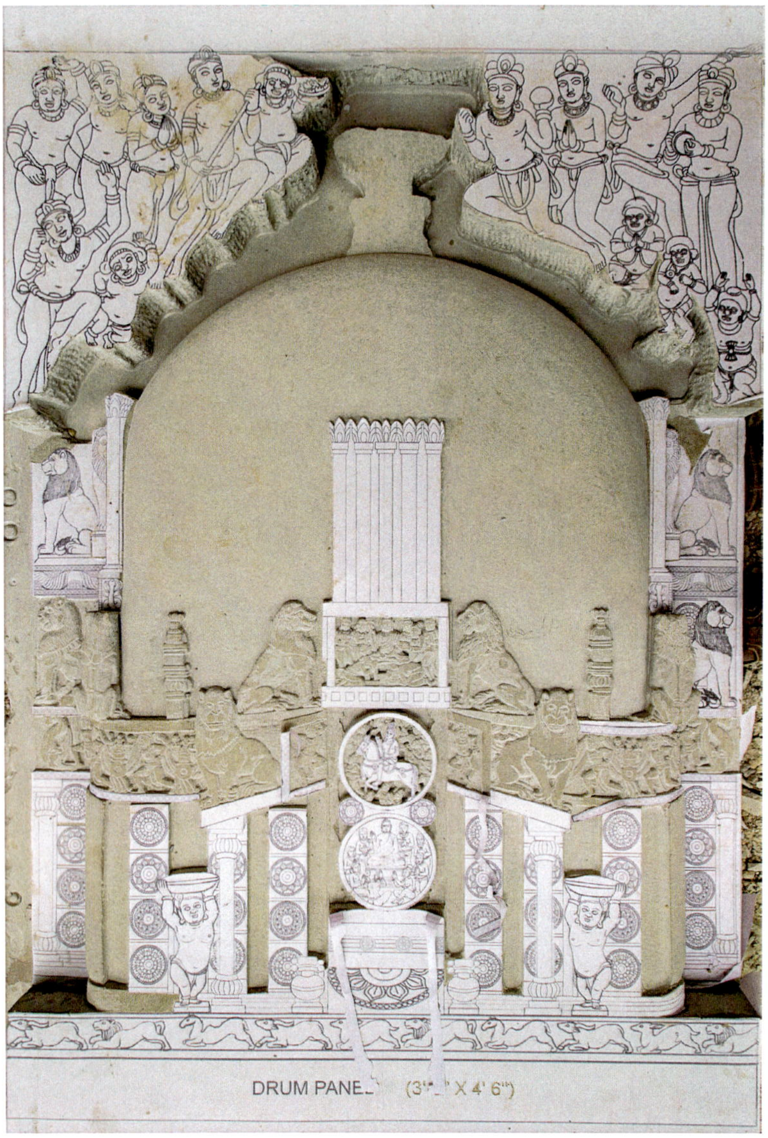

Figure 145 Drum slab in final stages of carving at the sculptors' workshop, 2014

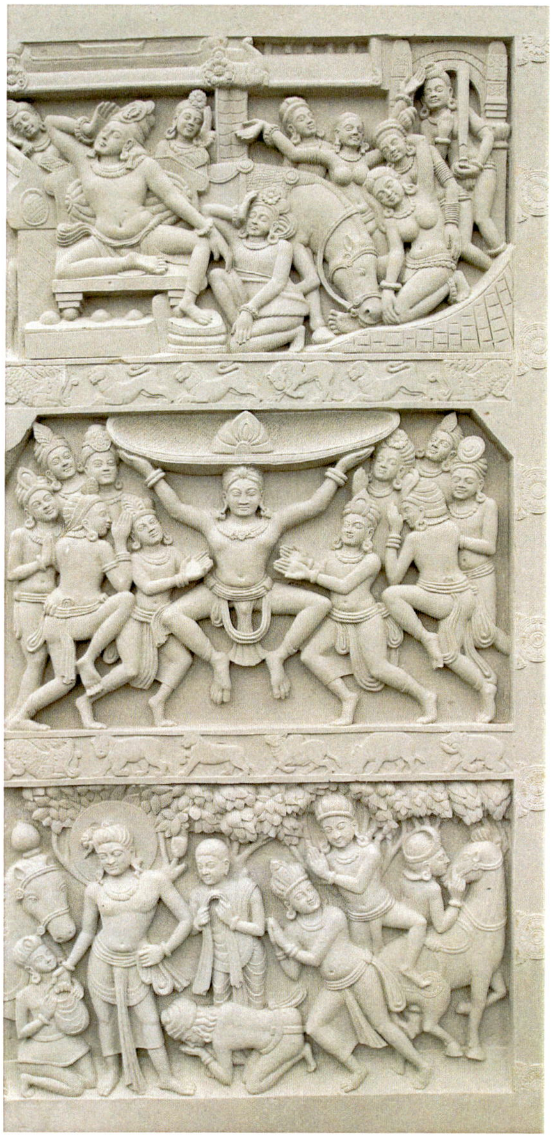

Figure 146 Dome slab of the *Mahāstūpa*, the Sriparvata Arama, Nagarjunasagar, 2015

eyes, nails, hair and drapery are intricately carved with fine pointed diamond-coated tools in order to bring the work to completion. The finished slabs are transported from the workshop to the Sriparvata Arama project site and are veneered on the *Mahāstūpa*. Once attached to the *stūpa*, final corrections are made, if necessary, to make a seamless and cohesive whole.

Training the sculptors

Since the Amaravati school of Buddhist art declined after the 4th century CE and gave way to Hindu art traditions, we had to train traditional stone sculptors who usually work for Hindu temples to accomplish our project. With an initial six months spent on training, a team of around 100 sculptors has been created. They are provided with high-quality reference photographs to understand the plasticity of the original slabs. For a better understanding of the style of the sculptures they were going to recreate, they visited the Archaeological Museums at Amaravati and Nagarjunakonda, the Telangana State Archaeology Museum in Hyderabad, the Indian Museum in Kolkata, Government Museum, Chennai and the National Museum in New Delhi (**Fig. 147**). In addition to the collections in India, they studied Andhran collections at the British Museum, London and the Musée Guimet in Paris.

To recreate the animated compositions of the Amaravati sculptures requires a sound knowledge of the human anatomy, and gaining such knowledge is possible only through rigorous training and observation. Having gone through the training to understand the aesthetic standard of the original masterpieces of the Amaravati school, the sculptors believe that they need a much longer period of study and practice, probably decades, to achieve the standard of the mature phase of the Amaravati sculpture. In order to improve their skills and to achieve high aesthetic standards in their works, they aspire to continue their study of the Amaravati school of art.

Conclusion

The Sriparvata Arama project aims to rekindle interest in the forgotten tradition of the Amaravati school of Buddhist art among people of the Telugu country by recreating the sculptures and the great *stūpa*. The Arama intends to be a place of experiential learning of Buddhist art through the

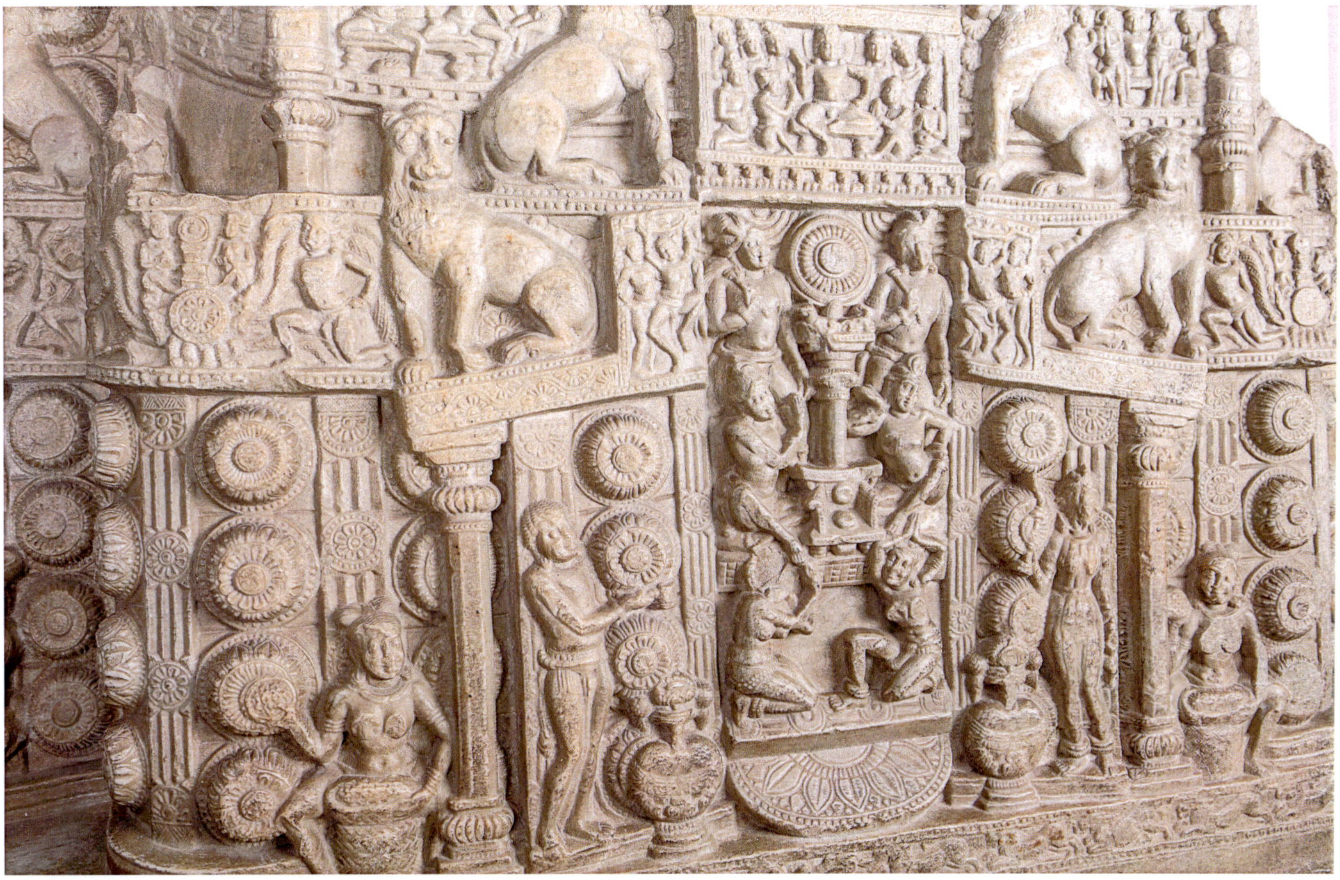

Figure 147 Detail of a drum slab from the Amaravati *stūpa*, c. 2nd–3rd century CE, Archaeological Museum, Amaravati, no. 1

medium of sculptures. People may study the Amaravati school of art by visiting museums in Andhra and Telangana. A significant part of the Amaravati collections are, however, located outside Andhra, for example in New Delhi, Kolkata and Chennai. Some collections are outside India. Moreoever, these museum collections do not exhibit the sculptures in their original architectural context. The Arama project hopes to fill this gap and to provide people of the Telugu country with a place where they may discover this lost tradition.

Supplementary remarks
Catherine Becker

Harsha Vardhan's discussion of the ongoing construction of the Sriparvata Arama, a 'Buddhist Theme Park' near the museum and reconstructed monuments associated with Nagarjunakonda, provides a fascinating insight into the use of sculptural and architectural forms from the distant past to fashion monuments that might be meaningful in the present. Specifically, Vardhan recounts how this park, which is the work of the Government of India and the State of Andhra Pradesh (and now Telangana), recreates the Amaravati *stūpa* with two aims: to provide visual evidence of the grandeur of the region's ancient Buddhist sculpture and to allow the public to study this fine sculpture in a recreation of its 'original' setting. In these brief remarks, I consider how these goals, which are somewhat inconsistently followed, not only replicate a colonial archaeological imperative that struggles to deal with the shifting nature of active sites of worship while attempting to expand regional tourism, but also how Vardhan's account of the challenges of working on the Sriparvata Arama might raise intriguing questions about how the sculptors of ancient Andhra approached their work on the region's Buddhist sites.

The goals underpinning this project highlight the colonial legacy of the approach to archaeological conservation and cultural heritage production in India. As scholars such as Tapati Guha-Thakurta (2004) and Maurizio Peleggi (2012) have outlined, archaeologists and academics have struggled to account for the inherent instability of sites of veneration, preferring to focus on locating the earliest form of a monument. For example, UNESCO's imperatives, which have recently attempted a more nuanced approach to heritage, have often rendered the architectural monuments it inscribes on the 'World Heritage' list as largely fixed and unchanging. The privileging of permanency demands that the ruined *stūpa*s of Andhra and Telangana – especially Amaravati and the Buddhist sites associated with the hastily excavated sites at Nagarjunakonda – remain relatively unreconstructed. An intact surrogate for these ruins, the new *stūpa* at the Sriparvata Arama purports to recreate the main *stūpa* at Amaravati. For scholars of the Buddhist art of South Asia, this stone-clad concrete *stūpa* serves as a striking reminder of the immense scale of the Amaravati *stūpa*, as the actual *stūpa* is presently lacking its once-towering dome.

Nevertheless, Vardhan's account of the construction and adornment of this *stūpa* demonstrates how the new monument – which on its surface and in the surrounding sculpture gardens creates a pastiche of Buddhist art from across India and Asia – is fundamentally a site stripped of an active ritual function. Over the centuries during which it was an object of veneration, the main *stūpa* at Amaravati was far from a static structure where the visitor could learn about 'Buddhist heritage'. Rather, the *stūpa* must have been periodically under construction; the existence of reused stone slabs – with early carving on one side and later carving on the other – testifies to such periods of enlargement and refurbishment. Given this evidence of the renovation of the Amaravati *stūpa*, a recreation of it must select which moment in the site's history to recreate, an act which necessarily prevents the visitor from apprehending the active and impermanent 'original' settings for the sculpture used to adorn Buddhist sites. Provocatively, the makers of the replica *stūpa* at the Sriparvata Arama, which, when finished, will include an inner sanctum, might be less interested in recreating the ancient *stūpa* than Vardhan's remarks suggest. As the main *stūpa* at Amaravati and all ancient *stūpa*s throughout the region were built as solid mounds, the creation of a *stūpa* that can be entered suggests a break with the past, perhaps even a desire to improve on the architecture of antiquity.

The Sriparvata Arama also responds to a larger drive to boost tourism in India and within the state of Andhra Pradesh. Elsewhere I have traced how a series of tourism brochures dating to the start of the new millennium attempts to market Andhra's Buddhist sites as evocative and stimulating tourist destinations (Becker 2015). In general, these documents employ rhetoric to suggest that the state's Buddhist sites are animated and capable of transforming the visitor. In part, the Sriparvata Arama provides the fantastic visual stimuli that might stoke the visitor's imagination (and which is not readily apparent at some of the more ruined Buddhist sites in Andhra Pradesh and Telangana) while also fulfilling a more practical role in supporting tourist activity. Visitors can refresh themselves at the snack shop, which was bustling during my visit on a holiday weekend in August 2013, before undertaking the journey home – by bus, automobile or motorbike. In dedicating resources to bolstering the visitor's experience at Buddhist sites, Andhra Pradesh and Telangana might appeal to tourists who have come to India to visit more well-known Buddhist sites such as Bodhgaya, which has also been repeatedly reshaped to appeal to a global Buddhist audience (Geary 2008: 11–14).

Finally, Harsha Vardhan's account, in exploring some of the challenges faced by artists and sculptors tasked with recreating an ancient monument that is no longer extant, also raises some questions about the processes employed by the artisans in this region during the 2nd and 3rd centuries CE. Vardhan notes the deeply collaborative process involved in creating the adornment for the main *stūpa* at the Sriparvata Arama. For example, archaeologists were consulted for their opinions, skilled artists, working with the assistance of computers, created drawings of the sculptures, and these were in turn used by teams of sculptors to carve the sandstone reliefs. A hierarchy governed the sculptors' process, with some sculptors roughing out the figures and more skilled sculptors providing more precise details. Vardhan records that a master sculptor attempted to ensure a uniform style across the sculptures and provided the finest finishing details. While ancient sculptors did not employ three-dimensional printing as part of their preparatory work, Vardhan's account encourages the reader to think carefully about the range of voices that determined the precise nature of the sculpture adorning the *stūpa*s. Vardhan elucidates how the artists and sculptors prepared for their work by visiting museums with collections of sculpture from Andhra and the spectacular *stūpa* of Kanaganahalli in Karnataka, which has more remains *in situ* than the contemporaneous sites in Andhra Pradesh and Telangana. Perhaps the sculptors engaged in work at Nagarjunakonda in the 3rd century CE also made occasional visits to nearby sites to study the sculptural remains of previous generations. While this must remain conjecture, Vardhan's analysis of his experience of working on the Sriparvata Arama reminds students of Buddhist art (myself included) to consider seriously the collaborative nature of the physical and intellectual work of the artists employed at the region's ancient *stūpa*s.

Bibliography

Abraham, S. 2003. Social complexity in Early Tamilakam: sites and ceramics from the Palghat Gap, unpublished PhD thesis, University of Pennsylvania, Philadelphia.

Allchin, B. and Allchin, F.R. 1982. *The Rise of Civilization in India and Pakistan*, Cambridge.

Allchin, F.R. 1956. The stone alignments of southern Hyderabad, *Man* 150: 133–6.

Almond, P. C. 1988. *The British Discovery of Buddhism*, Cambridge.

Anderson, J. 1883. *Catalogue and Hand-book of the Archaeological Collections in the Indian Museum*, 2 vols, Calcutta.

Aramaki, N., Dayalan, D. and Nakanishi, M. 2011. *A New Approach to the Origin of Mahāyānasūtra Movement on the Basis of Art Historical and Archaeological Evidence. A Preliminary Report on the Research* (Grant-in-Aid for Scientific Research, The Japan Society for Promotion of Science, Project (C), no. 20520050), Kyoto.

Aravamuthan T.G. 1938. A new type of punch marked coin, in *Transactions of the International Numismatic Congress, 1936* (ed. J. Allan, H. Mattingly and E.S.G. Robinson): 393–400, London.

Arlt, R. and Hiyama, S. 2015. Theatrical figures in the mural paintings of Kucha, *Journal of the International Association of Buddhist Studies* 38 (*Proceedings of the 17th Congress of the International Association of Buddhist Studies (IABS) 2014*, Vienna): 313–48.

Arunasiri, K. 2002. Mahāthūpa (2), in Weeraratne 2002: 486–99.

Babington, J. 1823. Description of the Pandoo coolies in Malabar, *Transaction of the Literary Society of Bombay* 3: 234–330.

Bachhofer, L. 1929 [1972], *Early Indian Sculpture*, Munich (reprinted New York, 1972).

Bagchi, P.C. 1941. The eight great caityas and their cult, *Indian Historical Quarterly* 17: 223–35 (reprinted in *Indological Studies: A Collection of Essays*: 138–53, Santiniketan, 1982).

Banerjee, N.R. 1965. *The Iron Age in India*, Delhi.

Barrett, D.E. 1954a. *Sculptures from Amaravati in the British Museum*, London.

Barrett, D.E. 1954b, The later school of Amaravati and its influences, *Arts and Letters* (*Journal of the India, Pakistan and Ceylon Society*) 28(2): 41–53.

Barrett, D.E. 1959. A rare sculpture from the Andhradeśa, *British Museum Quarterly* 21(4): 102–4.

Bauer, A.M. 2011. Producing the political landscape: monuments, labor, water, and place in Iron Age central Karnataka, in *The Archaeology of Politics: The Materiality of Political Practice and Action in the Past* (ed. P.G. Johansen and A.M. Bauer): 83–113, Newcastle upon Tyne.

Bauer, A.M. 2014. Impacts of mid- to late-Holocene land use on residual hill geomorphology: a remote sensing and archaeological evaluation of human-related soil erosion in Central Karnataka, South India, *Holocene* 24: 3–14.

Bauer, A.M. 2015. *Before Vijayanagara: Prehistoric Politics and Landscapes in the Tungabhadra Basin*, Vijayanagara Research Project Monograph Series, New Delhi.

Bauer, A.M. and Johansen, P.G. 2015. Prehistoric mortuary practices and the constitution of social relationships: implications of the first radiocarbon dates from Maski on a south Indian 'type site', *Radiocarbon* 57(4): 1–12.

Bauer, A.M. and Morrison, K.D. 2008. Water management and reservoirs in India and Sri Lanka, in *Encyclopaedia of the History of Science, Technology, and Medicine in Non-Western Cultures* (ed. H.L. Selin), 2nd edn: 2207–14, New York.

Bauer, A.M. and Trivedi, M. 2013. Contextualizing megalithic places: survey, mapping and surface documentation in the environs of Hire Benakal, *Man and Environment* 38(2): 46–61.

Bauer, A.M., Johansen, P.G. and Bauer, R.L. 2007. Toward a political ecology in early south India: preliminary considerations of the social context of land and animal use in the southern Deccan, Neolithic through Early Historic periods, *Asian Perspectives* 46(1): 1–38.

Bauer, R.L. 2007. *Animals in Social Life: Animal Use in Iron Age Southern India*, Saarbrücken.

Becker, C. 2009. Remembering the Amaravati stupa: the revival of a 'ruin', in Hawkes and Shimada 2009: 267–87.

Becker, C. 2015. *Shifting Stones, Shaping the Past: Sculpture from the Buddhist Stūpas of Andhra Pradesh*, New York.

Begley, W.E. 1968. The identification of the Ajanta fragment in the Boston Museum, *Oriental Art* 14: 24–33.

Bendall, C. (ed.) [1897–1902]. *Çikshāsamuccaya: a compendium of Buddhistic teaching compiled by Çāntideva chiefly from earlier Mahāyāna-Sūtras*, Bibliotheca Buddhica 1, St Petersburg (reprinted Delhi, 1992).
Bénisti, M. 1959. Nāgārjunakoṇḍa: Essai de 'caractérologie', *Arts Asiatiques* 6(3): 217–34.
Berkwitz, S. (trans.) 2007. *The History of the Buddha's Relic Shrine: A Translation of the Sinhala Thupavamsa*, New York.
Bhandare, S. 1999. Historical analysis of the Sātavāhana era: a study of coins, unpublished PhD thesis, University of Mumbai.
Bilbey, D. and Trusted, M. 2010. 'The question of casts': collecting and later reassessment of the cast collections at South Kensington, in *Plaster Casts: Making, Collecting, and Displaying from Classical Antiquity to the Present* (ed. R. Frederiksen and E. Marchand): 465–83, Berlin and New York.
Bird, J. 1847. *Historical Researches on the Origin and Principles of the Bauddha and Jaina Religions*, Bombay.
Birla Archaeological and Cultural Research Institute 1983. *Vaddamanu Excavations and Exploration in the Krishna Valley*, Hyderabad.
Boëthius, A. and Ward-Perkins, J.B. 1970. *Etruscan and Roman Architecture*, Harmondsworth.
Boivin, N., Fuller, D., Korisettar, R. and Petraglia, M. 2008. First farmers in south India: the role of internal processes and external influences in the emergence and transformation of south India's earliest settled societies, *Pragdhara* 18: 179–200.
Bopearachchi, O. 2008. Sculptures of Amaravati tradition in Sri Lanka, *Journal of the Asiatic Society* 50: 1–26.
Boswell, J.A.C. 1871. A letter from J.A.C. Boswell to the Acting Secretary to the Board of Revenue, dated Masulipatam, 31 March 1870, India Home Proceeding, Public, August 19 (no. 1301), 1871 (BL, IOR, P/507).
Branfill, B.R. 1881. On the Savandurga Rude stone cemetery, central Maisur, *Indian Antiquary* 10: 1–12.
Brilliant, R. 1963. *Gesture and Rank in Roman Art: The Use of Gestures to Denote Status in Roman Sculpture and Coinage*, Memoirs of the Connecticut Academy of Arts and Sciences 14, New Haven, Conn.
Brilliant, R. 1967. *The Arch of Septimius Severus in the Roman Forum*, Memoirs of the American Academy in Rome 29, Rome.
Brown, P. 1942. *Indian Architecture (Buddhist and Hindu Periods)*, 2nd edn, Bombay.
Brown, R.L. 2004. Vākāṭaka-period Hindu sculpture, in *The Vākāṭaka Heritage, Indian Culture at the Crossroads* (ed. H.T. Bakker): 59–69, Groningen.
Brown, R.L. 2014. *Carrying Buddhism: The Role of Metal Icons in the Spread and Development of Buddhism*, 20th J. Gonda lecture, 2012, Amsterdam.
Brubaker, R. 2001. Aspects of mortuary variability in the south Indian Iron Age, *Bulletin of Deccan College Post-Graduate and Research Institute* 60–1: 253–302.
Buchthal, H. 1943. The common classical sources of Buddhist and Christian art, *Journal of the Royal Asiatic Society of Great Britain and Ireland* ns 75: 137–48.
Burgess, J. 1882a. A letter from J. Burgess to the Secretary to the Government of India, dated 22 Seton Place, Edinburgh, 2 August 1882, Home Proceeding, Archaeology, September 1882 (BL, IOR, P/1681).
Burgess, J. 1882b. *Notes on the Amaravati Stupa*, Madras.
Burgess, J. 1887. *The Buddhist Stupas of Amaravati and Jaggayapeta in the Krishna District, Madras Presidency, Surveyed in 1882*, Archaeological Survey of Southern India 1, London (reprinted Varanasi, 1970).
Buswell, R.E. and Lopez, D.S. (eds). 2014. *The Princeton Dictionary of Buddhism*, Princeton, N.J.
Butcher, K. 2003. *Roman Syria and the Near East*, Los Angeles.
Casson, L. 1989. The 'Periplus Maris Erythraei', Princeton, N.J.
Chanda, R. 1925. Some unpublished Amaravati inscriptions, *EI* 15: 258–75.
Chattopadhyaya, B.D. 2003. Transition to the Early Historical phase in the Deccan: a note, in *Studying Early India: Archaeological Texts and Historical Issues* (ed. B.D. Chattopadhyaya): 39–47, New Delhi.
Childe, V.G. 1947. Megaliths, *Ancient India* 4: 4–13.
Chirapravati, P. 2008. Illustrating the lives of the Bodhisattva at Wat Si Chum, in *Past Lives of the Buddha: Wat Si Chum-Art, Architecture and Inscription* (ed. P. Skilling): 13–39, Bangkok.
Chowdhary, S.N. 2010. *Devnimori: Buddhist Monuments*, Maharaja Sayajirao University Archaeology Series 19, Vadodara, Gujarat.
Chung, Jin-Il and Schmidt, M. 2008. *Sanskrit-Wörterbuch der buddhistischen Texte aus den Turfan-Funden und der kanonischen Literatur der Sarvāstivāda-Schule*, fasc. 20, Göttingen.
Cimino, R.M. 1994. The 'Tabula Putingeriana', in *Ancient Rome and India: Commercial and Cultural Contacts between the Roman World and India* (ed. R.M. Cimino): 10–11, New Delhi.
Claridge, A. 1998. *Rome: An Oxford Archaeological Guide*, New York.
Cleveland Museum of Art, 1964. *Ancient Sculpture from India* (exhib. cat.), Cleveland, Ohio.
Coarelli, F. and Patterson, H. 2008. *La Colonna de Marco Aurelio*, Rome.
Cody, J.M. 1973. New evidence for the Republican *Aedes Vestae*, *American Journal of Archaeology* 77(1): 43–50.
Cole, H.H. 1872. *The Architecture of Ancient Delhi: Especially the Buildings around the Kutb Minar*, London.
Cole, H.H. 1882a. Memorandum of the present condition of Amaravati tope in Madras, India Home Proceedings, Archaeology, June 1882 (BL, IOR, P/1681).
Cole, H.H. 1882b. A letter from H.H. Cole to the Secretary to the Government of India, Home Department, Simla, dated Madras, 27 March 1882, Madras Public Proceedings, 16 June 1882, nos 412, 413 (BL, IOR, P/1925).
Cook, E. 1997. *The Stupa: Sacred Symbol of Enlightenment*, Crystal Mirror Series 12, Berkeley, Calif.
Coomaraswamy, A.K. 1908. *Mediaeval Sinhalese Art*, New York.
Coomaraswamy, A.K. 1927. *History of Indian and Indonesian Art*, New York.
Coomaraswamy, A. K. 1928a. *Yakṣas: Part I*, Washington, D.C.
Coomaraswamy, A.K. 1928b. Notes sur la sculpture bouddhique, *Révue des Arts Asiatiques* 5 : 244–52.
Coomaraswamy, A.K. 1929. Buddhist reliefs from Nāgārjunakoṇḍa and Amarāvatī, *Rupam* 38–39: 70–6.
Coomaraswamy, A.K. 1931. *Yakṣas: Part II*, Washington, D.C.
Cousins, L.S. 2003. 'Sākiyabhikkhu/Sakyabhikkhu/Śākyabhikṣu': a mistaken link to the Mahāyāna?, *Nagoya Studies in Indian Culture and Buddhism: Saṃbhāṣā* 23: 1–27.
Cowell, E.B. and Neil, R.A. 1886 (eds). *Divyāvadāna: A Collection of Early Buddhist Legends*, Cambridge (reprinted Delhi, 1987).
de Coral Rémusat, G. 1934. De l'origine commune des linteaux de l'Inde Pallava et des linteaux khmers préangkoriens, *Révue des Arts Asiatiques* 8(3): 242–50.
De Puma, R.D. 1991 Roman bronzes from Kolhapur, in *Rome and India. The Ancient Sea Trade* (ed. V. Begley and R.D. De Puma): 82–112, Madison, Wis.
DeCaroli, R. 2007. Text versus image: the implications of physical evidence for Buddhist history, in *Theoretical Approaches to the Archaeology of Religion: Belief in the Past* (ed. D.S. Whitley and K. Hays-Gilpin): 119–28, Walnut Creek, Calif.
Dehejia, V. 1997. *Discourses in Early Buddhist Art: Visual Narratives of India*, Delhi.
Delatour, C.R. 1996. Gabriel Jouveau-Dubreuil: l'érudit de Pondichéry, in *Âges et visages de l'Asie: un siècle d'exploration à travers les collections du musée Guimet* (ed. J.-P. Desroches, E. Starcky and C. Gras): 31–40, Dijon.
Deo, S.B. 1985. The megaliths: their culture, ecology, economy and technology, in *Recent Advances in Indian Archaeology, Proceedings of the Seminar Held in Poona in 1983* (ed. S.B. Deo and K. Paddayya): 89–99, Poona.
Deo, S.B. and Jamkhedkar, A.P. 1982. *Excavations at Naikund 1978–80*, Bombay.
Derrett, D.M. (trans.) 1983. *A Textbook for Novices: Jayarakṣita's 'Perspicuous Commentary on the Compendium of Conduct by Śrīghana'*, Pubblicazioni di 'Indologica Taurinensia' 15, Turin.
Desmond, R. 1982. *The India Museum, 1801–1879*, London.
Dewan, D. Deen Dayal, and Hutton, D. 2013 *Raja Deen Dayal: Artist-Photographer in 19th-Century India*, New Delhi.
Dimand, M.S. 1928. Two Indian reliefs of the Amarāvatī school, *Bulletin of Metropolitan Museum Art* 23(10): 238–44.
Disanayaka, J.B. 1987. *Mihintale: Cradle of Sinhala Buddhist Civilization*, Colombo.
Dowman, K. (trans.) 1973. Padmasambahava and Yeshe Tsogyal, *The Legend of the Great Stūpa (mChod-rten-chen-po-bya-rung-kha-shor-gyi-lo-*

rgyu-thos-pas-grol-ba), The Life Story of the Lotus Born Guru (Zab-pa-skor-bdon-las-O-rgyen-rnam-thar-dpag-bsam-lyon-sing), Berkeley, Calif.
EI = *Epigraphia Indica*
Ejima, Y. *et al.* 1985–93. *Index to the Saddharmapuṇḍarīkasūtra – Sanskrit, Tibetan, Chinese*, Tokyo.
Elliot, W. 1871. Letter from Sir Walter Elliot to the Secretary of State for India, Enclosure no. 2, Preservation of the important Buddhist remains at Amaravati, India Home Proceeding, 1871 (BL, IOR, P/507).
Elliot, W. 1872. Archaeology in the Krishna District, *The Indian Antiquary* 1: 346–8.
Elliott, W. [1886] 1976. *Coins of Southern India*, Varanasi (originally published London, 1886).
Elphinstone, M. 1815. *An Account of the Kingdom of Caubul and its Dependencies in Persia, Tartary and India*, London.
Emmerick, R.E. (ed.) 1967. *Tibetan Texts Concerning Khotan*, London.
Falk, H. 2012. A new Kuṣāna Bodhisattva from the time of Huviṣka, *ARIRIAB* 1: 13–18 and pl. 4.
Fergusson, J. 1867, Description of the Amravati tope in Guntur, *Journal of the Royal Asiatic Society of Great Britain and Ireland* 3: 132–66.
Fergusson, J. 1868. *Tree and Serpent Worship: Or, Illustrations of Mythology and Art in India in the First and Fourth Centuries after Christ. From the Sculptures of the Buddhist Topes at Sanchi and Amravati*, London.
Fergusson, J. 1873. *Tree and Serpent Worship: Or, Illustrations of Mythology and Art in India in the First and Fourth Centuries after Christ. From the Sculptures of the Buddhist Topes at Sanchi and Amravati*, 2nd edn, London.
Fergusson, J. 1891. *History of Indian and Eastern Architecture*, London.
Fogelin, L. 2006. *Archaeology of Early Buddhism*, Lanham, Md.
Foucher, A. 1928. Les sculptures d'Amarāvatī, *Révue des Arts Asiatiques* 5: 9–24.
Fuller, D.Q. 2005. Ceramics, seeds and culinary change in prehistoric India, *Antiquity* 79(4): 761–77.
Fuller, D.Q. 2006. Agricultural origins and frontiers in South Asia: a working synthesis, *Journal of World Prehistory* 20(1): 1–86.
Fuller, D.Q., Boivin, N. and Korisettar, R. 2007. Dating the Neolithic of south India: new radiometric evidence for key economic, social and ritual transformations, *Antiquity* 81(3): 755–78.
Fürer-Haimendorf, C. von 1953. New aspects of the Dravidian problem, *Tamil Culture* 2: 127–35.
Geary, D. 2008. Destination enlightenment: branding Buddhism and spiritual tourism in Bodhgaya, Bihar, *Anthropology Today* 24(3): 11–14.
Geiger, W. and Bode, M.H. (trans.) 1912. *The Mahāvaṃsa or The Great Chronicle of Ceylon*, Colombo.
Ghosh, A. 1979. The early phase of the stupa at Amaravati, south-east India, *Ancient Ceylon* 3:, 97–103.
Ghosh, A. and Sarkar, H. 1967. Beginning of sculptural art in south-east India: a stele from Amaravati, *Ancient India* 20–1 (1964–5): 168–77.
Ghosh, N.C. 1986. *Excavations at Satanikota 1977–80*, New Delhi.
Gnoli, R. (ed.) 1977. *The Gilgit Manuscript of the Saṅghabhedavastu: Part I*, Rome.
Gokhale, S. 1991. *Kanheri Inscriptions*, Pune.
Gordon, D.H. 1943. Early Indian terracottas, *Journal of the Indian Society of Oriental Art* 11: 136–95.
Gordon, D.H. 1958. *The Prehistoric Background to Indian Culture*, Bombay.
Government of India 1908. *Imperial Gazetteer of India: Vol. 19*, Oxford.
Guha-Thakurta, T. 2004. *Monuments, Objects, Histories: Institutions of Art in Colonial and Postcolonial India*, Delhi.
Gullapalli, P. 2009. Early metal in South India: copper and iron in megalithic contexts, *Journal of World Prehistory* 22: 439–59.
Gupta, P.L. 1963. *The Amarāvatī Hoard of Silver Punch-marked Coins*, Hyderabad.
Gupta, P.L. 1965. *Roman Coins from Andhra Pradesh*, Andhra Pradesh Government Museum Series 10, Hyderabad.
Gupta, P.L. and Hardaker, T. 1985. *Ancient Indian Silver Punch-marked Coins of the Magadha-Maurya Karshapana Series*, Nasik.
Gupta, S.S. 2008. *Sculptures and Antiquities in the Archaeological Museum, Amarāvatī*, New Delhi.
Gururaja Rao, B.K. 1972. *Megalithic Culture in South India*, Mysore.
Guy, J. 2000. Buddhist bronzes of southern India: discovering a lost history, *Arts of Asia* 30(6): 103–10.
Guy, J. (ed.) 2007a. *La escultura en los templos indios: el arte de la devoción*, Barcelona.
Guy, J. 2007b. *Indian Temple Sculpture*, London.
Guy, J. 2014. *Lost Kingdoms: Hindu-Buddhist Sculpture of Early Southeast Asia*, New York.
Hanson, J.A. 1969. *Roman Theater-Temples*, Princeton.
Hanumantha Rao, B.S.L. 1966. A lead coin from Chebrolu, *Proceedings of the Indian History Congress* (Mysore): 112–14.
Haque, E. 2001. *Chandraketugarh: A Treasure House of Bengal Terracottas: With 678 Illustrations*, Dhaka.
Hardy, E. (ed.) 1901. *Dhammapāla's Paramatthadīpanī: Part IV, Being the Commentary on the Vimāna-vatthu*, London.
Haricharan, S., Achyuthan, H. and Suresh, N. 2013. Situating burials in the Iron Age–Early Historic landscape of south India, *Antiquity* 87: 488–502.
Hawkes, J. and Shimada, A. (eds) 2009. *Buddhist Stupas in South Asia: Recent Archaeological, Art-historical and Historical Perspectives*, Delhi and Oxford.
Heitzman, J. 1984. Early Buddhism, trade and empire, in *Studies in the Archaeology and Palaeoanthropology of South Asia* (ed. A.R. Kenneth and G.L. Possehl): 121–37, New Delhi.
Holliday, P. 1997. Roman triumphal painting: its function, development, and reception, *Art Bulletin* 19(1): 130–47.
Horner, I.B. (trans.) 1974. *Vimānavatthu: Stories of the Mansions: New Translation of the Verses and Commentarial Excerpts*, The Minor Anthologies of the Pali Canon 4: 71–5, London.
Horsfall, J.G. 1880. From J.G. Horsfall Esq collector, Kistna District, to the Chief Secretary to Government, dated Masulipatam, 16 April 1880, no. 794, Madras Proceedings 1881 (BL, IOR, P/1746).
Howes, J. 2002. Colin Mackenzie and the stupa at Amaravati, *South Asian Studies* 18: 53–64.
Howes, J. 2009. The colonial history of sculptures from the Amaravati stupa, in Hawkes and Shimada 2009: 20–37.
Howes, J. 2010. *Illustrating India: The Early Colonial Investigations of Colin Mackenzie (1784–1821)*, New Delhi.
Hultzsch, E. 1883. Amarāvatī-Inschriften, *Zeitschrift der Deutschen Morgenländischen Gesellschaft* 37: 548–61.
Hultzsch, E. 1886. Berichtigungen und Nachträge zu den Amarāvatī-Inschriften, *Zeitschrift der Deutschen Morgenländischen Gesellschaft* 40: 343–46.
Hultzsch, E. 1925. *Inscriptions of Aśoka, New Edition, CII*, Oxford.
Hunt, E.H. 1912. The regulation of body temperature in extremes of dry heat, *Journal of Hygiene* 12(4): 479–88.
Hunt, E.H. 1916. Hyderabad cairns (their problems), *Journal of Hyderabad Archaeology Society* 2: 180–224.
Hunt, E.H. 1924. Hyderabad cairn burials and their significance, *Journal of the Royal Anthropological Institute of Great Britain and Ireland* 54: 140–56 and plates.
Huntington, S.L. 1985 (with contributions by J.C. Huntington). *The Art of Ancient India: Buddhist, Hindu, Jain*, Tokyo and New York.
IAR: *Indian Archaeology: A Review*
Ippel, A. 1929. *Indische Kunst und Triumphalbild*, Leipzig.
Ireland, J.D. (trans.) 1996. Sesavatī's mansion, *Buddhist Studies Review* 13(2): 107–8.
Jayaswal, K.P. 1927. The Hathigumpha inscription of the emperor Kharavela, *Journal of the Bihar and Orissa Research Society* 13: 221–46.
Jayawickrama, N.A. (ed. and trans.) 1971. *The Chronicle of the Thūpa and the Thūpavaṃsa, Being a Translation and Edition of Vācissaratthera's Thūpavaṃsa*, London.
Jayawickrama, N.A. (ed.) 1977. *Vimānavatthu and Petavatthu*, London.
Jha, A.K. and Garg, S. (eds) 1998. *Ex Moneta: Essays on Numismatics, History and Archaeology in honour of Dr. David W. McDowall*, 2 vols, New Delhi.
Johansen, P.G. 2003. Recasting the foundations: new approaches to regional understandings of South Asian archaeology and the problem of culture history, *Asian Perspectives* 42(2): 193–206.
Johansen, P.G. 2009. Site structure and settlement organization at Iron Age Bukkasagara and Rampuram: results from surface collections and documentation, *Man and Environment: Journal of the Indian Society for Prehistoric and Quaternary Studies* XXXIV (1): 17–29.
Johansen, P.G. 2010. Site maintenance practices and settlement social organization in Iron Age Karnataka, India: inferring settlement places and landscapes from surface distributions of ceramic assemblage attributes, *Journal of Anthropological Archaeology* 29(4): 432–54.

Johansen, P.G. 2011. Practising social difference, producing social space: the political architectonics of Iron Age settlement places, in *The Archaeology of Politics: The Materiality of Political Practice and Action in the Past* (ed. P.G. Johansen and A.M. Bauer): 186–220, Newcastle upon Tyne.

Johansen, P.G. 2014a. 'Early iron working in Iron Age South India: new evidence for the social organization of production from northern Karnataka, *Journal of Field Archaeology* 39(3): 256–75.

Johansen, P.G. 2014b. The politics of spatial renovation: reconfiguring ritual places and practice in Iron Age and Early Historic South India, *Journal of Social Archaeology* 14(1): 59–86.

Johansen, P.G. and Bauer, A.M. 2015. Beyond culture history at Maski: land use, settlement and social differences in Neolithic through medieval South India, *Archaeological Research in Asia* 1–2: 6–16.

Jongeward, D., Errington, E., Salomon, R. and Baums, S. 2012. *Gandharan Buddhist Reliquaries*, Seattle, Wash.

Jouveau-Dubreuil, G. 1932. L'architecture d'Amaravati, *Bulletin de l'association des amis de l'orient* 12: 5–16.

Kaimal, P. 2012. *Scattered Goddesses: Travels with the Yoginis*, Ann Arbor, Mich.

Kajale, M.D. 1984. Appendix: botanical remains from Veerapuram, in *Veerapuram: A Type Site for Cultural Study in the Krishna Valley* (ed. T.V.G. Sastri, M. Kasturi Bai and J. Vara Prasada Rao): i–xi, Hyderabad.

Kajale, M.D. 1989. Ancient grains from excavations at Hallur (1976 Season), District Dharwar, Karnataka, *Bulletin of the Deccan College Post-Graduate and Research Institute* 47–8: 123–8.

Karunaratne, S. 1984. *Epigraphia Zeylanica, Being Lithic and Other Inscriptions of Ceylon* 7, Colombo.

Kasturi Bai, M. 1986. Sada – a new dynasty discovered at Vaddamanu, Guntur dist., in coastal Andhra Pradesh, *Journal of the Numismatic Society of India* 48: 14–23.

Kasturi Bai, M. 1987. Coins from Vaddamanu excavations, in *Numismatics and Archaeology* (ed. P.L. Gupta and A.K. Jha): 102–12, Nasik.

Kelly, G.I.O. 2013. Craft specialization, technology and social change: a study of material culture in Iron Age and Early Historic South India, unpublished PhD thesis, University of Wisconsin, Madison, Wisc.

Kempers, A.J.B. 1932. Note on an ancient sculpture from Amarāvatī, *Acta Orientalia* 10: 364–71.

Kennedy, K. 2000. *God-Apes and Fossil Men: Paleoanthropology in South Asia*, Ann Arbor, Mich.

Kern, H. and Nanjio, B. (eds) 1908–12. *Saddharmapuṇḍarīka*, St Petersburg (reprinted Delhi, 1992).

Khan, A.W. 1963. *A Monograph on Yeleswaram Excavations*, Hyderabad.

Khare, M. D. 1962. Ceylonese monks in Nagarjunakonda, *Mahā Bodhi* 72(11–12): 317–19.

Knox, R. 1992. *Amaravati: Buddhist Sculpture from the Great Stūpa*, London.

Koezuka, T. 1994. The Amaravati sculpture, in *Masterpieces of Buddhist and Hindu Sculpture from the British Museum* (exhib. cat.): 21–4, Tokyo.

Köhn, S. 1996. *Ariadne auf Naxos, Rezeption und Motivgeschichte von Antike bis 1600*, Munich.

Kottkamp, H. 1992. *Der Stūpa als Repräsentation des buddhistischen Heilsweges – Untersuchungen zur Entstehung und Entwicklung architektonischer Symbolik*, Wiesbaden.

Krishna Murthy, K. 1977. *Nāgārjunakoṇḍa: A Cultural Study*, Delhi.

Krishna Sastry, V.V. 1983. *The Proto- and Early Historical Cultures of Andhra Pradesh*, Hyderabad.

Krishna Sastry, V.V. 1998. Indo-Roman trading centers in Andhra Pradesh, in Jha and Garg 1998: II, 475–99.

Krishna Sastry, V.V. 2003. Megalithic cultures: the Iron Age, in *Pre- and Protohistoric Andhra Pradesh up to 500 BC* (ed. M.L.K. Murthy): 107–38, Hyderabad.

Krishna Sastry, V.V., Subrahmanyam, B. and Rama Krishna Rao, N. 1992. *Thotlakonda (A Buddhist Site in Andhra Pradesh)*, Andhra Pradesh Government Archaeology Series 68, Hyderabad.

Krishnamurthy, R. 1998. Imitation Roman gold coins from Tirukoilur hoard, Tamil Nadu, in Jha and Garg 1998: I, 145–9.

Krishnaswami Aiyangar, S. 1928. *Manimekhalai in its Historical Setting*, London.

Kudo, N. (ed.) 2004. *The Karmavibhaṅga: Transliterations and Annotations of the Original Sanskrit Manuscripts from Nepal*, Bibliotheca Philologica et Philosophica Buddhica 7, Tokyo.

Kuraishi, M.H. 1930. Trial excavations at Alluru, Gummadidurru and Nagarjunikonda, in *ARASI 1926–27*: 150–61, Calcutta.

Kuwayama, S. 1997. A hidden import from imperial Rome manifest in stūpas, in *Gandharan Art in Context: East–West Exchanges at the Crossroads of Asia* (ed. R. Allchin, B. Allchin and N. Kreitman): 119–71, New Delhi.

Lama Chimpa and Chattopadhyaya, A. (trans.) 1990. *Tāranātha's History of Buddhism in India*, Delhi.

Lamotte, É. 1958. *Histoire du bouddhisme indien, des origines à l'ère Śaka*, Louvain.

Leander-Touati, A. 1987. *The Great Trajanic Frieze: The Study of a Monument and the Mechanisms of Message Transmission in Roman Art*, Gothenburg.

Leshnik, L. 1974. *South Indian 'Megalithic' Burials: The Pandukal Complex*, Wiesbaden.

Lévi, S. (ed. and trans.) 1932. *Mahākarmavibhaṅga (La grande classification des actes) et Karmavibhaṅgopadeśa (Discussion sur le Mahā Karmavibhaṅga)*, Paris.

Liebert, G. 1986. *Iconographic Dictionary of the Indian Religions: Hinduism, Buddhism, Jainism*, Asian Arts and Archaeology Series 5, Delhi.

LIMC: *Lexicon iconographicum mythologiae classicae*, 1981–2009, Zürich/ Munich.

Linossier, R. 1930. Une légende d'Udena d'Amarāvatī, *Révue des Arts Asiatiques* 6: 101–2.

Lippe, A. de 1978. *Indian Mediaeval Sculpture*, Amsterdam, New York and Oxford.

Longhurst, A.H. 1931. Excavations at Nāgārjunikonda, in *ARASI 1927–28*: 113–21, Calcutta.

Longhurst, A.H. 1938. *The Buddhist Antiquities of Nāgārjunakoṇḍa, Madras Presidency, MASI* 54, Delhi.

Lüders, H. 1912. A list of *brāhmī* inscriptions from the earliest times to about AD 400 with the exception of those of Aśoka, Appendix to *EI* 10 (1909–10).

Lüders, H., Waldschmidt, E. and Mehendale, M.A. 1963. *Bharhut Inscriptions*, Ootacamund.

McIntosh, J. 1985. Dating the South Indian megaliths, in *South Asian Archaeology 1983* (ed. J. Schotsmans and M. Taddei): 467–93, Naples.

Mackenzie, C. 1807. Account of extracts of a journal, *Asiatick Researches* 9: 272–8.

Mackenzie, C. 1823. Ruins of Amurvarty, Depaldina, and Durnakotta, *Asiatic Journal* 15, 464–78.

Mackintosh, M.C. 1973. Roman influences on the victory reliefs of Shapur I of Persia, *California Studies in Classical Antiquity* 6: 181–203.

Margabandhu, C. 1985. *Archaeology of the Satavahana Kshatrapa Times*, New Delhi.

Marshak, B. with Grenet, F. 2006. Une peinture kouchane sur toile, *Comptes rendus des séances de l'Académie des Inscriptions et Belles-Lettres* 150(2): 947–63, Paris.

Masefield, P. (trans., assisted by N.A. Jayawickrama) 1989. *Elucidation of the Intrinsic Meaning So Named, The Commentary on the Vimāna Stories (Paramattha-dīpanī nāma Vimānavatthu-aṭṭhakathā)*, Pali Text Soc 11, Oxford.

McNally, S. 1985. Ariadne and others: images of sleep in Greek and early Roman art, *Classical Antiquity* 4(2): 152–92.

Mehta, R.N. and Chowdhary, S.N. 1966. *Excavation at Devnimori (A Report of the Excavation Conducted from 1960 to 1963)*, Baroda.

Metzler, D. 1989. Kaiserkult ausserhalb der Reichsgrenzen und römischer Fernhandel, in *Migratio et Commutatio* (ed. H.-J. Drexhage and J. Sünskes): 196–200, St Katharinen.

Middleton, A.P. 1992. Appendix III. A note on the examination of some surface coatings on the Amarāvatī sculptures, in Knox 1992: 232.

Mirashi, V.V. 1941. A ship-type coin of Yajna Satakarni, *Journal of the Numismatic Society of India* 3, 43–4.

Misra, B.N. 2000. Some newly discovered *Jatakas* at Nagarjunakonda, in *South Indian Archaeology* (ed. G. Kamalakar, M. Veerender and A. Vijaya Kumar Babu): 100–9, Delhi.

Mitter, P. 1977. *Much Maligned Monsters: A History of European Reactions to Indian Art*, Oxford.

Mitterwallner, G. von 1987. The Brussels Buddha from Gandhara of the year 5, in *Investigating Indian Art: Proceedings of a Symposium on the Development of Early Buddhist and Hindu Iconography Held at the Museum of Indian Art, Berlin, in May 1986* (ed. M. Yaldiz and W. Lobo): 213–47, Berlin.

Miyaji, A. 1992. Minami indo Amaravati no setsuwa nehanzu: "shaka saigo no tabi" no setsuwazu (The narrative scene of Parinirvāṇa as represented in Amarāvatī art of South India), in *Nehan to Miroku no zuzogaku* (A. Miyaji): 85–112, Tokyo.

Moorti, U.S. 1994. *Megalithic Culture of South India: Socio-economic Perspectives*, Varanasi.

Morrison, K.D. 2009. *Daroji Valley: Landscape History, Place and the Making of a Dryland Reservoir System*, Vijayanagara Research Project Monograph Series 18, Delhi.

Morrison, K.D., Lycett, M.T. and Trivedi, M. 2016. Megaliths and memory: excavations at Kadebakele and the megaliths of northern Karnataka, in *Proceedings of the 20th Conference of the European Association for South Asian Archaeology and Art, Vienna, 2010*, vol. 2: Contextualizing Material Culture in South and Central Asia in Pre-Modern Times (ed. Widorn, Verena and Ute Franke): 241–52, Turnhout.

Morrison, K.D., Reddy, S.N. and Kashyap, A. forthcoming. Agrarian transitions in Iron Age Southern India: social and environmental implications, in *South Asian Archaeology 2012* (ed. V. Lefèvre), Paris.

Mudhol, M.S. 1997. *A Technical Study of Megalithic Metal Objects*, Mysore.

Mudiyanse, N. 2002. Mahāthūpa (1), in Weeraratne 2002: 481–6.

Nagar, S.L. 1993. *Jātakas in Indian Art*, Delhi.

Nagaraja Rao, M.S. 1971. *Protohistoric Cultures of the Tungabhadra Valley*, Delhi.

Nagaswamy, R. 1981. Roman sites in Tamil Nadu: recent discoveries – Shri M.N. Deshpande festschrift, in *Madhu: Recent Researches in Indian Archaeology and Art History* (ed. M.S. Nagaraja Rao): 337–9, Delhi.

Nagaswamy, R. 1995. *Roman Karur: A Peep into Tamils' Past*, Madras (the author also appears under the name Nākacāmi, Irā).

Nakamura, H. 1980. The Aṣṭamahāsthānacaityastotra and the Chinese and Tibetan versions of a text similar to it, in *Indianisme et bouddhisme: Mélanges offerts à Mgr Étienne Lamotte*, Publications de Institut Orientaliste de Louvain 23: 259–65, Louvain-la-Neuve.

Nakanishi, M. and von Hinüber, O. 2014. *Kanaganahalli Inscriptions*, *ARIRIAB* 17 (2013), Supplement, Tokyo.

Nilakanta Sastri, K.A. 1966. *A History of South India*, Oxford.

Okada, A. 2000. *Sculptures indiennes du musée Guimet*, Paris.

Padma, S. 2008. Material culture and the emergence of urban Buddhism in Andhra, in Padma and Barber 2008: 11–39.

Padma, S. and Barber, A.W. (eds) 2008. *Buddhism in the Krishna River Valley of Andhra*, Albany, N.Y.

Padma, S. and Holt, J.C. 2008. Buddhism in Andhra and its influence on Buddhism in Sri Lanka, in Padma and Barber 2008: 105–26.

Pagel, U. 2007. Stūpa festivals in Buddhist narrative literature, in *Indica et Tibetica. Festschrift für Michael Hahn zum 65. Geburtstag von Freunden und Schülern überreicht* (ed. K. Klaus and J.-U. Hartmann): 369–94, Vienna.

Paranavitana, S. 1935. Gadaladeniya rock-inscription of Dharmmakīrtti Sthavira, *Epigraphia Zeylanica* 4 (1934–41), 90–110.

Paranavitana, S. 1946. *The Stūpa in Ceylon*, Colombo.

Paranavitana, S. 1983. *Inscriptions of Ceylon: Vol. 2, Part 1, Containing Rock and Other Inscriptions from the Reign of Kuṭakaṇṇa Abhaya (41 B.C.–19 B.C.) to Bhātiya II (140–164 A.D.)* [Colombo].

Paranavitana, S. 2001. *Inscriptions of Ceylon: Vol. 2, Part 2, Containing Rock and Other Inscriptions from the Reign of Kaniṭṭhatissa (164–192 A.D.) to Mahāsena (276–303 A.D.)* [Colombo].

Parasher-Sen, A. 1991. Social structure and economy of settlements in the central Deccan (200 BC – AD 200), in *The City in Indian History: Urban Demography, Society and Politics* (ed. I. Banga): 19–46, New Delhi.

Parasher-Sen, A. 2007. Localities, coins and the transition to the early state in the Deccan, *Studies in History* 23(2): 231–69.

Parimoo, R. 1982. *Life of Buddha in Indian Sculpture: An Iconological Analysis*, New Delhi.

Parimoo, R. 1995. On re-identification of Āndhra Buddhist *Jātaka* relief sculptures, *Artibus Asiae* 55: 125–54.

Parimoo, R. 2010. *Life of Buddha in Indian Sculpture (Aṣṭa-Mahā-Pratihārya)*, rev. edn, New Delhi.

Pearsall, J. 2001. *New Oxford Dictionary of English*, Oxford.

Peleggi, M. 2012. The unbearable impermanence of things: reflections on Buddhism, cultural memory and heritage conservation, in Winter and Daly 2012: 55–68.

Pliny, 1942 [2006]. *Natural History*, Books 3–7, English translation by H. Rackham, Cambridge, Mass.

Pollen, J.H. 1874. *A Description of the Architecture and Monumental Sculpture in the South-east Court of the South Kensington Museum*, London.

Poonacha, K.P. 2011. *Excavations at Kanaganahalli (Sannati), Taluk Chitapur, Dist. Gulbarga, Karnataka*, *MASI* 106, New Delhi.

Prakong Nimanhaemind 2012. Taman Phra Chao Liap Loke (the legend of the Buddha's travels around the world): Lan Na Monastic Wisdom, in Skilling and McDaniel 2012: II, 109–19.

Prasad, P.R.K. 1993a. Sada coins in coastal Andhra, *Studies in South Indian Coins* 3: 53–63, Madras.

Prasad, P.R.K. 1993b. A new coin of Asaka Sada from Amarāvatī, *Journal of the Numismatic Society of India* 55: 44–9.

Prasad, P.R.K. 1999a. A hoard of miniature copper coins from Amarāvatī, in Shastri 1999: II, 312–26.

Prasad, P.R.K. 1999b. Pre-Satavahana phase at Amarāvatī – Dharanikota, in Shastri 1999: II, 327–40.

Price, M. 1981. Paintings as a source of inspiration for ancient die engravers, in *Culture and History in the Ancient World: Numismatic and Other Studies in Honor of Bluma L. Trell* (ed. L. Casson and M. Price): 69–75, Detroit.

Prinsep, J. 1837. Facsimiles of ancient inscriptions, *Journal of the Asiatic Society of Bengal* 6(1): 218–23.

Puljal, A. and Reddy, D. Raja 2005. Andhra Janapada coins from Singavaram, *Journal of the Oriental Numismatic Society* 185: 8–18.

Rajgor, D. 2001. *Punch-marked Coins of Early Historic India*, San José, Calif.

Rama Rao, M. 1942. A new lead coin from Amaravathi, *Journal of Andhra Historical Culture* 1: 92.

Rama Rao, M. 1961. *Satavahana Coins in the Andhra Pradesh Government Museum*, Andhra Pradesh Government Series 2, Hyderabad.

Rama, K. 1995. *Buddhist Art of Nāgārjunakoṇḍa*, Delhi.

Ramachandra Rao, P.R. 1956. *The Art of Nāgārjunikoṇḍa*, Madras.

Ramachandra Rao, P.R. 1984. *Andhra Sculpture*, Hyderabad.

Ramachandra Rao, P.R. 2001. *The Art of Nāgārjunikonda*, 2nd edn, Hyderabad.

Ramachandran, T.N. 1929. *Buddhist Sculptures from a Stupa near Goli Village, Guntur District*, Bulletin of the Madras Government Museum, ns, 1(1), Madras.

Ramachandran, T.N. 1932. An inscribed pillar-carving from Amarāvatī, *Acta Orientalia* 10, 135–53.

Ramachandran, T.N. 1953. *Nāgārjunakoṇḍa 1938*, *MASI* 71, Delhi (reprinted 1999).

Rao, K.P. 1988. *Deccan Megaliths*, New Delhi.

Rao, N.K. and Thakur, P. 2010. The astronomical significance of megalithic stone alignments at Vibuthihalli, *Journal of Astronomical History and Heritage* 13(1): 74–82.

Rapson, E.J. 1908. *Catalogue of Indian Coins in the British Museum: A Catalogue of the Coins of the Andhra Dynasty, the Western Ksatrapas, the Traikutaka Dynasty and the 'Bodhi' Dynasty*, London.

Raschke, M.G. 1975. Papyrological evidence for Ptolemaic and Roman trade with India, in *Proceedings of the XIV International Congress of Papyrologists, Oxford, 24–31 July 1974* (ed. P.J. Parsons): 241–6, London.

Ray, A. 1965. Sculptures of Nagarjunikonda, *Marg* 18(2): 9–40.

Ray, A. 1983. *Life and Art of the Early Andhradeśa*, Delhi.

Ray, H.P. 1988. Early trade in the bay of Bengal, *Indian Historical Review* 14: 79–89.

Ray, H.P. 1994. *The Winds of Change: Buddhism and the Maritime Links of Early South Asia*, New Delhi.

Ray, H.P. 1997. Networks of power: maritime history and archaeology of early Andhra, *Proceedings of the Andhra Pradesh History Congress, 21st Session*, 8–16.

Ray, H.P. 2008. Providing for the Buddha: monastic centres in eastern India, *Arts Asiatiques* 63: 119–38.

Rea, A. 1894. *South Indian Buddhist Antiquities, Including the Stûpas of Bhattiprôlu, Gudivâda and Ghantasâlâ and Other Ancient Sites in the Krishna District, Madras Presidency*, Madras.

Rea, A. 1909. Excavations at Amaravati, *ARASI (1905–6)*, 116–19.

Rea, A. 1912. Excavations at Amaravati, *ARASI (1908–9)*, 88–91.
Reddy, D.R. and Reddy, P.S. 1985. *Coins of the Megha Vahana Dynasty of Coastal Andhra*, Hyderabad.
Reddy, P.C., Subrahmanyam, B., Viyaja Kumar, J., Rama Krishna Rao, G.V., Kesava, K.S.B. Phanigiri 2008: *A Buddhist Site in Andhra Pradesh (An Interim Report 2001–2007)*, Hyderabad.
Rhi, J. 2005. Images, relics, and jewels: the assimilation of images in the Buddhist relic cult of Gandhāra – or vice versa, *Artibus Asiae* 65(2): 169–211.
Roberts, P., Boivin, N., Petraglia, M., Masser, P., Meece, S., Weisskopf, A., Silva, F., Korisettar, R. and Fuller, D.Q. 2015. Local diversity in settlement, demography and subsistence across the southern Indian Neolithic–Iron Age transition: site growth and abandonment at Sanganakallu-Kupgal, *Archaeological and Anthropological Sciences*: 1–25, doi: 10.1007/s12520-0150240-9.
Roth, G. 1980. Symbolism of the Buddhist stūpa, in *The Stūpa: Its Religious, Historical, and Architectural Significance* (ed. A.L. Dallapiccola with S. Zingel-Avé Lallemant): 183–209, Wiesbaden.
Rotman, A. 2008. *Divine Stories: Divyāvadāna: Part I*, Boston, Mass.
Rowland, B. 1953. *Art and Architecture of India: Buddhist, Hindu, Jain*, rev. 3rd edn, Harmondsworth.
Roy, A. 1994. *Amarāvatī Stūpa, Critical Comparison of Epigraphic, Architectural, and Sculptural Evidence*, 2 vols, Delhi.
Salomon, R. 1991. Epigraphic remains of Indian traders in Egypt, *Journal of the American Oriental Society* 3(4): 731–6.
Salomon, R. with Glass, A. 2008. *Two Gāndhārī Manuscripts of the Songs of Lake Anavatapta (Anavatapta-gāthā): British Library Kharoṣṭhī Fragment 1 and Senior Scroll 14*, Gandhāran Buddist Texts 5, Seattle, Wash.
Sarkar, H. 1960. Some aspects of Buddhist monuments at Nagarjunakonda, *Ancient India* 16: 65–84.
Sarkar, H. 1966. *Studies in Early Buddhist Architecture of India*, Delhi.
Sarkar, H. 1971. Some early inscriptions in the Amaravati museum, *Journal of Ancient Indian History* 4 (1–2), 1–13.
Sarkar, H. 1987. Emergence of urban centres in Early Historical Andhradesa, in *Archaeology and History*, 2 vols (ed. B.M. Pande and B.D. Chattopadyaya): 2, 631–42, Delhi.
Sarkar, H. and Misra, B.N. 1966. *Nagarjunakonda*, New Delhi.
Sarkar, H. and Misra, B.N. 2006 (reprint). *Nagarjunakonda*, New Delhi.
Sarkar, S.S. 1972. *Ancient Races of the Deccan*, New Delhi.
Sarma, I.K. 1975. Some more inscriptions from Amarāvatī excavations and the chronology of the mahāstūpa, *Studies in Indian Epigraphy* 1: 60–74.
Sarma, I.K. 1980a. More Prakrit inscriptions from Amaravati, *Journal of the Epigraphical Society of India* 7: 18–21.
Sarma, I. K. 1980b. *Coinage of the Satavahana Empire*, Delhi.
Sarma, I.K. 1985. Early sculptures and epigraphs from south-east India: new evidence from Amarāvatī', in *Indian Epigraphy: Its Bearing on the History of Art* (ed. F.M. Asher and G.S. Gai): 15–23, New Delhi.
Sarma, I.K. 1998. Coins from Amarāvatī excavations, *Studies in South Indian Coins* 8: 44–57.
Sarma, I.K. 2000. *Numismatic Researches: Critical Studies from Excavated Contexts*, Delhi.
Sasisekaran, B. and Raghunatha Rao, B. 2001. Iron in ancient Tamil Nadu, in *Metallurgy in India: A Retrospective* (ed. R. Rao and N.G. Goswami): 92–103, New Delhi.
Sastri, T.V.G. 1992. *Excavations of Vaddamanu and Exploration in the Krishna Valley*, Hyderabad.
Sastri, T.V.G., Kasturi Bai, M. and Vara Prasada Rao, J. 1984. *Veerapuram: A Type Site for Cultural Study in the Krishna Valley*, Hyderabad.
Sastry, D.L.N. 2000. *Paidigutta Excavations: A Proto-Historic Site in Lower Tungabhadra Valley, Mehaboobnagar District, Andhra Pradesh*, Jaipur.
Schlingloff, D. 2000. *Ajanta – Handbuch der Malereien: 1, Erzählende Wandmalereien*, 3 vols, Wiesbaden.
Schlingloff, D. 2013. *Ajanta – Handbook of the Paintings: 1, Narrative Wall-paintings* (English translation), 3 vols, New Delhi.
Schopen, G. 1988. On the Buddha and his bones: the conception of a relic in the inscriptions of Nāgārjunakoṇḍa, *Journal of the American Oriental Society* 108, 527–37 (also included in G. Schopen, 1997, *Bones, Stones, and Buddhist Monks*: 148–64, Honolulu, Hawaii).
Schopen, G. 1991 [1997]. An old inscription from Amarāvatī and the cult of the local monastic dead in Indian Buddhist monasteries, *Journal of the International Association of Buddhist Studies* 14(2): 281–329 (also included in G. Schopen, 1997, *Bones, Stones, and Buddhist Monks*: 165–203, Honolulu, Hawaii).
Schopen, G. [1994] 2004. Ritual rites and bones of contention: more on monastic funerals and relics in the *Mūlasarvāstivāda-vinaya*, in G. Schopen, *Buddhist Monks and Business Matters: Still More Papers on Monastic Buddhism in India*: 285–328, Honolulu, Hawaii (originally published in *Journal of Indian Philosophy* 22: 31–80).
Schopen, G. 1997. On the Buddha and his bones, in G. Schopen, *Bones, Stones, and Buddhist Monks*: 148–64, Honolulu, Hawaii.
Schopen, G. 2004 [1996]. Immigrant monks and the protohistoric dead: the Buddhist occupation of early burial sites in India, in G. Schopen, *Buddhist Monks and Business Matters: Still More Papers on Monastic Buddhism in India*: 360–81, Honolulu, Hawaii (originally published in *Festschrift Dieter Schlingloff zur Vollendung des 65. Lebensjahres dargebracht von Schülern, Freunden und Kollegen* (ed. F. Wilhelm): 215–38, Reinbeck.
Schopen, G. 2005. Mahāyāna in Indian inscriptions, in G. Schopen, *Figments and Fragments of Mahāyāna Buddhism in India: More Collected Papers*: Ch. 8, Honolulu, Hawaii (originally published in *Indo-Iranian Journal* 21 (1979): 1–19).
Schopen, G. 2014. 'Celebrating odd moments: the biography of the Buddha in some Mūlasarvāstivādin cycles of religious festivals', in G. Schopen, *Buddhist Nuns, Monks, and Other Worldly Matters: Recent Papers on Monastic Buddhism in India*: 361–89, Honolulu.
Selvakumar, V. 2000. Investigations into the Iron Age–Early Historic Cultures of the Upper Gundar Basin, Madurai District, Tamil Nadu, India, *Asian Studies* 16: 119–32.
Senart, E. 1905–6, The inscriptions in the caves at Nasik, *EI* 8: 59–96.
Sewell, R. 1880. *Report on the Amaravati Tope, and Excavations on its Site in 1877*, London.
Sewell, R. 1904. Roman coins found in India, *Journal of the Royal Asiatic Society of Great Britain and Ireland*: 591–637.
Shastri, A.M. 1993. On the Velpuru inscription of Maha Sada, *Journal of the Epigraphical Society of India* 19: 13–18.
Shastri, A.M. (ed.) 1999. *The Age of the Satavahanas*, 2 vols, New Delhi.
Shimada, A. 2006. The great railing at Amarāvatī: an architectural and archaeological reconstruction, *Artibus Asiae* 66(1), 89–141.
Shimada, A. 2013. *Early Buddhist Architecture in Context: The Great Stūpa at Amaravati (ca. 300 BCE – 300CE)*, Leiden and Boston.
Sidebotham, S.E. 2011. *Berenike and the Ancient Maritime Spice Route*, Berkeley, Calif.
Silva, K.M. de 2005. *A History of Sri Lanka*, rev. edn, New Delhi.
Silva, R. 1988. *Religious Architecture in Early and Medieval Sri Lanka: A Study of the Thūpa, Bodhimaṇḍa, Uposathaghara and Paṭimāghara*, Meppel.
Silva, R. 2007. Architecture of the thūpa, bodhimaṇḍa, uposathaghara and paṭimāghara, in *The Art and Archaeology of Sri Lanka: Vol. 1, Archaeology, Architecture, Sculpture* (ed. L. Prematilleke): 463–526, Colombo.
Singh, S. 1983. *A Study of the Sphuṭārthā Śrīghanācārasaṅgraha-ṭīkā*, 2nd edn, Tibetan Sanskrit Works Series 24, Patna.
Singh, U. 2001. The dismembering of the Amaravati stupa, *South Asian Studies* 17: 19–40.
Singh, U. 2008. *A History of Ancient and Early Medieval India from the Stone Age to the 12th Century*, Delhi.
Sinopoli, C. M. 2009. Late prehistoric landscapes of the Tungabhadra Corridor: recent excavations at Kadebakele (Koppal District, Karnataka), in *Recent Research Trends in South Asian Archaeology: Proceedings of the Professor H.D. Sankalia Birth Centenary Seminar* (ed. K. Paddayya and H.D. Sankalia): 279–94, Pune.
Sinopoli, C.M. and Morrison, K.D. 2007. *The Vijayanagara Metropolitan Survey: Vol. I*, Ann Arbor, Mich.
Sircar, D.C. 1951. The Sātavāhanas and the Chedis, in *The Age of Imperial Unity, The History and Cultura of the Indian People*, vol. 2 (ed. R.C. Majumdar): 191–16,
Sircar, D.C. 1957. Two inscriptions from Guntur District, *EI* 32: 82–90.
Sircar, D.C. 1961–2. Some Brahmi inscriptions, *EI* 34: 207–11.
Sircar, D.C. 1965. *Select Inscriptions Bearing on Indian History and Civilization: Vol. 1*, Calcutta.
Siva Naga Reddy, E. 1998. *Evolution of Building Technology: Early and Medieval Period: Vol. 1*, Delhi.

Sivaramamurti, C. 1942 *Amaravati Sculptures in the Madras Government Museum*, Bulletin of Madras Government Museum, ns, general section, 4, Madras.

Sivaramamurti, C. 1976. *The Amaravati Mode of Sculpture*, Bulletin of Madras Government Museum, ns, general section, 11(1), Madras.

Sivaramamurti, C. 1979. *Early Andhra Art and Iconography*, Mallampalli Somasekhera Sarma Memorial Lectures; Archaeology Series 53, Hyderabad.

Skilling, P. 1992. The Rakṣā literature of the Śrāvakayāna, *Journal of the Pali Text Society* 16: 109–69.

Skilling, P. 2003 [2546]. Ideology and law: the three seals code on crimes related to relics, images, and bodhi-trees, in *Sichamai-achan: Phiphit niphon chert chu kiat satsadachan dr. prasert na nakhon — satsadachan wisuth butsayakun nuang nai okat mi ayu 88 pi nai pho. so 2546 [Sichamai-achan: Articles in Honour of Prof. Dr. Prasert Na Nagara and Prof. Visuddh Busyakul on the Occasion of their 84th Birthdays in BE 2546]* (ed. W. Phongsipian): 287–307, Bangkok.

Skilling, P. 2005. Cutting across categories: the ideology of relics in Buddhism, *ARIRIAB* 8: 269–322.

Skilling, P. 2008. New discoveries from south India: the life of the Buddha at Phanigiri, Andhra Pradesh, *Arts Asiatiques* 63: 96–118.

Skilling, P. 2009. Redaction, recitation, and writing: transmission of the Buddha's teachings in India in the early period, in *Buddhist Manuscript Cultures: Knowledge, Ritual, and Art* (ed. S.C. Berkwitz, J. Schober and C. Brown): 53–75, London.

Skilling, P. 2010a. Scriptural authenticity and the Śrāvaka schools: an essay towards an Indian perspective, *The Eastern Buddhist* 41(2): 1–47.

Skilling, P. 2010b. Lumbinī: liturgy and devotion, in *The Birth of the Buddha. Proceedings of the Seminar held in Lumbini, Nepal, October 2004* (ed. C. Cüppers, M. Deeg and H. Durt): 345–54 (text); 459–60 (pls 1, 2). Lumbini.

Skilling, P. 2013. Vaidalya, Mahāyāna, and Bodhisatva in India: an essay towards historical understanding, in *The Bodhisattva Ideal: Essays on the Emergence of the Mahāyāna* (ed. Bhikkhu Nyanatusita): 69–162, Kandy.

Skilling, P. forthcoming a. Relics: the heart of Buddhist veneration, in *Relics and Relic Worship in the Early Buddhism of India and Burma* (ed. J. Stargardt), London.

Skilling, P. forthcoming b. The Buddhist cosmopolis: universal welfare, universal outreach, universal message, *Proceedings of the Conference 'L'universalisme bouddhique dans l'histoire des civilisations asiatiques', held at Kyoto, 3–5 October 2014*.

Skilling, P. and von Hinüber, O. 2011. An epigraphical Buddhist poem from Phanigiri (Andhra Pradesh) from the time of Rudrapuruṣadatta, *ARIRIAB* 14: 7–12.

Skilling, P. and McDaniel, J. (eds) 2012. *Buddhist Narrative in Asia and Beyond*, 2 vols, Bangkok.

Skilling, P. and Santi Pakdeekham 2010. Imaginaires of late Ayutthaya pilgrimage: the seven and eight great sites at Wat Ko Kaeo Suttharam, Phetchaburi, *Aséanie* 25: 147–94.

Skorupski, T. 2001. Two eulogies of the eight great *caityas*, in *The Buddhist Forum* VI (ed. T. Skorupski): 37–55, Tring.

Sotheby's 1990. *Indian and Southeast Asian Sculpture from the Pan-Asian Collection*, New York.

Soundara Rajan, K.V. 1981. *Cave Temples of the Deccan*, New Delhi.

Soundara Rajan, K.V. (ed) 2006. *Nagarjunakonda (1954–1960): Vol. II, The Historical Period, MASI* 75, New Delhi.

Spink, W.M. 2008. *Ajanta: History and Development of Painting, Sculpture, Architecture: Year by Year*, Leiden.

Spink, W.M. 1958. On the development of early Buddhist art in India, *Art Bulletin* 40: 95–104.

Srinivasan, K.R. 1983. Pan-Indian style: south India, *c.* 200 BC to 400 AD, Andhras, Iksvakus and literary sources, in *Encyclopaedia of Indian Temple Architecture: Vol. 1, South India: Part 1, Lower Dravidadesa (200 B.C.–A.D. 1324)* (ed. M. Meister): 3–21, New Delhi.

Srinivasan, P.R. 1971–3. Some Brahmi inscriptions from Guntupalli, *EI* 39: 247–52.

Srinivasan, S., Sinopoli, C.M., Morrison, K.D., Gopal, R. and Ranganathan, R. 2009. South Indian iron and higher carbon steel: with reference to Kadebakele and comparative insights from Mel-siruvalur, in *Metallurgy and Civilization: Eurasia and Beyond* (ed. J. Mei and T. Rehren): 116–21, London.

Stahl, A. 2013. Archaeological insights into aesthetic communities of practice in the Western Volta Basin, *African Arts* 43(3): 54–67.

Stern, P. and Bénisti, M. 1957. Évolution du stūpa figuré dans les sculptures d'Amarāvatī, *Bulletin de la Société des Études Indochinoises* 27 : 375–80.

Stern, P. and Bénisti, M. 1961. *Évolution du style indien d'Amarāvatī*, Publications du Musée Guimet, Recherches et documents d'art et d'archéologie 7, Paris.

Stone, E.R. 1985. A dated memorial pillar from Nāgārjunakoṇḍa, in *Indian Epigraphy: Its Bearing on the History of Art* (ed. F. Asher and G.S. Gai): 35–40, New Delhi.

Stone, E.R. 1994. *The Buddhist Art of Nāgārjunakoṇḍa*, Delhi.

Stone, E.R. 2004. A Buddhist incense burner from Gandhara, *Metropolitan Museum Journal* 39: 69–99.

Stone, E.R. 2005. Spatial conventions in the art of Andhra Pradesh: classical influence?, in *Buddhism: Art, Architecture, Literature & Philosophy*, 2 vols (ed. G. Kamalakar): I, 67–72.

Stone, E.R. 2006. The Amarāvatī master?: spatial conventions in the art of Amarāvatī, in *Hari Smriti: Studies in Art, Archaeology and Indology: Papers Presented in Memory of Dr Haribishnu Sarkar*, 2 vols (ed. A. Banerji): I, 51–60, New Delhi.

Stone, E.R. 2008. The sculpture of Andhra Pradesh and Roman imperial imagery, in *Krishnabhinandana: Archaeological, Historical and Cultural Studies (Festschrift to Dr V.V. Krishna Sastry)* (ed. P. Chenna Reddy): 100–6, New Delhi.

Strong, J.S. 2004. *Relics of the Buddha*, Princeton, N.J.

Sugandhi, N.S. 2013. Conquests of dharma: network models and the study of ancient polities, *Archaeological Papers of the American Anthropological Association* 22(1): 145–63.

Sugimoto, T. 2001. Jātakas from Amaravati, *Kanazawa-daigaku Bungakubu Ronshū, Kōdō-kagaku-Tetugaku hen [Studies and Essays, Behavioral Sciences and Philosophy, Faculty of Letters, Kanazawa University]* 21: 97–47.

Sundara, A. 1969–70. A new type of Neolithic burial in Terdal, Mysore State, *Puratattva* 3: 23–33.

Sundara, A. 1975. *The Early Chamber Tombs of South India: A Study of the Iron Age Megalithic Monuments of Northern Karnataka*, Delhi.

Takata, O. 1971. (photographs by M. Taeda) *Ajanta*, Tokyo.

Talbert, R.J.A. 2010. *Rome's World: The Peutinger Map Reconsidered*, Cambridge.

Taylor, M. 1853. Notices of cromlechs, cairns, and other ancient Scytho-Druidical remains in the principality of Shorapur, *Journal of the Bombay Branch of the Royal Asiatic Society* 17(4): 380–429.

Taylor, W. 1856. *On the Elliot Marbles, being a Report by the Reverend William Taylor*, Madras.

Thapar, B.K. 1957. Maski 1954: a chalcolithic site of the southern Deccan, *Ancient India* 13: 4–142.

Thomas, P.K. 1984. Appendix C: faunal assemblage of Veerapuram, in *Veerapuram: A Type Site for Cultural Study in the Krishna Valley* (ed. T.V.G. Sastri, M. Kasturi Bai and J.V.P. Rao): i–xi, Hyderabad.

Thomas, P.K. 1992. The faunal background of the Iron Age culture of Maharashtra, *Man and Environment* 17(2): 75–9.

Tomber, R. 2008. *Indo-Roman Roman Trade: From Pots to Pepper*, London.

Tomeanko, M. 1999. *Monumental Coins: Buildings and Structures on Ancient Coinage*, Iola, Wis.

Trainor, K. 1997. *Relics, Ritual, and Representation in Buddhism: Rematerializing the Sri Lankan Theravāda Tradition*, Cambridge.

Trautmann, T. 1997. *Aryans and British India*, Berkeley, Calif.

Trautmann, T. 2015. *Elephants and Kings: An Environmental History*, Chicago, Ill.

Tripe, L. 1859. *Photographs of the Elliot Marbles and of Other Subjects in the Central Government Museum, Madras* [Bangalore].

Tseng, V. (ed. and trans.) 2010. *A Unique Collection of Twenty Sūtras in a Sanskrit Manuscript from the Potala*, 2 vols, Vienna and Beijing.

Tsukamoto, K. 1996. *Indo bukkyo himei no kenkyu [A Comprehensive Study of the Indian Buddhist Inscriptions]*, 2 vols, Kyoto.

Tsukamoto, K. 2007. *Source Elements of the Lotus Sutra: Buddhist Integration of Religion, Thought, and Culture*, Tokyo.

Turner, R.L. [1966] 1999. *A Comparative Dictionary of the Indo-Aryan Languages: Vol. I, Text*, reprinted, Delhi.

Vaidya, P.L. (ed.) 1959. *Avadāna-Kalpalatā of Kṣemendra*, Buddhist Sanskrit Texts, nos 22 and 23, 2 vols, Durbhanga.

Varadpande, M.L. 1973. Nagarjunakonda amphitheatre, *Sangeet Natak* 30: 26–37.
Veerender, M. and Kamalakar, G. 2010. Numismatic finds from Garapadu excavations, *Studies in South Indian Coins* 20: 29–32.
Vogel, J.P. 1926. *Indian Serpent Lore, or the Nagas in Hindu Legend and Art*, London.
Vogel, J.P. 1930–1. Additional Prakrit Inscriptions from Nagarjunakonda, *EI* 21: 61–71.
Vogel, J.P. 1955. Een belangrijke aanwinst van het Museum van Aziatische Kunst, *Bulletin van het Rijksmuseum* 3: 51–8.
von Schroeder, U. 1990. *Buddhist Sculptures of Sri Lanka*, Hong Kong.
Walburg, R. 2005. The earliest inscribed 'coins' from Tissamaharama: why they are not truly coins, in *South Asian Archaeology 2003* (ed. U. Frank-Vogt and H-J. Weisshaar): 369–78, Aachen.
Waldschmidt, E. (ed.) 1950–1. *Das Mahāparinirvāṇasūtra: Parts 1–3*, Berlin (reprinted Kyoto, 1986).
Walimbe, S.R., Gambhir P.B. and Venkatasubbaiah, P.C. 1991. Human skeletal remains from Balijapalle in the Central Pennar Basin, Cuddapah District (A.P.), *Bulletin of Deccan College Post-Graduate and Research Institute* 51–2: 679–84.
Warmington, E.H. 1928. *The Commerce between the Roman Empire and India*, Cambridge.
Watson, J.F. 1873. *Vienna Universal Exhibition, 1873. A Classified and Descriptive Catalogue of the Indian Department*, London.
Weeraratne, W.G. (ed.) 2002. *Encyclopaedia of Buddhism: Vol. 6, Fasc. 3, Lobha–Mahavamsa*, Colombo.
Wenger, E. 1998. *Communities of Practice: Learning, Meaning and Identity*, Cambridge.
Wheeler, R.E.M. 1948. Brahmagiri and Chandravalli 1947: megalithic and other cultures in Mysore state, *Ancient India* 4: 180–310.
Wilcox, K. 2015. New insights on the ritual use of animals in the South Indian Iron Age (1200–300 BCE): faunal analysis at Kadebakele, in *South Asian Archaeology and Art 2012* (ed. V. Lefèvre, A. Didier and B. Mutin): 363–84, Turnhout.
Willis, M.D. 1997. Sculpture from India, in *A.W. Franks: Nineteenth-century Collecting and the British Museum* (ed. M. Cargill and J.F. Cherry): 250–61, London.
Willis, M.D. 2000. *Buddhist Reliquaries from Ancient India*, London.
Wilson, H.H. 1841. *Ariana Antiqua: A Descriptive Account of the Antiques and Coins of Afghanistan, with a Memoir on the Buildings called Topes, by C. Masson*, London (reprinted New Delhi, 1997).
Winter, T. and Daly, P. (eds) 2012. *Routledge Handbook of Heritage in Asia*, London.
Wogihara, U. (ed.) 1971. *Bodhisattvabhūmi: A Statement of Whole Course of the Bodhisattva (Being Fifteenth Section of Yogācārabhūmi)*, Tokyo.
Yule, H. and Burnell, A.C. 1903. *Hobson-Jobson: A Glossary of Colloquial Anglo-Indian Words and Phrases, and of Kindred Terms, Etymological, Historical, Geographical and Discursive*, new edn (ed. W. Crooke), London (reprinted New Delhi, 1984).
Zin, M. 1998. Der Vidūṣaka jenseits der Bühne, *Indo-Asiatiasche Zeitschrift* 2: 30–41.
Zin, M. 2004a. Die altindischen *vīṇās*, in *Studien zur Musikarchäologie IV. Orient-Archäologie* (ed. E. Hickmann and R. Eichmann): 321–62, Bonn.
Zin, M. 2004b. The Mūkapaṅgu story in the Madras Government Museum: the problem of the textual affiliations of the narrative reliefs in Amaravati and Nagarjunikonda, *Annali dell' Istituto Universitario Orientale* 64: 157–80.
Zin, M. 2011. The parable of 'The man in the well'. Its travels and its pictorial traditions from Amaravati to today, *Art, Myths and Visual Culture of South Asia* (ed. P. Balcerowicz and J. Malinowski): 33–93, Delhi.
Zin, M. 2012. Māndhātar, the universal monarch, and the meaning of representations of the *cakravartin* in the Amaravati school, and of the kings on the Kanganhalli *stūpa*, in Skilling and McDaniel 2012: I, 149–64.
Zin, M. 2014. Non-Buddhist narrative scenes at Nagarjunakonda, *Changing Forms and Cultural Identity: Religious and Secular Iconographies. Papers from the 20th Conference of the European Association for South Asian Archaeology and Art held in Vienna, 4–9 July 2010)* (ed. D. Klimburg-Salter and L. Lojda): 77–89, Vienna.
Zin, M. 2015a. Nur Gandhara? Zu Motiven der klassischen Antike in Andhra (einschließlich Kanaganahalli), *Tribus, Jahrbuch des Linden-Museums, Stuttgart* 64: 178–205.
Zin, M. 2015b. The jester and the vidūṣaka, *In ihrer rechten Hand hielt sie ein silbernes Messer mit Glöckchen. Setubandhinīvandanakaumudī, Festschrift für Heidrun Brückner* (ed. A.A. Esposito, H. Oberlin, K.J. Steiner and V. Rai): 379–96, Wiesbaden.
Zin, M. 2015c. The one who was against the Pavvajjā, *Sanmati, Essays Felicitating Professor Hampa Nagarajaiah on the Occasion of his 80th Birthday* (ed. L. Soni and J. Soni): 437–47, Bengaluru.
Zin, M. forthcoming a. Gandhara and Andhra: varying traditions of narrative representations (some observations on the arrangement of scenes citing the example of the Bodhisatva crossing the river Nairañjanā), *Proceedings of the International Conference on the Archaeology of Buddhism in Asia, Archaeological Survey of India, New Delhi, Delhi, 17–19 February 2012* (ed. B.R. Mani), Delhi.
Zin, M. forthcoming b. Gandhara iconography: dissemination & impact, *Gandhara: De l'Oxus au Ganges. Etudes en l'honneur de Francine Tissot. Actes du colloque en l'honneur de Francine Tissot organisé par Jessie Pons et Osmund Bopearachchi, à l'Ecole Normale Supérieur, Paris, le 8 juin 2013* (ed. J. Pons avec le concours d'O. Bopearachchi), Turnhout.
Zin, M. forthcoming c. Heavenly relics – The Bodhisatva's turban and bowl in the reliefs of Gandhara and Andhra (including Kanaganahalli), *Festschrift for Doris Meth Srinivasan* (ed. G.J.R. Mevissen, A. Banerji and V. K. Gupta), New Delhi.
Zin, M. forthcoming d. The Buddha's relics and the nāgas, an attempt to throw light on some depictions in the Amaravati school, in *Proceedings of the 21st Meeting of the European Association of South Asian Archaeology*, Paris.
Zwalf, W. 1996. *A Catalogue of the Gandhara Sculpture in the British Museum*, 2 vols, London.

Contributors

Nick Barnard is Curator, Asian Department, Victoria and Albert Museum, UK.

Catherine Becker is Associate Professor, Department of Art History, University of Illinois at Chicago, USA.

Shailendra Bhandare is Assistant Keeper, Numismatics, Ashmolean Museum, Oxford University, UK.

Peter G. Johansen is Visiting Assistant Professor, McGill University, Canada.

Akira Shimada is an Associate Professor in the Department of History at the State University of New York, New Paltz, USA.

Peter Skilling is Directeur d'études with l'École française d'Extrême-Orient (Bangkok and Paris) and a Special Lecturer at Chulalongkorn University (Bangkok).

Anna A. Ślączka is Curator, Department of Asian Art, Rijksmuseum, Amsterdam, Netherlands.

Elizabeth Rosen Stone is an independent scholar from New York, USA.

Harsha D. Vardhan is an artist from New Delhi, India.

Michael Willis is leading *Beyond Boundaries: Religion, Region, Language and the State*, a project funded by the European Research Council that is based in the British Museum, the British Library and the School of Oriental and African Studies.

Monika Zin is Professor, the Saxon Academy of Sciences, University of Leipzig, Germany.

Illustration Credits

Map by Jason Hawkes: 1–2; photograph: author: 3; © The Trustees of the British Museum 2016: 5–8; map by the author: 9; photograph: author: 11; photograph: courtesy of Andrew Bauer: 12; © The British Library Board: 13; Paritta Chalermpow Koanantakool: 16–17; courtesy of Archaeological Survey of India, ASI permission no. F.20/1/2010-Pub: 18; photograph: Maiko Nakanishi, courtesy of Archaeological Survey of India, ASI permission no. F.15/2/2009EE): 19; courtesy of Archaeological Survey of India, ASI permission no. F.20/1/2010-Pub: 20; photograph: Akira Shimada: 21; photograph: Kurt Behrendt: 22; Freer Gallery of Art, Smithsonian Institution, Washington, D.C.: 23; photograph: Christian Luczanits: 24a–b; photograph: Raja Deen Dayal, after Dewan *et al.* 2013, fig. 31: 25c; photograph: Chaibancha Prachong 2015; courtesy of Jom Prachong 1971: 26; photograph: Christian Luczanits: 27; © The Trustees of the British Museum 2016: 28–9; photograph: author: 30; photograph: courtesy of Indian Institute of Research in Numismatic Studies, Nasik: 31; photograph: author: 32; photograph: after Rapson 1908: pl. 5, G.P.4: 33; © The Trustees of the British Museum 2016: 34–5; photograph: author: 36–8; photograph: courtesy of Indian Institute of Research in Numismatic Studies, Nasik: 39–40; © The Trustees of the British Museum 2016: 41–3; photograph: author: 44–5; © The Trustees of the British Museum 2016: 46–51; photograph: Maiko Nakanishi with the permission of the Archaeological Survey of India: 52–3; © The Trustees of the British Museum 2016: 54; © 2016. Photo Scala, Florence: 55; photograph: the author, courtesy of The Trustees of the British Museum 2016: 56; photograph: Wojtek Oczkowski with the permission of the Archaeological Survey of India: 57; photograph: the author, courtesy of The Trustees of the British Museum 2016: 58–60; photograph: Wojtek Oczkowski with the permission of the Archaeological Survey of India: 61; photograph: the author, courtesy of The Trustees of the British Museum 2016: 62; photograph: Wojtek Oczkowski with the permission of the Archaeological Survey of India: 63; photograph: after Stern and Bénisti 1961: pl. 24b: 64; photograph: the author, courtesy of The Trustees of the British Museum 2016: 65; photograph: author: 66; photograph: Wojtek Oczkowski with the permission of the Archaeological Survey of India: 67; photograph: the author, courtesy of The Trustees of the British Museum 2016: 68; photograph: Wojtek Oczkowski: 69; photograph: author: 70; photograph: the author, courtesy of The Trustees of the British Museum 2016: 71–3; photograph: Akira Shimada with the permission of the Archaeological Survey of India: 74; © The Trustees of the British Museum 2016: 75–7; photograph: courtesy of American Numismatic Society: 78; © The Trustees of the British Museum 2016: 79–80; photograph: courtesy of American Numismatic Society: 81; Image courtesy of The Metropolitan Museum of Art (www.metmuseum.org): 82; photograph: courtesy of American Numismatic Society: 83; © The Trustees of the British Museum 2016: 84; photograph: courtesy of American Numismatic Society: 85; © The Trustees of the British Museum 2016: 86; photograph: courtesy of American Numismatic Society: 87; photograph: Christian Luczanits: 88; photograph: courtesy of the Archaeological Survey of India: 89; photograph: courtesy of

Alinari/Art Resource, NY: 90; photograph: courtesy of the Archaeological Survey of India: 91; photograph: courtesy of Eric Lessing/Art Resource, NY: 92; photograph: Akira Shimada with the permission of the Archaeological Survey of India: 93; photograph: John C. Huntington, courtesy of the Huntington photographic archive at Ohio State University: 94–95a; photograph: courtesy of Eric Lessing/Art Resource, NY: 95b; photograph: Akira Shimada with the permission of the Archaeological Survey of India: 95c; photograph: author, with the permission of the Archaeological Survey of India: 96; photograph: Françis Ory for the Inventory of the Archaeological Museum, Anuradhapura: http://129.199.58.244/fmi/iwp/cgi?-db=Inventaire_Anuradhapura-Yatala&-loadframes: 97; © The Trustees of the British Museum 2016: 98; photograph: author, with the permission of the Archaeological Survey of India: 99; © The Trustees of the British Museum 2016: 100; photograph: author, with the permission of the Government of Andhra Pradesh Department of Archaeology and Museums: 101–4; © Victoria and Albert Museum, London: 105–15; © The Trustees of the British Museum 2016: 116; © Victoria and Albert Museum, London: 117–19; photograph: courtesy of the Rijksmuseum, Amsterdam: 120–2; photograph: courtesy of the Tokyo National Museum: 123; © The Trustees of the British Museum 2016: 125–7; photograph: J.E. van Lohuizen-de Leeuw, courtesy of Leiden University, Digital Special Collections, P-006502: 128; photograph: courtesy of Leiden University, Digital Special Collections, P-038041: 129; after Stone 1994, fig. 124: 130; photograph: courtesy of Leiden University, Digital Special Collections, P-038122: 131; photograph: courtesy of Leiden University, Digital Special Collections, P-042934: 132; © The Trustees of the British Museum 2016: 133–4; © Ashmolean Museum, University of Oxford: 135; © Victoria and Albert Museum, London: 136; photograph: author: 137; photograph: author: 138–43; photograph: author, with the permission of the Archaeological Survey of India: 144; photograph: author: 145–6; photograph: author, with the permission of the Archaeological Survey of India: 147

Index

Index notes: *italicised* page numbers refer to photographs and captions